Index to

Seamen's Protection Certificate Applications

Port of Philadelphia
1796–1823

With Supplement 1796–1851

Record Group 36
Records of the Bureau of Customs
National Archives and Records Administration
Washington, DC

Compiled by
Ruth Priest Dixon
and
Katherine George Eberly

CLEARFIELD

Printed for
Clearfield Company, Inc. by
Genealogical Publishing Co., Inc.
Baltimore, Maryland
1995

Reprinted, with Supplement 1796-1861, for
Clearfield Company, Inc. by
Genealogical Publishing Co., Inc.
Baltimore, Maryland
2001

International Standard Book Number: 0-8063-4589-6

Made in the United States of America

Other books by Ruth Priest Dixon:

Index to Seamen's Protection Certificate Applications, Port of Philadelphia, 1824-1861

Sims settlement, Our Squatter Ancestors, 1806-1818.
Northern Alabama Local History and Genealogy

DENHAM & TOWN, PRINTERS.

United States of America.

Be it Known, THAT on the day of the date hereof, before me, Richard Palmer, Esquire, one of the Justices of the Peace in and for the County of Philadelphia, personally appeared *Joseph Dickinson* an American seaman, aged *Twenty Two* years or thereabouts, of the height of *five* feet *2 1/4* inches, has *dark* hair, and *dark* complexion *and has three birds, two hearts, and several letters on the Right arms, and on the left arm the Masons Coat of Arms an Anchor and 1798 done with Indian Inks, and spotted on the face with the Small Pocks —* who being duly sworn did depose and say, that he is a native of *New Orleans* in *Louisiana* and a Citizen of the United States of America.

$$\text{Joseph} \overset{\text{his}}{\times} \text{Dickinson}$$
Clark

And *John Langos* being also duly sworn, did depose and say, That the facts above stated are true, according to the best of his knowledge and belief.

$$\text{John} \overset{\text{His}}{\text{nm}} \text{Langos}$$
Clark

In Testimony whereof, I have hereunto set my Hand and Seal, this *twenty fifth* day of *June* *1807*

R Palmer

1597

On this Third Day of January
in the Year of our Lord One Thousand Eight Hundred and Six
Before me Clement Biddle, Esquire, Notary Public, dwelling
in the City of Philadelphia, Personally came John
Delaunay ———— and made Oath that he
is a Native of Native of France, But a Citizen of the
United States by virtue of his father Peter Delaunay being
made a Citizen of these U States before he was age, as appears
by his Certificate of Citizenship to me produced —
and a Citizen of the United States, that he is aged Twenty four
Years, of the Height of 5 Feet 6½ Inches Brown Hair, —
Hazel Eyes, Fresh Complexion, a
Mole to the right

John Jouffron being also duly
made Oath that he is well acquainted with John
Delaunay ——and verily believes he was born in France
But is a Citizen of these United
States, by virtue of his father Peter Delaunay
being made a Citizen as appear by Cert.
of Citizenship produced ——— John Jouffront
Sworn as above before me,
Clement Biddle
Notary
1805.

INTRODUCTION

This index to the names of merchant seamen who made application for a Seaman's Protection Certificate (SPC) at the Port of Philadelphia between 1796 and 1823 is a companion volume to the index to applications made between 1824 and 1861, published in 1994. These two volumes contain a complete index to the names of all of the merchant seamen whose applications were made at Philadelphia which have been preserved at the National Archives in Washington, D C. The names of 14,397 seamen appear in this index; 18,354 were indexed in the earlier volume. An index to applications made in New Orleans and smaller ports is being compiled. Applications for the Port of New York were destroyed, but a card index to those names is on file in the Civil Records Branch of the National Archives.

Seamen's Protection Certificates were authorized by Congress in 1796 to identify American merchant seamen as citizens of the United States and as such entitled to protection against impressment. As early as 1791, similar documents were issued and the applications for them were preserved with the post-1796 ones. They are included in this work.

These applications contain information of great significance to genealogists, sociologists, and historians. As a group, seamen were unlikely to own land and so would not appear in land or tax records. Often they were at sea when the decennial census was taken, and so are missing from census records. These applications may be the only record available for men serving in the early American merchant marine. The **index** gives the name, date of application, age at that time, color of complexion if of Afro-American or Indian descent, and state or country of birth. The **applications** contain additional information: city and/or county of birth; color of eyes, hair and skin; height; and identifying physical marks such as tattoos, scars, injuries, deformities. All applications were witnessed by someone who swore to or affirmed the information given. A few examples of significant information from the applications annotate the index.

Stories which appear on the applications make it abundantly clear why Congress was moved to take action to protect American merchant seamen. Both the British and French were guilty of seizing American seamen during the Napoleonic wars. The dispute over this practice of taking by "impressment" men on land or at sea to serve in the British navy became acute in 1806. It reached crisis level in 1807 when the British frigate *Leopard* removed four seamen, three of them Americans, from the U.S.S. *Chesapeake*. The war declared in 1812 ended with the Treaty of Ghent signed on 24 December 1814. The greatest number of "protections" was issued in this period -- 1809, 1815, 1810, and 1811, in that order.

Some stories of Seamen's Protection Certificates being taken by foreign powers are illustrative.

- 1798 SPC issued to Robert Kelsay was taken by a French privateer
- 1806 SPC issued to John Norris destroyed by an officer of the British sloop of war *Hornet* who boarded schooner *Nancy* in Port of Spain, Trinidad
- 1812 SPC issued to James McNullidge lost when he was captured on board ship *Ponona* of Philadelphia 7 August last by British frigate *Eolens*, when said ship was burned.
- 1812 Charles Mein's SPC was "torn to pieces" by lieutenant of British frigate *Shannon*.

During the war, many SPC were lost when seamen were captured and imprisoned, and their stories were told when they were free and applied for new "protections." The practice did not end with peace in 1815.

- 1817 SPC issued to James Francis was torn up and destroyed by a British captain when at sea.

The number of applications made for lost certificates jumped from 83 in 1809 to 132 in 1810 and reached a high of 169 in 1811, then 126 in 1815. In later years, the number dwindled from 56 to zero. Many were lost due to British and French actions; some were lost when a captain and a sailor parted company; some were lost through disasters at sea or carelessness; and there appears to be a real possiblity that some were sold.

Names of witnesses provide the most valuable clues for genealogists to follow. Witnesses described as a mother or father of the seaman number 365. Interestingly, many of the mothers had a different surname. An additional 122 were brothers, sisters, aunts, uncles, cousins, grandmother or grandfather, and inlaws. Over a thousand seamen and their witnesses had the same surname. In all, over 11% of the witnesses give direction for further family research. For example:

- 1798 Capt Eves of Philadelphia witnessed for his sons Robert, 21, and William, 20
- 1811 Obadiah Stevens' witnesses were his aunt Jane Allen, brother William Stevens, and cousin Elizabeth Thompson.
- 1812 father of John Baker was George A. Baker, Esq., late treasurer of Philadelphia

2

- 1823 Gabriel O'Brien, son of Richard O'Brien, born in Algiers during the time his father was Consul General of U. S. to Barbary Powers.

After 1800, 2% to 7% of the merchant seamen applying for an SPC in Philadelphia were foreign born, naturalized citizens. Their proof of citizenship when making application provides a wealth of information in this difficult-to-research field. Some early seamen even relinquished their naturalization certificates and they are on file with the applications. Normally, the application simply shows the date and place of naturalization, most often Philadelphia but on occasion New York, Charleston, Baltimore, and other cities. A variety of courts granted citizenship: the Court of Common Pleas, U. S. District Court, Mayor's Court, Supreme Court of Pennsylvania, Court of Nisi Prius -- to name the most common ones.

Citizenship was fairly easy to obtain in the early years of the Republic. Seamen claimed citizenship by being a resident when Independence was declared, during the Revolution, or when the peace treaty was signed on 3 September 1783. In 1790, Congress authorized the courts to grant citizenship to free white aliens who had resided in the country for two years, were of good character, and supported the Constitution. The Louisiana Purchase in 1803 granted citizenship to inhabitants of that territory; however, they were required to pledge allegiance to the U. S. in order to receive a "protection."

Some interesting examples of naturalization information on applications:
- No date given. Peter Greer arrived Wilmington, DE, on Ship *Mary* August 1782. Served apprentice to Capt. James Jefferson until 19 years old.
- 1801 John Allwine lived here during all of the Revolution and is thus a citizen.
- 1810 Robert Pearce came to the U. S. from England at the age of 4; was naturalized in Philadelphia on 16 February 1798 with his father who was a painter and glazier in Philadelphia.
- 1811 John Battis, free mulatto born in Territory of New Orleans, signs pledge of allegiance to U. S.

Afro-Americans appeared in the merchant marine in Philadelphia from before 1796, but the number was small, around 4%. That number grew rapidly and by 1800 had reached 10%. From 1804 to 1823, Afro-Americans accounted for up to 20% of the seamen making applications. In 1812 there were 30%, and by 1822, 33%. The percentage was higher in the period 1824-1861.

3

Some stories told on applications made by Afro-Americans are significant:

- 1797 James Philips' mother, a free woman, resided on estate of Col Churchill in VA; father a white man lived on his own small farm. James educated as a free boy.
- 1806 Cato Shewbert "This may certify that Cato Shewbert was born in my house Septm. 1, 1775 his father Cato and mother Zilpha both belonged to me." /s/ William Turner
- 1810 Heeler Jones, slave to Marcellous Jones of Sommerset County, MD, goes to sea with master's consent.
- 1818 Simon Harris, a black man, born Mount Vernon, VA
- 1820 William Purnell manumitted by his present master, Dr. Henry Neill of Philadelphia

Some seamen reported having been born in Africa when they made application:
- 1797   John Lynch Oliver
- 1815   Francis Johnston
- 1817   Evan Nepean

John Harris, in 1811, reported that he was born at sea on passage from coast of Africa. Apparently all of these men were granted SPCs. Not all Africans were so fortunate.
- 1810 John Thompson born in Africa and not entitled to protection. Claimed birth in Baltimore.

While the American-born seamen made application for an SPC in Philadelphia, their places of birth ranged up and down the east coast. The states represented in 1796 were Connecticut, Delaware, Georgia, Massachusetts, Maryland, North Carolina, New Hampshire, New Jersey, New York, Pennsylvania, Rhode Island, South Carolina, and Virginia. Maine was added in 1798; at that time it was still a part of Massachusetts. Seamen from the New Orleans area began appearing in 1804 and by 1806 many seamen came from there. In the index they are shown as having been born in Louisiana. The District of Columbia appeared in 1805. Kentucky and Vermont followed in 1806.

The age of merchant seaman was much as would be expected. Only three were under ten years of age. The percentages by age groups was as follows:

	10-19 years old	22.5%
	20-29	60.6
	30-39	13.2
	40-49	2.9
	50-59	.6

4

There were only four seamen in their 60s, and only two in their 70s.

The practice of learning a trade through apprenticeship is evident in the applications. Many seamen state the name of their master and the trade they were apprenticed in. The term "indenture" is used both for apprenticeship and for servitude. Some seamen went to sea as indentured servants: some accompanied their master, some earned wages for their master's benefit.

The given names of seamen provide food for thought and amusement. Statesmen were popular: there are many George Washingtons and Thomas Jeffersons, at least one Alexander Hamilton, and a Caesar Augustus. A man born at sea was named Neptune. Most men have only one given name; others have two or more:

Christopher Toppan Bayley
John Christopher Behncke
Albert Gallatin Bowling
Asahill Purnell Brittingham
Thomas Chamberlain Chase
Hewlett Townsend Coles
Michael Christopher Darling
Henry Payton Randolph Dayton
Andrew Donaldson Evans
Redman Lawrence Foushee
Matthias Hanson Goldaere
Jonathan Hamilton Haven
Christopher Stewart Henderson
Francis Hopkinson Hodgkinson

Lodowick Spogell Humphreys
Richard Tilghman Kennard
Joseph Stewart Liautier
John Baptiste Eugene Martin
Myles Thornton McLeveen
Thomas Pinckney McMahon
William Greves McMeaken
William Henry Odenheimer
Thomas Greenwich Robeson
Gustaf Rainholdt Salonius
Thomas Whittemore Thomas
Elie Augustus Frederick Vallette
Thomas Vaughan Whelldin
Laois Frederick Winkelmann

A cursory glance will show that such names are a genealogical gold mine, as are the witnesses, naturalization, apprenticeship, and Afro-American information.

Additional information on these records:

Ruth Priest Dixon. "Genealogical Fallout from the War of 1812," *Prologue*, Vol. 24, Spring 1992, pp. 70-76.

Index to Seamen's Protection Certificate Applications, Port of Philadelphia, 1824-1861, Baltimore: Clearfield Company, 1994.

Ira Dye. "The Philadelphia Seamen's Protection Certificate Applications," *Prologue*, Vol. 18, Spring, 1986, pp. 46-55, reprinted by the Archives in *Our Family, Our Town*.

"Seafarers of 1812 - A Profile," *Prologue*, Vol. 5, Spring 1973, pp. 3-13.

Guide to Genealogical Research in the National Archives. Washington, DC: National Archives Trust Fund Board, 1985, pp. 189-191.

Reginald Horsman. *Causes of the War of 1812*, Philadelphia: University of Pennsylvania Press, 1962.

Martha S. Putney. *Black Sailors, Afro-American Merchant Seamen and Whalemen Prior to the Civil War, New York: Greenwood Press, 1987.*

James Fulton Zimmerman. *Impressment of American Seamen*, Studies of History, Economics and Public Law, Columbia University Political Science Faculty, New York: Columbia University, 1925.

INDEX

SEAMEN'S PROTECTION CERTIFICATE APPLICATIONS

PORT OF PHILADELPHIA
1796-1823

Data in this index is given in this order:

| Seaman's name | Year | Age | Color | State | Country |

Key to Data:

Seaman's name:	last, first, middle
Year:	year application was submitted
Age:	age at time of application
	00 = no age given
Color:	b = black c = colored m = mulatto
	s = sambo y = yellow I = Indian
	blank = Caucasian
State:	state of birth
	blank = none given
Country:	country of birth
	none given = foreign born but no country given

Note: Applications made for lost certificates often lack much of the above information, but these applications frequently have interesting accounts of how the original SPC was lost.

No surname, Jesse 1806 30 b MD
Free black man, servant to Littleton Dennis, Jr.,
Ship *Young Elias* enroute to Bordeaux.

Abbot, Isaac 1800 21 b MD
Abbott, Benjamin 1797 25
Abbott, Curtis 1821 21 DE
Abel, George C. 1822 20 PA
Abels, William 1805 26 PA
Abels, William 1813 34 none given
Abercrombie, James, Jr
    1810 19 PA
Abercrombie, John B. 1814 18 c PA
Abott, John 1808 21 PA
Abraham, James 1809 22 NJ
Abraham, William 1818 23 MA
Ackley, William 1822 21 NJ
Acres, William Four 1810 22 DE
Adams, Alexander 1796 30 PA
Adams, Alexander 1804 0
Adams, Benjamin 1806 20 NJ
Adams, Benjamin 1810 0
Adams, Benjamin 1810 36 b NJ
Adams, Charles 1804 32 b MD
Adams, Charles 1808 18 PA
Adams, Charles 1809 0
Adams, David 1812 22 m DE
Adams, Henry 1818 18 CT
Adams, Howe 1818 30 b MD
Adams, Isaac 1816 22 MA
Adams, James 1816 38 MA
Adams, James 1818 20 PA
Adams, John 1801 25
Adams, John 1804 24 VA
Adams, John 1807 00
Adams, John 1807 26 y MD
Adams, John 1809 26 y NY
Adams, John 1811 29 NY
Adams, John 1817 33 b
Adams, John 1818 23 NJ
Adams, John 1821 28 NY
Adams, Robert 1818 20 PA
Adams, Robert 1823 17 PA
Adams, Samuel 1801 21 PA
Adams, Samuel 1815 26 b MA
Adams, Thomas 1807 20 y NC
Adams, Thomas 1808 24 MA
Adams, William 1801 27 PA
Adams, William 1804 24 PA
Adams, William 1804 19 SC
Adams, William 1808 27 PA
Adams, William 1816 20 MA

Adamson, Barnet 1800 18 PA
Adan, Thomas 1801 37 MA
Adderly, Robert 1796 0 PA
Addeson, George 1804 23 CT
Addington, Henry 1804 21 CT
Addington, William 1800 26 PA
Addison, Robert 1804 23 NY
Adley, John 1806 24 MD
Adlum, Richard 1801 20 PA
Adlur, John 1805 25 PA
Adye, Robert 1805 24 GA
Aekins, Archibald 1800 28 PA
Aertsen, William 1818 17 SC
Afford, Peter 1822 15 m PA
Ager, William 1809 22 PA
Agnew, James 1808 27 SC
Agnew, Joseph 1819 18 NJ
Agnew, Thomas 1801 17 NY

Agustus, Amer 1812 17 y DE
Indented servant of John Warner

Aiken, David 1805 23 m PA
Aikens, David 1816 26 y
Aikin, Robert 1817 36 none given
Ailes, Milford 1805 26 b PA
Aitken, John 1804 30 PA
Aitken, Robert L. 1809 21 PA
Akerley, Obadiah 1817 27 NY
Akeroyde, William 1804 22 NY
Akers, Thomas 1804 33 MD
Aland, Lois 1808 23 MS
Alberger, George 1821 22 PA
Albert, Henry 1820 21 b PA
Albert, John 1818 51 RI
Alberti, George, Jr. F. 1809 20 PA
Albertson, Aaron 1815 19 NJ
Albertson, William 1804 22 NJ
Albertson, William 1805 0
Albro, Benjn. 1798 17 RI
Alcock, William Ball, Jr. 1817 20 PA
Alcorn, George 1807 16 DE
Alcorn, Robert Reed 1818 25 none given
Alderman, Joel 1809 22 NJ
Aldershaw, John 1817 23 NH
Aldert, Sikke 1822 28 none given
Aldrige, William 1803 24 NJ
Alexander, Amos 1819 37 PA
Alexander, Benjamin 1807 21 b DE
Alexander, Charles 1810 23 NJ
Alexander, Daniel 1798 24 b PA
Alexander, Ellabuis 1798 73 NJ

Name	Year	Age	State	Note	Name	Year	Age	State	Note
Alexander, George	1807	18	PA		Allen, John	1818	32	PA	
Alexander, George	1813	0			Allen, John	1819	18	PA	
Alexander, James	1806	23	NY		Allen, John	1820	30	MA	
Alexander, James	1818	17	DE		Allen, John	1823	33	VA	
Alexander, John	1804	34	NJ		Allen, Jonathan	1814	22 c	PA	
Alexander, John	1807	21	PA		Allen, Jonathan	1815	0		
Alexander, John	1812	27		none given	Allen, Joseph	1809	23	PA	
Alexander, Joseph	1804	14	PA		Allen, Joseph	1809	20	MD	
Alexander, Joseph	1807	13	PA		Allen, Joseph	1811	32		none given
Alexander, Joseph	1810	22 b	DE		Allen, Joseph	1822	26	CT	
Alexander, Joseph	1815	18	LA		Allen, Michael	1813	19	GA	
Alexander, Lebuis	1806	0			Allen, Nathaniel	1817	27 b	MD	
Alexander, Peter	1821	19 c	PA		Allen, Noble	1821	30	MA	
Alexander, Richard Franks	1801	18	PA		Allen, Reuben	1806	57	MA	
Alexander, William	1804	19 m	MD		Allen, Reuben	1807	17	MA	
Alexander, William	1822	19	DE		Allen, Richard	1811	24	VA	
Alexanders, William	1810	26	PA		Allen, Richard	1815	20 s	PA	
Alexon, Daniel	1817	27	NY		Allen, Richard	1815	0		
Alftan, John	1798	0		Sweden	Allen, Richard	1819	0		
Algeo, John	1809	0		none given	Allen, Robert	1810	16	PA	
Alibos, Martin	1807	30	LA		Allen, Samuel	1809	25 b	PA	
Allardice, Joseph	1815	21	PA		Allen, Samuel	1810	38 b	DE	
Allbright, John	1798	26	NJ		Allen, Samuel	1815	26	RI	
Allcorn, James	1809	30		none given	Allen, Samuel	1820	21	NJ	
Allen, Alexander	1800	23	NY		Allen, Silvanus	1817	28	MA	
Allen, Alexander	1803	34	VA		Allen, Thomas	1807	37	PA	
Allen, Alexander	1818	18	MD		Allen, Thomas	1817	24	VA	
Allen, Andrew	1811	16	MA		Allen, Thomas W.	1821	32	NJ	
Allen, Anthony	1811	40 b	MD		Allen, Tiddeman	1807	23	NY	
Allen, Augustus	1810	26 m	CT		Allen, William	1804	20	PA	
Allen, Benjamin	1811	28	NJ		Allen, William Carll	1809	23	NJ	
Allen, Christian	1810	18	MA		Allen, William	1815	22	NY	
Allen, David	1810	18	PA		Allen, William	1815	31		
Allen, David	1812	00			Allen, William	1818	14	PA	
Allen, David	1815	0			Allen, William	1821	40 b	VA	
Allen, David	1819	32	NJ		Alley, John	1810	26	MA	
Allen, Elisha	1809	27	CT		Alligood, Thomas	1815	17	PA	
Allen, Francis	1815	21 m	NY		Allison, Cornelious	1798	25	NY	
Allen, George	1815	19	MA		Allison, George	1804	24	MD	
Allen, George	1821	20 y	MA		Allison, Thomas	1805	24	PA	
Allen, Henry	1801	26	MA		Alloway, Samuel,Jr.	1822	22	PA	
Allen, Ira	1810	24	CT		Allsop, Mack	1821	28	MD	
Allen, Isaac	1810	24 b	DE		Allwine, John	1801	32		Germany
Allen, Isaac	1815	29	Pa		Almendis, Francis	1807	31	LA	
Allen, James	1804	18	RI		Alpine, Thomas M.	1804	22	PA	
Allen, James	1810	23	CT		Alquest, Adam	1815	22	MA	
Allen, James	1817	19 b	PA		Alsieux, John C.	1818	16		St Thomas
Allen, John	1797	28	DE		Alvord, John	1809	24	NJ	
Allen, John	1798	19 b	PA		Ambelman, Thomas	1822	23 b	NY	
Allen, John	1804	21	PA		Ambruster, Caspar	1809	21	PA	
Allen, John	1815	23	NY		America, James	1806	30 b	MD	
Allen, John	1818	20 s	PA		America, James	1808	0 b		

Ames, John	1820	20	ME
Ames, Sears	1811	24	MA
Ames, Sears	1818	31	MA
Amor, Manuel	1808	23 y	DE
Amos, Daniel	1807	35 y	NY
Amy, John	1813	23 m	NY
And, Joseph	1810	24 b	NJ
Anderson, Aaron	1812	38 b	PA
Anderson, Abraham	1805	28 m	MD
Anderson, Abraham	1822	35 s	PA
Anderson, Alexander	1796	0	DE
Anderson, Alexander	1822	24 b	RI
Anderson, Andrew	1806	21	NJ
Anderson, Andrew	1814	39	LA
Anderson, Andrew	1817	27	LA
Anderson, Charles	1797	28 b	MD
Anderson, Charles	1810	16 c	DE
Anderson, Charles	1817	21 b	VA
Anderson, Cornelius	1815	15	NY
Anderson, David	1804	40 b	VA
Anderson, David Levi	1807	27 b	NY
Anderson, David	1809	23	NY
Anderson, George	1809	17	PA
Anderson, George	1811	24 b	MA
Anderson, George	1812	00	
Anderson, George	1815	23	PA
Anderson, Henry	1811	27 b	DE
Anderson, Henry	1812	00 b	DE
Anderson, Henry	1821	24 y	MD
Anderson, Hugh	1806	24	PA
Anderson, Issacha	1797	22	MA
Anderson, Jacob	1803	24	PA
Anderson, Jacob	1806	28	NJ
Anderson, James	1801	23	PA
Anderson, James	1805	22 b	MD
Anderson, James	1805	21	PA
Anderson, James	1808	22 b	PA
Anderson, James	1810	19	RI
Anderson, James	1817	27 b	DE
Anderson, James	1821	19	PA
Anderson, James	1823	21	PA
Anderson, John	1794	23	DE
Anderson, John	1803	29	MA
Anderson, John	1806	36	PA
Anderson, John	1806	30	NY
Anderson, John	1807	24	PA
Anderson, John	1809	25	DE
Anderson, John	1811	00	
Anderson, John	1817	25	VA
Anderson, John	1817	28	NC
Anderson, John	1818	27 b	NY
Anderson, John	1818	26 b	PA

Anderson, John	1822	28 y	MD
Anderson, Joseph	1805	18	DE
Anderson, Magnus	1810	35	PA
Anderson, Mosses	1795	29 b	PA
Anderson, Nathaniel	1804	26 m	NC
Anderson, Nicholas	1808	30	
Anderson, Peter	1809	23 b	PA
Anderson, Peter	1809	0	
Anderson, Reuben	1811	20	DE
Anderson, Robert	1809	28	RI
Anderson, Robert,Jr.	1815	12	PA
Anderson, Robert	1815	20	MA
Anderson, Robert	1823	26	NJ
Anderson, Rubin	1815	22 c	VA
Anderson, Samuel	1804	26	MD
Anderson, Samuel	1815	22 b	VA
Anderson, Samuel	1815	25	NY
Anderson, Samuel	1816	25	NJ
Anderson, Thomas	1804	18	PA
Anderson, Thomas	1806	21	NJ
Anderson, Thomas	1807	31	PA
Anderson, Thomas	1809	29	DE
Anderson, Thomas, Jr.	1812	00	
Anderson, Thomas	1813	17	PA
Anderson, Thomas	1823	12	PA
Anderson, William	1806	25	VA
Anderson, William	1806	30	LA
Anderson, William	1807	22	VA
Anderson, William	1810	27	SC
Anderson, William	1816	0	SC
Anderson, William E.	1818	24	NC
Anderson, William	1818	35 b	DE
Anderson, Wm.	1807	00	
Andreas, John	1805	0	
Andreas, John	1807	20	LA
Andreas, John	1810	32	PA
Andress, Lammuel	1811	21	MA
Andrew, John	1809	25 b	NC
Andrew, John B.	1811	18 c	PA
Andrew, Josiah B.	1811	18	MA
Andrew, Thomas M.	1822	20	NY
Andrews, Abraham	1815	22	Pa
Andrews, Alonzo R.	1820	16	PA
Andrews, Anthony	1805	29	SC
Andrews, Daniel	1811	23	PA
Andrews, David	1818	25	NJ
Andrews, Ezekiel	1815	35	MA
Andrews, Henry	1820	19	PA
Andrews, John	1800	15	NJ
Andrews, John	1800	15	NJ
Andrews, John	1807	23	RI
Andrews, John	1810	23	RI

11

Name	Year	Age		Place
Andrews, John	1811	30		NY
Andrews, John	1812	37		none given
Andrews, John	1818	32		MA
Andrews, Joseph	1807	26		PA
Andrews, Peter, Jr.	1815	20		PA
Andrews, Peter, Jr.	1817	27		PA
Andrews, Robert	1809	26		NY
Andrews, Seth	1804	53		MA
Andrews, William, Jr.	1823	24		MA
Andron, Peter	1807	27		VA
Andrup, Christian	1815	30		
Angell, Amos	1817	16		PA
Angelo, David	1810	21		NJ
Anger, Johnan	1806	29		NJ
Angle, John	1804	51		PA
Angus, Samuel	1807	22		PA
Annan, John	1815	20		NJ
Annar, Charles	1809	20		NY
Annely, William	1798	21		NY
Ansbey, Charles	1810	16		PA
Ansdell, Thomas	1804	22		MA
Ansley, Andrew	1805	14		NY
Anson, Peter	1803	32		MA
Anspach, Philip	1815	27		PA
Anthony, Abraham	1806	21		CT
Anthony, Abram	1806	21 b		CT
Anthony, Enos	1805	30		LA
Anthony, Frank	1805	25		GA
Anthony, John	1809	0		
Anthony, John	1815	21 c		PA
Anthony, Joseph	1813	32		none given
Anthony, Noah	1808	24 b		PA
Antoine, John	1806	23		LA
Antoine, John	1807	27		LA
Antoine, Joseph	1810	33		LA
Antonio, Alexander	1807	30		LA
Antonio, Joseph	1810	25		LA
Antonio, Joseph	1812	00		
Antonio, Peter Thomas	1810	20		LA
Antony, Jack	1817	20 b		LA
Antony, John	1809	21		LA
Antony, Joseph	1809	29		LA
Anwood, Elijah	1816	35 b		MD
Apeny, Anthony	1815	28 b		LA
Apple, George	1796	0		PA
SPC from Timothy Pickering,				
Secretary of State				
Apple, George	1811	00		
Apple, George	1811	39		PA
Apple, Henry	1822	13		PA
Applegate, James	1821	27		NJ
Applegate, Richard	1823	24		NJ
Appleton, Charles	1818	22		MA
Appleton, John	1809	22		PA
Appleton, John	1815	0		PA
Appleton, John H.	1818	28		DE
Appleton, William	1818	27		NY
Applewhite, Benjamin	1806	22 y		MA
Arbutton, William	1798	0		Ireland
Archer, Benjamin	1799	25		NJ
Archer, James	1806	14		
Archer, James	1810	18		MA
Archer, Robert	1822	22 b		DE
Archibald, Bartholomew	1809	57		PA
Ardis, George	1810	22		VA
Ardis, John W.	1798	24		VA
Ardley, Ernest	1823	15		PA
Arentrue, John	1823	15		PA
Arentrue, William, Jr.	1823	18		PA
Arey, Samuel	1818	30		NJ
Arffmann, John Jacob	1807	17		PA
Argus, John	1804	25 b		NY
Argus, John	1810	0		
Armand, John	1805	39		PA
Armor, George	1807	33 b		NJ
Armour, William	1811	22		NY
Armstead, George	1823	22		VA
Armstid, John	1823	50 y		SC
Armstrong, Abraham M.	1811	15		PA
Armstrong, Alexander	1805	21		PA
Armstrong, Alexander	1822	27		RI
Armstrong, Andrew	1823	15		PA
Armstrong, Elijah	1817	35		MD
Armstrong, George L.	1815	24		NJ
Armstrong, George H.	1818	16		PA
Armstrong, James	1803	33		PA
Armstrong, James	1805	24 y		MD
Armstrong, James	1819	22 b		DE
Armstrong, John	1798	30		England
Armstrong, John	1800	25		RI
Armstrong, John	1818	21		PA
Armstrong, Jonathan	1804	26		MD
Armstrong, Joseph G.	1823	20 y		MD
Armstrong, Lazarus	1805	24 b		MD
Armstrong, Nicholas C.	1812	16		PA
Armstrong, Nicholas C.	1813	0		
Armstrong, Richard	1816	16		NC
Armstrong, Theodore	1823	15		PA
Armstrong, Thomas M.	1817	14		PA
Armstrong, William	1811	25 c		MA
Armstrong, Wm.	1817	49 c		PA
Arnel, William, Jr.	1821	17		NJ

Name	Year	Age	State	Note
Arnold, Benedick	1806	31	PA	
Arnold, Charles D.	1815	18	NJ	
Arnold, James	1814	16 c	DE	
Arnold, James	1817	0		
Arnold, John	1804	25	CT	
Arnold, John	1809	0		
Arnold, John M.	1819	14	PA	
Arry, John	1805	35	LA	
Art, James	1811	21	PA	
Arthur, Robert	1807	18	NY	
Ash, Charles	1803	23	PA	
Ash, Charles	1810	0		
Ash, James, Jr.	1803	22 m	VA	
Ash, William	1810	29 b	DE	
Ashburn, John	1815	29	VA	
Ashburn, Thomas	1798	0	PA	
Ashfield, Henry	1811	18	NY	
Ashford, James	1808	20	PA	
Ashley, John	1798	23	CT	
Ashley, Thomas	1821	35		none given
Ashmead, Thomas	0000	21	PA	
Ashmead, Thomas	1800	21	PA	
Ashmore, Jabesh	1812	23	NJ	
Ashmore, Jebiz	1822	22	NC	
Ashton, Isaac L.	1814	16	PA	
Ashton, James	1823	26		England
Ashton, John	1810	0		
Ashton, John	1822	20	NY	
Ashton, Joseph H.	1806	22	PA	
Ashton, Joseph H.	1812	00		

SPC issued 1806 taken from him by British

Name	Year	Age	State	Note
Ashton, William	1807	20	PA	
Ashton, William	1809	22	PA	
Askin, Francis	1823	17	PA	
Askin, James	1811	23	DE	
Askin, John	1818	15		none given
Askins, Thomas	1820	31 b	DE	
Aspin, George	1805	25	CT	
Asquith, Henry	1812	19 b	MD	
Asquith, Henry	1818	26 b	MD	
Astick, Entonio	1817	23 y	LA	
Astill, Joseph	1815	16	NJ	
Aston, David	1811	21	PA	
Aston, John	1810	28 y	VA	
Aston, John	1811	00		
Astram, John	1812	00		
Astrea, Anthony	1808	45	LA	
Athroun, Samuel	1810	29		Gr.Br.
Atiane, John	1817	26	NJ	
Aticheson, John	1808	20	NY	

Name	Year	Age	State	Note
Atkins, John	1811	33	CT	
Atkins, Robet	1819	29	PA	
Atkins, Solomon	1810	23	MD	
Atkins, William	1810	28	PA	
Atkins, William	1811	21	PA	
Atkinson, Charles	1798	22		England
Atkinson, Henry	1809	16 b	MD	
Atkinson, Henry	1815	31	MD	
Atkinson, John	1806	28	PA	
Atkinson, Joseph	1809	16	NJ	
Atkinson, Levy	1809	23	NJ	
Atkinson, William	1803	28	NJ	
Atkinson, William	1809	20	NJ	
Atwell, Nathaniel	1821	22	NY	
Atwood, William	1798	32	SC	
Auchinleck, Alexr.	1806	17	PA	
Augustine, John	1815	0		
Augustus, Abraham	1815	28 y	DE	
Augustus, John	1805	29 b	PA	
Auld, William	1821	20	MD	
Aull, Joseph	1821	24	DE	
Austen, James	1800	23		
Austin, David	1810	22	MA	
Austin, Jacob	1815	22	NJ	
Austin, James	1797	21		
Austin, Joseph	1811	24	RI	
Auston, John	1804	32	NY	
Auterbridge, David	1808	24 y	RI	
Auterbridge, David	1811	00		
Auzou, Peter	1809	27	LA	
Averlin, Jacob	1803	30	PA	
Avery, Charles	1822	24	NY	
Avery, James	1807	27	PA	
Avery, John	1806	0		
Avis, Levi	1815	27	CT	
Avry, John	1803	21	DE	
Axford, Charles	1803	18	PA	
Axford, William	1804	35	NJ	
Axford, William	1807	31	NJ	
Aydelott, Eber	1810	24	DE	
Aydelott, John	1810	23	MD	
Aydelott, Samuel	1811	27	DE	
Ayers, John	1813	25	NY	
Ayers, Robert	1820	46 b	DE	
Aylmere, George	1796	28		
Ayres, Benjamin	1819	19 y	PA	
Ayres, Daniel	1801	15	NJ	
Ayres, David	1820	25 c	PA	
Ayres, George	1815	23 b	PA	
Ayres, George	1822	28	MA	
Ayrs, John William	1822	19	MA	
Azen, John	1816	31 b	MA	

13

Babb, Jacob	1798	20	PA	
Babbidge, William	1809	18	NJ	
Babcock, Bradford	1811	30	MA	
Babcock, Jacob	1804	28	NJ	
Babcock, Joseph	1823	29	NJ	
Babcock, Oliver	1818	27	RI	
Babcock, William	1807	25 m	NY	
Babino, David	1815	24	Va	
Babson, John	1817	31	MA	
Baccus, Thomas	1812	22 b	NJ	
Bache, Benjamin Franklin	1816	15	VA	
Bachtold, Daniel	1817	32	MA	
Backman, Lawrence	1817	44		none given
Backus, Isaac	1804	21 b	NJ	
Bacon, Job	1806	20	PA	
Bacon, Job	1815	20	NJ	
Bacon, Nathan	1810	18	NJ	
Bade, Frederick	1804	36	DE	
Bade, Frederick	1808	0		
Badger, Bela	1807	39	CT	
Bador, Gibson H.	1807	24	MA	
Bagendorf, Christopher	1807	25	PA	
Baggs, James	1809	16	PA	
Baggs, James	1810	0		
Baggs, James	1810	0		
Baggs, John	1806	40	PA	
Baggs, William	1807	20	PA	
Bagret, Henry	1823	25	NY	
Bagshaw, Joseph	1805	17	PA	
Bailey, Bennett	1810	30	MA	
Bailey, George	1805	27	PA	
Bailey, James	1809	29		none given
Bailey, John	1805	16	PA	
Bailey, John	1806	22	MD	
Bailey, Joseph	1809	20	NJ	
Bailey, Richard	1805	21 b	NY	
Bailey, Richard	1812	28 b	MA	
Bailey, Thomas	1797	20	MA	
Bailie, William	1821	25	MA	
Baily, William	1811	19	NY	

Baish, John George   1800 21   PA
Born 23 Sept. 1779; baptised German Lutheran
Church, Phila, 10 Oct 1779, son of Martin & Maria
Magdalena Baish

Baker, Albert G.	1817	16	PA
Baker, Bowman	1823	25	VA
Baker, Cleophas	1807	28	MA
Baker, Daniel	1823	19	DE
Baker, Edward	1817	27	LA
Baker, Edward	1819	21	PA

Baker, Frederick	1817	18	PA
Baker, Fredrick	1815	32	PA
Baker, George	1804	18	VA
Baker, Harrison	1815	18 c	VA
Baker, Hilary	1810	19	PA
Baker, Horace	1822	22	NY
Baker, Jacob	1823	27	NJ
Baker, James	1800	23	PA
Baker, James	1811	17	PA
Baker, James	1823	29	VA
Baker, John W.	1805	26	PA
Baker, John	1808	20	PA
Baker, John	1809	19	NH
Baker, John	1809	26	PA
Baker, John	1809	0	PA
Baker, John	1810	18	PA
Baker, John	1810	0	
Baker, John Burton	1810	20	MD
Baker, John Christopher	1812	22	PA
Baker, John Hilary, Jr	1822	16	PA
Baker, Jonathan	1819	20	MA
Baker, Joseph	1810	23	NY
Baker, Joseph	1813	0	
Baker, Lewis	1809	23 b	PA
Baker, Martin	1822	24	MA
Baker, Noah	1805	21	DE
Baker, Robert	1820	24	SC
Baker, Samuel	1809	16	PA
Baker, Samuel	1814	15	PA
Baker, Samuel	1819	21	NJ
Baker, Thomas	1810	44	MA
Baker, Thomas	1820	30	NC
Baker, William	1798	22	MA
Baker, William	1818	22	NC
Baker, William	1823	29 y	NY
Balant, Reuben	1822	19	NC
Bald, John Rice	1815	14	PA
Baldwin, Jesse	1809	38	CT
Baldwin, Samuel	1801	16	PA
Baldwin, Samuel	1807	22	PA
Baldwin, William	1804	26	PA
Bale, Joseph	1811	26	MD
Balfield, Thomas	1815	18	NC
Balflower, John	1810	29	LA
Balfour, Antoine	1818	18 y	LA
Balk, William	1803	29	MA
Ball, Isaac	1805	28 b	NJ
Ball, William	1807	28	SC
Ballentime, James	1804	14	PA
Balls, William	1804	23	PA
Balls, William	1810	29	PA
Balm, Jacob	1809	21	PA

Balos, Andrew	1809	32	LA		Barker, James	1806	30 b	DE
Ban, John	1810	23 b	NY		Barker, James	1815	19	PA
Banan, Nicholas	1805	22	MD		Barker, John Douglass	1820	20	MA
Bancraft, Samuel	1823	15	MA		Barker, Joseph	1805	33	VA
Bandick, Robert	1812	19 c	VA		Barker, Samuel	1815	29	MA
Banfield, James	1819	27	NY		Barker, Thomas	1815	20	MA
Banger, Samuel	1820	18	PA		Barkinbile, Matthias	1804	40	PA
Banister, John W.	1822	21	RI		Barkinlile, Matthias	1807	00	
Banjonah, William	1815	24 y	PA		Barkinson, Peter	1804	21 b	VA
Banker, Peter	1808	22	NY		Barling, Aaron	1818	26	MD
Banks, David	1804	23 y	MD		Barling, William	1822	27	PA
Banks, James E.	1815	14	MD		Barlow, George	1822	39	none given
Banks, Thomas	1801	24	CT		Barlow, Joseph	1816	26	VA
Banks, Thomas	1807	26 b	MD		Barlow, Josiah	1809	24	DE
Bankson, William G.	1813	17	MD		Barlow, Robert	1809	30	VA
Banner, William	1809	34 b	VA		Barlow, Robert	1810	0	
Bannerman, William W.	1823	19	MD		Barmetior, John	1817	29	PA
Baptist, John	1820	21	SC		Barnabar, Joshua	1811	00	SC
Baptiste, John	1807	21	LA		Barnabas, Joshua	1807	25 b	SC
Baptiste, John	1807	22 m	SC		Barnaby, William	1798	27	MD
Baptiste, John	1809	38	LA		Barnard, William	1815	26	PA
Barbara, Anthony	1821	33			Barnes, Aaron	1809	22	PA
Barbara, Anthony	1822	33	LA		Barnes, Charles	1806	25 b	PA
Barber, Ephraim	1810	31	MA		Barnes, Dangill	1804	21	NH
Barber, John C.	1814	25	PA		Barnes, Dangill	1804	21	NH
Barber, Michael	1807	29	LA		Barnes, George	1810	25	MD
Barber, Oliver	1804	32	MA					
Barber, Saloman	1796	23	MA		Barnes, James, Jr.	1816	15	PA
Barbier, Stephen	1807	19	MA		Barnes, John	1816	21	PA
Barchelai, Stephen	1807	24	NY		James Barnes, Sr., is father of James & John			
Barclay, David W.	1811	17	PA					
Barclay, James	1805	21 y	NY		Barnes, James	1818	27	NJ
Barclay, James	1806	0			Barnes, John	1798	29	MD
Barclay, John	1817	17	PA		Barnes, John	1811	25	MD
Barclay, Joseph	1812	20	PA		Barnes, John	1818	19	PA
Barclay, Joseph	1819	21	PA		Barnes, John B.	1818	23	NY
Barclay, Samuel, Jr.	1799	18	PA		Barnes, Joseph	1804	21	NJ
Barclay, William	1809	19	MD		Barnes, Joseph	1812	00	
Barcley, Tobias	1810	34 b	DE		Barnes, Joseph	1815	0	
Bardell, William	1806	10	PA		Barnes, Paul	1809	24	PA
Barden, Michael	1801	21	PA		Barnes, Paul	1809	24	PA
Bardin, Levi	1805	28	MA		Barnes, Peter	1804	21	PA
Baret, Elijah	1817	22	NJ		Barnes, Philip	1823	32	PA
Barger, William	1796	22	PA		Barnes, Robert	1800	16	PA
Barhhill, Robert	1815	19	PA		Barnes, Robert	1807	28	NY
Bari, Swen	1807	40	none given		Barnes, Thomas	1798	33	VA
Baright, Henry	1811	24	NY		Barnes, William	1801	21	PA
Barker, Augustus	1810	16	MA		Barnes, William	1807	21	MA
Barker, George	1811	23	RI		Barnes, William	1818	38	DE
Barker, George	1818	10 c	NJ		Barnes, William	1820	21	VA
Barker, James	1804	22 y	PA		Barnes, Wm.	1823	18	PA
Barker, James	1805	0			Barnet, John	1803	18	DE

15

Barnet, John	1806	22	MD
Barnet, Toby	1798	24	DE
Barnett, John	1803	18	
Barnett, John	1803	18	MA
Barnett, John	1812	00	
Barnett, William	1805	19	
Barney, William	1810	21 b	PA
Barnhart, Philander	1822	26	PA
Barns, Henry	1809	14	PA
Barns, Livingston	1805	32	MA
Barnwell, William	1809	22 b	SC
Barnwell, William	1812	00	
Baron, James	1804	27	VA
Baron, Lewis	1807	20	LA
Barr, John	1804	23	CT
Barr, William S.	1815	20	DE
Barrat, Tobias	1806	32 b	DE
Barrell, Jeremiah	1822	22	PA
Barrett, Edward	1805	34	PA
Barrett, George	1815	22 b	DE
Barrett, James	1799	18	NY
Barrett, James	1809	23	DE
Barrett, John	1807	21	PA
Barrett, John	1815	25	CT
Barrett, Robert	1809	22	PA
Barrett, William	1798	15	PA
Barrie, Peter	1797	0		Scotland
Barrington, Oliver	1809	30	NY
Barrington, Thomas	1810	37	PA
Barron, John	1809	21 y	NC
Barron, John	1815	29 c	NC
Barrow, Andrew D.	1815	25	MD
Barrows, Isaac	1801	18	PA
Barry, James	1798	26	CT
Barry, James	1807	00	
Barry, James	1807	21	VA
Barry, James	1809	24	MD
Barry, Jesse	1807	00	
Barry, John	1806	25	MD
Barry, John	1806	11	PA
Barry, John	1810	20	PA
Barry, John	1811	21 b	DE
Barry, John	1812	00	PA
Barry, John	1817	26	PA
Barry, John	1819	27	NC
Barry, Ruben	1817	27 s	MA
Barry, William	1804	19	VA
Bartel, John	1809	23	
Bartelson, Peter K.	1817	17	PA
Bartholmew, John	1797	22	CT
Bartholomew, Benjamin			
	1806	15	PA

Bartholomew, Thomas			
	1804	15	PA
Bartist, John	1806	26	LA
Bartle, George	1815	22	PA
Bartleson, Charles M.	1811	16	PA
Bartleson, Charles M.	1816	23	PA
Bartleson, John	1802	22	PA
Bartlet, James	1798	22	MD
Bartlet, Peleg,Jr.	1815	14	MA
Bartlett, Benjamin	1811	00	
Bartlett, Benjamin	1812	00	
Bartlett, Benjamin	1813	0	
Bartlett, George	1815	28	DE
Bartlett, Nichoas	1807	00	
Bartlett, Nicholas	1799	19	MA
Bartlett, Zephaniah	1805	38	MA
Bartling, David	1807	20	PA
Bartlit, Ethelbert	1815	22	CT
Bartlum, James	1811	31	MD
Bartol, Samuel	1811	21	MA
Barton, Benjamin	1815	41	RI
Barton, George	1804	22	PA
Barton, John	1805	21	PA
Barton, Joseph	1804	0		Italy
Barton, Joseph	1804	38		none given
Barton, Joseph L.	1823	20	PA
Barton, Luther	1823	38	ME
Barton, Samuel	1810	28	MA
Barton, William	1823	29	DE
Bartram, Lewis	1813	25		none given
Barttell, Benjamin	1810	23	MA
Bascome, Nathaniel	1809	23	NY
Basell, Francis	1807	21	LA
Bashford, Norbury	1811	21	PA
Basset, Ensigne	1803	22	MA
Bassett, James	1808	15	PA
Bassett, Samuel	1811	32	NH
Bassett, Samuel	1813	0	
Bassett, William	1812	21 b	PA
Batchelder, Stephen	1823	23	ME
Bateman, Enos	1814	0	
Bateman, Enos	1817	0	
Bateman, Robert W.	1818	18		none given
Batemen, Enos	1809	20	NJ
Bates, Charles	1811	21	NJ
Bates, Isaac	1807	23	NJ
Bates, James	1815	31	NJ
Bates, Lewis	1819	16	MA
Batson, James	1815	17	DE
Batson, Thomas	1798	23	DE
Batt, James	1798	27	PA
Batt, James	1804	33	PA

Batt, John	1803	23 y	MA
Batt, William	1809	18	NJ
Battess, John	1821	36 y	KY
Battis, Claybourn B.	1807	27	VA
Battis, George	1812	33 b	MT
Battis, John	1801	22	MD
Battis, John	1804	30 b	DE
Battis, John	1811	27 c	LA
Battis, John	1811	22 c	NY
Battis, John	1812	50 b	LA
Battis, John	1815	25 b	PA
Battis, John	1817	43	none given
Battis, John	1821	23	PA
Battle, John	1808	22	DE
Battles, Nathaniel	1799	21	PA
Baum, George	1816	27	PA
Baungard, Jacob	1814	24	PA
Baven, David	1817	34	VA
Baxby, Richard G.	1809	26	RI
Baxter, Allen	1812	13	MA
Baxter, Franklin	1823	32	MA
Baxter, Henry	1823	27	MA
Baxter, John	1813	23	NJ
Baxter, Moses	1809	20	DE
Baxter, Samuel	1818	21	PA
Baxter, William	1818	19	PA
Bayard, Adam	1811	16	PA
Bayard, Charles	1817	17	PA
Bayard, Charles	1821	20	PA
Bayard, Thomas	1811	26 y	NY
Bayard, Walton	1804	17	PA
Bayard, Walton	1807	19	PA
Bayley, Christopher Toppan			
	1815	24	MA
Bayley, George	1805	26	PA
Bayment, John	1799	0	MD
Baynard, Jacob	1822	26 b	DE
Bazillie, Elijah	1811	22	NJ
Beaden, William	1800	30	PA
Beal, John	1815	25	PA
Beal, Seth, Jr.	1820	22	MA
Beal, Thomas	1804	21	DE
Beal, Thomas	1806	18	PA
Beale, Thomas	1809	21	PA
Beale, William	1806	16	SC
Beale, William Golden	1813	21	PA
Beales, Joseph	1807	31	LA
Beaman, Joseph	1823	29	ME
Bean, John	1813	29	PA
Beardsley, Lewis	1811	18	CT
Bears, Watson	1823	19	MA
Beasley, Edward	1806	17	MD

Beasley, Edward	1807	00	MD
Beasley, Moses	1820	23	MD
Beatty, Robert	1820	21	NY
Beaty, James	1805	13	NY
Beaty, James	1812	00	
Beaty, James	1815	0	
Beaty, John	1805	15	NY
Beaumant, Joel	1805	23	PA
Beavis, John	1800	16	PA
Beazley, James	1807	39	MD
Beazley, Robert	1813	23	DE
Beazley, Robert	1813	0	
Bebster, John Lee	1817	22 b	PA
Bechtel, John	1823	20	PA
Beck, John	1799	16	PA
Beck, John	1803	20	DE
Beck, John	1804	0	
Beck, John	1812	00	
Beck, John, Jr.	1813	21	PA
Beck, Joseph F.	1820	16	PA
Beck, Michael	1806	30	PA
Beck, Peter F.	1807	24	PA
Becket, Henry	1815	30 b	VA
Becket, William	1815	28	MA
Beckets, Joseph	1804	21 b	PA
Beckets, Peter	1823	30	VA
Beckett, James	1809	20	NJ
Beckett, James	1810	0	
Beckett, Joseph	1809	25	NJ
Beckett, Timothy	1815	22 b	DE
Becks, Peter John	1816	31 b	LA
Bedford, Joseph	1811	24 b	DE
Bedlow, Francis	1817	32	LA
Bedwell, John	1809	21	PA
Bedwell, John	1815	0	

SPC lost when Schooner *Hamilton* went over on
Lake Ontario two years ago.

Bedwell, William	1805	17	PA
Bedwell, William	1815	0	
Bedwell, William	1815	0	
Bee, Samuel J.	1809	31	NJ
Beebe, David	1810	17	NY
Beech, Jehu	1819	26 b	DE
Beeman, Joel	1809	28	MA
Beeson, John	1804	22	DE
Beggs, William	1804	27	NY
Behncke, John Christopher			
	1809	0	
Beish, Jacob	1807	19	PA
Beish, Jacob	1812	00	

Name	Year	Age		State
Beish, Joseph	1818	22		PA
Bell, David	1817	27		MA
Bell, George	1807	21		VA
Bell, George	1809	0		
Bell, George	1817	18	b	VA
Bell, James	1817	32		PA
Bell, John	1810	15		NJ
Bell, John M.	1811	15		PA
Bell, Joseph	1816	30	c	SC
Bell, Nicholas	1809	31		NY
Bell, Peter, Jr.	1810	14		PA
Bell, Richard	1810	22	y	MA
Bell, Samuel	1809	21		VA
Bell, Stewart	1806	23		VA
Bell, William	1805	20		PA
Bell, William	1818	14		PA
Bell, William	1818	20		NH
Bellam, William	1796	0		VA
Bellangee, Isaac	1807	18		NJ
Bellangee, Isaac	1815	25		NJ
Bellangee, William	1811	20		NJ
Bellangee, William	1812	00		
Bellas, John	1810	24	b	VA
Bellow, Johathan	1805	30		RI
Bellows, Davius	1811	30		MA
Bellypere, Ambrose	1811	21	y	NY
Belmy, William	1806	20		PA
Beltz, Crawford	1807	22		PA
Ben, Peter	1809	34	b	LA
Bence, Francis	1820	27		LA
Bender, Isaiah	1813	19		PA
Bender, William	1809	22		PA
Benderman, John	1809	22		DE
Benedict, Charles I.	1823	18		VA
Benjamin, John	1804	28	b	PA
Benjamin, Joseph	1818	38	b	PA
Benn, Thomas	1817	34	b	VA
Bennae, Joseph	1806	20		none given
Bennall, Lewis	1822	21	y	NY
Bennenat, William	1807	22		MA
Benners, Henry	1807	11		PA
Bennest, Thomas	1807	27		DE
Bennet, David	1820	17		PA
Bennet, John	1811	23		VA
Bennet, Robert	1821	31		VA
Bennet, William	1804	28		NY
Bennet, William	1807	25		NJ
Bennet, William	1807	25		NJ
Bennet, William W.	1820	18		PA
Bennett, Benjamin	1818	21		NJ
Bennett, Christopher	1804	23		RI
Bennett, Frederick	1822	24		ME
Bennett, George	1822	20		NJ
Bennett, James	1810	28	b	DE
Bennett, John	1805	18		PA
Bennett, John	1809	22		PA
Bennett, John	1811	00		
Bennett, Mahlon	1798	26		PA
Bennett, Peter	1807	22		VA
Bennett, Samuel	1815	18		Va
Bennett, Stephen	1807	17		PA
Bennett, Thomas	1809	21		DE
Bennett, Thomas	1812	00		
Bennett, William	1809	20		NJ
Bennett, William	1822	19		DE
Benneville, Vincent	1809	20		DE
Benney, John	1809	18		PA
Bennie, Alexander	1805	28		MA
Bennitt, Ely S.	1823	25	y	PA
Bensen, George	1814	20	b	MD
Benson, Cesar	1815	23	b	DE
Benson, George	1805	25	b	MD
Benson, George	1805	37		VA
Benson, George	1809	25		VA
Benson, Isaac	1822	19	n	PA
Benson, John	1814	19		MA
Benson, John	1815	23	b	NY
Benson, Levi	1821	21	b	MD
Benson, Robert	1799	26	b	NY
Benson, William	1806	21		VA
Benson, William	1809	21		DE
Bensted, Richard H.	1809	23		VA
Benthall, John	1817	16		SC
Benthur, Anthony	1809	25		LA
Bentley, Amos	1816	20	b	NJ
Bentley, Thomas	1816	21	b	NJ
Benton, Charles B.	1821	21		NY
Berey, Henry	1809	28		Sweden
Bernard, John	1815	14		PA
Berniard, Joseph	1806	25		none given
Berrien, William	1814	21		NY
Berriman, William	1816	30		PA
Berry, Christopher	1817	45		none given
Berry, Edward	1818	25		PA
Berry, James	1810	23		NY
Berry, James	1821	39	b	PA
Berry, Jesse	1804	24		MA
Berry, John	1804	17		DE
Berry, John	1809	31		MD
Berry, John	1809	31		MD
Berry, John	1819	20	y	PA
Berry, Joseph	1815	33		
Berry, Joseph	1820	21	y	PA
Berry, Kent	1806	40	b	PA

Berry, Robert 1815 26 b PA
Berry, Thomas 1799 24 NY
Berry, Thomas 1809 25 MA
Berryman, Edmond J. 1823 16 NY
Berthou, Joseph 1810 22 LA
Bertram, John 1807 22 b DE
Beson, John 1804 22 DE
Besricks, John 1799 23 y DE
Bethell, John 1810 21 NJ
Bethell, John 1820 28 PA
Bettell, Dennis 1815 28 PA
Bettle, William 1807 16 PA
Bettle, William 1808 0 PA

Bettle, William 1809 0
SPC lost when cast away in brig *Sea Blown*

Bettle, William 1810 0
Betton, Samuel, Jr. 1805 20
Bevan, David 1800 37 PA
Bevans, John 1823 27 MD
Bianch, Pietro 1817 25 LA
Bickee, John Christopher
1807 26 PA
Bickerton, Robert 1805 39 PA
Bickham, Thomas D. 1822 20 PA
Bickley, Daniel, Jr. 1804 15 PA
Bicknell, Samuel 1810 29 MA
Biddle, Abraham 1818 17 DE
Biddle, George 1810 19 NJ
Biddle, James 1807 24 PA
Biddle, Thomas 1809 18 PA
Biddle, William 1807 26 y MD
Biddle, William 1808 23 PA
Bigaby, William 1816 24 VA
Bigalow, Charles 1815 12 PA
Bigalow, Isaac 1823 21 NJ
Bigan, John 1811 20 PA
Biggs, Abraham 1823 16 NJ
Biggs, David 1798 21 DE
Biggs, David 1805 28 DE
Biggs, James 1811 17 PA
Biggs, John 1810 24 PA
Biggs, Joseph L 1807 15 PA
Biggs, Thomas 1810 21 PA
Bigler, William 1821 18 PA
Bignell, William 1821 39 DE
Bilderback, Charles 1811 32 NJ
Bill, Peter 1818 24 b PA
Billings, Benjamin 1819 38 PA
Billings, John P. 1804 23 NH
Billings, John 1811 40 MD

Billington, Charles B. 1812 24 PA
Bills, John 1811 21 PA
Binder, Martin 1821 19 PA
Bingham, Peter 0000 0 MA
Bingham, Peter 0000 0 MA
Bingham, Peter 1794 23
Bioren, Benjamin W. 1823 23 PA
Birch, Henry 1798 29 VA
Birch, Jonathan 1816 18 PA
Birckhead, Christopher
1815 20 MD
Bird, Charles 1811 19 PA
Bird, Comfort 1806 15 MA
Bird, Conrad L. 1820 17 PA
Bird, Edward 1812 27 b NJ
Bird, John 1817 22 b NJ
Bird, Samuel 1811 22 PA
Birley, George 1799 21 PA
Bisbee, Charles 1823 23 MA
Biscoe, James 1822 27 MD
Bishop, Edward 1807 27 m NY
Bishop, Isaac 1805 22 NJ
Bishop, Isaac 1806 0
Bishop, John 1801 23 RI
Bishop, William 1823 20 NJ
Biting, Charles 1821 19 NJ
Bitters, John 1805 22 NJ
Bitters, John 1810 0
Bituel, Francis 1807 33 LA
Biven, Joseph 1809 35 VA
Bixler, Jacob 1805 20 PA
Black, Bristor 1812 32 b DE
Black, Brittainham 1821 28 b MD
Black, Charles 1805 23 PA
Black, Charles 1811 33 GA
Black, Charles 1815 22 b NJ
Black, Charles 1819 25 b DE
Black, Jesse 1818 26 y DE
Black, John 1803 22 b PA
Black, John 1806 23 PA
Black, John 1806 21 SC
Black, John 1809 26 NY
Black, John 1809 0
Black, John 1821 18 PA
Black, Joseph 1821 42 none given
Black, Martin 1798 23 none given
Black, Nicholas 1805 22 MD
Black, Peter 1805 28 MA
Black, Rhoad 1812 24 c DE
Black, Richard 1823 27 NY
Black, Thomas 1805 21 b PA
Black, Thomas 1809 26 b PA

Black, William	1815	38	MA	Blish, George	1813	17	MA
Blackman, Enoch	1807	21	NJ	Bliss, Francis	1818	25	MA
Blacks, Robert	1820	25	none given	Bliss, William	1801	21	RI
Blackshier, Robert	1810	17	DE	Blizard, Silas	1822	30	MD
Blackwood, Joseph	1809	24	PA	Blizerd, Henry	1805	24	NY
Blackwood, William	1815	23	NY	Block, Edward	1810	19	MA
Blackwood, William	1815	27	PA	Block, Edward	1813	0	
Blaclock, Henry	1803	17	PA	Bloom, Joseph	1810	0	PA
Bladen, John	1815	22	VA	Bloomer, Benjamin	1820	27	MA
Bladen, William	1805	22 b	PA	Bloomfield, Benjamin	1798	20	NJ
Blain, William	1804	25	MA	Bloomfield, John	1806	16	PA
Blair, William, Jr.	1809	14	PA	Bloomfield, John	1812	00	
Blair, William, Jr.	1810	0		Bloomfield, John	1821	32	PA
Blake, Andrew	1821	36 b	DE	Bloxen, Stephen	1822	33	DE
Blake, Burden	1818	36 c	MD	Bloxson, John B.	1822	23	VA
Blake, Dobbin	1816	34	PA	Blume, George	1809	19	PA
Blake, Edward	1821	25 b	PA	Blume, George	1812	00	
Blake, Elsey	1803	30 b	DE	Blume, John	1804	21	PA
Blake, James	1808	28	PA	Blume, Joseph	1815	27	PA
Blake, James	1811	25 c	PA	Blush, Owen	1810	13	MA
Blake, James	1816	29 s	NY	Bly, James	1807	28	MA
Blake, John	1805	21	PA	Blye, John	1805	18	PA
Blake, John Davis	1809	23 b	PA	Boardley, George	1797	0	MD
Blake, John	1812	17 b	PA	Boardman, Walter S.	1823	18	CT
Blake, Mitchell	1820	22 b	MD	Bockholt, Andrew	1815	46	Sweden
Blake, Pernel	1816	24 b	DE	Bockius, Daniel	1809	23	PA
Blake, Pernel	1817	0		Bodine, Simes	1804	23	PA
Blake, Perry	1815	32 b	MD	Boger, William	1810	18	NJ
Blake, Purnel	1797	30 m	DE	Boger, William	1811	00	
Blake, Purnell	1810	18 b	DE	Boggs, Henry	1821	18 c	MD
Blake, Warner	1817	23 y	MD	Boggs, James	1804	51	none given
Blake, William	1811	39	MD	Boggs, James	1810	0	
Blake, William	1818		xx	Boggs, James	1812	00	
Blake, William	1823	23 b	MD	Boggs, James	1812	00	
Blakeman, William	1807	24	NY	Boggs, William	1803	27	PA
Blakeman, William	1808	0		Bohler, John	1809	21	PA
Blan, John	1816	16	PA	Bohler, William	1803	20	PA
Blanchard, Ebenezer	1823	33	MA	Boice, William	1805	18	DE
Blanchard, George W.	1820	14	PA	Boidren, Peter	1807	26	LA
Blanchard, James	1821	18	ME	Boiles, Caleb	1803	15	NJ
Blanchard, Jason	1821	24	ME	Boiviet, James	1806	30	MA
Blanchard, Leni	1821	26	ME	Bolan, William	1823	34	PA
Blanchard, Samuel	1814	26	MA	Bolderston, David	1800	35	DE
Bland, Peter	1805	22	VA	Bole, John	1818	22	PA
Blandorne, Joseph	1810	22	LA	Bolins, John	1803	25 y	MD
Blannchard, John D.	1813	23	PA	Bolster, William	1821	33	MD
Blayney, Willis Henry	1815	15	PA	Bolt, James	1815	39	
Bleaksley, Abraham P.	1814	29	CT	Bolton, John	1804	24	MD
Bletterman, George	1810	21	PA	Boman, William	1807	20 b	MD
Bligh, Michael	1808	23	VA	Bomman, Jonas	1811	33	Sweden
Blight, John	1818	31	PA	Bonage, Philip	1815	26	LA
Blinn, Charles	1823	28	NY	Bonamano, Andrew	1811	25	LA

20

Bond, Burr J.	1811	18	NJ	
Bond, James	1808	25 y	MD	
Bond, James	1815	22	MD	
Bond, John	1807	40 b	SC	
Bond, John	1815	18	PA	
Bond, Joseph	1815	21	PA	
Bond, Lewis	1819	26	PA	
Bond, Samuel	1798	25	PA	
Bond, Samuel	1807	27	NJ	
Bond, William	1817	23		
Bondy, Killes	1818	21 y	PA	
Bongerss, Peter C.	1809	23	MD	
Bonner, James	1805	21	NJ	
Bonsall, Edwin	1820	16	PA	
Bonticue, Henry	1823	23	NY	
Booker, Henry	1809	13	DE	
Boon, Henry	1818	21 b	DE	
Booth, George	1815	25	MD	
Booth, Joseph	1817	38 b	MD	
Booth, Richard	1818	22	DE	
Bordley, Adam	1809	28 y	DE	
Bordley, George	1805	23 b	DE	
Boret, Simon	1810	27		none given
Borman, Alexander	1820	21	NY	
Borradaile, Thos.	1812	21	NJ	
Borton, Jacob	1806	29	NJ	
Bos, Garret	1801	28	PA	
Bosman, Daniel	1820	17	NY	
Bossman, Thomas	1823	26	VA	
Boston, Jefferson	1805	23 b	MD	
Boston, Jefferson	1807	00	MD	
Boston, Peter	1811	29 y	MD	
Boswell, John	1817	29	DC	
Botewills, Rudolph	1810	29	MD	
Botner, James	1812	25	PA	
Bottomen, Thomas	1809	22	PA	
Boucher, George	1811	20	PA	
Bough, Paul	1806	26 b	MA	
Bourke, Hugh	1815	18	PA	
Bousquet, Frederick	1809	18		France
Boutcher, James Anders				
	1803	32	VA	
Bowden, Johathan	1803	27	MA	
Bowen, Charles Douglas				
	1801	27	MD	
Bowen, George W.	1817	17	PA	
Bowen, Isaac	1804	18	RI	
Bowen, John	1809	22	VA	
Bowen, Lewis	1805	20	NY	
Bowen, Lewis	1806	18	SC	
Bowen, Nathaniel	1809	23	MD	
Bowen, Nathaniel	1810	23	MD	

Bowen, Nathaniel	1811	00		
Bowen, Nathaniel	1811	00		
Bowen, Obadiah	1818	26	RI	
Bowen, Zacheus	1813	17	NJ	
Bowers, David	1823	27	NJ	
Bowers, Isaac	1811	18	DE	
Bowers, John	1809	36 b	MA	
Bowers, Robert	1817	25	PA	
Bowie, Alexander	1806	28	PA	
Bowie, Henry	1801	24	PA	
Bowker, Francis	1809	27	NJ	
Bowles, Hugh	1798	23		
spprenticed to Thomas Robins, blockmaker, for ten years				
Bowles, John, Jr.	1805	28	NH	
Bowles, William	1821	21	VA	
Bowling, Albert Gallatin				
	1821	21	VA	
Bowman, Isaac	1809	21	PA	
Bowman, John Henry	1806	32	NY	
Bowman, Jonas	1809	21	PA	
Bowman, Jonas	1809	31	PA	
Bowman, Thomas	1822	25 y	VA	
Bowzer, Philip	1807	30 b	PA	
Boyce, Pennel	1810	24 b	DE	
Boyd, Charles	1815	42	LA	
Boyd, Copeland	1809	20	PA	
Boyd, Dennis	1816	21	LA	
Boyd, George	1798	24	NY	
Boyd, George	1804	0		
Boyd, James	1818	22	DE	
Boyd, Jesse	1802	20	PA	
Boyd, John J.	1812	11	KY	
Boyd, John	1817	32	NY	
Boyd, John	1818	22	MD	
Boyd, John	1821	23 c	NY	
Boyd, Robert	1795	17	PA	
Boyd, Robert	1804	21	NJ	
Boyd, Robert	1804	21	NJ	
Boyd, Thomas	1804	28	PA	
Boyd, Thomas	1804	0		
Boyd, William	1803	25	PA	
Boyde, George	1804	0		
Boyer, Benjamin	1811	27	PA	
Boyer, Caleb	1811	21 b	DE	
Boyer, David	1804	18	NH	
Boyer, Evans	1822	23	NJ	
Boyer, John	1809	33 b	DE	
Boyer, Noah	1817	21	PA	
Boyer, Samuel	1803	23	PA	

Name	Year	Age		State	
Boyer, Samuel H.	1821	17		PA	
Boyer, Thomas	1823	39	b	MD	
Boyle, James	1804	35	b	MD	
Boyle, James	1820	21		PA	
Boyle, John	1801	19		PA	
Boyle, Michael	1812	24			none given
Boyle, Thomas	1804	28		PA	
Boyne, Peter	1810	15		NJ	
Boyne, Peter	1810	15		NJ	
Boyton, Thomas	1811	26		MA	
Brack, Joseph	1801	22		PA	
Bracket, James	1818	22	b	VA	
Braden, John	1811	23		PA	
Braden, Thomas	1816	24		MD	
Bradfield, Benjamin, Jr.					
	1823	16		PA	
Bradford, Benjamin	1811	17	b	MD	
indented black boy to Elijah Miller					
Bradford, George	1821	24		MA	
Bradford, Henry	1817	29	b	MD	
Bradford, James	1808	18	b	MD	
Bradford, James	1809	0	b	PA	
Bradford, James	1811	00			
Bradford, John	1816	20		PA	
Bradford, William	1809	23		NH	
Bradley, Ansel	1817	24		MA	
Bradley, Daniel	1800	21		PA	
Bradley, Daniel	1810	17		PA	
Bradley, Daniel	1811	00			
Bradley, Hugh	1800	16		PA	
Bradley, James	1819	20		PA	
Bradley, John	1811	25		VA	
Bradley, John	1821	22		MA	
Bradley, Newton	1806	20		MA	
Bradley, Samuel	1820	18		MA	
Bradley, Syies	1817	21	c	DE	
Bradshaw, Benjamin	1800	18		PA	
Bradshaw, Thomas	1803	22		NY	
Bradshaw, Thomas	1806	0		NY	
Bradshaw, Thomas	1806	0			
Bradshaw, William	1814	15		NY	
Brady, George	1804	25	b	MD	
Bragdon, Amos	1821	22		ME	
Bragg, John	1818	21		NJ	
Bragg, Phineas	1822	25		NJ	
Bragger, Henry	1812	31			none given
Braham, John	1823	25		NY	
Brainard, Russel	1809	21		CT	
Brakel, Edward	1805	34		NY	
Brame, Henry	1813	20		PA	
Branch, Anthony	1809	22		PA	
Branch, Cyrus	1811	18		VA	
Brandis, John	1812	23		LA	
Branham, Stephen	1814	0			
Brankam, Stephen	1808	27		PA	
Brannan, Anthony	1805	32		MD	
Branner, Christopher	1805	26		PA	
Brano, Joseph	1809	0			none given
Brant, John	1803	28		PA	
Brawn, John	1806	27		NY	
Bray, Henry	1798	28	b	MA	
Bray, James	1809	11	y	PA	
Bray, James	1818	21		PA	
Bray, John	1815	16		DE	
Bray, Joseph E.	1816	40			
Brayee, John	1807	45		NY	
Brayly, William	1807	25		PA	
Brazier, James	1823	32		PA	
Brearley, David	1807	21		NJ	
Breintnall, Thomas	1807	18		PA	
Brekfoard, John	1811	27		PA	
Brelesford, Shaperd	1804	23		PA	
Brelsfoard, Edward C.	1810	22		PA	
Brelsford, Thomas	1804	22		PA	
Brenand, Thomas	1807	18		MA	
Brent, John Saunders	1823	21		PA	
Brereton, James	1813	21		DE	
Brewer, George Harman					
	1815	14		PA	
Brewer, Cornelius	1811	19		NJ	
Brewing, Whiteman	1799	20		DE	
Brewington, Thomas	1812	20		NC	
Brewster, Martin, Jr.	1810	16		MA	
Brewster, William	1811	31		NJ	
Brewton, Robert	1820	17		PA	
Brewton, William	1810	18		PA	
Briant, Eli	1820	18		NJ	
Brice, David	1812	30	y	MD	
Brice, William	1823	35	b	NJ	
Brick, John	1815	26		NJ	
Brickell, William	1807	21		NY	
Brickwell, William	1807	21		NY	
Bride, James	1805	19		VA	
Bridge, Prince	1816	40	b	CT	
Brien, Peter	1798	21		PA	
Briggs, Jeremiah	1807	36		RI	
Briggs, John	1809	23		PA	
Briggs, John	1811	25		RI	
Briggs, John	1817	26		MA	
Briggs, John	1821	33		MA	
Briggs, Nathaniel	1805	19		MA	
Briggs, Thomas W.	1821	18		MA	
Briggs, William	1800	16		PA	

Name	Year	Age	State
Briggs, William John	1820	23	MA
Brigham, Samuel	1805	36	MA
Bright, George	1809	20	NJ
Bright, Thomas Jefferson	1818	17	NJ
Bright, William	1810	22	NJ
Bright, William	1811	35 b	NY
Brine, Daniel	1803	34	NY
Brink, Daniel	1807	24	NJ
Brinson, John	1814	23	DE
Brinton, Ethan	1810	20	PA
Brinton, William	1806	23	DE
Briscoe, Frederick G.	1817	18	MD
Brison, John	1810	25 b	MD
Bristol, James	1807	23 y	NJ
Bristol, Moses	1810	26 b	MD
Britt, William	1822	24	VA
Brittain, Charles	1805	22	NJ
Brittingham, Asahill Purnell	1810	21	MD
Brittingham, Joshua	1815	24	MD
Britton, Charles R.	1819	16	PA
Britton, George W.	1818	19	MD
Britton, John	1801	17	MD
Broad, Richard	1810	19	PA
Broderson, John	1810	27	PA
Brodie, Ludovick	1806	33	VA
Brooke, George	1810	0	
Brooke, Thomas	1813	35	PA
Brooke, William Porter	1821	16	PA
Brooks, David	1809	21	NJ
Brooks, Edward	1806	25	PA
Brooks, Edward	1812	00	
Brooks, Edward	1819	21	PA
Brooks, George	1809	21	PA
Brooks, George	1823	29	NY
Brooks, James	1803	25	NY
Brooks, James	1810	19	CT
Brooks, James E.	1823	24	NH
Brooks, John	1798	21	PA
Brooks, John	1809	20 y	PA
Brooks, John	1811	22	PA
Brooks, John, Jr.	1817	15	PA
Brooks, John	1819	17	Pa
Brooks, Robert	1815	27	MA
Brooks, Thomas	1807	23	MD
Brooks, Thomas	1810	36	NJ
Broom, Elias	1809	41	PA
Broom, Thomas	1819	21	PA
Brothers, Richard	1797	19	DE
Brothers, Richard	1805	25	DE
Brothers, Richard	1805	25	DE
Brotherton, George	1809	21	PA
Broughton, Samuel	1818	21 b	PA
Broughton, Samuel	1819	25 b	PA
Brown, Abia W.	1815	15	NJ
Brown, Abraham	1805	23 b	NY
Brown, Abraham	1812	24	NJ
Brown, Abram	1804	39	MA
Brown, Adam	1816	20 b	PA
Brown, Adam	1819	23 b	PA
Brown, Alexander	1804	25	PA
Brown, Americus	1816	23	NH
Brown, Andrew	1817	24 m	PA
Brown, Andrew	1822	39	none given
Brown, Baptist	1805	18 b	MD
Brown, Benjamin	1805	39	PA
Brown, Benjamin	1808	21	VA
Brown, Benjamin	1815	27 b	PA
Brown, Benjamin	1821	31	PA
Brown, Burwell	1810	33	VA
Brown, Cesar	1822	33 y	NJ
Brown, Charles	1809	22 b	SC
Brown, Charles	1810	38	MS
Brown, Charles	1815	42	MS
Brown, Charles	1819	22	DE
Brown, Charles	1821	23 b	PA
Brown, Clemeth	1818	24 b	DE
Brown, Constant	1822	35 b	DE
Brown, Cornelius	1811	24	NY
Brown, Daniel Morse	1796	36	MA
Brown, Daniel C.	1805	37	RI
Brown, Daniel	1821	20	NJ
Brown, David	1809	20	MD
Brown, Ebenezer	1810	16 b	RI
Brown, Edward	1809	36	NC
Brown, Edward L.	1809	24	NH
Brown, Edward P.	1809	20	MA
Brown, Edward	1813	20	NY
Brown, Edward P.	1820	14	NY
Brown, Elias	1814	28 b	NY
Brown, Ellis	1815	37 b	DE
Brown, Even	1809	22	PA
Brown, Ezakiah	1815	0	
Brown, Francis	1798	39	
Brown, Francis	1803	19 m	PA
Brown, Friday	1804	21 b	DE
Brown, Friday	1813	0	
Brown, George Washington	1803	22	PA
Brown, George	1804	33 b	DE
Brown, George	1804	29 b	MD
Brown, George	1805	22	MA
Brown, George	1805	0	

Name	Year	Age		State
Brown, George	1807	16		PA
Brown, George	1809	20		PA
Brown, George	1809	22	b	NJ
Brown, George	1811	21	b	NJ
Brown, George	1813	23		VA
Brown, George	1815	32		MD
Brown, George	1820	28	c	LA
Brown, Geroge	1805	20		PA
Brown, Henry	1805	17		PA
Brown, Henry	1806	24	b	MD
Brown, Henry	1815	26		PA
Brown, Henry	1817	20		PA
Brown, Henry	1819	19	b	PA
Brown, Henry	1821	25	s	PA
Brown, Hezekiah	1809	34		NJ
Brown, Isaac	1819	24		MD
Brown, Isaiah	1818	19		MA
Brown, Jacob	1804	32	b	MD
Brown, Jacob	1809	23		NJ
Brown, James	1803	25		VA
Brown, James	1803	26		MD
Brown, James	1805	0		
Brown, James	1806	36	b	DE
Brown, James	1807	26	b	DE
Brown, James	1808	34	b	NJ
Brown, James	1809	23		PA
Brown, James	1809	45	m	MD
Brown, James	1809	33	b	DE
Brown, James	1809	0	m	MD
Brown, James	1809	35	m	MD
Brown, James	1810	20		VA
Brown, James	1810	35	c	NY
Brown, James	1811	00		MD
Brown, James	1811	45	b	DE
Brown, James	1811	33		CT
Brown, James	1811	00		
Brown, James	1815	18		NY
Brown, James	1818	20		SC
Brown, James	1819	15		PA
Brown, James	1820	20		NY
Brown, James	1822	29	s	PA
Brown, James	1823	28		NY
Brown, James	1823	18		PA
Brown, John	1797	0		
Brown, John	1798	0		RI
Brown, John	1798	39	b	VA
Brown, John	1798	19	m	PA
Brown, John	1798	39		
Brown, John	1798	29		NY
Brown, John	1798	0	b	PA
Brown, John	1800	22		PA
Brown, John	1801	24		PA

Name	Year	Age		State
Brown, John	1805	22		VA
Brown, John	1805	18		PA
Brown, John	1805	21		PA
Brown, John	1805	21	y	DE
Brown, John	1805	25		MD
Brown, John	1806	21		PA
Brown, John	1806	42		PA
Brown, John	1807	00		
Brown, John	1807	22		PA
Brown, John	1807	23		NJ
Brown, John	1807	23		LA
Brown, John	1807	31		MA
Brown, John	1807	38	m	PA
Brown, John	1807	25		PA
Brown, John	1807	25	b	PA
Brown, John	1807	30		LA
Brown, John	1807	18		PA
Brown, John	1809	0		PA
Brown, John	1809	35	b	CT
Brown, John	1809	23	b	MD
Brown, John	1809	29		LA
Brown, John	1809	38		NY
Brown, John	1809	21		MA
Brown, John	1809	0		MA
Brown, John	1809	21		MA
Brown, John	1810	26	b	DE
Brown, John	1810	0		
Brown, John	1810	12	b	PA
Brown, John	1810	23		NY
Brown, John	1810	25	b	NJ
Brown, John	1810	35	b	NJ
Brown, John	1810	24	b	DE
Brown, John	1810	30		NJ
Brown, John	1811	20		NY
Brown, John	1811	32		LA
Brown, John	1811	25		PA
Brown, John	1811	25		Hispaniola
Brown, John	1812	27	b	DE
Brown, John	1812	00		
Brown, John	1812	00		DE
Brown, John	1812	27	b	NY
Brown, John	1812	23		PA
Brown, John	1813	23	b	MD
Brown, John	1815	25	b	LA
Brown, John	1815	17		NY
Brown, John	1815	15	y	MD
Brown, John	1815	31		MD
Brown, John	1815	32	b	MD
Brown, John	1816	0		LA
Brown, John	1816	20		NJ
Brown, John	1817	46	b	NY
Brown, John, II	1817	29		NY

Brown, John	1817	44 b	MD
Brown, John	1818	22	PA
Brown, John	1818	19	PA
Brown, John	1818	23 y	PA
Brown, John	1819	27 b	PA
Brown, John	1821	26 b	PA
Brown, John	1821	20	PA
Brown, John	1822	37 y	VA
Brown, John M.	1823	22	PA
Brown, John	1823	20	NY
Brown, Joseph	1805	21	MD
Brown, Joseph	1806	23 b	PA
Brown, Joseph	1806	37	LA
Brown, Joseph	1809	17 b	PA
Brown, Joseph	1809	19	NJ
Brown, Joseph	1810	26 y	MD
Brown, Joseph	1810	27	SC
Brown, Joseph	1811	19 b	PA
Brown, Joseph	1812	21	PA
Brown, Lewis R.	1805	22	PA
Brown, Liberty	1807	22 b	NC
Brown, Liberty	1815	0	
Brown, Liberty	1817	35 b	PA
Brown, Manuel	1816	21 b	PA
Brown, Mark	1818	26 b	DE
Brown, Martin	1812	29	PA
Brown, Mathew	1798	38	NJ
Brown, Nathan	1801	30	VA
Brown, Peter	1806	0	
Brown, Peter	1807	20 b	NY
Brown, Peter	1812	25 b	NY
Brown, Peter	1815	21	MA
Brown, Peter	1815	32	NY
Brown, Peter	1818	00	MA
Brown, Philip	1807	23	NY
Brown, Randle	1804	28	PA
Brown, Randle	1806	0	
Brown, Reuben	1804	25	NJ
Brown, Richard	1812	36 b	NJ
Brown, Richard	1821	17 b	MD
Brown, Richard	1823	44 b	PA
Brown, Richd.	1809	28 b	DE
Brown, Robert	1809	22 b	DE
Brown, Robert	1811	27	NY
Brown, Robert	1813	0	
Brown, Robert	1815	30	MA
Brown, Robert	1816	24	MA
Brown, Robert	1820	25 y	MA
Brown, Russell	1807	35	RI
Brown, Saml.	1796	20 y	SC
Brown, Samuel	1806	27	PA
Brown, Samuel D.	1809	30	CT

Brown, Samuel	1814	48	NY
Brown, Samuel	1814	23	NJ
Brown, Samuel	1815	52 b	PA
Brown, Samuel	1815	27 b	PA
Brown, Samuel	1821	20	PA
Brown, Samuel	1822	34	ME
Brown, Seth	1818	35	MA
On board *Constitution* at sinking of Syann and Levant sloops of war			
Brown, Sylvester	1807	22	NY
Brown, Thomas	1798	29	PA
Brown, Thomas	1798	24	PA
Brown, Thomas	1799	27	PA
Brown, Thomas	1803	32	PA
Brown, Thomas	1803	26	PA
Brown, Thomas	1805	22	NY
Brown, Thomas	1805	0	
Brown, Thomas	1806	29	MA
Brown, Thomas	1807	20 b	MD
Brown, Thomas	1809	28	LA
Brown, Thomas	1809	26	NY
Brown, Thomas	1809	36	LA
Brown, Thomas	1809	26	NJ
Brown, Thomas	1810	25	DE
Brown, Thomas	1812	40 b	VA
Brown, Thomas	1815	26	MA
Brown, Thomas	1815	17	VA
Brown, Thomas N.	1815	21	PA
Brown, Thomas	1815	0	SC
Brown, Thomas, Jr.	1817	14	PA
Brown, Thomas, Jr.	1818	15	PA
Brown, Thomas	1818	36	MD
Brown, Thomas	1818	16	PA
Brown, Thomas	1818	23	MD
Brown, William	1801	19 b	NY
Brown, William	1804	23	NY
Brown, William	1804	28	GA
Brown, William	1804	30	PA
Brown, William	1806	24	NJ
Brown, William	1806	17 m	SC
Brown, William	1807	28 m	PA
Brown, William	1807	18 b	NJ
Brown, William	1809	25 b	NY
Brown, William	1809	38	VA
Brown, William	1809	19	PA
Brown, William	1810	26	NJ
Brown, William	1812	26	RI
Brown, William	1812	21	NY
Brown, William H.	1815	0	
Brown, William	1815	44	CT

Name	Year	Age	State
Brown, William H.	1815	23	NJ
Brown, William	1816	35	MD
Brown, William	1816	32 b	NY
Brown, William	1817	18	NY
Brown, William	1818	18	VA
Brown, William	1819	22	PA
Brown, William	1820	27 b	RI
Brown, William	1821	26	NJ
Brown, William	1822	42	NC
Brown, William A.	1822	29 b	CT
Brownburk, David	1809	26	PA
Browne, Charles Cresap			
	1815	16	MD
Browne, Joseph	1815	0	
Browne, William	1812	00	
Brownell, Joseph	1811	30	MA
Brownell, Samuel	1820	21	MA
Brownett, John	1798	30	PA
Browning, Benjamin	1811	21	NJ
Browning, John	1818	37 b	DE
Brownn, Peter	1798	30	PA
Bruce, George	1801	16	PA
Bruce, John	1809	18	VA
Bruce, John	1815	21 m	MD
Bruce, Thomas	1818	25	NJ
Brumby, John	1808	29	MA
Brumby, John	1808	26	CT
Brumengen, Samuel	1817	29 b	DE
Brumley, John	1823	24	NJ
Brumley, Samuel	1807	25	NJ
Brunell, Andrew	1811	28	NY
Brunson, Nathaniel	1815	21	MA
Bruorton, George	1815	20	England
Brusstar, Henry	1817	21	PA
Brusstar, James S.	1811	21	PA
Bryan, George	1815	23	VA
Bryan, Joel, Jr.	1805	18	PA
Bryan, Perry	1811	24 m	PA
Bryan, Thomas	1806	28 b	MA
Bryan, William	1798	17	PA
Bryan, William	1801	25 b	VA
Bryan, William	1805	21	PA
Bryant, James	1811	15	PA
Bryant, John	1805	12	PA
Bryant, Thomas	1806	28 m	VA
Bryant, Thomas	1820	27	CT
Bryant, William	1805	25	MA
Bryon, George W.	1822	22	PA
Buchan, George	1816	20	MA
Buchanan, John	1798	14	MD
Buck, Edward	1804	30 b	PA
Buck, Isaac	1809	18	NJ

Name	Year	Age	State
Buckless, Henry	1810	30	MD
Buckley, Edward	1801	20	PA
Buckley, James	1809	19	NJ
Buckley, Samuel	1811	00	
Buckley, Samuel	1811	25	PA
Buckman, Thomas	1823	21	NJ
Buckwater, Abraham	1814	25	PA
Budd, Joseph	1803	29	NY
Budden, John	1805	21	PA
Buell, Isaac	1809	22	NY
Buffington, John	1806	0	
Buffum, Joshua	1810	28	MA
Bufington, John	1801	23	DE
Bulfinch, Samuel	1803	20	PA
Bull, John Baptist	1810	29	LA
Bull, Joseph	1797	25	NY

son of Joseph Bull, Sr. late of NY, rope maker; married niece of John Springor

Name	Year	Age	State
Bulley, Andrew	1806	20	VA
Bulley, William	1798	0	MA
Bullock, David	1809	24	NJ
Bullock, Joseph, Jr.	1810	25	PA
Bullock, Joseph	1814	45	MA
Bullus, Samuel H.	1807	15	NJ
Bundick, Ruben	1815	22 b	
Bundy, Silas	1817	23 b	NC
Bunker, Christopher	1818	50	MA
Bunker, Freeman	1805	22	MA
Bunker, John	1805	23	MA
Bunn, William	1811	27	NJ
Bunting, Isaac	1820	24	PA
Bunyan, Joseph	1811	22 b	NY
Bunyie, John	1811	21	PA
Burbage, Peter L.	1822	20	MD
Burbbage, John	1822	30	MD
Burbeck, Joseph	1810	27	MA
Burbeck, William	1809	23	MA
Burckhard, William	1810	20	NJ
Burckhardt, John	1810	23	PA
Burckhardt, John	1811	00	
Burckhardt, William	1811	00	
Burden, Derrick	1822	24 b	NJ
Burdon, John	1805	22 m	NJ
Burgess, Francis	1805	30	GA
Burgess, Joshua	1818	29	MA
Burk, Edward	1799	24	DE
Burk, James	1803	25	MD
Burk, James	1823	20	PA
Burk, John	1807	20	PA
Burk, John	1807	33	PA

Burk, Michael	1798	19	PA	
Burk, Thomas	1798	16	PA	
Burk, William	1809	38	PA	
Burkat, Moses	1809	20 y	PA	
Burke, Michael	1800	0		
Burkinshew, John Green				
	1810	13	NY	
Burl, Benjamin	1810	17	DE	
Burlage, Simeon	1821	23	MD	
Burls, John	1809	21	DE	
Burman, Richard	1815	19	NJ	
Burmesster, Johan	1809	30	PA	
Burn, Farmer	1809	17	PA	
Burn, John	1810	24	PA	
Burn, John	1817	26	PA	
Burnes, Thomas	1805	27	PA	
Burnes, William	1823	26	MD	
Burnet, James	1804	27	SC	
Burnet, John	1815	28	PA	
Burnet, Moses	1815	21	NJ	
Burnet, Moses	1815	22	NJ	
Burney, James	1815	19 b	DE	
Burnham, Daniel	1798	26	MA	
Burnman, John	1810	32		none given
Burnman, Thomas	1799	27	PA	
Burns, Aaron	1807	18	PA	
Burns, Aaron	1810	0		
Burns, Aaron	1816	0		
Burns, Daniel	1803	21	NH	
Burns, George	1815	30	PA	
Burns, Isaac W.	1818	25	NJ	
Burns, James	1814	28	PA	
Burns, Matthias	1806	15	PA	
Burns, Robert	1818	20	PA	
Burns, Solomon	1815	26 b	NY	
Burr, Joseph B.	1810	15	NJ	
Burr, Moses	1820	25 b	PA	
Burr, Nathan	1804	23	CT	
Burr, William	1810	19	CT	
Burrel, Benjamin	1809	17	DE	
Burrell, Thomas	1805	17	MA	
Burrill, Samuel	1823	23	MA	
Burrite, Henry	1820	28	NY	
Burrough, Charles	1809	26	NJ	
Burrough, Joseph	1809	25	NJ	
Burroughs, Gideon	1815	21	NJ	
Burroughs, Jonnathan B.				
	1809	21	DE	
Burrows, John	1812	18	PA	
Burrows, William	1811	26	PA	
Burrus, Robert	1810	29 b	DE	
Burton, Albertus	1812	24	DE	

Burton, David	1822	26 s	DE	
Burton, Henry	1815	22 b	PA	
Burton, James	1796	27	NJ	
Burton, John	1807	38	NJ	
Burton, Peter	1801	21 y	DE	
Burton, Peter	1812	22 y	DE	
Burton, Robert	1809	23	DE	
Burton, William	1805	28	PA	
Burton, William	1809	19	VA	
Burton, William	1811	20	MD	
Buruis, John	1818	39	PA	
Burveal, John	1817	21	DE	
Burwis, Mahlon	1807	25	PA	
Bush, Frederick	1804	25	PA	
Bush, John	1806	23	PA	
Bush, Mathias M.	1811	19	PA	
Bushe, Moses	1818	60		none given
Busher, Thomas	1804	14	PA	
Buskirk, Joseph	1804	19	PA	
Bussier, John	1809	18	PA	
Bussy, John	1807	25 b	MA	
Butcher, James	1810	20	CT	
Butcher, James	1810	21	PA	
Butcher, James	1811	00		
Butcher, James	1811	00		
Butcher, James	1815	0		
Butcher, James	1817	0		
Butcher, John	1813	18	PA	
Butcher, Joseph	1804	24	PA	
Butcher, William	1807	16	PA	
Butcher, William	1815	27	MA	
Butler, Aaron	1809	24	NY	
Butler, Charles	1806	26 b	MD	
Butler, Francis	1814	17	PA	
Butler, George	1811	21 b	MD	
Butler, Henry	1810	27 b	NY	
Butler, Henry	1821	24 b	PA	
Butler, Henry Robinson				
	1823	16	PA	
Butler, James	1809	54		none given
Butler, James	1813	26	MD	
Butler, John	1805	37 b	PA	
Butler, John	1806	22	PA	
Butler, John	1807	00 b	NY	
Butler, John	1807	12	PA	
Butler, John	1807	19	NY	
Butler, John	1809	0		
Butler, John Mifflin	1811	18	PA	
Butler, John O.	1815	16	MD	
Butler, John	1817	36	MA	
Butler, John	1821	32 b	PA	
Butler, John	1823	35 s	MD	

Butler, Joshua M.	1823	23		NJ	Cain, John	1807	22		PA
Butler, Lawrence R.	1817	19		PA	Cain, Nathaniel	1816	26 b	NJ
Butler, Levi	1818	27		CT	Cain, Peter	1815	28		CT
Butler, Nicholas	1810	22		PA	Cain, Samuel	1821	21 y	PA
Butler, Patrick	1816	27 b	MD	Cairns, William	1813	17		DE
Butler, Samuel	1807	22		PA	Caktion, Daniel	1818	17		MA
Butler, Samuel	1809	20		CT	Calder, Alexander	1818	22		MD
Butler, Thomas	1815	36		MD	Calder, Andrew	1808	21		NY
Butler, William	1803	22 b	PA	Caldwell, Benjamin	1804	22		PA
Butler, William	1809	36 b	NY	Caldwell, David Maffit	1815	15		PA
Butler, William	1810	21 b	NY	Caldwell, George	1811	31 b	DE
Butler, William,Jr.	1815	23		NY	Caldwell, John	1796	42		Ireland
Butterfield, Elishu	1818	22		NY	Caldwell, Jonathan	1809	29		DE
Butterworth, Joseph, Jr.					Caldwell, Thomas	1798	17		PA
	1800	35		NJ	Caldwell, William	1805	27		DE
Buvet, John	1811	21 b	MS	Caldwell, William	1809	20		PA
Buzby, Joseph	1810	21		NJ	Cale, Timothy	1796	0		CT
Byard, Charles	1809	20 b	MD	Calhoon, James	1817	60		PA
Byard, Robert	1811	28 b	MD	Callaghan, James	1810	0		DE
Byram, Beals	1803	22		MA	Callaghan, James	1812	00	
Byran, Edward	1805	22		MA	Callaghan, Michael	1810	39		Ireland
Byran, John	1805	41		RI	Callahan, James	1807	24 y	DE
Byrch, John Isaac	1817	22		PA	Callanan, Cornelius	1807	48		Ireland
Byrn, John	1814	18		PA	Callanan, John	1810	26		NY
Byrn, Mathias	1804	0			Callaw, Edward	1797	28		Gr.Br.
Byrn, Matthias	1803	28		MD	Callen, William	1815	16		PA
Byrne, Edmund	1810	15		PA	Callender, John	1822	42		none given
Byrne, Gerald	1807	35		none given	Callum, David	1815	29		MA
Byrne, John	1803	24		MA	Callwell, Barswell	1812	17 y	NJ
Byrne, Thomas	1810	25		PA	Calm, Jacob	1809	23		NJ
Byrnes, Henry	1823	20		MD	Calm, Jacob	1816	31		NJ
Byrt, Francis	1810	23		PA	Calm, John	1806	24		NJ
Byrum, James	1805	23		NC	Calm, John	1809	28		NJ
Cabert, Paul	1810	10 y	LA	Calson, John	1811	25		PA
Caddern, Peter	1815	24		MD	Calverley, Edward	1805	0	
Caddick, Henry	1807	37		MD	Calverley, Edward	1805	0	
Cade, Turvil	1811	31		DE	Calverly, Edward	1804	28		MA
Cadet, John	1823	21 c	MA	Calverly, Edward	1822	17		PA
Cadett, James	1811	24		NY	Calwell, Daniel	1798	24 b	DE
Cadozo, Antonio	1809	21		LA	Calwell, William	1805	25		PA
Cady, Horace	1815	24		VT	Cambell, John	1814	16		NC
Cahoon, William	1818	42		PA	Camble, Archabald	1803	27		DE
Cain, Adam	1816	23 y	NJ	Camble, Jeremiah	1804	20 b	MA
Cain, Anthony	1811	20		PA	Cameron, David W.	1815	18	
Cain, Charles	1801	22		PA	Cameron, Richard	1809	23		SC
Cain, Charles	1806	36		SC	Cameron, William	1823	20		NC
Cain, Charles	1811	20		PA	Cammek, William	1818	19		PA
Cain, Dennis	1809	17		NJ	Cammron, Andrew	1809	25		DE
Cain, Dennis	1813	0			Camp, Braddock	1817	25		NY
Cain, George	1818	26 y	NJ	Camp, David	1815	28		NJ
Cain, George	1821	26 y	NJ	Camp, John	1804	24		NJ
Cain, James	1811	35 b	NY	Campbel, John	1815	23 y	PA

Name	Year	Age		State
Campbell, Alexander Hamilton	1819	23		MA
Campbell, Alexander	1820	20		PA
Campbell, Anthony	1810	38		none given
Campbell, Arthur	1805	21		NY
Campbell, Benjamin	1804	17		PA
Campbell, Benjamin	1807	35	b	MD
Campbell, Cornelius	1811	25		NJ
Campbell, David, Jr.	1818	16		PA
Campbell, Edward	1809	16		PA
Campbell, Edward	1818	00		
Campbell, Felix	1805	23		PA
Campbell, George Washington	1807	19		SC
Campbell, George H.	1809	25		NY
Campbell, George H.	1809	0		
Campbell, Henry	1817	14		MA
Campbell, Jacob	1804	25		NY
Campbell, James	1815	23	b	NY
Campbell, James	1822	21		PA
Campbell, John	1798	22		PA
Campbell, John	1798	24		NY
Campbell, John	1798	28		PA
Campbell, John	1799	31		PA
Campbell, John	1800	19		VA
Campbell, John	1803	23		MA
Campbell, John	1804	28		NJ
Campbell, John	1805	22		MD
Campbell, John	1809	20		PA
Campbell, John	1810	0		PA
Campbell, John	1812	25	b	NJ
Campbell, John	1815	22		MD
Campbell, Lewis	1817	23	y	VA
Campbell, Moses	1811	24		NJ
Campbell, Philip	1804	20		PA
Campbell, Robert	1808	16		PA
Campbell, Thomas	1804	23	y	PA
Campbell, Thomas	1807	32		none given
Campbell, Thomas	1809	25	b	VA
Campbell, William	1809	22		NJ
Campbell, William	1811	00		
Campbell, William H.	1814	17		PA
Campbell, William	1817	24		RI
Campble, James	1821	20		NY
Camper, Moses	1811	30	b	MD
Canacano, John	1804	22		none given
Canacanos, John	1806	0		
Canby, Joseph	1809	42		DE
Canely, Samuel T.	1811	13		PA
Caner, Charles C.	1817	15		PA
Cannan, Joseph	1805	21		MD
Cannan, Joseph	1806	0		
Cannon, Charles	1801	21		PA
Cannon, Damiel	1799	18		PA
Cannon, James	1807	37	b	DE
Cannon, James	1819	18		PA
Cannon, Joseph S.	1815	25		DE
Cannon, Robert	1804	21		PA
Canoll, Thomas	1815	23		PA
Canon, George	1810	20		PA
Canon, William	1811	31		NJ
Cantey, John A.	1815	18		NY
Cantile, Simon	1809	25		LA
Canton, Joseph	1821	51		LA
Cantrell, John A.	1823	11		PA
Capan, Richard	1811	00		
Capey, Joseph	1815	27	l	MA
Capiane, Richard	1815	0		
Caplin, Robert	1798	26		MD
Capple, John	1804	24		PA
Caragan, William	1798	18		PA
Carbonne, Jacob	1807	33		LA
Carefull, Edward	1807	19		NY
Carey, Jeremiah	1804	18	b	DE
Carey, Jeremiah	1807	00		
Carey, John	1810	36		PA
Carey, Levi	1822	21	Y	PA
Carey, Moses	1800	25	b	MD
Carey, Richard	1806	25		PA
Carey, Richard	1807	00		
Carey, Wilson	1816	23		PA
Carey, Wm.	1807	00		PA
Cargill, Robert	1807	21		VA
Cargill, Robert	1809	0		
Carl, Thomas	1810	22		NJ
Carlin, H. J.	1821	22		PA
Carlin, John	1809	23		PA
Carling, John Alfred	1811	29		NJ
Carling, John Alfred	1815	0		
Carlisle, Joseph Donley	1810	13		MD
Carlisle, Joseph	1818	32		NY
Carlisle, Pemberton	1818	23		DE
Carlisle, Thomas	1804	20		DE
Carmick, Stephen	1821	17		NJ
Carmod, Henry	1818	25		NJ
Carmody, John	1817	17		NY
Carnar, William	1816	24		PA
Carney, Charles	1815	21		NY
Carney, James M.	1823	34		Ireland
Carney, John	1804	24	m	DE
Carney, John	1804	24	m	DE
Carney, John	1805	0		
Carney, Samuel	1805	22		PA

Carney, Samuel	1805	22		PA	Carson, Joseph	1810	22	PA
Carney, Thomas	1810	48	b	MD	Carson, Joseph	1812	41	NJ
Carns, John	1809	51		PA	Carson, Joseph	1818	24	PA
Carns, Richard, Jr.	1812	16		PA	Carson, William	1806	25	MA
Carns, Richard	1815	0		PA	Carson, William	1817	37	PA
Carpenter, Benjamin	1811	13		PA	Carswell, Samuel K.	1818	16	PA
Carpenter, Benjamin	1818	21		PA	Cart, Joseph	1808	21	PA
Carpenter, Caleb	1815	24	c	MD	Cart, Peter, Jr.	1806	23	PA
Carpenter, Edwin	1821	17		PA	Carter, Jacob	1799	12	DE
Carpenter, Jacob	1810	19	b	DE	Carter, Jehu	1814	29	NJ
Carpenter, James	1818	23	b	DE	Carter, John	1805	20	VA
Carpenter, John	1815	21		DE	Carter, John	1810	0	
Carpenter, John	1819	26		MD	Carter, John	1810	23 c	DE
Carpenter, John	1821	22	s	MD	Carter, Joseph	1823	29	NY
Carpenter, Lewis	1823	14	b	PA	Carter, Michael	1814	48	NY
Carpenter, Randall	1815	27	y	VA	Carter, Philip	1809	33 b	PA
Carpenter, Samuel M.	1815	15		PA	Carter, Robert	1801	26	DE
Carpenter, Tobias	1805	21	y	DE	Carter, Thaddeus	1807	31	MA
Carpenter, Tobias	1809	0			Carter, Thomas	1814	31	PA
Carpenter, Walter	1819	27		NY	Carter, William	1810	23	PA
Carpenter, William	1806	19		PA	Carter, William	1823	29 b	MD
Carpenter, William	1807	25		NY	Cartwright, William	1805	23	MA
Carpenter, William	1815	23	b	VA	Carty, Charles	1821	17	PA
Carr, Charles	1804	18		NY	Carty, John	1815	23 y	NY
Carr, James	1805	25		NJ	Carty, Samuel	1798	0	DE
Carr, James	1813	18		PA	Carty, Solomon	1810	22 b	DE
Carr, Joseph	1803	29		PA	Cary, Robert	1811	25 y	PA
Carr, Obed	1817	14		MA	Cary, Robert	1811	00	
Carr, Samuel	1821	33		MA	Cary, William	1804	30	PA
Carr, Thomas	1799	25		PA	Caryer, Richard	1801	26	PA
Carr, William	1818	21		PA	Caryer, Richard	1804	0	
Carragan, Thomas	1804	19		NJ	Casdorf, John	1811	00	
Carran, James	1811	00			Casdorp, John	1805	19	SC
Carrell, James	1815	20		DE	Caseman, Francis	1810	22 y	LA
Carrell, John	1801	18		PA	Casey, Jacob	1820	14	PA
Carrell, John	1804	18		PA	Casey, John	1806	23 m	NY
Carrell, John	1805	0						
Carrell, John	1805	0			Casey, Samuel	1804	20	PA
Carrell, John	1809	0		PA	Casey, Samuel	1807	00	PA
Carrell, John	1809	28		PA	cast away on board Schooner *Active* on			
Carrell, John	1817	37		PA	voyage from Curracoa to Aruba			
Carrell, Joseph	1823	17		PA				
Carrol, Charles Henry	1822	24	b	MD	Cash, Edmund Jefferson			
Carroll, Thomas	1801	22		PA		1819	18	PA
Carrot, Patrick	1800	26		PA	Caslan, Robert	1803	22	PA
Carsey, James	1816	24		DE	Casmir, Francis	1811	00	
Carson, Abraham	1803	32		NJ	Cass, Joseph	1823	21	PA
Carson, David	1805	23		SC	Cassady, Humphrey	1815	22	PA
Carson, John	1805	23		MD	Cassan, Samuel	1803	22	PA
Carson, John	1809	22		PA	Casseau, Richard	1809	21 y	SC
Carson, John	1809	32		none given	Cassedy, Henry	1798	0	Ireland
Carson, John	1811	00			Cassedy, Henry	1804	30	none given

Cassedy, Patrick 1821 30 Ireland
Cassel, Edward 1822 22 Y DE
Cassin, Stephen 1810 28 PA
Casson, John 1804 28 DE
Casson, William 1798 23 PA
Castagnet, John 1809 17 PA
Castagnet, Paul, Jr. 1810 15 PA
Casteell, James 1811 28 b MA
Castledine, Charles 1823 19 PA
Castledine, Thomas 1823 17 PA
Castro, Thomas 1807 36 LA
Caswell, Samuel 1821 39 MA
Cathcart, William 1809 28 MA
Cathrall, Edward, Jr. 1810 23 PA
Catnach, Daniel 1820 19 PA
Cauffman, Joseph W. 1815 16 PA
Caufield, John 1817 0 xx
Caulk, Norris J. 1822 16 DE
Causey, William 1805 25 b VA
Cavender, Charles 1804 20 m DE
Cavender, John 1812 27 DE
Cavll, Phinehas 1811 20 NJ
Cavtes, Philip 1811 00
Celson, John 1812 00
Cemmitt, James 1811 18 PA
Chabrera, Giuseppe 1810 22 LA
Chace, Thomas R. 1820 20 MA
Chadwick, James W. 1806 20 NJ
Chadwick, John 1815 25 MA
Chaloner, Ambrose 1800 14 PA
Chamberlain, Aaron 1796 0 MA

Chamberlain, David 1804 20 b MD
bound servant to Thomas Hood; goes to sea
with his consent

Chamberlain, David 1806 0
Chamberlain, David 1810 0 MD
Chamberlain, Enoch 1800 26 NJ
Chamberlain, Enoch 1800 28 NJ
Chamberlain, George 1805 25 MA
Chamberlain, George 1806 0
Chamberlain, George 1817 20 PA
Chamberlain, James G.1805 29 NJ
Chamberlain, Jonathan
 1810 24 MD
Chamberlain, William 1817 21 PA
Chamberlain, Wm. F. R.
 1821 24 NH
Chamberland, James 1804 18 b MD
apprenticed to Henry Molier of Phil. and is a free man at
expiration of indenture

Chamberlin, John 1809 21 DE
Chambers, Charles 1810 25 b DE
Chambers, George 1815 17 PA
Chambers, James 1798 30 none given
Chambers, John 1816 32 MA
Chambers, John 1822 29 MA
Chambers, Joseph 1808 23 NJ
Chambers, Robert 1810 22 PA
Chambers, Robert 1810 22 PA
Chambers, Samuel 1800 22 PA
Chance, John 1819 26 MD
Chandler, David 1810 32 DE
Chandler, John 1815 17 PA
Chandler, John 1815 0
Chandler, Samuel V. 1810 26 MA
Channell, Britton 1801 20 b MD
Chapels, William 1811 18 PA
Chaplen, Peter 1810 25
Chaplen, Peter 1815 0
Chaplle, John 1803 22 NJ
Chapman, John 1811 12 PA
Chapman, Samuel 1809 21 VA
Chappell, David 1798 23 CT
Chappell, John 1809 17 PA
Chard, Benjamin 1806 23 NJ
Chard, William 1804 25 NJ
Chard, William 1804 25 NJ
Chardon, Anthony, Jr. 1823 18 PA
Chare, Frederick 1807 19 b PA
Charles, George 1823 19 y PA
Charles, Henrey 1810 23 NJ
Charles, James 1823 16 y PA
Charles, Jeremiah 1823 22 y DE
Charles, John 1810 20 b PA
Charli, John 1810 35 b LA
Charruer, Peter Joseph
 1811 20 LA
Chase, George 1803 22 PA
Chase, George 1810 25 MA
Chase, Henry 1810 25 b DE
Chase, Henry 1811 26 MA
Chase, Jacob 1822 21 y MD
Chase, Jacob 1822 32 y MA
Chase, John 1809 23 MA
Chase, John 1810 39 NH
Chase, John 1816 22 MA
Chase, Joseph 1821 31 RI
Chase, Robert 1805 21 m DE
Chase, Samuel 1822 23 b MD
Chase, Thomas 1815 23 NH

Chase, Thomas Chamberlain				
	1818	23 b	MD	
Chasserian, John	1815	40		
Chasseriau, John	1809	0		none given
Chasson, George	1823	21	PA	
Chatfield, Oliver	1798	28	MA	
Chatterton, Jas	1823	32	NY	
Chattles, John	1823	36	MD	
Chauvell, Mitchell	1804	21 m	MD	
Check, Stephen	1798	15 y	NY	
Chedsey, Jacob	1811	24	CT	
Cheessen, John	1804	30 c	PA	
Cheever, Samuel	1815	26	MA	
Cherington, John	1810	24	PA	
Cherricks, William	1809	22	VA	
Cherry, William	1809	26	VA	
Chesebrough, Jabez	1819	21	CT	
Chesnut, William	1810	23		Ireland
Chester, Benjamin	1811	15	NJ	
Chester, Christopher	1807	37	RI	
Chester, Elijah	1815	19 b	NJ	
Chester, John	1805	20	PA	
Chester, John	1810	21	NJ	
Chester, John	1821	21 m	PA	
Chester, Pompey	1804	30 b	NJ	
Chester, Pompy	1807	30 b	NJ	
Chester, Samuel	1804	21 b	PA	
Chew, Joseph	1819	38 b	DE	
Cheyney, John H	1822	22	PA	
Chidsey, Abraham	1812	20	CT	
Childs, Henry	1815	23	PA	
Childs, James	1804	22	PA	
Childs, John, Jr.	1811	17	PA	
Childs, Jonathan F.	1813	29	NY	
Childs, William R.	1821	33	ME	
Chis, Daniel	1800	24	PA	
Choate, Joseph	1818	21	NJ	
Chohoon, William	1819	20	DE	
Cholbet, David	1807	24	PA	
Chollet, David	1804	22	PA	
Chollet, David	1809	0		
Chollet, David	1809	28	PA	
Christian, Daniel	1809	27	PA	
Christian, Ezekiel	1804	22 b	GA	
Christian, Jere	1815	26 b	VA	
Christian, John	1809	23 b	LA	
Christian, John	1821	45	PA	
Christian, Lawrence	1801	19	PA	
Christianin, Soloman	1823	43		Sweden
Christie, John	1815	32	PA	
Christopher, Issac Abbott				
	1822	54 b	VA	

Christopher, James	1803	25	PA
Christopher, John	1807	30	VA
Christy, David	1821	23	PA
Chubb, Thomas	1807	21	NJ
Church, Abraham	1821	25 b	VA
Church, Elisha	1819	28 y	CT
Church, Ezekiel	1809	24 b	VA
Church, Humphrey	1805	20	NJ
Church, Justice	1803	16	PA
Church, Nathan	1807	22	NJ
Church, Nathan	1807	22	NJ
Church, Nathan	1813	0	NJ
Church, Samuel T.	1805	39	RI
Church, Thomas	1815	33 y	CT
Chute, David	1811	30	MA
Cibben, John Battie	1811	21 b	LA
Cinel, Joseph	1806	29	PA
Clampit, William	1822	15	DE
Clare, Charles	1806	37	PA
Clark, Aaron	1815	24	CT
Clark, Abraham D.	1809	24	NY
Clark, Charles J.	1819	19	NJ
Clark, David	1809	19	DE
Clark, Elezear	1815	38	MA
Clark, Elijah	1814	27	NJ
Clark, Elisha	1807	24	MA
Clark, Esau	1806	23	DE
Clark, Francis Wayne	1823	17	PA
Clark, George	1806	18	NC
Clark, George	1807	21 b	DE
Clark, George	1818	32	NY
Clark, George W.	1823	14	NY
Clark, Henry	1810	22	MA
Clark, Israel	1810	20 b	DE
Clark, James	1811	22	NY
Clark, John	1798	23	NJ
Clark, John	1804	22	PA
Clark, John	1806	24	NY
Clark, John	1807	27	MA
Clark, John	1811	26	NJ
Clark, John	1811	34	MA
Clark, John	1812	28	MA
Clark, John	1812	25	MA
Clark, John	1813	0	
Clark, John	1818	21	MD
Clark, John	1822	30	PA
Clark, John	1822	22	MA
Clark, John	1823	21	PA
Clark, Joseph, Jr.	1809	29	MA
Clark, Joseph	1812	29	NH
Clark, Laurence	1818	18	VA
Clark, Layman	1807	22	NY

Clark, Myers	1811	21	DE
Clark, Nathaniel	1811	18 y	DE
Clark, Nathaniel	1818		
Clark, Peter	1804	27	NH
Clark, Philip	1807	37	MD
Clark, Robert	1801	24	MD
Clark, Robert	1803	22	DE
Clark, Robert	1811	22 b	NY
Clark, Samuel	1810	25	NH
Clark, Samuel	1821	18	PA
Clark, Samuel	1822	19	PA
Clark, Samuel	1823	18	ME
Clark, Sparrow	1815	26	MA
Clark, Spencer	1815	20	VA
Clark, Stephen	1804	23	DE
Clark, Stephen	1805	22	NJ
Clark, Stephen	1809	0	
Clark, Stephen	1819	15	PA
Clark, Thomas	1805	25	PA
Clark, Thomas	1806	23 b	PA
Clark, Thomas	1807	22	NY
Clark, Thomas	1808	24	PA
Clark, Thomas	1821	48	NJ
Clark, William	1804	33	VA
Clark, William	1810	23	NJ
Clark, William Young	1811	18	PA
Clark, William	1815	38	NJ
Clark, William	1815	23	NY
Clark, William	1818	20	NH
Clarke, John	1804	21	PA
Clarke, John	1807	21	MD
Clarke, John	1810	23	VA
Clarke, John	1812	00	
Clarke, Matthias	1817	27	NJ
Clarke, Michael	1820	41 y	PA
Clarke, Peter	1815	18	NY
Clarke, Thomas	1815	25	MA
Clarke, William	1818	22	PA
Clarke, William	1819	23	VA
Clarkson, Jack	1798	24 b	MD
Clarkson, John	1804	26 b	PA
Clarkson, John	1806	28 b	PA
Clarkson, John	1817	45 c	PA
Clary, James	1815	29	PA
Clary, Jose	1811	32	MS
Clasby, Frederick	1817	20	MA
Claskey, Charles	1813	18 c	NJ
Clavey, John	1809	29	none given
Clay, Edward W.	1817	18	PA
Claypoole, John	1817	14	MD
Clayton, Henry	1803	29	PA
Clayton, Henry	1809	24 b	DE

Clayton, Levi	1822	21 y	MD
Clayton, Maston	1819	21	PA
Clear, Benjamin	1809	23	MD
Cleary, James	1809	21	PA
Clefton, Aaron	1809	0	
Cleghorn, Thomas	1801	37	PA
Clemens, John	1812	37	PA
Clement, Arthur H.	1817	22	NJ
Clement, Edward	1821	27 y	PA
Clement, George	1805	38	SC
Clement, Jacob B.	1811	26	NJ
Clement, Peter	1817	32 y	LA
Clement, Tolbert	1822	20	NJ
Clements, Hugh	1815	16	PA
Clements, Michael	1803	27	NY
Clemming, Benjamin	1819	21	MA
Clemont, Edward	1809	13 m	PA
Clerr, John	1809	19	PA
Clever, Christian	1806	22	PA
Cleves, Robert	1798	22	MA
Clifford, William	1806	19	MA
Clifford, William	1819	22	MA
Clift, John	1807	19	MA
Clifton, Aaron	1807	21	DE
Cline, Jacob Read	1818	21	DE
Cline, John	1815	21	NJ
Cline, Thomas	1813	24	DE
Clinger, Frederick	1807	25	PA
Clinton, Joseph	1822	33 y	PA
Clocker, William	1810	25	MD
Clothier, Samuel	1810	28	PA
Clouds, James Ellis	1805	28 b	MD
Clover, Benjamin	1822	24 b	NJ
Clover, Elijah	1811	22 c	DE
Clunn, Charles	1814	27	NJ
Clyde, Alexander	1819	26	MA
Coakley, Benjamin Dale			
	1807	19	NC
Coates, George	1815	30 b	PA
Coates, Thomas W.	1821	14	PA
Coats, Alexander	1812	20 m	DE
Coats, Asa	1819	19	NJ
Coats, John	1805	21	PA
Cob, Alfred	1822	24	CT
Cobb, Zurial T.	1817	22	MA
Coburn, William	1815	24	RI
Cochran, George	1812	23 b	NC
Cochran, John	1810	26	NJ
Cock, William J.	1818	16	PA
Cockayne, John	1809	25	DE
Cockrill, William	1809	19	PA
Cocks, James	1817	19 c	LA

Cockshalt, James	1807	14		PA	Coleman, Charles S.	1823	12		PA
Cody, John	1804	21		PA	Coleman, Daniel	1810	0		
Cody, John	1804	21		PA	Coleman, Daniel	1810	35		PA
Coff, Daniel	1817	37	b	DE	Coleman, Isaiah	1809	23	y	NJ
Coffield, William	1806	25		PA	Coleman, Perry	1822	28	b	PA
Coffin, Albert	1804	31		MA	Coleman, William	1803	26		VA
Coffin, John	1801	30		NY	Coleman, William P.	1817	16		PA
Coffin, John	1818	26		NY	Coles, Daniel	1809	28		NJ
Coffin, Peter	1821	40		MA	Coles, Hewlett Townsend				
Coffin, Robert	1797	30		MA		1815	15		NY
Coffin, Samuel	1811	27	y	MA	Colesberry, William	1806	22		DE
Cofield, John	1816	21		NJ	Colesman, Armond	1814	24	c	PA
Coggins, Wallis	1811	18		MA	Colguhoun, John	1801	41		MA
Cohee, Clement	1816	21		DE	Colhoun, John	1818	16		PA
Coke, John Pinder	1809	23		MD	Colhoun, Thomas	1804	44		none given
Cokely, Joseph	1821	21		CT	Colladay, Daniel	1798	26		PA
Colbert, John	1813	26		DE	Collar, William	1809	21		PA
Colburt, John	1809	18		NJ	Collet, Cato	1819	30	b	DE
Colby, Enoch	1819	32		MA	Collick, Charles	1811	22	b	DE
					Collier, Peter	0000	30		PA
Coldwell, Amos	1804	19	b	PA	Collings, Dennis	1798	26		

Coldwell, Amos 1804 19 b PA
negro, born free, apprentice to Smith &
Carpenter, sail makers

Cole, Asel	1820	21		MA	Collings, John	1823	21		DE
Cole, Christopher	1814	21		DE	Collings, Tillinghast	1810	0		
Cole, George	1823	26	b	DE	Collingwood, William	1798	23		NY
Cole, Henry	1822	17		DE	Collins, Charles	1815	29		MA
Cole, James	1805	49	b	VA	Collins, David R.	1818	19		DE
Cole, Jeremiah	1822	26		ME	Collins, Earl	1804	23		NY
Cole, John	1809	17		MA	Collins, Frederick	1811	30		none given
Cole, John	1810	31		ME	Collins, Freeman	1806	38		CT
Cole, John	1811	21		MD	Collins, George	1804	37	y	MD
Cole, John	1815	32	b	NY	Collins, George	1806	26		VA
Cole, John	1817	21		NY	Collins, George	1807	16		DE
Cole, John	1823	20	b	MD	Collins, Henry	1815	35		PA
Cole, John	1823	25		NJ	Collins, Isaac	1805	25	b	MD
Cole, Joseph R.	1817	19		DE	Collins, Jacob	1811	16		VA
Cole, Perry	1810	19	b	MD	Collins, James B.	1803	17		PA
Cole, Peter	1805	16		PA	Collins, James	1816	22		DE
Cole, Richard	1810	21		PA	Collins, James L.	1821	17		DE
Cole, Robert	1807	21		MA	Collins, John	1807	27		LA
Cole, Samuel	1801	21		NJ	Collins, John	1809	23		DE
Cole, Stephen	1816	26		MA	Collins, John	1815	26		NY
					Collins, Jonathan	1804	14		MA
					Collins, Joshua	1798	16		PA
					Collins, Jr., Thomas	1814	21		PA

Cole, Thomas 1795 0
"emanumitted" by Caley Boyer, Talbot
County, MD

					Collins, Ralph	1815	24	b	VA
					Collins, Samuel	1803	24		PA
					Collins, Thomas	1803	23		PA
					Collins, Thomas	1806	26		MA
					Collins, Thomas	1811	00		
Cole, William	1808	26		VA	Collins, Tillinghast	1806	33		RI
Cole, William	1810	12	b	PA	Collins, Tillinghast	1807	00		RI
Cole, William	1812	28	y	MD	Collins, William	1809	22		VA

Collison, James	1811	22	PA		Conner, David	1810	19	PA
Collison, William E.	1815	24	PA		Conner, Edward	1806	23	PA
Collister, Daniel	1799	0	PA		Conner, Garrison	1821	22 b	DE
Collom, Clement	1799	26	PA		Conner, James	1811	19	PA
Colton, Joseph	1809	19	MA		Conner, John	0000	34	PA
Colvin, John	1809	19	DE		Conner, John	0000	34	PA
Colvin, John	1816	21	MA		Conner, John	1806	25 b	NY
Colvin, Robert	1809	21	DE		Conner, John	1812	00	
Colwell, John	1808	24 b	DE		Conner, John	1812	25	MD
Colwell, John	1810	21	NY		Conner, Lewis	1801	22 b	MD
Colwick, Tennis	1810	51	none given		Connier, Peter	1810	41	none given
Colyer, Jonathan	1809	24	PA		Connor, Bernard Jr.	1822	14	PA
Comble, Spiro	1804	22			Connor, Charles C.	1819	20	NY
Combs, John	1810	13	PA		Connor, Daniel	1818	47	PA
Combs, Richard	1812	22 b	PA		Connor, Felix	1818	16	PA
Combs, Thomas	1807	21 b	PA		Connor, James	1817	23	NC
Comly, Iredell	1812	16	PA		Connor, John	1810	23	VA
Comly, John	1806	22	PA		Connor, Joseph	1811	16 b	MD
Comly, William	1816	23 c	PA		Connor, Michael	1810	24	PA
Compart, John	1812	00			Connor, Michael	1810	18	PA
Comport, James	1810	20	PA		Connor, Peter	1810	21	DE
Comport, James	1810	0			Connor, Richard	1798	19	NJ
Comport, John	1810	17	PA		Connor, Samuel	1809	18	PA
Comport, John	1818				Connor, Thomas	1815	20	NY
Conckland, John	1814	17	MD					
Condon, Benjamin	1818	19	NJ		Connor, William	1796	15	PA
Condon, John	1808	19	PA		baptised St Mary's church July 1781; son of			
					Edmund and Bridget Connor			

Condon, John   1812 00
SPC lost when cast away in Brig *Africa* on
Gulf of Finland in 1810

					Conover, John	1813	23	NJ
					Conover, Micajah	1809	25	NJ
					Conover, Samuel	1805	20	NJ
Condon, John	1813	0			Conover, Samuel	1809	24	NJ
Condon, William, Jr.	1809	21	PA		Conover, Samuel	1809	0	
Condon, William	1816	22	PA		Conovor, Micajah	1811	00	
Coney, Thomas	1811	17	NY		Conrad, Ephraim	1806	15	PA
Congdill, Simon	1810	37 b	RI		Conrad, John, Jr.	1806	21	PA
Congdon, George	1821	21	MA		Conrow, Eber.	1821	25	NJ
Congle, Pero	1804	27 y	VA		Conser, George	1811	34	PA
Conklin, Joseph	1809	21	NJ		Constantin, Martin	1795	0	France
Conley, James	1819	23	MA		Conway, Henry	1820	39	NY
Conn, James	1805	50	DE		Conway, Jacob, Jr.	1804	28 m	MD
Connell, Henry	1811	18	PA		Conway, John	1812	38	PA
Connell, Robert	1806	30	MD		Conway, Scipio	1799	21 b	VA
Connell, Robert	1816	35	PA		Conyers, David	1817	23 b	PA
Connell, William	1800	40	NJ		Conyers, John	1823	27 y	PA
Connelly, Andrew	1823	20	MD		Conyngham, David	1811	16	PA
Connelly, John	1823	20	DE		Cooch, William	1818	17	DE
Connelly, Joseph	1806	26	PA		Cood, John	1807	15	MD
Connelly, Thomas	1804	19	PA		Cook, Abraham, Jr.	1805	14	PA
Connelly, Thomas L.	1815	23	PA		Cook, Ansel	1810	34	CT
Connely, Peter	1805	26	PA		Cook, Charles	1803	20	MA

Cook, Charles	1823	18	MA
Cook, Ebenezer	1809	39	NJ
Cook, Ebenezer	1815	45	NY
Cook, Edward A.	1814	24 y	MA
Cook, George	1810	19 y	DE
Cook, Henry	1807	21	NJ
Cook, Henry	1810	19 y	PA
Cook, Henry	1811	00	
Cook, Henry	1815	0	
Cook, Jacob	1823	31	NJ
Cook, John	1810	27	MA
Cook, John	1815	29	CT
Cook, Jonathan	1817	22 b	NJ
Cook, Joseph	1815	18 b	CT
Cook, Justin	1815	26	MA
Cook, Nathaniel B.	1818	13	RI
Cook, Peter	1807	19 b	MD
Cook, Peter	1810	0	
Cook, Robert	1799	28	MD
Cook, Thomas	1796	0	PA
Cook, Thomas Leston	1820	15	PA
Cook, William	1809	28	NJ
Cook, William	1809	26 b	DE
Cook, William	1810	16	SC
Cook, William	1811	21 y	MD
Cooke, John	1809	24	PA
Cooke, John	1811	24 b	NY
Cooke, Thomas	1822	21	NJ
Cooke, William	1804	22	PA
Cooke, William	1807	32	MA
Cooley, Thomas	1819	22	DE
Coombs, Peter	1822	21	ME
Coombs, Richard	1819	28 b	MD
Cooney, Samuel	1822	24 b	NC
Cooper, Allen	1822	20 s	PA
Cooper, Daniel	1807	21 b	MD
Cooper, Daniel	1814	20	NJ
Cooper, David	1812	22	PA
Cooper, Francis	1798	33	PA
Cooper, Francis	1806	0	
Cooper, George	1815	16	NJ
Cooper, Griffith Morgan			
	1809	18	NJ
Cooper, Isaac	1807	32 b	PA
Cooper, Jacob	1807	16	NJ
Cooper, Jacob L.	1809	19	NJ
Cooper, James	1799	21	
Cooper, James	1809	20	MA
Cooper, James M.	1817	18	NJ
Cooper, Jessey	1823	28 s	NY
Cooper, John C.	1800	21	PA
Cooper, John	1804	28	NJ

Cooper, John	1815	23	MD
Cooper, John	1821	16 y	MD
Cooper, Peter	1804	21	PA
Cooper, Thomas	1810	22 b	MD
Cooper, Timothy	1819	31	MA
Cooper, William	1806	22	MA
Cooper, William	1807	24	PA
Cooper, William	1814	0	
Cope, George	1810	22	NY
Cope, George A.	1814	0	
SPC burned on board British ship while a			
prisoner on board			
Cope, George	1806	20	PA
Cope, John Jacob	1810	21	PA
Cope, John	1815	28	NJ
Cope, John	1815	23	PA
Cope, Samuel	1811	24	DE
Copeland, George	1810	20	PA
Copeland, James	1805	17	PA
Coperthwait, Theodore		1817	17
			DE
Copes, Daniel	1822	23	NC
Copeu, Bartholomew	1811	25	MS
Copland, James	1818	28	NY
Coply, Jeremiah	1801	17	PA
Copper, Abraham George			
	1817	13	PA
Coppinger, John	1807	36	PA
Corban, Christopher	1805	22	PA
Corbet, John	1812	26	PA
Corbett, Archibald	1805	25	MA
Corbit, Henry	1819	22	PA
Corbit, John	1806	17	PA
Cordier, Moses	1818	28 m	MA
Coren, Isaac	1796	0	PA
Corgae, Thomas,Jr.	1811	24	PA
Corgee, Arthur F.	1812	21	PA
Corgie, George	1812	30	NJ
Corgie, William	1812	18	NJ
Cork, Isaac	1809	18 b	MD
Corkry, Edmund	1797	23	NH
Corlis, Edward	1803	19	NY
Corlis, William	1809	39	MA
Cormick, David, Jr.	1818	14	PA
Cornelius, Michael	1812	28	NJ
Cornelius, Peter	1815	21	NJ
Cornelius, Robert	1818	33	VA
Cornell, Amos	1805	28 m	NY
Cornell, John	1796	0	RI
Corner, John	1804	28	NJ

Cornet, John	1810	0			Couret, Francis	1811	16	PA
Cornet, John	1810	25	PA		Course, Isaac J.	1821	18	SC
Cornfoot, Alexander	1807	23	PA		Coursey, George D.	1820	20 b	DE
Cornforth, Cornelius	1798	29	NY		Coursey, John	1810	24	PA
Cornick, Henry	1811	21 b	MD		Courtney, James	1808	16	PA
Cornish, Daniel	1809	20	NJ		Courtney, John	1804	23	CT
Cornish, Daniel	1810	0 c	NJ		Courtney, John	1810	0	
Cornish, Elzy	1801	24 y	DE		Courtois, John Baptist	1807		
Cornish, James,Jr.	1815	17	PA		Cousland, William	1819	17	PA
Cornish, John	1807	15 b	DE		Coutie, Charles	1807	23	LA
Cornish, John	1812	28 m	MD		Covel, Daniel	1807	25	NH
Cornish, John	1817	23 y	DE		Covenhoven, Jacob	1809	21	NY
Cornish, Joseph	1815	0			Coverdill, Luke	1807	24	DE
Cornish, Joseph	1821	27 b	MD		Covert, John	1809	20	NY
Cornish, Samuel	1805	0			Covinton, William	1810	16	VA
Cornish, Samuel	1805	23 b	MD		Cowan, Oliver	1807	26	none given
Cornish, Samuel	1806	0			Cowell, Ebenezar	1804	20	NJ
Cornish, William	1805	22	VA		Cowell, George	1815	31	
Cornish, William	1810	28 y	DE		Cowen, William	1804	19	PA
Cornish, William	1811	27 b	DE		Cowlin, Frederick	1804	26	MA
Cornwell, Eleanah	1807	18	NY		Cowpland, William	1804	13	PA
Cornwell, Joseph	1813	31	MD		Cowpland, William	1807	17	PA
Cornwell, Robert	1806	21	PA		Cox, Alexander	1809	22 b	NJ
Cornwell, Robert	1815	28	PA		Cox, Edward R.	1819	18	PA
Corra, Joseph	1796	0	Genoa		Cox, Jacob L.	1821	21	PA
Corran, James	1801	33	NY		Cox, James	1811	14 b	VA
Corry, James	1811	22	NJ		Cox, James	1819	24	PA
Corson, Allen	1815	24	NJ		Cox, John W	1818	14	LA
Corson, Henry	1810	19	NJ		Cox, Joseph	1805	22	MA
Corson, Jacob	1809	19	NJ		Cox, Michael	1803	27	PA
Corson, Jacob	1810	23	NJ		Cox, Michael	1809	34	none given
Corson, James	1810	17	NJ		Cox, Moses	1804	36	MA
Corson, John	1810	22	NJ		Cox, William	1804	27	PA
Corson, John	1811	00			Cox, William	1806	27	NY
Corson, Joseph,Jr.	1815	27	NJ		Cox, William	1807	16	PA
Corson, Seth	1809	19	NJ		Cox, William Hiram	1814	16	PA
Coso, Josef	1806	25	LA		Coxe, George	1819	26	NY
Costen, Thomas	1815	21 b	VA		Coyles, John	1810	15	PA
Costigin, Francis Jay	1805	26	NY		Cozens, Homer	1818	19	NJ
Coston, Nicholas	1815	39 b	DE		Cozens, Ivory L.	1815	18	MA
Coston, Thomas	1816	25 b	NY		Cozers, George	1799	0	NJ
Cotterell, William	1809	22	MD		Crabb, Thomas	1811	23	Md
Cotton, Samuel	1817	29 c	MA		Craft, William	1823	35	RI
Cottrell, Roswell W.	1822	21	NY		Crafton, John	1809	21	NJ
Cottrell, Thomas	1798	36	NJ		Craig, Andrew	1798	0	
Couch, Hezekiah	1815	17	CT		Craig, Andrew	1798	30	PA
Couch, Robert	1798	21	PA		Craig, George	1798	28	PA
Coulbourn, John	1811	31	MD		Craig, Hugh	1815	15	NY
Coulon, Joseph	1818	13	PA		Craig, James	1809	34	PA
Coulter, John	1817	15	PA		Craig, James	1814	42	DE
Council, James	1798	31	DE		Craig, John	1804	18	PA
Council, William	1817	13	PA		Craig, John	1805	23	PA

Craig, John	1813	20	MA	
Craig, Peter	1812	15	NJ	
Craig, Robert	1816	27	SC	
Craighead, Joseph	1809	27	NJ	
Crall, Edmund	1819	20	MA	
Crandal, Barton	1809	28	RI	
Crandall, William	1812	21	NY	
Crandell, Jeremiah	1805	16	PA	
Crandell, John	1811	27	NY	
Crandell, William	1806	24	PA	
Crane, Alexander	1807	26	NY	
Crane, John	1798	18	MD	
Crane, Samuel	1823	22	NJ	
Craneman, Levi	1805	18	PA	
Crannier, Jonathan	1803	23	DE	
Crannier, Jonathan	1803	23	DE	
Cranston, Gardner L.	1818	16	PA	
Cranston, George	1807	20	NY	
Cranston, John	1798	20	RI	
Crap, Samuel	1818	14	PA	
Crappen, Smith	1809	18	MD	
Crawford, Barnes	1815	25	NJ	
Crawford, George	1810	23	NJ	
Crawford, John	1796	0	CT	
Crawford, John	1805	52	NY	
Crawford, John	1812	23	PA	
Crawford, Nelson	1812	25 y	VA	
Crawford, Richard	1805	17	RI	
Crawford, Samuel H.	1811	20	PA	
Crawford, Thomas	1804	19	NY	
Crawford, William	1805	19	DE	
Crawford, William	1815	38	CT	
Crawley, Samuel	1813	25	MA	
Craycroft, Richard	1813	23	MD	
Crayton, Emanuel	1806	18	PA	
Crayton, Emanuel	1806	19	PA	
Creaghead, Job	1809	11	PA	
Creaghead, Joseph	1806	22	NJ	
Crearin, James	1816	16	PA	
Creery, William	1804	21	DE	
Creery, William	1806	23	DE	
Creighton, George	1820	14	PA	
Creighton, John L.	1816	33	MA	
Creighton, Samuel	1807	40 b	SC	
Cremen, John	1809	34	MA	
Cress, George	1806	20	PA	
Cress, John	1806	30	NY	
Creten, Paul	1812	27		none given
Crippin, James	1818	28 c	VA	
Cripps, Samuel	1807	15	NJ	
Cripps, Samuel	1809	19	NJ	
Crips, Richard, Jr.	1804	16	PA	
Crips, Richard, Jr.	1804	16	PA	
Crips, Richard	1805	0		
Criss, Joseph	1803	35	PA	
Crisswell, Samuel	1797	29		
Crocker, Edward	1816	26	VA	
Croft, James	1809	25 b	MD	
Croft, James	1812	00		
Croft, Thomas	1809	25	PA	
Croft, Thomas	1812	00		
Cromstock, John	1811	27	NY	
Cromwall, George W.	1820	22 y	NJ	
Croneman, Levi	1807	18	PA	
Cronmiller, John	1821	21	MD	
Crooks, Robert	1804	26 m	SC	
Crop, James	1804	15	PA	
Crop, John Peter	1809	22	PA	
Cropper, Cato	1804	24 b	DE	
Cropper, Charles	1807	18 b	DE	
Cropper, Charles	1815	0		
Cropper, Isaac	1815	53	MD	
Cropper, John	1811	26 b	DE	
Cropper, Lemuel	1823	50 b	MD	
Cropper, London	1811	19 b	DE	
Cropper, Moses	1809	22 b	DE	
Cropper, Samuel	1807	44	MD	
Cropper, William	1809	22	MD	
Crosbey, Henry	1821	39	PA	
Crosby, Andrew Doz	1815	19	PA	
Crosby, Barnabas	1809	20	MA	
Crosby, George	1806	16	CT	
Crosby, George	1812	00		
Crosby, George	1818	00	CT	
Crosby, Josiah	1815	23	MA	
Crosby, Peirce, Jr.	1821	16	PA	
Crosby, Richard	1799	19	PA	
Crosby, Thomas	1821	14	MA	
Crosdell, Joseph	1820	20 b	NY	
Crosen, John	1817	25 m	NJ	
Crosfield, Reuben	1808	44	VA	
Cross, Charles	1811	27 b	LA	
Cross, Frederick	1798	27	PA	
Cross, James J.	1820	31	PA	
Cross, John	1811	18	PA	
Cross, Joseph	1810	21	PA	
Cross, Thomas	1804	21 b	PA	
Cross, Thomas	1809	24 b	PA	
Crosser, David	1798	26	PA	
Crossman, Hiram	1811	20	CT	
Crouch, James	1815	26	MA	
Crousillat, Joseph	1809	17	PA	
Crowan, Robert	1805	23	MD	
Crowell, Benjamin	1821	21	NJ	

Crowell, Nathaniel	1811	22		PA	Curris, James	1806	13	NY
Crowell, Obed	1823	23		MA	Curry, George	1811	23 y	SC
Crowell, William S.	1820	15		PA	Curry, Thomas	1815	20	CT
Crowell, Yelveton	1809	31		NJ	Curry, William	1819	28 b	NY
Crowninshield, Caleb	1811	21		MA	Curtin, William	1804	24	PA
Crozer, John	1809	22		PA	Curtin, William	1805	0	
Crue, John	1821	21 b		VA	Curtis, Asa	1822	28	MA
Crumb, John	1818	29		NY	Curtis, Eli	1821	23	MA
Crumback, Godfrey	1807	28		PA	Curtis, Geroge	1822	29	MA
Crumpton, William	1818	24		PA	Curtis, Isaac Antrim	1809	21	NJ
Cruse, Peter	1822	37		none given	Curtis, James	1807	20	NJ
Cruseman, Francis	1804	30		PA	Curtis, John	1807	23	MA
Cuffburt, Enanus	1822	21 b		MD	Curtis, Jonathan T.	1805	20	NJ
Culbert, Thomas	1804	23		MD	Curtis, Martin	1817	21	MA
Cullen, Jonathan	1817	21		NJ	Curtis, Martin	1818		
Cumber, Walter	1815	21		VT	Curtis, Samuel	1810	19 c	PA
Cummas, George	1811	27		LA	Curtis, Samuel	1811	00	
Cummingham, William					Curtis, Thomas R.	1821	34	NJ
	1808	0		PA	Curtis, William	1807	32	MA
Cummings, Alexander	1796	0		PA	Curtis, William	1809	23 m	PA
Cummings, Alexander	1797	17			Curtis, William	1809	22 y	PA
Cummings, John	1823	25		England	Curtis, Zebina, II	1813	24	VT
Cummings, Robert	1811	30 b		NJ	Curwen, Joseph	1796	0	Gr.Br.
Cummings, Samuel	1815	17		PA	Curzine, William	1812	46	PA
Cummings, Thomas	1806	24		MD	Cushing, John	1812	15	PA
Cummings, William	1799	22		DE	Cushing, Marrquis	1815	36	MA
Cummings, William	1809	20		PA	Cushman, John	1817	18	MA
Cummins, Cyrus	1806	14 m		PA	Custilon, William	1804	62	VA
Cummins, Isaac	1809	21 y		PA	Custis, George	1812	23 c	PA
Cummins, Isaac	1811	00			Custis, Joseph	1823	16	MA
Cummins, John	1815	20		PA	Cuthbert, Robert	1820	23	PA
Cummins, Robert	1818	15		PA	Cuthbert, Samuel	1822	16	PA
Cummiskey, John	1809	21		PA	Cutler, James	1809	26	DE
Cumpton, Crawford	1804	20		NJ	Cutley, James	1810	21	MA
Cuningham, John	1804	28		PA	Cylus, James	1798	22 b	PA
Cuningham, John	1809	25		PA	Cylus, James	1810	0	
Cunningham, Andrew	1803	24		PA	Cyrus, Peter	1811	00	
Cunningham, James	1809	21		CT	Dabney, Marks	1813	25	NY
Cunningham, James	1809	30		NY	DaCosta, George T	1816	17	PA
Cunningham, John	1814	21		DE	DaCosta, Joseph	1806	26	LA
Cunningham, Matthew					DaCosta, Manuel	1807	18	LA
	1804	21		PA	Dag, Enoch	1804	25	NJ
Cunningham, William	1801	18		PA	Dailey, Joseph	1807	22 m	VA
Curphy, Matthew	1804	33		PA	Dailey, Joseph	1810	0	
Currace, James	1808	0			Dailey, Joseph	1812	00	
Curren, Peter	1798	0		Ireland	Dalahan, John	1804	30	DE
Currey, Edward	1821	39		MD	Dalavau, Abraham	1815	23	PA
Currey, John	1809	22 b		MD	Dalby, Owen	1810	19	NJ
Currie, William M.	1820	17		PA	Dale, James	1810	21	NJ
Currier, Samuel	1822	43		MA	Dalstead, Matthew	1822	27 b	MA
Currin, Martin	1804	24		PA	Dalton, Nathaniel	1805	21	NY
Currin, Martin	1804	24		PA	Daly, John	1795	23	PA

Name	Year	Age		Location
Dame, James	1818	24		NH
Dampier, George	1807	24		DE
Dan, Gabriel	1815	26	b	LA
Danford, Stephen	1818	18		MA
Danham, William	1798	36		VA
Daniel, James	1811	21	b	PA
Daniel, James	1812	00		
Daniel, James	1816	0		
Daniel, William	1811	23		NJ
Danielly, Jesse	1820	20		NJ
Daniels, Henry	1807	00		NJ
Daniels, Henry	1807	19		NJ
Daniels, Henry	1813	0		
Daniels, John	1822	23		CT
Daniels, Owen	1812	22		NJ
Daniels, Thomas	1810	28		MA
Daniels, Whittenton	1815	22	b	NJ
Daniels, William	1812	24	b	VA
Daniels, William	1815	0		
Daniels, William	1815	14		PA
Dankin, Charles	1822	26		PA
Dannacker, George	1809	19		PA
Danterochis, Alex C.	1823	21		NJ
Dardayon, John Lewis	1806	32		none given
Dare, Charles	1810	24		NJ
Daring, Jacob	1812	00		
Darling, Gamaliel	1809	19		NJ
Darling, Gamaliel	1811	00		
Darling, Mitchell Christopher				
	1811	24		
Darrack, John	1809	27		PA
Darrack, John	1811	00		
Darragh, Archibald	1819	23	b	PA
Darram, Thomas	1809	32	y	DE
Darrow, James	1820	24		CT
Darvin, John	1816	23		NJ
Darwin, William	1809	18		NY
Dary, Fortune	1804	32	b	PA
Dashiell, Isaac	1820	21		MD
Dasimore, Adam	1801	18	m	PA
DaSylva, Manuel	1807	25		LA
Daton, Nathaniel	1806	0		NY
Daudy, Francis	1811	21		France
Daugherty, James	1798	28		MA
Daulton, Henry	1817	21		NJ
Daumas, Francis L.	1816	19		NJ
Daumas, James	1807	17		LA
Davaus, Aime	1815	29		
Davenport, James	1798	24		PA
Davenport, Robert	1815	31		NY
Davenport, Robert	1817	00		xx
Davenport, William	1815	19		NY

Name	Year	Age		Location
Davenport, William, Jr.				
	1821	14		PA
Daversen, Cornelius	1803	18		PA
David, Benjamin	1798	20		DE
David, Benjamin	1807	00		DE
David, Benjamin	1811	34		DE
David, Thomas	1806	23		NY
David, Thomas	1807	00		
Davids, Matachia	1819	21		PA
Davidson, Andrew	1801	21		PA
Davidson, Bebe	1813	18		NY
Davidson, James	1809	22		PA
Davidson, John	1797	0		Gr.Br.
Davidson, William	1810	23		PA
Davidson, Wm	1817	21		MD
Davies, Edward	1810	27		NC
Davies, Edward	1810	27		England
claimed to have been born Beaufort, NC; confessed				
to being an Englishman; captain returned SPC				
Davies, Noble	1807	21		MD
Davies, Thomas	1805	22		SC
Davinson, Hugh	1800	25		NY
Davis, Ashton	1804	21		PA
Davis, Ashton	1804	21		PA
Davis, Benjamin	1809	27	y	PA
Davis, Benjamin L.	1815	29		MA
Davis, Benjamin	1818	21		NY
Davis, Cato	1815	24	y	DE
Davis, Charles	1808	23		VA
Davis, Charles	1809	17		PA
Davis, Charles	1809	38	b	NY
Davis, Daniel	1815	36		PA
Davis, David	1821	17	y	DE
Davis, Davis	1809	23		PA
Davis, Edmond	1806	21		CT
Davis, Francis	1818	22	c	MD
Davis, George	1809	22		MA
Davis, George P.	1809	18		PA
Davis, George, Jr.	1810	19		PA
Davis, George P.	1810	0		
Davis, George	1811	16	b	VA
Davis, George	1813	24		PA
Davis, George	1816	14		PA
Davis, George P.	1818			
Davis, Henry	1815	19		PA
Davis, Henry	1818	28	b	PA
Davis, Henry	1823	26		PA
Davis, James	1798	20		VA
Davis, James	1800	21		PA
Davis, James	1801	25		VA

Davis, James	1806	24	NY
Davis, James	1809	17	MD
Davis, James	1810	31	RI
Davis, John	1798	27	NJ
Davis, John	1803	22	NY
Davis, John	1803	23 m	VA
Davis, John	1804	16 b	DE
Davis, John	1804	27 b	NY
Davis, John	1806	25	SC
Davis, John	1807	25	SC
Davis, John	1807	28	RI
Davis, John	1808	29	DE
Davis, John	1809	22	MD
Davis, John	1809	17	PA
Davis, John	1810	20	DE
Davis, John	1810	22	RI
Davis, John	1810	22 m	PA
Davis, John	1810	0	
Davis, John	1811	56 b	VA
Davis, John	1811	35	PA
Davis, John	1815	27 m	VA
Davis, John	1817	57 b	VA
Davis, John B.	1819	31 b	PA
Davis, John	1819	45 b	RI
Davis, John	1821	21 b	MD
Davis, Jonathan	1805	31	DE
Davis, Joseph	1810	24	LA
Davis, Kendal	1809	19	MD
Davis, Kendal	1817	21	DE
Davis, Levin	1807	22 b	DE
Davis, Levin	1807	22 b	DE
Davis, Levin	1818	27 c	MD
Davis, Lewis	1807	22	LA
Davis, Moses	1811	24	MA
Davis, Nathan	1818	28	MA
Davis, Nicholas	1811	27	none given
Davis, Richard	1798	21	NY
Davis, Richard	1809	23 b	DE
Davis, Samuel	1804	16	PA
Davis, Samuel	1805	21 b	MD
Davis, Samuel	1810	22 b	MD
Davis, Samuel	1815	19	PA
Davis, Samuel	1817	26	VT
Davis, Samuel B.	1822	28	VA
Davis, Stephen	1798	0	NH
Davis, Stephen	1810	21	NJ
Davis, Thomas	1801	20	NY
Davis, Thomas	1801	24	MA
Davis, Thomas	1803	50 b	PA
Davis, Thomas B.	1804	29	PA
Davis, Thomas	1804	34 b	NY
Davis, Thomas C.	1804	22	VA

Davis, Thomas	1805	26	PA
Davis, Thomas	1809	23 b	DE
Davis, Thomas	1809	16	PA
Davis, Thomas	1811	37	MD
Davis, Thomas	1815	24	NY
Davis, Thomas	1818	27 y	NJ
Davis, Thomas	1818	30 b	DE
Davis, Thomas	1819	36	MA
Davis, Thomas	1820	21	NH
Davis, William	1800	0	NY
Davis, William	1803	30	VA
Davis, William	1806	26	VA
Davis, William	1808	25	PA
Davis, William	1809	29 y	NC
Davis, William	1809	0	VA
Davis, William	1811	19 b	PA
Davis, William	1811	26	MD
Davis, William	1812	00	
Davis, William	1815	24	NC
Davis, William	1816	32	VA
Davis, William	1817	29 b	MD
Davis, William	1821	23 b	LA
Davis, William	1822	32	MA
Davis, William N.	1822	23 s	SC
Davison, Jack	1803	26 c	MA
Davison, James	1808	21	MD
Davison, Samuel	1798	22	DE
Davisson, Mathias	1798	22	VA
Davnay, John	1804	22	PA
Davy, James	1801	24 b	VA
Davy, Josiah	1815	17	PA
Davy, Thomas	1804	20	none given
Dawes, Edward	1809	20	PA
Dawes, Edward	1813	0	
Dawson, George	1810	25	MD
Dawson, John	1796	0	MD
Dawson, Levy	1818	28 s	NJ
Dawson, Matthias	1807	18	NJ
Dawson, Matthias	1809	0	
Dawson, Matthias	1810	0	
Dawson, Richard	1815	33	MD
Dawson, Thomas	1796	0	NJ
Dawson, William	1815	18	PA
Day, Charles	1815	23	PA
Day, David	1804	21	MA
Day, Henry	1809	26 b	MD
Day, Henry	1810	0 b	
Day, James	1809	14	NY
Day, John	1804	28	MA
Day, John	1804	28	MA
Day, John	1805	0	
Day, John	1805	37	NY

41

Day, John	1815	18		RI
Day, Joseph	1810	22		NJ
Day, Richard	1805	19		NC
Day, Robert	1810	27 b		PA
Day, Samuel	1811	25		LA
Day, Samuel	1817	22		MA
Day, Thomas	1809	23		PA
Dayley, Michael	1809	16		PA
Dayley, Michael	1809	15		PA
Daymon, Florey	1798	21		PA
Days, Jacob	1804	25		NJ
Days, Jacob	1804	25		NJ
Dayton, Henry Payton Randolph				
	1809	18		RI
Dayton, Henry	1809	18		RI
Dayton, Henry R.	1809	0		
Dayton, Henry	1810	19		RI
Dayton, William	1804	21		RI
Dayton, William	1806	0		
Dayton, William	1810	0		
De Frettos, Francis	1796	0		Portugal
Deacon, David	1806	23		NJ
Deacon, Thomas	1806	28		MA
Deal, Jacob	1817	24		PA
Dealy, Richard	1808	25		NY
Deamey, William	1822	46 y		Va
Dean, Eli	1806	25		MA
Dean, Eli	1809	28		MA
Dean, Henry	1811	14		CT
Dean, William	1805	20		MD
Deanel, William	1799	20		PA
Dearing, Jacob	1810	26		PA
Dearing, Noah	1819	25		MA
Deats, Martin	1805	21		PA
Deauine, John, Jr.	1818	23		PA
Debans, Peter	1823	20		PA
DeBaptist, John	1803	30		VA
Debest, Philip	1809	23		MS
Debeust, John	1815	33		NY
DeBock, Augustine	1798	23		
deBosch, Charles	1806	28		none given
Deboss, Joseph	1809	35 y		NY
DeBow, Samuel Quay	1821	16		NJ
DeBredeka, Andries	1806	24		NH
Decatur, John	1803	17		PA
Decatur, Stephen	1818	29 b		PA
Decker, Edward	1822	18 m		PA
Deckes, Richard	1823	19 y		PA
Decosta, James	1821	34		MA
DeCosta, Cato	1818	49 c		MD
DeCosta, Emanuel	1806	22		LA
Decoster, Charles	1818	30		PA

Decrous, Anthony	1818	21 c		Portugal
Deer, William	1804	16		GA
Dees, Manuel	1806	22		LA
DeHart, Robeson	1810	23		PA
Dela, Forbes	1815	26		MA
Delahan, John	1806	0		
Delainy, Greenberry	1812	28 b		MD
Delaney, Manuel	1809	0		
Delaney, Peter	1805	54		PA
Delano, Charles	1804	26		MA
Delano, Ezekiel	1817	19		MA
Delano, Thomas	1805	25		MA
Delanoy, Abraham	1823	25		NY
Delany, James W.	1807	21		PA
Delany, John	1811	17		PA
Delany, John	1817	00		xx
Delany, Manuel	1807	22 b		NY
Delany, Peter	1795	0		MD
Delany, Peter	1806	0		
Delany, Peter	1811	00		
Delany, Philip	1803	25 b		MD
Delap, William	1810	23		NJ
Delaporte, Antoine	1809	30		MS
Delaunay, John	1806	24		France
Delavon, Charles	1801	22		NJ
Delavon, Charles	1816	37		NJ
Delavou, Charles	1808	0		
Delibou, Abraham	1807	19		PA
Dellaney, William	1804	30		MA
Dellon, John -	1809	21		NY
Delone, Emanuel	1815	34		LA
Demarest, Martin	1805	18		NY
Demarlour, Francis	1809	17 y		NY
Deming, Basilly	1807	39		CT
Demont, Thomas	1817	23 b		NJ
Dempsey, Maurice	1804	41		DE
Dempsey, Thomas	1822	16		PA
Denbey, John	1821	49 b		MD
Denby, Richard	1823	29 b		MD
Denby, Samuel	1811	38 b		MD
Denckla, Christian	1815	20		PA
Denight, Samuel	1812	25		NJ
Denike, Davis	1810	48		NJ
Denike, Robert	1807	40		NJ
Denn, James, Jr.	1809	25		NJ
Dennett, George	1820	25		MA
Denney, Charles	1804	26 m		DE
Denney, Evan	1809	16		DE
Denney, John	1813	34		NC
Dennis, John	1804	23		NJ
Dennis, John	1804	25		NJ
Dennis, John	1805	32		LA

Dennis, John	1806	0	
Dennis, John	1810	20 b	MD
Dennis, John	1811	32	MD
Dennis, John	1822	22	Pa
Dennis, Joseph	1804	30	NJ
Dennis, Joshua	1817	20 b	DE
Dennis, Littleton, Jr.	1806	22	MD
Dennis, Peter	1810	22	MD
Dennis, Peter	1810	22	MD
Dennison, Edward	1815	24	CT
Dennison, John	1810	23	MA
Denniston, William	1815	17	PA
Denny, Patrick	1815	31 y	DE
Denver, Arthur	1810	22	VA
Denver, Arthur	1815	0	
deOlibeira, Peter	1807	26	LA
Deosel, Francis Samuel			
	1809	20	LA
Depool, Francis V.	1811	22	LA
Depsey, Morris	1804	52	DE
Derby, John	1812	21 b	PA
DeRego, Francis	1807	26	LA
Derham, John	1811	24 y	DE
Derrick, James	1818	23 b	MD
Derrickson, Solomon	1810	25 b	DE
Derry, Isaac	1803	20	PA
Desaugue, Francis	1823	22	PA
Desberry, Thomas	1804	29 b	PA
Desilva, Thomas	1806	27	SC
Detrickson, John	1809	26	PA
Deurver, Cornelius	1809	21	PA
Devany, Francis	1815	18 m	SC
Devereux, James	1809	45	RI
Devereux, James	1818	15	PA
Devereux, John	1796	0	PA
Devereux, John, Jr.	1815	15	PA
Devereux, Phillip	1803	21	MD
Deviez, Thomas	1810	38	MA
Devoe, Henry A.	1809	30	NY
Devoe, Richard	1805	18	NY
Devoe, Richard	1809	0	NY
Devoll, Stephen	1798	25	MA
Devon, James	1823	21	NY
Dew, Edward	1801	16	
Dewees, Reuben	1821	24 b	PA
Dewey, Christopher	1823	35	RI
Dewey, George	1819	23	CT
Dewey, Jonathan	1804	21	PA
Dewist, Thomas	1804	21	PA
Dewist, Thomas	1805	0	
DeWitt, William	1822	23 b	NY
Dexter, John	1815	23	NY

Dialogue, George	1821	21	PA
Diamond, John Francis			
	1807	35 b	MD
Dible, John	1801	21	PA
Dick, Charles	1814	16	PA
Dick, Charles	1816	0	PA
Dick, Edward	1809	21 b	SC
Dick, Elisha	1806	21 b	DE
Dick, Hamilton R.	1809	17	PA
Dick, Richard	1804	41 b	DE
Dickenson, Isaac	1805	0	MD
Dickenson, Samuel	1820	22 b	MD
Dickerson, Isaac	1804	22 b	MD
Dickerson, Isaac	1811	28	NY
Dickerson, John	1809	23	NJ
Dickey, Casper	1823	23	NY
Dickey, William C.	1813	17	PA
Dickin, Richard	1803	28	PA
Dickinson, Alfred	1822	24	SC
Dickinson, Benjamin	1822	23 y	DE
Dickinson, Francis	1810	15	PA
Dickinson, Isaac	1812	0	
Dickinson, John	1811	22	PA
Dickinson, John	1815	20	PA
Dickinson, Joseph	1807	26	LA
Dickinson, Joseph	1808	0	
Dickinson, Richard C.	1809	15	NY
Dickinson, William	1799	23	NJ
Dickinson, William	1823	26	NY
Dickison, Nicholas	1816	26	PA
Dickson, Aaron	1811	26	DE
Dickson, John	1798	24	PA
Dickson, John	1807	40	MD
Dickson, Richard	1811	24 b	NY
Dickson, William	1810	24	NY
Dickson, William	1811	22 b	DE
Dickson, William	1811	00	
Dieffenbach, John L.	1806	35	none given
Dien, James	1818	21 b	DE
Digenoe, James	1798	31	NC
Diggs, John	1817		DE
Diggs, William	1814	22	NY
Dilkes, Elijah	1823	23	NJ
Dilkes, James	1809	25	NJ
Dilks, Josiah	1811	21	NJ
Dilks, Josiah	1817	29	NJ
Dill, Adam Albert	1805	22 b	MD
Dill, Anthony	1807	23 b	NJ
Dill, Edward	1817	18 b	PA
Dill, Elberd	1809	26 b	MD
Dill, Elbert	1816	33 b	MD
Dill, Isaac	1815	24 b	DE

Dill, Isaac	1817	00	xx
Dill, Samuel	1820	24 b	DE
Dill, Soloman	1819	22	MA
Dillet, Charles	1815	21 y	MA
Dillin, William	1821	15	PA
Dillingham, John	1815	14	MA
Dillivon, Isaac	1804	22	NJ
Dillon, Samuel	1815	27 b	NJ
Dillon, Thomas	1807	17	PA
Dillon, William	1810	34	PA
Dilworth, John	1821	16	NJ
Dilworth, Reese	1821	17	PA
Dilworth, Samuel	1812	20	PA
Dilworth, Thomas	1807	22 b	PA
Dimmick, Francis	1805	26	GA
Dine, Martin	1795	0	
Dingee, William	1815	28	NY
Dio, Francis	1809	28	MS
Dippoldt, John	1811	25	NJ
Ditmar, Enoch	1811	22 b	NJ
Ditterline, Charles	1809	22	PA
Divine, John	1822	21 y	NJ
Dixey, Thomas, Jr.	1803	17	PA
Dixon, Archibald	1815	18	PA
Dixon, Charles Ampy Harrison			
	1818	22 b	VA
Dixon, George	1806	19	PA
Dixon, George	1814	27	DE
Dixon, Henry	1803	22	PA
Dixon, James	1803	20	NY
Dixon, James	1805	25	Ma
Dixon, James	1806	21	NY
Dixon, James	1809	39 b	NJ
Dixon, James	1810	29	PA
Dixon, John	1804	18	MA
Dixon, John	1805	21	MA
Dixon, Jonathan	1809	27 b	DE
Dixon, Richard	1811	00	
Dixon, Richard	1811	20	MD
Dixon, Robert	1804	21	NY
Dixon, William	1807	27	NY
Dixson, Robert	1806	23	NY
Doane, Isaiah	1810	25	MA
Dobbins, Silas H.	1820	17	PA
Dobbins, Thomas, Jr.	1811	16	PA
Dobson, Robert	1808	28	PA
Doda, Peter	1815	26 y	LA
Doda, Peter	1816	0	
Dodd, John	1798	29	RI
Dodds, John	1809	22	NY
Dodds, John	1814	19	PA
Dodge, Andrew	1809	26	NY

Dodge, William R.	1822	30	MA	
Doland, Isaac	1819	21 b	DE	
Dolbon, Daniel	1809	0		
Dolbow, Daniel	1805	23	NJ	
Dolby, Joseph R.	1810	14	PA	
Dolby, Owen	1814	0		
Dolley, Samuel	1821	19	PA	
Dolman, John	1810	18	DE	
Domingo, Thomas	1807	22	LA	
Domingue, Manoel	1807	28	LA	
Dominick, Edward	1819	15 y	PA	
Dominick, James	1821	26 y	NY	
Dominick, John	1820	35	LA	
Dominick, John W.	1822	28	NY	
Donagan, James	1810	18	PA	
Donagan, Thomas, Jr.	1817	17	PA	
Donahoo, Matthew	1805	32	PA	
Donald, William	1812	18	PA	
Donalds, Charles	1822	45	NY	
Donaldson, Richard Martin				
	1804	16	PA	
Donall, George	1816	0		none given
Done, Jacob	1810	30 b	NY	
Donehue, John	1817	18	NY	
Donelson, Andrew	1796	0		Ireland
Donimick, John	1815	36	LA	
Donlap, James	1805	18	MA	
Donlevy, Henry	0000	45	PA	
Donlevy, Henry	0000	45	PA	
Donnald, Thomas	1803	20	NJ	
Donnell, Benjamin L.	1808	14	NJ	
Donnell, Benjamin L.	1814	19	NJ	
Donnell, Lester F.	1806	21	NJ	
Donnell, Lester F.	1812	00		
Donnell, Nathaniel	1815	17	NJ	
Donnelly, George	1814	22	PA	
Donnelly, George	1820	43	NJ	
Donovan, James B.	1809	19	PA	
Donovan, James B.	1809	19	PA	
Donovan, John	1819	13	PA	
Donovan, Richard B.	1803	24	VA	
Doras, Richard	1812	23 b	PA	
Doras, William	1809	19	PA	
Dore, Daniel	1805	40	NH	
Dore, Daniel	1815	0		
Doroty, Joseph	1805	40 b	MD	
Dorrington, James	1811	22	NY	
Dorsey, John	1822	27 s	MD	
Dorson, John	1820	26	PA	
Dorton, Henry	1805	27	NJ	
Dorus, Richard	1813	0		
Dory, Forten	1799	28 b	PA	

Dote, Jonathan	1811	17 y	Pa		Downs, Charles	1812	00	
Dougherty, Charles	1823	32	NY		Downs, John	1801	22	DE
Dougherty, Daniel	1822	24		none given	Downs, John	1810	21	NH
Dougherty, John	1809	19	NJ		Downsen, Charles	1815	27 b	NC
Dougherty, John	1810	0			Doyel, Edward	1818	25	NJ
Dougherty, Joseph	1814	20 b	PA		Doyle, George	1815	16	PA
Dougherty, Joseph	1815	21 b	PA		Doyle, James	1812	15	PA
Dougherty, William	1799	20	NJ		Doyle, James	1813	40	Ireland
Dougherty, William	1799	20	NJ		Doyle, John	1807	21	MD
Dougherty, William	1803	22	NY		Doyle, Matthew	1796	34	PA
Doughlass, Richard	1816	24 s	PA		Doyle, Matthew	1796	0	PA
Doughlass, Thomas	1810	21 b	RI		Doyle, Peter	1811	26 y	VA
Doughty, David	1816	17	MA		Doyle, Thomas	1814	18	PA
Doughty, Lemuel	1805	16	PA		Doyle, William	1800	30	PA
Doughty, Lemuel	1809	0	PA		Drake, Peter	1811	44	none given
Douglass, Abner	1811	47 b	DE		Drake, William	1809	27	NJ
Douglass, Charles	1804	36		Gr. Br.	Draper, George	1806	76 b	DE
Douglass, David	1817	24 b	DE		Draper, William	1818	33 c	DE
Douglass, Francis	1798	31			Dredger, Isaac	1823	16	PA
Douglass, George	1823	37	NY		Dreeger, John	1804	20	PA
Douglass, John	1815	20	NY		Drew, Benjamin	1797	22 m	PA
Douglass, John	1817	20 b	RI		Drew, John	1809	37	PA
Douglass, Joseph M.	1820	20	PA		Drew, John	1815	0	
Douglass, Neals	1806	21	PA		Drew, Peter	1805	31	PA
Douglass, Neuls	1807	00			Drew, Samuel	1811	24	MA
Douglass, Richard	1817	24 s	PA		Drinker, Jr., Joseph D.	1814	17	PA
Douglass, Septimus	1810	21 b	PA		Drinkwater, Andrew	1817	22	MA
Douglass, Septimus	1815	27 c	PA		Drinkwater, James	1809	21	MA
Douglass, William	1809	25 y	NJ		Drinkwater, James	1812	00	
Douglass, William	1818	21	NY		Drinkwater, Reuben	1811	15	MA
Dous, Simon	1819	25 m	PA		Driscoll, Jeremiah	1806	17	DE
Douse, Richard A.	1809	21 y	PA		Drummon, William	1815	30 b	MD
Douse, William	1817	22 m	PA		Drummond, Hill	1809	25	MD
Douty, Peter	1805	22	PA		Drummond, John	1810	22	VA
Dove, John	1811	14	PA		Drummond, John	1810	44 b	DE
Dove, Samuel	1815	15 b	NC		Drummond, John K.	1819	40	NJ
Dowe, George	1815	23 y	PA		Drummond, Parker	1815	22	MA
Dowerman, Mathias	1807	21	PA		Drummond, Samuel	1810	26	NJ
Dowers, John	1800	38	NJ		Dsahiell, Mathias	1814	24	MD
Dowling, John	1811	27	PA		Dubernet, Theodore	1809	21	LA
Down, Philip	1817	00	xx		Dublin, Morris	1810	22 b	NJ
Downes, James	1820	25	PA		Dublin, Perrey	1818	25 b	MD
Downes, John	1807	37	DE		Dubosq, Theodore	1821	16	PA
Downey, John	1814	19	PA		Dubree, John	1814	24	PA
Downey, John	1819	21	PA		Ducart, John	1809	35	LA
Downey, Peter	1804	20	PA		Ducet, Lewis G.	1816	21	
Downey, Terence	1803	0		none given	Duck, Ebenezar	1810	24 b	NJ
Downie, Daniel	1814	24	PA		Duckerfield, William	1809	33	MA
Downing, Benjamin	1818	22	MA		Ducoing, Francis	1823	16	PA
Downing, Howard	1821	26 b	VA		Ducomb, John B.	1812	15	PA
Downing, Mahlon M.	1810	13	NJ		Dudley, William S.	1823	21	NH
Downs, Charles	1811	21 m	PA		Duffee, Phillip	1821	25	none given

Duffel, James	1812	29	PA		Dunn, Richard	1809	0	
Duffel, John	1821	23	NJ		Dunn, Richard	1809	22	PA
Duffour, Augustes	1818	17	NY		Dunn, Robert	1818	34	PA
Duffy, Andrew	1804	24	PA		Dunn, William R.	1813	27	PA
Duffy, John	1806	21	PA		Dunn, William	1817	24	NY
Duffy, Moses	1808	21			Dunnis, John	1817	28 b	RI
Dugal, James	1801	19	VA		Dunphy, James	1806	13	PA
Dugee, Samuel	1815	32	PA		Dunphy, John	1810	13	PA
Duggan, John A.	1823	23	MA		Dunscomb, Richard	1804	21	PA
Duggan, William	1810	14	PA		Dunsdon, Joseph	1805	18	MD
Dulany, Hugh	1822	26	SC		Dunton, George	1803	23	PA
Duling, Jacob	1814	13	PA		Dunton, George	1807	0	
Duling, Jacob	1817	0	xx		Dunwoody, David	1805	23	PA
Duling, Thomas	1819	10	PA		Duplex, Robert Wharton			
Dumay, Lewis	1811	21		none given		1801	22	MA
Dumont, Benjamin	1809	22 b	NJ		Duran, John	1809	25	MS
Dumphy, Thomas	1822	23	PA		Durant, Robert R.	1821	22	NH
Dunaway, John	1815	22	NJ		Durbie, Lawrence Joseph			
Dunbar, Edward	1805	30 b	PA			1809	15	PA
Dunbar, George	1817	32 m	PA		Durfee, Daniel	1810	20	CT
Dunbar, James Forten	1810	11 y	PA		Durkin, William	1823	21	VA
Dunbar, Joseph	1804	20	MA		Durrant, John	1808	20	MA
Dunbar, Nicholas	1810	24 m	PA		Dutilh, Peter	1817	28	VA
Dunbar, Reuben	1819	21 b	NJ		Duton, Cyrus	1807	36 b	DE
Duncan, James N.	1810	16	PA		Dutton, Absalom	1821	14 y	PA
Duncan, James	1813	26	PA		Dutton, Cyrus	1822	19 y	Pa
Duncan, John	1807	26	MD		Dutton, Isaac	1817	19	MD
Duncan, John	1809	25	DE		Duvall, John	1823	20	FL
Duncan, John	1820	18	PA		Dwine, John	1809	28	MD
Dundas, James	1810	24	NY		Dyche, Joseph B.	1804	14	PA
Dungan, William	1804	19	PA		Dyche, Joseph B.	1808	19	PA
Dunham, Gershom	1804	14	MA		Dyckman, William	1810	37	NY
Dunham, Wing	1819	35	RI		Dyer, Benjamin	1806	21	PA
Dunkel, John	1820	33	MD		Dyer, Benjamin	1818	31	MA
Dunker, Joseph,Jr. D.	1815	0			Dyer, Richard T.	1805	20	NY
Dunkin, Anthony	1804	28 b	DE		Dyer, Samuel	1810	25	MA
Dunkin, John	1818	30	NY		Dyer, Thomas James	1801	17	NJ
Dunkin, Thomas	1823	24 b	SC		Dyer, Thomas J.	1806	0	
Dunlap, Edward	1804	29	MA		Dyer, Thomas	1810	21	MA
Dunlap, John	1823	26	DE		Dyer, William	1811	27	MA
Dunlap, Nathaniel	1814	22	NJ		Dymock, Daniel	1809	22	MD
Dunleavy, Andrew	1798	34	PA		Dymon, Benjamin	1822	24 y	MD
Dunn, Benjamin	1800	20	PA		Dyne, Martin	1801	30	PA
Dunn, Edward	1815	16	PA		Dyson, Christopher	1813	33		none given
Dunn, Hezekiah	1820	31	MD		Dyson, Christopher	1815	0	
Dunn, John	1809	17	PA		Eaden, William	1818	25		none given
Dunn, John	1810	22	MD		Eakin, John	1809	16	DE
Dunn, John	1811	24	NY		Earheart, George	1814	17	PA
Dunn, John	1812	00			Earick, Michael	1805	35	NJ
Dunn, Michael	1809	24			Earl, James	1807	27	MD
Dunn, Peter	1809	25			Earl, James	1809	0	MD
Dunn, Peter	1811	27		none given	Earl, James	1823	25	NJ

Earl, William Henry	1817	18	PA	Edwards, John J.	1811	21 b	MD
Earle, John	1796	17	PA				
Earnest, Bynard	1805	23	NJ	Edwards, John	1811	00	
Earnest, Thomas	1809	12	PA	SPC taken by Capt Page, ship *Robert Wilson*,			
Eastburn, John	1814	16	NJ	when Edwards put in debtors prison			
Eastburn, John	1819	21	NJ				
Eastburn, John	1819	0		Edwards, John	1815	25	CT
Eastburn, Robert	1804	22	NJ	Edwards, John	1818	38	MA
Eastburn, Robert	1809	27	NJ	Edwards, Joseph H.	1801	26	PA
Eastburn, Samuel	1815	21	PA	Edwards, Joseph, Jr.	1809	30	NJ
Eastburn, Thomas	1810	24	PA	Edwards, Nicholas	1807	20	LA
Eastman, Richard	1807	23	MA	Edwards, Peter	1818	33	PA
Eastman, Richard	1811	00		Edwards, Rickloff	1807	34	PA
Easton, John	1798	24	MA	Edwards, Standish Ford			
Easton, Samuel	1818	23 y	PA		1809	16	PA
Eaton, David	1804	22	PA	Edwards, Thomas	1801	17	PA
Eaton, David	1808	25	PA	Edwards, Thomas	1812	21	PA
Eaton, Thomas	1806	20	PA	Edwards, Thomas	1817	25	CT
Ebbins, John	1807	21 b	NH	Edwards, William	1818	28	DE
Ebeling, Roelof William				Edwards, William	1819	34	NY
	1808	21		Egbert, Peter	1810	23	NY
Ebeling, Roelof William				Eickholtz, Simon	1821	17	PA
	1809	22		Ekin, David	1815	37	
Eccles, John	1810	25	MD	Elare, Joseph	1811	23 y	LA
Eck, Jacob	1806	19	PA	Elberson, Charles	1809	23	NJ
Eckart, George	1809	45		Elberson, John	1811	33	NJ
Eckfeldt, John	1809	16	PA	Elbert, Henry	1807	23 b	PA
Eckford, Walter	1811	15	PA	Elbert, Henry	1811	14	PA
Eckford, Walter	1815	0		Elbert, Samuel	1811	21 b	MD
Eckley, Joseph	1819	23	PA	Elbort, Charles	1807	25 b	MD
Eddo, James	1821	24	NJ	Elder, Crawford	1800	22	PA
Eddy, James	1817	18	PA	Elder, Henry S.	1813	20	PA
Edgar, William	1810	17	PA	Elder, William T.	1808	23	PA
Edgar, William	1815	0		Elders, William	1819	37 b	NY
Edgrley, Ebenezer	1810	27	NH	Eldred, Benjamin	1821	27	RI
Edmonds, Thomas	1801	23	RI	Eldredge, Anthony	1810	15	PA
Edmonds, Thomas	1805	26	NJ	Eldredge, Elijah	1810	18	MA
Edmondson, Francis	1796	0	England	Eldredge, Phineas	1822	32	PA
Edson, Isaiah	1805	25	MA	Eldredge, Reuben	1820	21	MA
Edward, William	1813	22	DE	Eldridge, Anthony	1812	00	PA
Edwards, David	1815	25	MA	Eldridge, Elijah	1815	0	
Edwards, David	1823	21	NJ	Eldridge, Elisha	1806	17	MA
Edwards, James	1809	15	MA	Eldridge, Jamed	1803	18	PA
Edwards, James	1811	23	NY	Eldridge, Joseph	1811	21	NJ
Edwards, James	1812	20	NY	Eldridge, William	1812	15	NJ
Edwards, James	1812	00		Elesberry, Charles	1806	30 b	DE
Edwards, John	1806	28	MA	Elford, Thomas	1808	29 y	RI
Edwards, John Peter	1807	20	SC	Elfreth, Isaac Cathrall	1820	29	PA
Edwards, John	1809	26	PA	Elhinton, Joseph P.	1821	25	NJ
Edwards, John	1810	0		Elis, Francis	1815	27 b	CT
Edwards, John P.	1811	00		Eliston, William	1810	22	PA
Edwards, John J.	1811	20	SC	Elkins, Joseph	1810	21	MA

Ellenwood, Joseph	1804	25		MA	Emerson, John	1813	22	NJ
Elliot, Isarel L.	1817	26		PA	Emery, George	1815	20 y	PA
Elliot, Jacob	1807	33 m		NY	Emery, James	1821	21	NY
					Emery, John	1822	20 b	PA
Elliot, Lindsay C.	1819	22		PA	Emery, Joseph	1810	23	NH
son of William Elliot who keeps the Hark					Emery, Samuel	1815	20	MA
and Eagle, North 3rd Street					Emig, John Christian	1805	35	PA
					Emig, John Christian	1809	0	
Elliot, William Henry	1823	22		PA	Emmell, George A.	1821	28	NJ
Elliott, Francis	1808	19		PA	Emmin, John	1804	24	PA
Elliott, Francis	1809	0			Emmins, Thomas	1805	28 b	NY
Elliott, Francis	1811	00			Emmons, Jesse	1811	29 b	NJ
Elliott, Francis	1812	00			Emmons, Jesse	1812	00	
Elliott, Francis	1815	0			Emmons, Jesse	1815	0	
Elliott, Jacob	1805	26		PA	Endicott, John	1820	16	PA
Elliott, John	1810	24		DE	Endicott, Samuel	1807	28	PA
Elliott, John	1813	21		PA	Engel, John P.	1807	25	PA
Elliott, Robert	1809	23		PA	England, Elias	1806	19	NJ
Elliott, Robert M	1821	28		MA	England, Michael	1813	23	DE
Elliott, Stephen	1809	25 b		MA	England, Thomas, Jr.	1810	28 b	DE
Elliott, William	1813	18		DE	Engle, Isaac E.	1818	19	PA
Elliott, William	1815	0			Englebert, Oliver H.	1820	16	NJ
Elliotts, Francis	1818	21		RI	Englefreath, Charles	1822	19	PA
Ellis, Abel	1810	22		MA	Engles, Edward	1823	35	none given
Ellis, Charles D.	1819	21		VT	Engles, George	1822	21	PA
Ellis, George	1822	23 b		GA	Engles, Thomas, Jr.	1799	22	PA
Ellis, James	1809	23		PA	English, Elisha N.	1805	19	NJ
Ellis, John	1805	21		NC	English, John	1809	23	PA
Ellis, John	1811	24		LA	Engvolson, Peter	1809	36	NC
Ellis, Martin	1809	33		PA	Ennis, John	1796	45	
Ellis, Peter	1796	30 m		MA	Ennis, John	1796	0	
Ellis, Stephen	1810	19 b		DE	Enox, Isaac	1799	25	PA
Ellis, Thomas	1800	24		PA	Ensworth, John	1805	21	PA
Ellis, William Goe	1816	16		PA	Errington, Thomas Bell	1805	28	PA
Ellis, William S.	1817	16		MA	Erskin, George	1821	24	ME
Ellison, Edward	1810	22		NJ	Erven, Samuel	1804	21	DE
Ellwood, James	1820	19		MA	Ervin, William H.	1810	26	NY
Elm, William	1820	21		NY	Ervin, William	1813	0	
Elmer, John	1823	20		NJ	Erwin, John	1797	20	NY
Elmes, Jas.	1797	35		MA	Erwin, John, Jr.	1810	18	NY
Elsley, John	1803	24		SC	Erwin, John W.	1815	19	PA
Elston, James	1809	48		PA	Erwin, Robert	1812	15	PA
Elston, James	1818	21		PA	Erwin, Samuel	1805	21 m	PA
Elston, Thomas	1810	44	none given		Erwin, Samuel	1805	18	DE
Elston, Thomas	1816	24		PA	Erwin, Samuel	1807	0	
Elsworth, Jacob	1804	40		NY	Erwin, Samuel	1809	0	DE
Elton, John H.	1806	21		NJ	Escott, Edward	1798	25	MD
Eltonhead, Peter	1810	18		PA	Esdall, Richard	1798	0	NJ
Elwine, Michael	1809	21			Esders, Henry	1809	29	NJ
Ely, Joseph	1812	00			Eskrige, Noah	1798	0	MD
Emanuel, Augustine	1807	26 c		MD	Esling, Paul	1806	20	PA
Emanuel, Charles	1811	24 b		NY	Espey, Andrew	1805	23	PA

Essex, Albion	1815	22 y	PA	
Essex, Robert	1820	47 b	PA	
Estel, Samuel	1806	20	NJ	
Estel, Samuel	1807	0		
Esterlon, Andrew	1809	30		Sweden
Esters, Michael	1807	32	MA	
Estes, John	1804	30	MA	
Estill, John	1810	19	NJ	
Etiene, John	1810	21	NJ	
Eton, Thomas	1807	0		
Etting, Edward J.	1819	16	MD	
Ettinger, William	1815	24	PA	
Eunson, Samuel H.	1810	25	MA	
Evans, Andrew Donaldson				
	1817	15	PA	
Evans, Arthur	1813	0		
Evans, Benjaman	1806	15	MA	
Evans, Charles	1814	26 b	VA	
Evans, Daniel	1804	21 b	VA	
Evans, David	1799	23	PA	
Evans, David	1815	19	PA	
Evans, George	1804	25	PA	
Evans, Henry	1806	22	NY	
Evans, Jacob	1815	27	PA	
Evans, James	1811	22	SC	
Evans, James	1813	0		
SPC issued 1811 taken by an officer on				
British ship *Spartan*				
Evans, John	1803	22	PA	
Evans, John	1813	21	VA	
Evans, John	1817	28 b	MA	
Evans, Jonathan	1815	28	PA	
Evans, Joseph	1804	27	PA	
Evans, Joseph Ogden	1807	19	PA	
Evans, Leonard,Jr.	1809	24	MA	
Evans, Lewis	1806	21	LA	
Evans, Lewis	1806	21	PA	
Evans, Peter	1812	20	PA	
Evans, Richard	1809	35	DE	
Evans, Ruben	1798	21 m	PA	
Evans, Samuel	1807	29	NJ	
Evans, Seth W.	1815	17	PA	
Evans, Thomas L.	1800	15	PA	
Evans, Thomas L.	1804	18	PA	
Evans, Thomas M.	1805	18	MD	
Evans, Thomas	1810	24	PA	
Evans, Thomas	1812	20	SC	
Evans, Wallace	1811	22	MD	
Evans, William	0000	0		
Evans, William	1799	0	MD	

Evans, William	1805	28	PA	
Evans, William R.	1810	17	DE	
Evans, William	1817	43	MD	
Evans, William	1817	26	NJ	
Evans, William Henry	1818	20	DE	
Eveleigh, William	1815	21	CT	
Evens, Adam	1807	27 b	PA	
Evens, Arthur	1804	16	NJ	
Evens, Arthur	1809	0		
Evens, George B.	1799	20	MD	
Everitt, John	1811	27	NY	
Everly, George	1811	16	PA	
Everly, Jacob	1809	45	PA	
Everly, Samuel	1819	19	PA	
Evers, Hinrich	1809	23	PA	
Eves, Robert	1798	21	PA	
Eves, William	1798	20	PA	
Sons of Capt. Eves of Philadelphia				
Eves, William	1798	0		
Evetts, Levi	1807	20	MA	
Ewalt, Carl Friedrich	1804	30	PA	
Ewalt, Charles Frederick				
	1807	0	PA	
Ewan, John	1809	23	NJ	
Ewen, John	1804	22	PA	
Ewing, James	1810	35		none given
Ewing, John	1803	19	NJ	
Ewington, John	1801	16	NJ	
Exeter, John	1799	20 y	PA	
Exeter, John	1805	0		
Exeter, John	1811	00		
Exeter, John	1815	0		
Eyre, Samuel	1810	15	PA	
Eyres, Thomas	1818	39 b	PA	
Fabian, Joseph	1809	22	NJ	
Fabler, Benjmin	1816	32 b	DE	
Fackney, John	1813	24	MD	
Fagan, Peter	1811	27 b	PA	
Fagundus, Thomas Jefferson				
	1818	16	PA	
Fairbrother, James	1804	21	DE	
Fairbrothers, James	1809	21	NJ	
Fairchild, Abner	1806	24	NJ	
Fairfield, Joseph	1811	26	MD	
Fairfowl, James	1819	24	NY	
Fanning, David	1812	29	CT	
Fanning, Joseph L.	1804	25 b	SC	
Fanning, Philip	1805	19	ME	
Farden, David	1812	21	PA	
Farker, John	1799	20	NY	

Name	Year	Age		State/Note
Farley, John	1807	22	b	NJ
Farley, John	1810	0	b	NJ
Farley, John	1812	00		
Farman, Daniel H.	1816	18		RI
Farmat, John	1807	24		LA
Farmer, Ceaser	1812	00		
Farmer, Cesar	1811	19	b	NJ
Farmer, Samuel	1803	18		RI
Farnham, Elias	1823	46		CT
Farr, John	1813	26		NY
Farr, Thomas	1805	20		PA
Farr, William	1820	42		VA
Farrell, Francis	1809	21		PA
Farrell, Henry A.	1818	21		PA
Farren, James	1807	23		CT
Farren, Michael	1806	18		MA
Farriah, Joseph A.	1817	21		PA
Farrier, Baptiste	1813	0		
Farrington, Charles	1819	21		MA
Farris, Washington	1815	19		MA
Farriss, John	1809	21	b	NJ
Farson, Henry	1817	24		DE
Farson, James B.	1818	17		DE
Farthin, William	1816	29		none given
Fassitt, Theodore	1823	19		MD
Faulk, George	1805	15		PA
Faulk, George	1813	0		PA
Faulkner, John	1804	22		NJ
Fauver, Robert	1810	31		NJ
Favier, John	1820	23		PA
Fawsett, Robert	1812	28		MD
Fayette, William	1809	25	m	NJ
Fear, John	1799	15		
Fear, Philip	1797	27		PA
Feathears, John	1801	24		PA
Feddia, Henry	1809	37		MD
Feinour, Joseph	1804	26		PA
Feinour, Joseph, Jr.	1819	15		PA
Feleson, James	1804	30	b	MD
Fell, John Thorntwaite	1803	41		NY
Fell, John Thornthwaite	1805	0		
Felleni, James	1814	20		PA
Fells, Emanuel	1807	23		LA
Felt, John	1801	29		VA
Felton, Christian	1816	37		none given
Felton, George	1804	23		PA
Felty, Jacob C.	1808	34		PA
Fenimore, Anthony L.	1823	14		PA
Fenimore, John Girard	1815	14		PA
Fenimore, Stephen Girard				
	1820	13		PA
Fenimore, Thomas E.	1809	15		NJ
Fenimore, William Gordon				
	1822	15		NJ
Fening, Philip	1806	0		
Feniny, Philip	1809	0		
Fennell, Edmond	1804	14		PA
Fennell, Edmond	1806	14		PA
Fennell, Edmund	1809	0		PA
Fennell, Thomas Pratt	1819	17		PA
Fennemore, John	1804	22	m	NJ
Fennemore, Reuben	1804	21		NJ
Fenner, John	1813	24		PA
Fenno, Henry	1807	18		MA
Fenton, John	1803	30		NY
Fenton, John	1808	35		NY
Fenton, Thomas	1821	16		PA
Fenton, William	1809	21		PA
Fenton, William C.	1815	20		MD
Feran, John	1809	18		PA
Feran, John	1811	00		
Feran, John	1811	00		
Ferara, Antonio	1807	42		LA
Ferara, Joachim	1807	36		LA
Fereira, Joseph	1808	30		MS
Ferer, Peter	1807	32		LA
Fergurson, Thomas	1821	40	y	MA
Ferguson, Abbot Sayre				
	1822	19		PA
Ferguson, Andrew	1809	16		PA
Ferguson, Andrew	1811	00		
Ferguson, Andrew	1817	0		xx
Ferguson, George	1810	23		NY
Ferguson, James	1811	23	b	DE
Ferguson, James G.	1816	24		PA
Ferguson, John L.	1804	21		PA
Ferguson, John	1816	16		CT
Ferguson, John	1818	16		MD
Ferguson, Jonathan	1811	23	b	DE
Ferguson, Joseph	1806	23	y	PA
Ferguson, Normand	1795	23		NC
Ferguson, Richard	1804	20	b	MA
Ferguson, William	1801	31		NJ
Fering, Henry	1808	26		SC
Fernald, Dennis	1809	28		MA
Fernald, Nathaniel	1823	24		ME
Fernandes, Julian	1806	28		LA
Fernandes, Manuel	1806	24		LA
Fernandez, Anthony	1810	28		LA
Fernandez, Antonio	1807	22		LA
Fernandez, Emanuel	1810	58		LA
Fernandez, Joseph	1809	41		MS
Fernandez, Joseph	1823	57		Portugal
Fernandez, Manuel	1809	18		MS

Fernandos, Francis	1805	27	LA
Fernans, Anthony	1805	38	LA
Fero, James	1810	16	PA
Ferrady, James	1807	11	PA
Ferrand, Charles Louis	1807	28	LA
Ferrell, John	1806	22	LA
Ferrell, Joseph	1811	27 y	PA
Ferren, Thomas	1809	24	PA
Ferrier, George	1809	23	SC
Ferris, John	1823	20	NY
Fessenden, Thomas	1812	36	MA
Fetters, Peter	1810	21	PA
Fick, John	1817	17	PA
Field, Aaron	1807	22 b	PA
Field, Aaron	1807	28 b	PA
Field, Aron	1809	0	
Field, Aron	1809	24 b	MD

Field, David 1810 19 m DE
indented mulatto servant to Samuel Keith;
goes to sea with his consent

Field, Dwelle	1815	21	MA
Field, Joseph	1811	31	PA
Field, Nehemiah	1820	16	DE
Field, Rubus	1809	18	NH
Field, William G.	1820	24	NY
Fieldden, Henry	1806	35	PA
Fielding, Samuel	1804	20	MD
Fields, Henry	1806	21	NJ
Fields, Joel	1815	20	CT
Fields, Moses	1821	19 b	PA
Fields, William W.	1822	26 b	NY
Fife, John	1819	29	MD
Fife, Thomas	1806	14	PA
Fillena, John	1798	36	none given
Filler, Robert	1802	30	DE
Fillesson, James	1810	0	
Fillman, Adam	1810	17	PA
Finch, John	1815	35	LA
Finch, William	1812	25	NJ
Finch, William	1814	0	
Fincho, Camino	1809	20	CT
Findley, Hugh	1807	22	NY
Fine, William	1815	24	NY
Finess, Isaac	1812	25 b	NY
Fink, George	1816	25	VA
Finley, Eli	1818	34	DE
Finley, Henry	1823	27 y	MD
Finley, Nathan	1809	24	DE
Finney, James	1816	22 c	DE
Finnix, John	1807	30	MA

Finny, John	1799	27	PA
Finour, George	1804	14	PA
Finucane, John	1805	28	MA
Finucane, John	1805	28	MA
Fish, Isaac	1805	22	NJ
Fish, Isaac	1809	26	NJ
Fisher, Caeser	1815	16 b	PA
Fisher, Charles	1807	25 b	DE
Fisher, Charles	1817	25	MA
Fisher, David	1821	23	PA
Fisher, Frederick	1807	18	PA
Fisher, George	1804	23	PA
Fisher, George	1805	30	Ireland
Fisher, George	1809	21	PA
Fisher, George	1810	23	NJ
Fisher, Jacob	1821	27 b	DE
Fisher, James	1815	21	NJ
Fisher, James	1816	23 b	DE
Fisher, Jeremiah	1815	20 b	MA
Fisher, John	1798	23	NY
Fisher, John Philip	1803	29	PA
Fisher, John	1810	22	none given
Fisher, John	1810	24	VA
Fisher, John	1810	14	PA
Fisher, John	1815	22	VA
Fisher, John	1823	19	NJ
Fisher, Michael	1815	25	MD
Fisher, Orange	1805	22 b	DE
Fisher, Robert Young	1801	18	PA
Fisher, Robert Y.	1804	21	PA
Fisher, Thomas M.	1809	20	PA
Fisher, Thomas P.	1817	19	DE
Fisher, William	1809	30	NJ
Fisher, William W.	1820	18	PA
Fisk, John	1797	24	NY
Fiske, Edmund	1821	32	RI
Fiss, Joseph	1810	21	PA
Fithian, Lawrence	1820	22	NJ
Fithion, Thomas	1798	0	NJ
Fitzgerald, David	1801	24 b	DE
Fitzgerald, Jacob	1805	18 b	DE
Fitzgerald, Samuel	1821	15 b	NJ
Fitzgerald, Tilghman	1815	30 b	DE
Fitzgerald, Tillman	1807	25	MD
FitzSimmons, John	1812	29	MD
Fitzsomons, Henry	1800	27	PA
Flake, Samuel	1817	29	NJ
Flanagan, John	1821	16	PA
Flanagan, Thomas	1807	20	MD
Flanders, Daniel	1823	34	MA
Flaxon, Charles	1807	17	PA
Flecher, Simon	1807	38 b	VA

Name	Year	Age		State/Note
Fleetwood, Palmer	1805	22		DE
Fleming, Alexander	1809	19		NJ
Fleming, Archibald	1803	0		
Fleming, Benjamin	1807	22		DE
Fleming, Farltton	1809	0		
Fleming, James	1803	0		
Fleming, James	1803	33		SC
Fleming, John	1805	25		PA
Fleming, John	1809	24		RI
Fleming, John	1809	18		PA
Fleming, John	1812	00		
Fleming, Tarlton	1807	48	b	VA
Fleming, Thomas	1804	25		NJ
Flemming, William	1817	23		SC
Fleng, Pearce	1812	20		SC
Fletchard, William	1800	22		PA
Fletcher, Foxwell C.	1815	25		MA
Fletcher, John	0000	15		PA
Fletcher, John	1806	36		none given
Fletcher, John	1811	20		VA
Fletcher, Joshua	1815	32		DE
Fletcher, Samuel	1810	22		MA
Fletcher, Thomas	1823	27		MD
Fletcher, William	1813	19		MD
Flick, John	1815	23		PA
Flick, William	1817	27		PA
Fling, John	1807	19		MA
Fling, John	1807	19		MA
Fling, Robert	1820	16		PA
Flinn, Thomas	1820	29		PA
Flintham, William, Jr.	1823	19		NJ
Flood, Benjamin	1818	24	c	NC
Flood, Francis	1820	30		DC
Flood, Isaac	1813	26		NY
Flood, John	1815	24		
Flood, Thomas	1815	19		PA
Florance, John	1818	51		MA
Florenzo, Augustus Charles				
	1807	25		LA
Flower, John	1798	16		PA
Floyd, David	1796	20		NJ
Floyd, George	1817	35		NJ
Floyd, Peter	1822	28	b	VA
Floyd, Samuel	1809	18		DE
Fodery, Joseph	1803	22		VA
Fogarty, Archibald	1807	25		MA
Fogel, Jacob	1814	16		PA
Folder, William	1806	21		LA
Foldridge, John	1805	34		LA
Foley, John D.	1823	36		NC
Folger, Giles	1819	33		MA
Folk, Thomas	1818	26		MA
Folk, William J.	1811	15		PA
Folley, John	1800	22		PA
Folsom, Nathanial	1815	0		
Folsom, Nathaniel	1805	14		NH
Folster, James	1798	0		CT
Folwell, Job W.	1814	20		NJ
Folwell, Joseph	1813	19		NJ
Fontaine, Francis	1818	35		none given
Fontan, Frank	1811	36		LA
Foote, Benjamin	1821	22		ME
Forbes, Benjamin	1804	21	b	DE
Forbes, James	1803	19		PA
Forbes, Robert	1809	25		NJ
Forbes, Samuel	1806	25		MA
Forbes, Samuel	1815	0		
Ford, James	1810	19		NJ
Ford, John	1815	20		MA
Ford, Joseph	1801	21		MD
Ford, Joseph	1807	30	b	NY
Ford, Nace	1808	26	b	MD
Ford, Philip	1806	21		NY
Ford, Robert	1815	17		PA
Ford, Samuel	1801	22		MD
Ford, Thomas	1809	23		MD
Ford, William	1809	24		DE
Ford, William P.	1811	21		PA
Forde, Joseph	1807	22	b	NJ
Foreman, Amos	1820	42		MD
Forks, William	1818	27		NJ
Forkum, William	1809	22		DE
Forlavy, Joseph	1811	00		
Forman, William	1814	17		NJ
Forman, William	1814	0		
Forney, Peter	1815	33		LA
Forrest, James	1796	22		PA
Forrest, Joseph	1810	25	y	LA
Forrest, Lorman	1823	26		PA
Forrier, Baptist	1811	00		Genoa
Forrier, Baptiste	1810	30		none given
Forshew, John	1809	24		MA
Forsyth, William	1817	14		PA
Fort, Cleyteman M.	1804	21		NJ
Fort, William	1809	49		NJ
Fortescue, Joseph	1809	16		PA
Fortescue, Joseph	1817	0		xx
Fortescue, Thomas S.	1815	25		PA
Fortis, Anthony	1805	21	b	SC
Fortman, Anthony	1806	23		NY
Fortner, Charles	1823	21		MD
Fosis, John	1810	21	b	NJ
Fossat, Ellis	1812	00		
Fosset, Ellis	1811	21		NJ

Fosset, Ellis	1818	26 b	NJ
Fossis, Francis	1820	23 b	PA
Foster, Adam	1816	24	NY
Foster, Beriah	1807	40	NJ
Foster, Cornwell	1803	25 b	MA
Foster, Daniel W.	1818	20	NJ
Foster, Henry	1823	28 y	MA
Foster, James	1821	17	PA
Foster, John	1807	20	NY
Foster, John	1812	22	NJ
Foster, Nathaniel	1811	19	MA
Foster, Robert	1810	18	MA
Foster, Robert	1821	16	PA
Foster, Samuel	1806	17	NJ
Foster, Silas, Jr.	1804	13	PA
Foster, Thomas	1817	26	MA
Foster, William	1797	21	NC
Foster, William	1814	15	PA
Foudray, Saml. G.	1813	20	PA
Foudray, William	1811	16	DE
Foulk, George	1810	0	
Foulton, William	1809	26	
Fountain, Daniel	1807	18	NY
Fountain, Nicholas	1809	21	MD
Fountain, William	1805	24	VA
Fountain, William	1807	25	VA
Fountain, William	1812	20	GA
Fouquet, Charles	1822	18	PA
Foushee, Redman Lawrence			
	1823	15	PA
Fow, William	1810	17	PA
Fowler, David	1821	33	DE
Fowler, James	1809	27	MD
Fowler, Michael	1806	18	NJ
Fowler, Robert	1818	25 b	NJ
Fowler, Samuel	1807	21	NJ
Fowler, Vincent	1809	20 b	NJ
Fox, Frederick	1812	22	NY
Fox, George	1805	24	MA
Fox, George	1809	20	PA
Fox, George	1812	21	PA
Fox, George	1822	45 b	PA
Fox, James	1817	36 b	VA
Fox, William	1809	18	NJ
Foxe, Thomas	1804	35	MD
Foy, John	1801	21 b	PA
Foy, William	1806	28	PA
Foy, William	1807	00	
Fraiser, Thomas	1812	32	PA
Frame, George	1813	19	PA
Frame, Turner	1823	30 b	DE
France, William	1804	27	NY

Francis, Alexander	1810	25 m	LA	
Francis, Barnett	1823	35	PA	
Francis, Edward	1815	24	PA	
Francis, Edward	1815	0		
Francis, Emanuel	1808	30	LA	
Francis, Frank	1810	27	NY	
Francis, Gamaliel	1815	19	PA	
Francis, George	1818	21	MD	
Francis, George	1823	25 y	VA	
Francis, Henry	1812	27 b	SC	
Francis, James	1801	22	NJ	
Francis, James	1806	17	PA	
Francis, James	1815	25	PA	
Francis, James	1817	26	PA	
Francis, John	1803	28 b	NY	
Francis, John	1806	26 b	MD	
Francis, John	1807	00		
Francis, John	1807	23 b	MD	
Francis, John	1807	19	LA	
Francis, John	1807	22	LA	
Francis, John	1809	25	LA	
Francis, John	1809	21 b	PA	
Francis, John	1809	25	LA	
Francis, John	1809	23 b	MA	
Francis, John	1809	33 b	VA	
Francis, John	1811	00		
Francis, John	1811	24 b	MA	
Francis, John	1811	22 b	LA	
Francis, John	1812	28 y	LA	
Francis, John	1815	30 b	LA	
"rendered a free man by the cession of				
New Orleans to U. S."				
Francis, John	1815	25 b	MD	
Francis, John	1817	18	MA	
Francis, John	1818	31		none given
Francis, John	1819	21 y	MS	
Francis, John	1821	17 b	PA	
Francis, John	1821	23 y	PA	
Francis, John C.	1823	21 b	NY	
Francis, Julius	1817	27 y	LA	
Francis, Lewis	1815	19 c	NY	
Francis, Mark	1815	16 y	PA	
Francis, Michael	1805	21	PA	
Francis, Samuel	1807	17	PA	
Francis, Samuel	1809	19	PA	
Francis, Silas	1811	31 b	DE	
Francis, Thomas	1806	22	NH	
Francis, Thomas	1823	20 y	VA	
Francis, William	1805	26 b	DE	
Francis, William	1806	0	DE	

Francis, William	1812	31 b	VA		Freeman, George	1823	28 m	MD
Francis, William	1818	23	RI		Freeman, Geroge	1809	21 y	MD
Francisco, John	1807	24	LA		Freeman, Harry	1809	18 b	MD
Francisco, Joseph	1817	28		Sicily	Freeman, Harry	1811	20 b	MD
Frank, Anthony	1810	22	LA		Freeman, Isaac	1817	25 b	NY
Frank, George	1806	26	PA		Freeman, Jacob	1809	24 y	MD
Frank, John	1807	26	PA		Freeman, Jacob	1810	24 b	MD
Frank, Levi	1815	23	MA		Freeman, Jacob	1812	00	
Frankford, Alexander	1809	20	PA		Freeman, Jeptha	1809	25	NJ
Frankland, Stephen	1804	22	PA		Freeman, John	1803	20 b	PA
Frankland, Stephen	1804	22	PA		Freeman, John	1815	35 b	PA
Franklin, Francis	1805	22	PA		Freeman, John	1817	25	MD
Franklin, George	1805	26	LA		Freeman, John	1823	21 b	NY
Franklin, Henry	1815	15	PA		Freeman, Philemon	1821	35	NC
Franklin, Hiram	1799	23	CT		Freeman, Pollidore	1801	21 b	NY
Franklin, Jacob	1809	27	PA		Freeman, Rodrick	1805	26 b	NY
Franklin, James	1805	28	PA		Freeman, Thomas	1809	25 b	MD
Franklin, James	1810	0			Freeman, William	1801	26	PA
Franklin, John	1810	20	MD		Freeman, William	1816	21 y	PA
Franklin, John	1815	16	PA		French, David	1806	25	DE
Franklin, John	1818	18 b	NJ		French, John	1809	19	PA
Franklin, Samuel	1796	23	RI		French, Robert	1805	21	PA
Franklin, Stephen	1805	0			French, Samuel	1806	16	NY
Franks, Francis	1815	37	NY		French, William	1815	23	MA
Frasure, John	1816	25	CT		French, William	1815	23 b	NJ
Frazer, Charles	1809	38	NY		Freys, William	1817	27	MD
Frazer, David	1807	21	MA		Freys, William	1817	27	MD
Frazer, James	1805	22	PA		Friberg, Andrew Gabriel			
Frazer, James	1816	19	VA			1811	25		Sweden
Frazer, Thomas	1805	25			Frick, Jacob	1797	18	PA
Frazer, Thomas	1809	23	PA		Fricke, Charles	1815	15	PA
Frazer, William	1808	29	MA		Fricke, Charles	1816	0	
Frazier, Alexander	1820	20	PA		Fricke, Henry C.	1814	18	PA
Frazier, John	1804	23	MA		Friedrisch, Charles	1807	23	PA
Frazier, John	1807	25	LA		Friend, Peter	1808	22	MS
Frazier, John	1815	13	PA		Friend, Samuel	1805	26	NJ
Frazier, William	1797	29	NJ		Friend, Samuel	1806	29	NJ
Fredd, William	1805	21	PA		Frisby, Ranson	1817	25	CT
Freddele, Stephen	1815	24 y	NY		Fritz, Jeremiah	1813	21	PA
Frederic, John	1809	25	DE		Frogwell, Edward	1812	23	NY
Frederic, John	1809	38	PA		Frost, Joseph	1807	16	MA
Frederick, Charles	1809	38	MA		Frost, Joseph	1809	22 y	NY
Frederick, John	1807	20	LA		Fruct, Richard	1810	0	
Fredericks, Charles	1815	40	PA		Fry, Jacob	1804	19	PA
Fredericks, Charles	1817	00	PA		Fry, John	1821	21	PA
Fredrickson, John	1815	20	PA		Fry, William	1806	22	PA
Fredrickson, William	1822	18	Pa		Frye, Benjamin	1815	21	MA
Freeborn, Joseph	1811	23	PA		Fryer, Henry	1800	21	NJ
Freeman, Charles	1811	20 y	DE		Fryer, John	1805	22	PA
Freeman, Garrison	1809	20 y	MD		Fryer, John	1808	0	
Freeman, Garrison	1811	00			Fulcher, John	1815	23	NC
Freeman, George	1809	21 b	DE		Fulcher, John	1823	33	VA

54

Fullensby, Samuel	1804	20	PA		Ganes, William	1805	24	NY
Fuller, Peter	1804	14	NY		Ganno, James	1799	0	PA
Fuller, William	1823	31 y	MA		Ganson, Robert	1815	35 b	PA
Fullerton, James	1803	30	PA		Ganzey, Levi	1822	39 b	PA
Fullerton, John	1815	27	Pa		Garcia, Felix	1820	24	NJ
Fullerton, Richard Alex	1807	15	PA		Gardener, John	1815	31	
Fullerton, Robert	1804	36	none given	Gardette, Joseph C.	1818	18	PA
Fullingsbe, Andrew	1820	44	NJ		Gardiner, George J.	1821	23 y	PA
Fullington, Adam	1806	21	NJ		Gardiner, John	1806	26 b	VA
Fullman, Philip	1810	28 b	DE		Gardiner, Jonathan	1808	38	NC
Funck, John M.	1806	21	PA		Gardiner, Joseph	1813	20 b	MA
Funk, Charles	1810	19	PA		Gardner, Clement	1812	29	MD
Funk, Henry, Jr.	1809	25	PA		Gardner, Clement	1818	28	MD
Funk, James	1815	23	PA		Gardner, Edward C.	1817	14	PA
Fure, William	1804	19	NY		Gardner, Henry	1808	20	PA
Furgerson, John Lindsay					Gardner, James	1800	19	PA
	1805	21	PA		Gardner, James	1810	22 c	DE
Fyelt, William	1807	24	NJ		Gardner, James	1817	19 y	LA
Gable, Samuel	1803	21	PA		Gardner, James	1806	22 b	RI
Gabriel, Andrew	1804	23	NY		Gardner, John	1806	22 b	RI
Gabriel, Andrew	1807	00	NY		Gardner, John	1807	00	RI
Gad, Thomas	1821	26	PA		Gardner, John	1809	25	MA
Gage, Samuel	1810	34	NY		Gardner, John	1809	27 b	MD
Gagjino, Batista	1801	30	PA		Gardner, John	1816	35	PA
Galbraith, James	1816	0			Gardner, John	1821	48	PA
Galbreath, James	1796	0	MD		Gardner, Jonathan	1810	0	
Galbreath, James	1815	17	PA		Gardner, Peter	1809	19	NY
Gale, Amos	1818	22	NJ		Gardner, Richard	1815	43 b	RI
Gale, George	1811	15	PA		Gardner, Robert	1812	28 b	CT
Gale, John .	1803	30	GA		Gardner, Samuel	1803	33 b	MA
Gale, John	1807	20	NJ		Gardner, Scipio	1819	21 c	PA
Gale, Stephen	1810	40 m	MD		Gardner, William	1801	21	NY
Gale, Thaddeus	1801	28	MA		Gardner, William H.	1815	16	MA
Gall, Frederick	1811	18	RI		Gariel, Francis	1809	29	
Gallagher, Michael	1812	00			Garin, John	1814	18	NY
Gallagher, Stephen	1805	22	PA		Garner, Jeremiah	1807	24 b	MD
Gallagher, Stephen	1808	0			Garner, Jeremiah	1813	0	
Gallagher, Thomas A	1822	24	PA		Garner, William	1804	23	RI
Gallaher, Michael	1811	14	PA		Garner, William	1804	23	RI
Gallay, Henry	1811	21	PA		Garns, William	1811	13	PA
Gallen, James	1816	16	NJ		Garrard, Joseph	1809	19	NY
Gallon, James	1798	21	MD		Garret, Jacob	1796	26	
Galvin, Joseph	1804	27	SC		Garret, John	1807	26	NJ
Gamble, Charles	1810	24	NJ		Garrete, William	1801	22	PA
Gamble, James, Jr.	1806	17	PA		Garretson, Joseph	1822	33	NJ
Gamble, James	1815	23	NJ		Garrick, Peter	1804	22	PA
Gamble, John	1806	24	PA		Garrigues, James Ralph			
Gamble, Samuel W.	1818	25	NJ			1809	16	PA
Gamble, William	1804	29	PA		Garrigues, James R.	1814	0	
Gamble, William	1805	0			Garrigues, Joseph	1807	22	DE
Gamble, William	1807	00			Garrigues, Joseph	1809	0	DE
Game, Mark	1807	37	MD		Garrison, Christopher	1807	23	NJ
					Garrison, Christopher	1809	0	

Garrison, David	1805	15	NJ	Gerard, Jacob	1806	19 b	DE
Garrison, Joseph Graves				Gerisher, Charles Henry			
	1809	26	NJ		1818	17	NY
Garrison, William	1801	21	NJ	German, John, Jr.	1800	16	PA
Garside, George	1811	23	NY	Gery, Henry	1809	19	DE
Gartley, Samuel	1801	0	PA	Gethen, Richard H.	1823	17	PA
Garvin, John	1798	33	MD	Getman, George	1805	21	PA
Garwood, George M.	1823	15	PA	Getman, George	1806	0	
Gary, John	1806	15	VA	Getman, George	1806	0	
Gash, Frederick	1814	22	PA	Gettoo, Petter	1798	16	MA
Gaskill, Enoch	1821	22	NJ	Getz, George	1818	32	PA
Gaskill, Robert Ralston				Getz, Henry	1811	25	PA
	1817	19	PA	Geyer, Henry C.	1821	34	MA
Gaskin, Thomas	1815	23	DE	Gibbon, Grant	1816	20	NJ
				Gibbons, David	1801	38	
Gatehele, David	1810	0		Gibbons, Edmond	1815	28	VA
lost SPC from Sloop *Hiland* when British				Gibbons, James	1817	30 c	DE
Frigate *Leander* took over				Gibbons, John	1822	36 b	DE
				Gibbons, Richard	1801	33 b	PA
Gates, Frederick G.	1810	18	MA	Gibbs, Abraham	1804	37 b	SC
Gatewood, Bennett	1798	0	VA	Gibbs, Abraham	1806	0	
Gatewood, Thomas	1803	34	VA	Gibbs, Abraham	1823	29 b	DE
Gaul, James	1810	17	PA	Gibbs, Abraham	1823	48 y	PA
Gaun, Jacob	1804	23	PA	Gibbs, Alfred	1810	33	MA
Gauntt, Charles S.	1811	20	NJ	Gibbs, Alfred	1810	33	MA
Gauntt, Samuel W.	1812	24	NJ	Gibbs, Constant	1804	15	MA
Gavin, James	1805	26	PA	Gibbs, George	1810	21 b	DE
Gaw, John	1817	17	PA	Gibbs, George	1810	21 b	DE
Gaylord, Myran	1822	14	PA	Gibbs, George	1822	26 b	VA
Gaynor, William	1818	20	NY	Gibbs, Henry	1817	18	MA
Geddes, George Henry				Gibbs, Isaac	1819	19	MA
	1798	16	DE	Gibbs, James	1812	29 y	MD
Geddes, James R.	1823	24	PA	Gibbs, Lewis	1822	26 b	DE
Geddes, William C.	1809	17	DE	Gibbs, Samuel	1812	19 y	DE
Geddes, William C.	1820	27	DE	Gibbs, William	1804	20	MA
Geddis, William Charles				Gibby, William	1822	16	PA
	1813	0		Giberson, Samuel	1815	22	NJ
Gee, Russell	1798	30	NJ	Gibson, Cyrus	1815	22 b	CT
Gee, Thomas	1822	33	PA	Gibson, Elijah	1804	23	NJ
Geen, James	1809	22	VA	Gibson, Henry	1805	23	PA
Geene, James	1818	27	NY	Gibson, John	1809	34	MA
Geiger, George	1809	23	PA	Gibson, Joseph	1809	24	DE
Genovich, Matthias	1811	36	LA	Gibson, Perry	1810	31 y	MD
Gentry, Benjamin	1809	27	NJ	Gibson, Robert	1809	25	NC
Gentry, David	1815	22	NJ	Gibson, Thomas	1815	46	Ireland
Gentry, Samuel	1805	21	PA	Gibson, William	1809	19	NY
George, John	1798	22	MD	Gibson, William	1811	28	NY
George, John	1803	24	NJ	Gidley, George	1807	14	MD
George, John	1811	32	none given	Gieve, George	1808	18	NY
George, Peter	1804	21	PA	Gifford, Alden	1817	45	MA
George, Samuel	1818	18 b	PA	Gifford, Anthony	1803	22	NJ
George, William	1807	33	PA	Gifford, Delany	1822	27	NJ

Gifford, Francis	1818	31	NJ
Gifford, George	1815	29	MA
Gifford, James B.	1811	14	PA
Gifford, John	1814	22	NJ
Gifford, Joseph	1817	25	MA
Gifford, Prince P.	1815	20	MA
Gifford, Robert	1821	16	DE
Gifford, William M.	1811	16	PA
Gifford, William	1815	0	
Gilbert, James	1809	48 m	MD
Gilbert, James	1815	24	MA
Gilbert, John	1810	24	LA
Gilbert, John	1815	21	NJ
Gilbert, Thomas	1809	23	NJ
Gilby, William	1803	33	PA
Gilby, William	1805	0	
Gilchrist, James	1815	27	NY
Gilder, Jacob	1812	23 b	DE
Gilder, James	1816	21 y	DE
Giles, Alexander	1798	21 b	DE
Giles, Charles Augustus			
	1815	24	NY
Giles, George	1806	25	NY
Giles, George	1807	25	NY
Giles, Jacob	1804	26 B	DE
Giles, Jeremiah	1817	22	MD
Giles, William	1817	33	CT
Gill, Abijah	1804	22	MA
Gill, James	1806	25	NJ
Gill, John	1804	21	NJ
Gillespey, John	1807	27	PA
Gillespie, George	1809	25	DE
Gillies, Edward R.	1820	34	NY
Gillilan, James	1817	48	none given
Gillingham, James, Jr.	1810	15	PA
Gillis, John	1806	22	VA
Gillmore, James	1807	25	LA
Gilmore, Isaac	1817	30 y	MD
Gilpin, James	1821	19 b	DE
Gilpin, Richard B.	1822	18	DE
Giltzow, George	1820	24	NY
Gines, Edward	1805	45	VA
Ginkins, Jacob	1818	23 b	DE
Ginnis, William	1812	22	PA
Girton, Bazilla	1815	25	NJ
Gitchell, David	1803	26	MD
Githaus, John	1812	24	NJ
Githens, Charles	1809	23	NJ
Gittyer, George	1819	25	PA
Gladding, George	1815	25 m	VA
Glading, James	1809	35	NJ
Glading, James	1811	00	

Glading, John, Jr.	1818	15	PA
Glagg, John	1806	25	PA
Glann, Benjamin	1805	41	PA
Glasgow, William	1804	22	PA
Glasier, Beamsley	1822	47	ME
Glassgow, Ceaser	1815	22 b	PA
Gleason, Peter	1810	23	NJ
Gleaves, John W.	1809	21	MD
Glem, James	1815	26	MA
Glen, Daniel	1800	32	DE
Glenn, Hanson W.	1821	48	MD
Glenn, William	1811	10	PA
Glenne, John	1779	22	PA
Glenton, Thomas	1815	21	NJ
Glentworth, James, Jr.			
	1817	23	PA
Glover, James	1813	24	PA
Glover, William	1803	19	PA
Glum, John	1799	22	PA
Goby, Maholon	1817	24 b	DE
Goddard, Charles	1804	11	Pa
Godfree, Moses	1810	23 b	VA
Godfrey, George	1806	18 y	VA
Godfrey, Joseph	1810	16	NJ
Godfrey, Joseph	1813	0	
Godfrey, Knowles	1811	21	MA
Godfrey, William	1811	27	NJ
Godfrey, William	1811	00	
Godin, Samuel	1807	45	MA
Godlips, John	1816	29	MA
Godshall, John	1811	16	PA
Godwin, Peter	1806	22	DE
Goff, Robert	1811	20	MA
Goff, Thomas	1818	47	PA
Goings, Peter Paul	1822	56 b	SC
Golan, Michael	1806	45	LA
Gold, John	1809	24	PA
Gold, Samuel	1810	24 y	NJ
Goldaere, Matthias Hanson			
	1810	26	Denmark
Goldar, John	1814	36	NJ
Golden, Crownshield	1821	25 y	NY
Golden, Jacob	1809	22	NJ
Golder, Jacob	1806	20	NJ
Goldsmith, John	1806	44	MD
Golifer, George	1815	30	PA
Gomez, Michael	1820	38	LA
Gongo, Enos	1815	28	NJ
Gonsalves, Francis	1807	27	LA
Gonsalves, Francis	1807	24	LA
Gonsalves, Pedro	1807	23	LA
Goodale, William	1815	24	MA

Name	Year	Age		State
Goodbartlet, William	1807	21		
Goodes, William	1815	48		MD
Goodfellow, Wm.	1821	24		PA
Goodin, John	1815	18		PA
Goodin, Thomas	1810	19		CT
Goodin, William	1822	26		PA
Goodine, George	1823	24	b	DE
Goodison, James	1820	28		MA
Goodman, George	1809	16		PA
Goodridge, Jewett	1817	22		MA
Goodwin, Benjamin	1804	17		MD
Goodwin, John	1798	36		MD
Goodwin, Thomas F.	1811	18		PA
Goodwin, Thomas J.	1820	17		ME
Goram, Philip	1807	20		LA
Gorden, Thomas	1819	22		MD
Gordon, Francis	1805	33		SC
Gordon, John	1798	0		PA
Gordon, John	1807	26		PA
Gordon, John	1819	29	b	PA
Gordon, Morgan S.	1811	18		MA
Gordon, Nathaniel	1809	25		MA
Gordon, Peter, Jr.	1802	26		PA
Gordon, Peter	1820	39		PA
Gordon, Robert	1820	22	b	DE
Gordon, Thomas	1817	18		PA

Gordon, Wickelmiller 1816 34 b MA
false statement to obtain SPC. Declared
himself an Englishman in Liverpool on Ship
Jane Ferguson

Name	Year	Age		State
Gordon, William	1817	33		MD
Gordon, William	1818	26		NY
Gordon, William	1818	27		VA
Gordon, William	1821	22		NY
Gordon, William	1823	19		DE
Gore, Thomas	1812	16		MA
Gorman, James	1798	24		NJ
Gormly, David	1806	20		VA
Gorton, James	1798	30		
Gosley, Joseph	1815	27		NY
Gosline, John	1823	21		PA
Gosner, Peter	1813	22		PA
Gosner, Peter	1814	0		
Goss, Charles	1815	18		SC
Gossage, Robert	1810	21		MD
Gossan, John	1805	18		MD
Gossman, Benjamin	1804	22		PA
Goto, John Augustim	1795	0		
Goucher, Samuel	1804	19		PA
Goudani, Francis	1813	24		MT

Name	Year	Age		State
Gould, Alexander	1804	21		England
Gould, Elizah	1815	24		NJ
Gould, John	1797	0		Gr.Br.
Gould, John	1811	25		MA
Gould, Samuel	1815	0		
Gould, Thomas	1821	21		MA
Goulden, Joseph	1809	31		PA
Goulding, Isaac	1811	26		MA
Goulding, Jack	1806	24	b	MD
Grace, Allen	1810	27	b	MD
Grace, Allen	1812	00		
Grace, John	1811	25	y	PA
Grace, John	1812	22		PA
Grace, Richard	1801	22	m	MD
Grace, Richard	1804	23	y	MD
Grace, Richard	1805	24	y	MD
Grace, Thomas	1807	18		MA
Grady, Thomas	1812	29		none given
Grady, Thomas	1812	29		none given
Graff, Andrew	1813	22		PA
Graff, Henry	1807	18		PA
Gragg, John	1806	25		PA
Graham, Henry	1812	21	c	NJ
Graham, James	1818	31		NJ
Graham, John	1796	0		NY
Graham, William	1803	35		NY
Graham, William	1812	18		DE
Gramsby, George	1823	46		NY
Grandison, Jeremiah	1817	00		xx
Grandson, Jeremiah	1816	40	b	VA
Granson, Peter	1798	16		PA
Grant, Darius	1820	23		CT
Grant, James	1823	23	c	MD
Grant, John	1809	16		DE
Grant, Joseph	1813	32		VA
Grant, Paul	1823	21	y	NY
Grant, Samuel	1807	25		MA
Grant, William	1821	21		PA
Grapevine, William	1822	25		NJ
Gravenstine, John	1815	15		PA
Graves, Thomas	1799	0		PA
Gravy, William	1820	19		PA
Gray, Archabald	1801	35		NJ
Gray, Donald	1801	21	b	PA
Gray, Edward	1818	28		NC
Gray, Gawn	1796	0		
Gray, George	1809	21		MD
Gray, Henry	1822	23	b	MD
Gray, Henry M.	1823	16		PA
Gray, James	1805	23		MD
Gray, James	1805	22		PA
Gray, James	1810	25	b	NJ

Gray, John	1798	32	VA
Gray, John	1800	15	PA
Gray, John	1804	19	MD
Gray, John	1815	19	NY
Gray, John	1822	25 b	MD
Gray, John	1822	42 y	SC
Gray, Joseph, Jr.	1806	15	PA
Gray, Joseph, Jr.	1810	19	PA
Gray, Samuel	1819	23	MD
Gray, Thomas	1803	26 b	VA
Gray, William C.	1818	34	RI
Gray, William	1822	23	PA
Grays, William	1820	18 m	PA
Graysberry, Benjamin, Jr.			
	1796	23	NJ
Greave, George	1821	18 b	PA
Greaves, Casper	1822	16	PA
Greaves, Joseph	1821	21	PA
Greble, Charles	1809	20	PA
Greble, William	1815	16	PA
Greeley, David	1809	27	MA
Green, Aaron	1815	28 y	PA
Green, Anthony	1820	28 b	DE
Green, Asa	1815	14	MA
Green, Charles	1801	25 b	NJ
Green, Charles	1806	28	NJ
Green, Charles	1806	0 b	
Green, Charles	1807	00	
Green, Charles	1807	00	NJ
Green, Charles	1811	21 b	NJ
Green, Charles	1815	0	
Green, Charles	1815	19 y	NJ
Green, Charles	1822	22 b	NY
Green, David	1807	22	NY
Green, Edward	1807	24 y	MD
Green, Elijah	1814	20	NJ
Green, George	1812	18	NY
Green, George	1816	26 m	NY
Green, George	1809	19 b	NJ
bound servant to John Meany; goes to sea with his consent			
Green, Gidian	1815	21 y	RI
Green, Henry	1819	28 b	NY
Green, Henry	1820	20	NY
Green, Isaac	1809	30	PA
Green, Isaac	1811	26 b	DE
Green, Isaac	1815	0	
Green, Isaac	1815	0	
Green, Jacob	1804	34	PA
Green, James	1804	24	PA

Green, James	1804	0	
Green, James	1805	22	MD
Green, James	1805	0	
Green, James Craig	1807	15	PA
Green, James	1814	36 b	RI
Green, James	1815	20	NY
Green, James	1822	17 y	PA
Green, Jeremiah	1807	18	MA
Green, John	1809	20 y	MD
Green, John	1810	30	MA
Green, John	1811	22	PA
Green, John	1812	22 y	LA
Green, John	1815	18	MA
Green, John	1815	19	MD
Green, John	1820	21	PA
Green, Joseph	1799	36	PA
Green, Joseph, Jr.	1801	25	PA
Green, Joseph	1811	00	
Green, Joseph	1811	36 b	PA
Green, Joseph	1818	22 b	PA
Green, Levi	1809	17 b	DE
Green, Levy	1811	00	
Green, Lymus	1804	27 b	NY
Green, Nathan	1811	17	VA
Green, Nathaniel	1818	26	PA
Green, Neal	1811	20	PA
Green, Peter	1808	38	
Green, Robert	1809	25	PA
Green, Samuel	1815	27 b	NJ
Green, William	1798	27	none given
Green, William	1804	16 m	PA
Green, William	1810	23 b	MD
Green, William	1822	22	MD
Greenchurch, Isaac	1808	49 b	RI
Greenick, Nicholas	1805	20 b	MD
Greenlief, Hannibal	1815	26	NY
Greenough, Robert	1810	25	MA
Greenough, William	1815	19	NH
Greenyer, William	1810	23	PA
Greer, Joseph	1807	33	LA
Greer, Peter	0000	0	Ireland
Greer, Peter	0000	21	Ireland
Gregg, Israle	1820	17 y	PA
Gregory, Alva	1815	20	Ct
Gregory, David	1811	22	PA
Gregory, Elijah	1803	17	NY
Gregory, Elijah	1805	0	
Gregson, Peter	1803	34	PA
Grenich, John	1811	26 b	DE
Grew, Edward	1812	34	PA
Grew, Edward	1817	39	PA
Gribb, George	1819	24	PA

Grice, Isaac	1815	15	PA
Grieggs, Cato	1819	27 b	DE
Grierson, Frederick	1812	18	PA
Griffee, Thomas	1809	21	NJ
Griffeth, Robert	1805	0	
Griffey, John	1814	0	
Griffin, Charles	1815	20	NY
Griffin, James	1820	34	MD
Griffin, John	1812	22 y	PA
Griffin, Joseph	1816	25 y	MD
Griffin, Thomas	1801	18	NY
Griffin, Thomas	1805	0	
Griffin, William	1804	39	DE
Griffin, William	1819	18	PA
Griffing, Joseph C.	1798	16	PA
Griffing, Samuel	1811	27	PA
Griffis, John L.	1822	18	PA
Griffis, Robert	1795	20	PA
Griffis, Robert	1796	0	PA
Griffis, Thomas	1823	36	NY
Griffith, John	1811	23 b	PA
Griffith, Robert	1804	21	PA
Griffith, William	1798	23	PA
Griffith, William R.	1815	16	NY
Griffith, William	1815	26	PA
Griffith, William	1818	19	PA
Griffiths, Abraham	1811	20	PA
Griffiths, Thomas	1810	44	NY
Griffy, John	1810	20 m	PA
Griffy, John	1812	00	
Griges, John	1810	19	LA
Griges, John	1815	0	
Griggs, David	1807	32	NJ
Grigous, William	1810	29 y	PA
Grime, George	1816	29	VA
Grimes, Charles	1803	16	NY
Grimes, George	1813	25	VA
Grimes, John	1820	21	PA
Grimes, Michael	1804	28	PA
Grimes, William	1822	16	PA
Grims, William	1801	20	MD
Grimson, John	1817	21	NC
Grimstone, John	1818		
Grinion, William	1808	21	PA
Groff, Jacob	1813	25	PA
Groombridge, Richard	1817	35	MA
Gros, Henry	1809	31	
Gross, Samuel	1822	19	PA
Gross, William	1810	24	DE
Grouard, John P.	1817	12	NH
Grover, Charles	1814	19	PA
Grover, Christopher	1808	21	PA

Grover, Curtis T.	1815	20	PA
Grover, John, Jr.	1805	17	PA
Grover, John	1817	16	PA

no SPC to be given unless Samuel Hagerman, to whom he is apprenticed, is present.

Grover, Robert	1807	18	PA
Groves, Charles	1821	25 y	NJ
Groves, David	1806	18	NJ
Groves, Harry	1803	17 m	NJ
Groves, Philas	1798	36 b	PA
Groves, Richard	1804	40	MA
Groves, Robert	1798	24	PA
Groves, Robert	1801	28	PA
Grow, Nathaniel	1810	40	MA
Grozer, William	1809	19	NY
Grub, Jacob	1809	21	PA
Grubb, George	1810	37	PA
Grubb, John	1810	29	DE
Grubb, John	1820	26	PA
Grubb, Samuel	1801	25	PA
Grueff, Henry	1821	19	PA
Gruiner, William	1815	0	
Grumman, Aaron	1818	34	CT
Guenk, John	1809	20	CT
Guerout, Louis Gregory			
	1809	35	MS
Guerten, Joseph	1804	25 m	DE
Guest, Henry	1815	20	MD
Guigue, Joseph	1816	22 y	PA
Guilds, Lanson	1807	25	CT
Guilles, Joseph	1805	16	MA
Guior, William	1798	22	MA
Guirey, Samuel	1805	24	PA
Gulager, Henry	1811	15	MA
Gullager, Christian	1815	25	MA
Gum, Jacob	1812	24	DE
Gumbo, James	1809	23 y	MD
Gunby, Daniel	1811	26 b	DE
Gunn, Alexander	1797	0	
Guss, Thomas H.	1820	31 b	MA
Gussall, John	1813	18	PA
Gussett, Peter	1807	32	LA
Gustard, William	1818	23	PA
Guthrie, William	1818	16	NC
Guthry, Thomas	1807	19	NY
Gutterson, Alexander	1817	18	PA
Gutthry, James	1810	22	MD
Guttrey, Isaac	1811	27 m	NY
Guy, John	1815	29 b	PA
Guy, Robert	1818	27	PA

Guy, Soloman Smith	1809	28 b	DE
Guyant, David	1810	22	PA
Gwabo, Peter	1807	23	LA
Gwisen, Lewis	1807	30	LA
Habacker, George	1807	22	PA
Habacker, William	1806	19	PA
Habacker, William	1807		PA
Habacker, William	1809	0	
Habacker, William	1812	00	
Hacker, Benjamin	1812	31	PA
Hackerson, James	0000	21	PA
Hackeson, James	0000	21	PA
Hacket, John	1809	48 b	MD
Hacket, Joseph	1805	25 b	DE
Hackett, Jonathan	1800	19 b	
Hacquin, William Noel	1797	0		Gr.Br.
Haddick, Simon	1816	38 b	
Haddock, Joseph Price			
	1805	30	MA
Hadley, John	1811	17	NY
Hadley, William	1806	21	NY
Haffard, William	1817	26	MA
Haffard, William	1822	31	
Haffee, Roddy	1806	25	CT

Haftpenny, Robert 1799 27 SC
was on board British ship *Defiance*; imprisoned
in Samur Prison; released to U. S. Consul,
Ports of Poole Cowes

Hagan, David	1806	24	PA
Hageston, John	1822	26	PA
Hagins, Peter	1811	21	DE
Haigg, James	1805	27	MD
Haight, Joseph	1811	19	PA
Haight, Joshua	1810	36	NY
Haight, Joshua	1811	00	
Haight, Joshua	1815	0	
Hailer, Frederick	1813	24	PA
Hailer, Joseph	1811	14	PA
Haines, John	1822	17	PA
Haines, Thomas	1812	29 y	PA
Haines, Thomas	1816	13	PA
Haines, Thomas	1817	14	PA
Hainey, Henry	1815	20	VA
Hains, Thomas	1797	0	DE
Hake, Robert	1816	22	PA
Halberstadt, John	1822	24	PA
Halbert, Peter	1803	26	SC
Hald, William	1815	26	NY
Hale, John	1815	23	NY
Hale, Joshua	1808	21	MD

Hale, Warwick	1810	22	PA
Hale, William	1811	20	NH
Hale, William	1823	28	ME
Halfpenny, Rob	1806	0	
Hall, Bartley	1800	30 b	MD
Hall, Benjamin	1820	29	MA
Hall, David	1805	22 b	DE
Hall, David	1810	23 b	DE
Hall, David	1819	27	CT
Hall, Ezekial	1806	19	PA
Hall, Greenfield	1810	24	MA
Hall, Henry	1807	26	NC
Hall, Henry	1809	24 b	Pa
Hall, Horatio H.	1811	11	MD
Hall, Isaac	1800	50	DE
Hall, Isaac	1805	21	PA
Hall, Isaac Norris	1809	19	NJ
Hall, Isaac	1810	24 b	PA
Hall, James	1796	13	PA
Hall, Jeremiah	1809	17	CT
Hall, John	1796	40	MD
Hall, John	1809	24	MA
Hall, John	1811	00	
Hall, John	1817	28 y	PA
Hall, John	1820	36	NH
Hall, John	1821	33 b	MA
Hall, John	1822	25 b	NJ
Hall, John	1822	21	CT
Hall, Joseph	1804	40	PA
Hall, Joseph	1805	0	
Hall, Joseph S.	1815	25	PA
Hall, Joseph	1815	12	DE
Hall, Joseph	1819	25	PA
Hall, Philip	1807	26	NY
Hall, Robert	1811	21	PA
Hall, Robert	1822	22	ME
Hall, Samuel	1821	32	VA
Hall, Spencer	1818	20 b	DE
Hall, Step	1805	19 b	MD
Hall, Thomas	1809	28	MD
Hall, Thomas	1821	42	NC

Hall, Thomas 1821 26 c MD
certificate signed Thomas Hood, Justice of the
Peace, Annie Arundelee County, states Hall was
born free

Hall, William	1815	21	MA
Hall, William	1815	21	MD
Hall, William	1818	14 c	PA
Haller, Isaac	1805	24	PA
Hallet, Allen	1805	16	MA

Hallett, Robert	1821	21	MA		Hammond, Joseph	1810	18	MA
Halliday, James	1820	20		Ireland	Hammons, John	1821	16	ME
Hallman, John S.	1816	23	PA		Hamond, Thomas	1801	29	NH
Halsam, Richard	1821	24	NY		Hamrick, Chrestean	1809	19	PA
Halsey, George	1817	15	NY		Hanagan, Peter	1804	21	PA
Halsey, Hezekiah	1810	23	NY		Hanagan, Peter	1807		PA
Halstat, Charles	1809	21	MA		Hance, Samuel	1807	30 b	DE
Halstead, James	1805	23	NY		Hance, William	1804	26	PA
Haman, Jesse	1812	00			Hancock, James	1811	28	NC
Hamilton, Charles	1804	33	NJ		Hancume, John	1805	37	SC
Hamilton, Columbus	1818	16	PA		Hand, Charles	1810	21	NJ
Hamilton, Elias	1815	22	MD		Hand, David	1809	20	NJ
Hamilton, George	1804	26 m	PA		Hand, Eldridge	1810	23	NJ
Hamilton, George	1810	23	CT		Hand, Ezekiel	1806	21	NJ
Hamilton, George	1823	27	NJ		Hand, George Chew	1823	17	PA
Hamilton, George	1823	22	DE		Hand, Jasper	1806	22	PA
Hamilton, James	1798	17	PA		Hand, Jessee	1806	30	NJ
Hamilton, James	1809	44	DE		Hand, John	1803	25	NJ
Hamilton, James	1811	25	MD		Hand, John	1804	25	NJ
Hamilton, John	1808	23	NY		Hand, John Keen	1823	16	DC
Hamilton, John	1811	00			Hand, Joseph	1815	20	NJ
Hamilton, John	1815	22	SC		Hand, Joseph L.	1816	24	NJ
Hamilton, John	1815	0			Hand, Joshua	1812	26	NJ
Hamilton, Magor	1809	22	DE		Handey, George	1815	27 b	PA
Hamilton, Robert	1813	28	PA		Handsey, Cary	1823	22 y	DE
Hamilton, Samuel	1823	19	PA		Handy, Barnabus	1818	19	MA
Hamilton, Thomas	1813	20	NJ		Handy, Otis	1811	20	MA
Hamilton, William	1809	27	NJ		Handy, William, Jr.	1823	18	ME
Hamilton, William	1810	25	NH		Hanekel, John Frederik			
Hamilton, William	1812	00				1817	42	Germany
Hamilton, William	1815	22	MA		Hanes, William	1813	18	NY
Hamilton, William	1823	24	PA		Haney, Edward	1803	26	PA
Hamlet, John	1811	26 m	NJ		Haney, Edward	1805	0	
Hamlet, John	1814	0			Haney, Edward	1805	0	
Hamlin, John	1809	20	MD		Haney, Edward	1809	32	PA
Hamlin, Thomas	1810	18	MA		Haney, Isaac	1814	22	VA
Hamm, Charles	1811	30	PA		Haney, Isaac	1815	0	
Hammel, Wm. H.	1817	25	MD		Haneyford, John	1811	23	MA
Hammelback, Philip	1805	21	PA		Hanford, Charles	1823	26	NY
Hammell, Seth A.	1822	20	NJ		Hanker, Henry	1819	21	PA
Hammet, Emanuel	1809	22	PA		Hankison, Benjamin	1805	0	
Hammett, George	1806	26	NY		Hankuson, Benjamin	1804	24 b	NJ
Hammett, Thomas	1811	44	MA		Hanlon, Henry	1804	16	PA
Hammit, John	1810	40			Hanlon, Henry	1815	0	
Hammitt, John	1817	20	NJ		Hanna, Alexander	1821	19	ME
Hammon, Crosby	1814	19	PA		Hanna, John	1810	22	DE
Hammon, Jesse	1813	0			Hanna, Thomas H.J.	1822	16	PA
Hammon, John	1804	17	NJ		Hanna, William	1823	15	PA
Hammond, Banjamin	1809	25	MD		Hannaford, George	1818	18	MA
Hammond, Barton	1808	31	Ma		Hannagan, Peter	1806	0	PA
Hammond, Barzillai	1815	49	MA		Hannagan, Peter	1809	0	
Hammond, John	1804	18	NJ		Hannah, Daniel	1810	28	SC

Hannah, David	1811	22	NJ
Hannah, John	1804	21	PA
Hanner, John	1804	21	NJ
Hannon, William	1805	21	PA
Hannum, Isaac Gill	1809	24	NJ
Hannum, James	1798	19	PA
Hanse, Peter	1806	22	NY
Hanse, William	1803	36	PA
Hanse, William	1809	43	PA
Hanse, William	1823	56	PA
Hansey, Jesse	1823	24 y	DE
Hansey, John	1821	28 m	DE
Hansford, Benjamin	1810	21	VA
Hansley, Jacob	1796	0	PA
Hanson, Abraham	1822	50	PA
Hanson, Andrew	1804	30	PA
Hanson, Andrew	1806	35	none given
Hanson, Andrew	1808	25	PA
Hanson, Andrew W.	1814	14	PA
Hanson, Christopher	1803	32	PA
Hanson, George	1805	0	
Hanson, George	1805	20	PA
Hanson, Henry	1809	28 b	VA
Hanson, Jacob	1813	20	DE
Hanson, James	1810	28	NY
Hanson, John	1809	16	PA
Hanson, John	1816	0	none given
Hanson, Laurence	1800	22	PA
Hanson, Marcus	1823	50	none given
Hanson, Mathias	1809	25	PA
Hanson, Peter	1809	24 b	NY
Hanson, Samuel	1805	21	DE
Hanson, William	1815	29	MA

Hany, Nicholas 1803 48
lived in U.S. at Independence and ever
since

Hany, Thomas	1817	23 m	MD
Hapeny, James D.	1816	22	PA
Harberger, George	1809	17	PA

Harbeson, Banjamin, Jr.

	1818	22	PA
Harborn, Joseph, Jr.	1821	36	VA
Harden, George	1813	23	PA
Harden, Peter	1812	31 b	DE
Harden, William	1821	23 b	NY
Harden, William	1821	34	NC
Hardie, John Charles	1816	33	LA
Hardin, James	1823	14	PA
Harding, Hezekiah	1809	18	NJ
Harding, Isaac	1806	18	NY

Harding, Isaac	1816	30 y	PA
Harding, Jacob	1809	16	MD
Harding, James	1804	23	PA
Harding, James	1821	21	PA
Harding, John	1815	21	PA
Harding, Peter	1812	00	DE
Harding, William	1805	27 y	PA
Harding, William	1806	0	
Harding, William	1821	27 b	NJ
Hardy, Alexander	1815	16	PA
Hardy, Francis	1799	0	PA
Hardy, Francis A.	1805	23	PA
Hardy, George	1807	42 b	MD
Hardy, John	1799	27	DE
Hardy, John	1817	22 m	NY
Hardy, Jonathan	1798	19	MA
Hardy, William	1805	28	NY
Hare, Robert	1810	22 y	NY
Harford, James	1805	26	MD
Harford, James	1807		
Harford, Thomas	1808	20	PA
Harford, Thomas	1811	00	

SPC lost when Schooner *Eliza* for Lisbon
foundered at sea

Hargesheimer, John, Jr.

	1820	20	PA

Hargesheimer, Jonathan

	1811	16	PA
Hargrave, Thomas	1809	23	CT
Harker, John	1813	19	PA
Harkes, William	1822	24	PA
Harkins, John	1804	21	PA
Harkins, John	1807	18	MA
Harkins, John William	1815	18	PA
Harkley, Thomas	1805	29	NJ
Harlan, Bazer	1812	31	PA
Harlan, James M.	1822	14	PA
Harlan, John	1804	33	PA
Harlan, William	1807	21	PA
Harley, Jacob	1805	19	PA
Harlow, Kimbell	1820	17	MA
Harman, Eli	1806	21 b	DE
Harman, Eli	1809	0	
Harman, Elisha	1822	22 b	PA
Harman, Henry	1813	17	DE
Harman, Isaac	1817	20 c	PA
Harman, Jacob	1809	36	none given
Harman, Jacob	1821	21 c	VA
Harman, Jacob	1823	31 y	VA
Harman, John	1804	0	DE

Harman, John	1809	23 y	DE	
Harman, John	1811	00	DE	
Harman, John	1811	00		
Harman, John	1816	0		
Harman, Joseph	1798	22	PA	
Harman, Kendel	1818	22	DE	
Harman, Levan	1822	27 b	NJ	
Harman, Luke	1822	23 s	DE	
Harman, William	1812	41		none given
Harmer, Samuel	1808	17	PA	
Harmer, Samuel	1810	18	PA	
Harmer, Samuel	1813	0		
Harmon, Ezekiel	1815	17 b	NJ	
Harmon, Ezekiel	1816	18 b	NJ	
Harmon, John	1803	18 m	MD	
Harmon, Solomon	1819	22 y	DE	
Harmond, Jess	1807	23 m	NC	
Harmony, Benjamin	1815	27	CT	
Haroah, Alexander	1800	27	PA	
Harod, David	1807	18 b	DE	
Harp, David	1801	24	DE	
Harper, John	1810	18	PA	
Harper, Peter	1816	18	PA	
Harper, Robert	1806	19	PA	
Harper, Robert	1807			
Harper, Robert	1813	25		none given
Harper, William	1805	23	NJ	
Harper, William	1816	16	PA	
Harrard, Jacob	1812	25 b	DE	
Harrington, Nathaniel	1810	0		
Harris, Benjamin	1815	22	NJ	
Harris, Charles B.	1813	21	NJ	
Harris, Charles	1821	25 b	PA	
Harris, Clayton	1804	20 m	DE	
Harris, David	1803	25	VA	
Harris, David	1809	0		
Harris, Francis	1815	18 y	PA	
Harris, Francis	1821	23 y	PA	
Harris, George L.	1815	22	PA	
Harris, George	1823	21 b	MD	
Harris, Jacob	1806	25 b	NC	
Harris, James	1816	20 c	NJ	
Harris, Jocob	1807	26 m	MD	
Harris, John	1799	25	VA	
Harris, John	1806	21 b	VA	
Harris, John	1807	21	NY	
Harris, John	1807	21	LA	

Harris, John   1811   27 b   at sea
free black man, born at sea on passage from
coast of Africa

Harris, John	1811	25 b	NJ	
Harris, John	1815	22	NJ	
Harris, John	1817	24 b	DE	
Harris, John	1817	39 b	NH	
Harris, John	1819	26	MA	
Harris, John H.	1821	25	PA	
Harris, Lemeul	1815	17 b	DE	
Harris, Lewis	1806	24	LA	
Harris, Nathan	1811	24 c	MD	
Harris, Nathan	1815	0		
Harris, Nehemiah	1805	27 y	DE	
Harris, Phillip	1818	18 b	PA	
Harris, Robert	1804	30	PA	
Harris, Robert Wire	1808	16	MA	
Harris, Samuel	1796	34	DE	
Harris, Simon	1818	36 b	VA	
Harris, Solomon	1823	23	NY	
Harris, Thomas	1800	18	PA	
Harris, Thomas	1809	24	CT	
Harris, Walter	1809	41 m	VA	
Harris, William	1807	23	NY	
Harris, William	1808	0		
Harris, William	1814	19	VA	
Harris, William	1815	26 b	PA	
Harrison, Anthony	1806	28	NC	
Harrison, Charles	1809	26	MD	
Harrison, Charles	1810	0	MD	
Harrison, Edward	1822	23 s	MD	
Harrison, Francis	1815	15	PA	
Harrison, Harry	1815	30 y	NY	
Harrison, Henry	1815	30	NY	
Harrison, James	1809	21	PA	
Harrison, James	1811	23 b	DE	
Harrison, James	1819	13	PA	
Harrison, John	1804	19	NY	
Harrison, Nathan	1809	32 b	MD	
Harrison, Richard	1812	19	PA	
Harrison, Thomas	1815	28 b	MD	
Harrison, William	1804	23	MD	
Harrison, William	1807	19	NY	
Harrison, William	1809	0		
Harrisson, John	1806	17	MA	
Harrisson, John	1821	18	PA	
Harrod, David	1807	b		
Harrod, James	1812	36	PA	
Harrodd, William	1818	22 b	DE	
Hart, David	1819	28 b	RI	
Hart, Henry	1815	39	NJ	
Hart, James	1817	36		none given
Hart, John	1808	21 b	NJ	
Hart, John	1815	19	PA	
Hart, John, Jr.	1817	20	PA	

Hart, John Moore	1817	21 b	PA		Hatch, James	1807	20		PA
Hart, Oliver, Jr.	1819	19	NH		Hatch, James	1808	22		PA
Hart, Richard	1810	19	NY		Hatch, James	1809	22		PA
Hart, Samuel	1809	24	NY		Hatch, Prince	1817	25		MA
Harten, William	1812	20 b	NC		Hatch, Samuel H.	1810	28		CT
Hartford, William	1811	21	MA		Hatcher, Thomas	1809	22		PA
Hartless, James	1815	29	CT		Hatfyld, Thomas	1803	22		DE
Hartley, Geroge	1794	0		Germany	Hathaway, Pardon	1807	21		MA
Hartley, Solomon	1803	28	PA		Hatherton, Samuel	1804	20		VA
Hartly, John	1806	22	PA		Hathway, Joseph	1809	23		MA
Hartman, Derrick	1807	45			Hatney, Zadock	1814	24 b		VA
Hartman, John	1809	21	PA		Hatstat, Charles	1812	00		
Hartshorn, Benjamin	1815	36 y	MA		Hatton, William	1804	22		PA
Hartshorne, Joseph	1806	27	VA		Hatts, Elisha	1805	25		VA
Hartshorne, Peter S.	1808	27	VA		Haulding, James	1811	24		NJ
Harvey, Alexander	1815	21	DE		Hautman, John	1817	39		PA
Harvey, Edward	1816	22	MA		Haven, Jonathan Hamilton				
Harvey, James	1807	22 b	NY			1820	14		NH
Harvey, James	1809	29	MA		Hawes, Jacob	1811	13		MA
Harvey, James	1813	26	MA		Hawk, Christian	1809	35		PA
Harvey, James	1818	43 y	MD		Hawke, Jacob	1805	19		NJ
Harvey, John	1798	25	PA		Hawkins, Abraham	1810	31		DE
					Hawkins, Daniel	1809	21 b		MD
Harvey, John	1799	34			Hawkins, Daniel	1812	31 m		MD
baptised Swedish Church of Phila. by rector					Hawkins, Elija	1822	17 b		PA
Nicholas Collin, as was brother William					Hawkins, George Washington				
						1819	22		DE
Harvey, Lewis	1815	30	LA		Hawkins, Isaac	1803	23 m		MD
Harvey, Robert	1805	22	NY		Hawkins, Isaac	1807	24 y		MD
Harvey, Thomas	1804	25	PA		Hawkins, James	1818	18		DE
Harvey, William	1808	32	MA		Hawkins, Jesse	1817	24		NC
Harvey, William	1811	20	VA		Hawkins, John	1810	21		DE
Harvy, John	1810	33	PA		Hawkins, Lewis	1805	38		SC
Harvy, John	1811	23	MA		Hawkins, Parker	1812	18		GA
Harwood, John	1804	19	NJ		Hawkins, Richard	1812	19 b		MD
Harwood, John	1809	23	NJ		Hawkins, Stephen	1809	21 y		DE
Harwood, John	1810	0			Hawkins, Stephen	1812	00		
Harwood, John	1811	00			Hawkins, Thomas	1805	47 b		MD
Harzard, Israel	1819	30	DE		Hawkins, Thomas	1815	26		Ct
Haskap, Henry	1809	27	PA		Hawksworth, John	1815	43		NY
Haskins, Benjamin	1815	28 b	MD		Hawley, Lemuel	1798	28		CT
Haslett, Caleb	1807	22 b	DE		Haws, Andrew	1801	26		DE
Haslop, George	1801	16	VA		Hawthorn, Thomas	1798	21		PA
Hassell, John	1811	40		Germany	Hawthorn, Thomas P.	1810	0		
Hassen, John	1804	21 b	MA		Hawthorn, Thomas P.	1815	0		
Hassett, John	1815	45		Germany	Hay, Michael	1809	33 m		MD
Hastings, John	1821	30	MA		Hayden, James	1809	16		MA
Hastings, William Havely					Haydock, William	1804	18		PA
	1817	22	NJ		Hayes, John	1797	0		Ireland
Hasy, Robert	1811	00	PA		Hayes, Thomas	1816	16		PA
Hatch, Elisha	1808	0			Hayes, William	1803	19		NY
Hatch, Henry	1807	29	CT		Haylander, Peter	1810	14		PA

Haylander, Peter F.	1810	14	PA		Hedeliers, Andrew	1800	42	PA
Haylander, Peter F.	1811	00			Hedelius, Andrew, Jr.	1813	15	PA
Haylander, Peter F.	1814	17	PA		Heeler, John	1805	20	PA
Hayley, John	1805	18	PA		Heffeton, Edward	1811	35	VA
Hayley, John	1807				Heft, John Frederick	1808	24	PA
Hayman, James	1806	19	MD		Heft, William	1820	16	PA
Hayman, William	1815	20	MA		Hegamin, John	1811	21 b	NJ
Haynes, Peter B.	1813	29 m	MA		Hegamin, William	1821	25 b	NJ
Haynes, William	1799	47	PA		Heifleigh, Jacob	1811	22	MD
Hayney, John	1815	15	NY		Heimberger, Peter	1803	16	PA
Hays, Abraham	1805	21	NJ		Heiney, John	1816	26	PA
Hays, Edward	1809	25	DC		Heiss, John	1810	27	PA
Hays, James	1823	22 b	DE		Hellet, Nathan	1811	18	NY
Hays, John	1816	30	MD		Hellon, Benjamin	1798	25	MD
Hays, Robert	1811	24	PA		Helmbold, Henry R.	1815	26	PA
Hayward, Alexander	1811	23	SC		Helmbold, Jacob	1809	16	PA
Hazard, Alfred	1815	0			Helmbold, Joseph K.	1810	18	PA
Hazard, Edwin	1810	19	NJ		Helms, Aaron	1818	25	PA
Hazard, Henry S.	1811	21	RI		Helms, Job	1819	19	PA
Hazard, Isaac	1815	23 b	DE		Helveston, John	1822	20	PA
Hazard, James	1815	28 y	MD		Hemmings, John	1811	29	PA
Hazard, John	1804	21	DE		Hemminous, Philip	1820	20 b	DE
Hazard, William	1801	22	MA		Hender, James	1822	21	
Hazard, Woolsey	1803	21	PA		Henderson, Alexander	1818	17	PA
Hazel, James	1811	23	MD		Henderson, Christopher Stewart			
Hazel, John	1806	22 c	DE			1817	16	PA
Hazelton, Joseph	1811	12	PA		Henderson, Francis	1799	17	
Hazle, James	1809	23 m	DE		Henderson, Frederick	1822	20 b	DE
Hazlet, Samuel	1798	32	PA		Henderson, George	1807	22	NY
Hazleton, John	1798	19	PA		Henderson, Henry	1810	21 b	MD
Hazzard, Seth	1812	20	DE		Henderson, Henry	1812	00	
Hazzard, Seth	1813	0			Henderson, James	1817	21	VA
Heachman, Gust Davis					Henderson, John L.	1798	20	PA
					Henderson, John	1817	24	NY
	1803	32	PA		Henderson, John	1817	48 b	MA
Heachman, Gust Davis	1803	32	PA		Henderson, Robert H.	1817	22	PA
Head, James	1804	22	NY		Henderson, Thomas	1796	28	GA
Headman, Gustavus	1806	0			Henderson, William	1804	21	PA
Headman, Simon M.	1819	43	MD		Henderson, William	1806	22	PA
Heard, Thomas	1805	20	NJ		Henderson, William	1809	0	
Heard, Thomas	1809	0			Hendfield, John Henry	1803	29	Prussia
Heartman, Charles Henry					Hendfield, John Henry	1803	0	Prussia
	1805	45	MA		Hendley, Elias	1819	52	MA
Heath, Teakle	1818	18	VA		Hendrick, Josiah	1798	21	MA
Heatney, Zadock	1815	24 b	VA		Hendricks, John	1817	39	Holland
Heavlo, John	1809	21	DE		Hendricks, William	1806	25	PA
Heavrien, William	1811	20	DE		Hendricks, William	1815	22	PA
Heazell, Daniel	1810	16	MD		Hendricks, William	1817	23	PA
Heazell, Daniel	1810	0			Hendrickson, John	1809	25	MD
Hebbard, Seth	1806	49	CT		Hendrickson, Jonas	1809	19	NJ
Hebden, John	1822	21	NY		Hendrickson, William	1804	20	NC
Hedden, George	1821	16	NJ		Hendrix, John	1816	22 b	NY

Hendy, William	1803	29	none given
Hendy, William	1805	0	
Henkel, Frederick	1809	19	PA
Henn, Frederick Christian			
	1810	19	MD
Henn, Frederick C.	1811	00	
Hennessy, John	1809	20 m	PA
Hennessy, John	1810	0	
Henry, Charles	1822	20 y	NJ
Henry, Daniel	1811	00	
Henry, Francis	1808	22 y	NY
Henry, George	1821	38	PA
Henry, Isaac	1822	21	PA
Henry, James	1805	23	DE
Henry, James	1805	30	PA
Henry, Jeremiah	1818	22 b	NY
Henry, John B.	1804	0	PA
Henry, John	1810	19	MD
Henry, John	1811	21	MD
Henry, John	1815	30	DE
Henry, Joseph	1815	22	MS
Henry, Peter	1812	51 b	LA
Henry, Robert	1810	28	DE
Henry, Thomas	1809	21 y	MD
Henry, Timothy	1823	21	MA
Henry, Volsey	1819	20	PA
Henry, William	1815	22 b	MD
Henry, William	1823	19 b	PA
Hensel, John	1813	26	PA
Hensey, Samuel	1809	23 c	DE
Henshaw, George	1809	27	MA
Hepburn, Robert	1812	26	VA
Heppard, William	1815	20	NJ
Hera, John	1809	21	PA
Herbert, William	1798	22	MD
Herd, William	1805	21 y	PA
Herdingbaugh, Jacob	1812	22	PA
Heritage, Samuel	1799	16	NJ
Herman, John	1809	20	PA
Herny, Francis	1808	0	
Herrenden, John	1812	25	MA
Herring, Benjamin	1823	29 y	VA
Herring, Thomas	1815	22	MD
Herrington, Ezekiah	1818	26 b	DE
Herrington, Nathaniel	1805	21	DE
Herron, Amos	1823	28	MA
Herron, Thomas	1810	26	NY
Herse, Michael	1820	12	PA
Herse, Michael	1821	30	PA
Hersey, Seth Stowers	1812	22	MA
Hersh, Philip	1810	26	PA
Hess, William	1817	38	PA

Heston, Daniel	1822	27	ME
Hesy, Robert	1809	26	PA
Hettrick, James	1822	16	NJ
Heuisler, John A.	1815	19	MD
Hewan, John	1810	54 c	MD
Hewes, James	1812	23	PA
Hewetson, Robert	1811	26	NY
Hewit, Aaron, Jr.	1821	24	NJ
Hewitt, Robert	1819	47	none given
Hewitt, Shamgar, Jr.	1810	21	NJ
Hewitts, William	1810	21	DE
Hewland, John	1810	22	PA
Hewlet, Cesar	1807	30 b	PA
Heyberger, John	1823	23	PA
Heydenrick, Frederick	1809	23	PA
Heyland, John	1819	25 y	PA
Heylin, Lucius Carter	1815	15	PA
Heysham, Hamilton	1818	14	PA
Hibbs, Abner	1811	20	PA
Hick, James	1811	00	
Hickey, Michael	1801	23	PA
Hicklin, James	1815	24 b	PA
Hickman, Daniel	1804	25	PA
Hickman, Joshua	1809	18	MD
Hickman, Nathaniel	1823	22	DE
Hickman, Return B.	1819	15	NJ
Hicks, Benjamin	1818	31	MA
Hicks, George	1806	22	MA
Hicks, John C.	1811	25	CT
Hicks, Richard	1801	24	PA
Hicks, Thomas	1816	29 m	MD
Hicks, William	1812	21	PA
Hide, Richard	1809	28 y	DE
Hide, Temple	1805	38	MA
Higbie, Joseph S.	1814	17	NJ
Higby, James L.	1823	23	MA
Higdon, James	1812	28	PA
Higgins, Jacob	1804	12	PA
Higgins, Jonathan	1822	21	ME
Higgins, Thomas	1805	26	MD
Higgins, William, Jr.	1805	22	CT
Higgins, William	1806	37	NH
Hight, Joseph	1820	26	DE
Hight, Thomas	1803	27	MA
Hilbourn, Charles	1808	36	
Hiler, George	1817	28	MA
Hill, Adam	1809	26 b	MA
Hill, Anthony	1817	21 b	VA
Hill, Arteman	1817	25	MA
Hill, Arthur	1809	24	DE
Hill, George	1803	22 b	MD
Hill, George	1808	27 b	MD

Hill, Isaac	1806	26		MA
Hill, Jacob	1811	26 b		PA
Hill, Jacob	1822	40 b		MD
Hill, John	1807	23 b		PA
Hill, John Truman	1807	24		NY
Hill, John	1808	32		PA
Hill, John	1809	19		MA
Hill, John	1812	21 m		PA
Hill, Joshua William	1801	26		DE
Hill, Joshua	1815	28 y		MD
Hill, Reilly	1815	19		DE
Hill, Richard	1811	36 y		VA
Hill, Richard F.	1821	21 b		PA
Hill, Robert	1815	29		GA
Hill, Thomas	1806	29 b		MD
Hill, Thomas	1809	15		PA
Hill, Thomas	1816	20 y		VA
Hill, Thomas	1818	38		VA
Hill, William	1804	23 m		MD
Hill, William Fenly	1807	26		SC
Hill, William	1807	22 b		NY
Hill, William F.	1811	00		
Hill, William	1811	23		PA
Hill, William	1812	00		
Hill, William	1815	24		DE
Hillard, Nathaniel Green				
	1798	14		RI
Hillers, Hillert	1811	48		Germany
Hillman, David	1805	23		NJ
Hillman, Eliakein	1822	31		MD
Hillman, Thomas	1823	22		PA
Hills, John	1809	25		PA
Hills, John Samuel	1823	16		PA
Hillyard, William	1811	22		PA
Hilton, James	1815	15 y		DE
Hilton, James	1817	19 y		DE
Hilton, William	1805	22		NY
Himes, Martin	1815	24		PA
Himes, Martin	1817	18		GA
Hinar, George	1811	19		MD
Hindman, Alfred Galbrath				
	1820	17		PA
Hine, Martin	1803	27		PA
Hiney, David	1810	22		PA
Hinkle, John	1804	21		PA
Hinkley, Jacob B.	1822	27		ME
Hinkly, Jeremiah	1807	29		MA
Hinsdale, Charles	1811	24		CT
Hinsey, John	1807	21		DE
Hinsey, John	1815	26		DE
Hinson, Stanley	1798	17		MD
Hinson, Thomas	1807	17		SC

Hirst, Wm.	1812	00		NJ
Hirth, MD, Stubbins	1804	22		NJ
Hitchingham, Thomas	1817	22		VT
Hitchman, Solomon	1804	18		MA
Hith, James	1821	21 s		MD
Hizer, William	1804	22		PA
Hobday, Charles	1815	21		VA
Hobson, Jeremiah	1813	22		NY
Hockaday, John	1815	21		NY
Hocker, Leonard	1815	23		PA
Hockley, Isaac	1804	22 b		VA
Hodgdon, Asa T.	1818	16		NH
Hodgdon, Daniel	1801	21		NH
Hodgdon, John	1810	22		NY
Hodge, John	1810	18 b		NJ
Hodge, Rufus	1818	25		MA
Hodge, William	1810	32		GA
Hodgkins, Philip	1822	34		ME
Hodgkinson, Francis Hopkinson				
	1807	14		NJ
Hodgkinson, Nathan	1819	22		NJ
Hoeckley, Frederick L	1818	21		PA
Hoey, Nicholas	1810	23		NY
Hoff, Samuel	1815	28		NY
Hoffman, Francis	1811	17		NJ
Hoffman, George	1818	17		PA
Hoffman, John	1806	21		PA
Hoffman, John	1807	18		PA
Hoffman, Nicholas, Jr.	1809	18		NY
Hoffman, Samuel	1822	38		Pa
Hoffner, Daniel J.	1815	0		
Hoffner, Richard	1817	22		PA
Hofman, Jacob	1809	36		PA
Hofman, John	1806	26		NY
Hofner, Daniel James	1809	15		PA
Hofton, John	1823	35		NJ
Hogan, Denis M.	1799	0		
Hoge, Ezekiel	1798	0		NY
Hogerbets, John	1808	21		PA
Hogg, James	1811	30		NY
Holahan, John	1823	21		PA
Holand, Joseph	1801	30		DE
Holbrook, Benjamin	1809	29		none given
Holbrook, David	1821	37		MA
Holbrook, Sumner	1817	42		MA
Holcombe, James G.	1820	18		GA
Holden, David	1806	20		MA
Holden, James	1809	21		MD
Holden, James	1815	23		DE
Holden, Jeremiah	1806	19		NJ
Holden, Jeremiah	1807			
Holden, Randal	1798	17		

Holden, Thomas	1797	19	NC
Holden, William	1806	12	PA
Holden, William	1823	47	NY
Holderson, Jeremiah	1810	18	ME
Holdsworth, Thomas	1823	20	NY
Holgen, Timothy	1806	0	MD
Holiday, Jeremiah	1823	33	MA
Holland, James T.	1809	23	PA
Holland, James M.	1823	25	MD
Holland, John	1811	22	DE
Holland, John	1821	21	DE
Holland, Joseph	1823	21 b	PA
Holland, Richard	1809	21	MD
Holland, Saunders	1822	22 b	DE
Holland, William	1801	21	VA
Holleger, George	1823	20	DE
Hollemstick, Andrew	1809	22	PA
Hollen, Sacker	1806	26 b	DE
Hollingsworth, John	1805	24	PA
Hollingsworth, John	1806	0	
Hollins, Jacob	1808	28	PA
Hollinshead, Samuel How			
	1810	23	NJ
Hollon, Issac	1810	20	MD
Holly, Willliam	1810	25	MA
Holmes, Charles	1818	22	NJ
Holmes, James	1814	35	PA
Holmes, James	1820	27	GA
Holmes, Jeremiah	1806	0	
Holmes, Jeremiah	1806	24	ME
Holmes, John	1809	27	PA
Holmes, John H.	1822	20	NY
Holmes, John	1823	38 y	SC
Holmes, Joseph	1804	0	VA
Holmes, William F.	1809	23	RI
Holmes, William	1810	25	PA
Holms, James	1811	24 b	NJ
Holms, John W.	1817	29	NY
Holster, Charles	1801	25	MD
Holt, Robert	1811	24	CT
Holt, William	1819	22	PA
Homan, Daniel	1805	17	PA
Homes, Henry	1807	35 b	NY
Homes, Joseph	1812	19 b	NJ
Hommedia, Richard L.	1823	24	NY
Hommell, Christopher	1810	40	SC
Hood, Albert	1810	16	PA
Hood, Geo. P.	1817	18	PA
Hood, Joseph	1801	16	PA
Hood, Robert	1801	28 b	DE
Hood, Samuel	1798	29	CT
Hoofnagle, Peter	1811	19	MD

Hook, John	1810	21	DE
Hook, William, Jr.	1821	15	PA
Hooker, Thomas	1809	21	PA
Hooper, Roger	1810	21	MD
Hooper, Rutis	1806	13	PA
Hoover, George	1810	19	NJ
Hoover, Jacob	1804	24	PA
Hoover, Jacob	1815	15	PA
Hoover, John	1803	34	DE
Hoover, William	1801	25	PA
Hope, James	1800	20	PA
Hopkins, Cornelius	1815	26	MD
Hopkins, Edmond	1811	30	MA
Hopkins, Jacob	1815	20	DE
Hopkins, James	1815	25	MA
Hopkins, John	1811	23	MD
Hopkins, John	1822	24 y	PA
Hopkins, Reuben	1817	16	MA
Hopkins, Reuben	1819	20	MA
Hopkins, Robert	1814	36	MD
Hopkins, Samuel	1810	29	MA
Hopkins, Thomas	1819	30	PA
Hoppel, Jr., George	1814	21	PA
Hopper, William	1817	24	NY
Horder, William	1807	33	NJ
Horgen, Timothy	1805	32	MD
Horn, Gerret	1818	33	NY
Horn, Peter	1817	21	PA
Horne, Jonathan	1809	16	VA
Horner, John	1806	22	NJ
Horner, William	1817	30	NJ
Hornor, William	1809	20	NJ
Hornsby, Asa	1811	19	VA
Horsey, Thomas W.	1809	24	MA
Horstman, Davis	1816	24	MD
Hort, Robert	1804	29 b	NY
Horton, David	1820	41	NJ
Horton, William	1817	24	PA
Hoskin, Roberet	1804	28	
Hoskins, Joshua	1820	30	MA
Hotz, Peter	1814	15	PA
Houard, Adolphus	1823	17	PA
Hough, Constant	1795	14	PA
Hough, Constant,Jr	1822	16	PA
Houlding, James	1812	00	
SPC taken by Capt. James Townsend, British			
ship Aolus, when lately captured in ship Mechanic			
Houlding, John	1810	31	PA
Hourie, Hugh	1800	23	PA
House, Peter	1813	19	PA

69

House, Stephen	1816	20	PA		Hoxse, Joseph S.	1810	23	RI
Houseman, Henry	1804	24	PA		Hoy, Cornelius	1804	23	PA
Houseman, John	1823	18	PA		Hoyle, Cornelius	1811	00	
Houston, Lucius	1815	23	DE		Hoyt, Divid	1822	31	MA
Houston, Perry L.	1809	22 b	DE		Hoyt, Enos	1803	36	CT
Hovey, Joseph	1819	38	MA		Hubbard, John	1804	26	NJ
Hovey, William	1810	25	MA		Hubbard, John	1816	44 b	VA
Hovington, William	1815	27 b	DE		Hubbard, John	1822	38	MD
How, John	1803	18	MA		Hubbart, William	1804	23	PA
Howard, Amos	1803	21 b	NY		Hubbell, William	1813	23	CT
Howard, Caleb N.	1811	23	PA		Hubbs, Daniel Gage	1812	16	MA
Howard, James	1808	27	MD		Huber, Adam	1804	23	PA
Howard, James	1815	32	MA		Hubert, William	1799	23	MD
Howard, James	1815	30 b	RI		Huckel, Jacob	1815	14	PA
Howard, John	1798	23	MD		Huddell, Samuel	1796	0	PA
Howard, John	1806	23	MD		Huddle, Joseph	1817	14	PA
Howard, John	1807				Huddle, Samuel	1795	24	PA
Howard, John	1810	22	DE		Hudibras, Edward	1817	25 b	NJ
Howard, John	1815	27	RI		Hudner, Samuel	1805	24	PA
Howard, John	1818	47 y	MD		Hudner, Samuel	1819	39	PA
Howard, Peter	1815	21	RI		Hudson, Daniel	1820	20	MA
Howard, Peter	1816	22 b	MA		Hudson, Evans	1815	29	MD
Howard, Richard	1817	26		Ireland	Hudson, James	1807	21	NY
Howard, Robert	1798	0	MA		Hudson, John	1804	20	SC
Howard, Robert	1821	22 b	DE		Hudson, John	1805	22	NY
Howard, Robert	1822	40 b	NY		Hudson, John	1809	26	NY
Howard, Robert	1822	23 b	DE		Hudson, William	1807		
Howard, Samuel	1810	25 b	DE		Hudson, William	1807	28	PA
Howard, Samuel	1821	23	MA		Hudson, William	1812	21	MD
Howard, William	1805	19	PA		Huel, William	1798	23	VA
Howard, William	1806	0			Huff, Isaac	1823	33	NJ
Howe, Phineas	1817	28 y	MA		Huff, John	1822	24	PA
Howell, Benjamin	1815	25 b	MD		Hufman, William	1819	36	MA
Howell, Franklin	1822	23 m	VA		Hugg, Charles W.	1817	20	NJ
Howell, Jacob S.	1811	15	PA		Hugg, Jacob	1818	19	MD
Howell, James	1809	23	DE		Hugg, Levy	1807	37	MD
Howell, John	1809	21	NJ		Hugg, William	1806	29	NJ
Howell, John	1810	21	PA		Hugg, William E.	1821	19	NJ
Howell, John	1815	0			Huggens, Robert	1810	19 y	DE
Howell, Michael	1818	18 c	PA		Huggins, John	1815	19 y	DE
Howell, Paschale	1807	18	NJ		Huggins, Samuel	1810	23	DE
Howell, Paschall	1809	0			Hughes, Benjamin	1823	19	DE
Howell, Richard	1798	36	PA		Hughes, Charles L.	1809	20	PA
Howell, Samuel	1818	26	MD		Hughes, Constant	1817	36	NJ
Howes, Daniel	1822	17	MA		Hughes, Humphrey	1805	21	NJ
Howes, Jeremiah	1822	21	MA		Hughes, Humphrey	1806	0	
Howland, Daniel	1815	35	MA		Hughes, James	1810	23	NJ
Howland, David	1803	24	MA		Hughes, James	1815	26	LA
Howland, Henry	1816	18	PA		Hughes, James	1823	33	none given
Howland, Isaac Jr. L.	1819	23	PA		Hughes, John	1803	18	VA
Howland, James.3rd	1801	19	MA		Hughes, John	1805	16	DE
Howley, Thomas	1823	28	MA		Hughes, John	1806	21	CT

Name	Year	Age	State
Hughes, John	1807		DE
Hughes, John E.	1810	21	VA
Hughes, Joseph	1817	29	MA
Hughes, Samuel	1806	0	
Hughes, Thomas	1815	42	Ireland
American prisoner of war at Dartmour Prison			
Hughes, William	1806	18	NJ
Hughes, William	1819	35	SC
Hughey, John	1820	37	PA
Hulins, Laurence	1811	00	
Hulins, Lawrence	1809	39	PA
Hull, Abraham H.	1818	25	CT
Hull, Daniel	1815	22	CT
Hull, James	1821	38 b	DE
Hull, John	1813	16	PA
Hull, William	1815	25	RI
Hull, William	1816	31	NY
Hulse, Ulysses	1823	24	NY
Hulson, Allen	1798	21	RI
Humell, John	1807	24	LA
Humpatch, John	1806	16	MA
Humphreys, Daniel	1810	0	
Humphreys, Daniel	1811	00	
Humphreys, Daniel	1819	23	PA
Humphreys, James	1812	28	PA
Humphreys, Lodowick Spogell			
	1815	20	PA
Humphreys, Tobias	1811	21 b	NJ
Humphreys, William	1811	19 c	PA
Humphries, William	1815	17	PA
Hunecker, Anthony	1810	0	
Hungary, William	1814	17	NJ
Hungeleer, Alexander	1807	35	PA
Hungerford, James	1809	19	NJ
Hungerford, John	1809	22	PA
Hungerford, Tlavel	1809	27	CT
Hunicker, Anthony	1810	33	PA
Hunt, Charles	1822	26 y	PA
Hunt, David	1803	19	MA
Hunt, David	1804	0	MA
Hunt, David	1804	0	
Hunt, Edward P.	1815	26	MA
Hunt, James P.	1803	25	NJ
Hunt, John	1805	22	PA
Hunt, John	1809	36	NJ
Hunt, John, Jr.	1817	21	NJ
Hunt, Samuel	1820	27	RI
Hunt, Sylvester	1799	17	
Hunt, Theodore	1807	26	NJ
Hunt, Thomas	1799	0	NY
Hunt, William	1796	0	MA
Hunter, Charles	1812	21	NJ
Hunter, Charles	1815	23	NJ
Hunter, Francis	1814	34	PA
Hunter, George	1807	21	MD
Hunter, George	1807	23	NH
Hunter, Jacob	1798	19 y	NC
Hunter, James	1805	17	NY
Hunter, James	1811	26	MA
Hunter, James	1811	21	NJ
Hunter, John L.	1816	0	PA
Hunter, Nathaniel E.	1818	31	RI
Hunter, William	1806	45	NJ
Hunter, William M.	1810	19	PA
Hunter, William	1821	24	NY
Huntress, Richard	1806	21	NH
Hurd, Abel	1810	0	
Hurd, Able	1810	31	MA
Hurd, Jacob	1819	24	MA
Hurd, William	1806	17	NY
Hurley, Isaac	1806	22	NJ
Hurley, Isaac	1810	0	
Hurley, Joseph R.	1815	15	PA
Hurley, Thomas	1800	19	PA
Hurn, Edward	1821	38	MD
Hurry, John	1822	23	PA
Hurry, Samuel	1820	18	PA
Hurst, Henry	1820	20	PA
Hurst, Isaac	1815	20	NJ
Hurst, Wm.	1811	26	NJ
Huse, Ebenezer	1804	31	MA
Huse, John	1807	23	CT
Huston, John	1821	40	PA
Huston, Samuel	1807	20	DE
Huston, William	1811	38	Ireland
Hutcheson, Thomas	1801	23	VA
Hutchfords, Charles	1822	28	ME
Hutchings, William	1803	22	SC
Hutchings, William	1823	19	NH
Hutchins, James L.	1814	22	NJ
Hutchins, James W.	1821	25	NH
Hutchins, Samuel H.	1818	21	PA
Hutchinson, Daniel	1811	32	MA
Hutchinson, Ephiraim	1810	21	PA
Hutchinson, Harry	1817	31 b	NY
Hutchinson, Henry	1815	20	DE
Hutchinson, John	1810	24	SC
Hutchiny, Charles	1807	23	NY
Hutson, George	1800	19	PA
Hutson, William	1818	26	NC
Hutt, James	1806	20 m	DE
Hutt, James	1807		

Hutton, Benjamin	1811	31	NJ
Hutton, Charles	1817	25 b	PA
Hutton, James	1823	41	MD
Huver, Jacob	1813	23	PA
Hyatt, James	1812	00	
Hyatt, William	1822	31	MD
Hyberg, Nicholas	1796	0	Denmark
Hybirger, Benjamin	1813	16	PA
Hyde, John	1818	45	RI
Hyett, James	1805	21 y	DE
Hyett, James	1805	0	
Hyitt, Samuel	1804	21	NY
Hyitt, Samuel	1804	21	NY
Hymand, Abraham	1809	27	NY
Hyneman, George	1803	21	PA
Hynson, Henry	1814	17	MD
Hynson, Joseph	1821	31 b	MD
Hysylbaugh, John	1812	22	PA
Ihrie, George	1812	21	PA
Iles, Jeremiah	1806	20	MA
Ilsley, Stephen	1822	22	MA
Imlay, Joseph	1798	27	NJ
Imlay, Joseph	1805	27 m	NJ
Imthurn, Barnard	1815	26	Switzerland
Ince, James	1798	55	PA
Incell, Artist	1815	25 l	NJ
native American			
Ingall, Thomas	1798	30	Gr.Br.
Ingersoll, William	1819	22	MA
Ingerson, Jacob	1804	23	NJ
Ingram, Edward	1805	24	PA
Ingram, Edward	1813	20 m	RI
Ingrum, Samuel	1804	19	DE
Innes, John	1817	23 b	NJ
Innis, Francis	1811	29	LA
Inskife, Issac	1822	21 b	PA
Ireland, Daniel	1820	21	NJ
Ireland, Henry	1812	22	PA
Ireland, Jacob	1811	24	NY
Ireland, James	1810	28	NY
Irons, Aron	1810	26	DE
Irons, John	1815	22	DE
Irons, Oliver	1804	21 b	DE
Irons, Oliver	1807		
Irons, William	1810	19	DE
Irvin, William	1819	22 b	PA

Irvine, William Nisbet 1810 35   none given
naturalized 8 Aug 1805, Chambersburg, Franklin
County, PA

Irving, David	1809	24	PA
Irving, William	1807	22	MA
Irwin, David	1809	24	DE
Irwin, George	1807	14	PA
Irwin, Magnus	1810	14	PA
Irwin, Mangus	1812	00	
Irwin, Robert	1810	29 b	PA
Irwin, William	1811	31	RI
Isarael, Jacob	1800	21	PA
Isbourn, John	1807	15	PA
Isdel, Alexander	1810	0	
Isdell, Alexander	1804	20	NJ
Isdell, Alexander	1804	20	NJ
Isgrig, Robert	1815	22	MD
Israel, George L.	1811	16	DE
Israel, John	1819	19	PA
Israel, Nathaniel	1805	25	DE
Israel, Nathaniel	1807		
Ives, Thomas	1806	23	NC
Ivey, John	1823	21	NC
Ivins, Ezekiel	1804	23	NJ
Ivins, Ezekiel	1804	23	NJ
Ivins, Izekiel	1805	23	NJ
Izatt, James	1798	31	PA
Iznard, John	1810	27	VA
Jack, Thomas	1809	38 b	CT
Jackaway, Samuel	1823	17	PA
Jackins, John	1821	21	ME
Jackson, Bemey	1807		NC
Jackson, Benjamin	1813	23	CT
Jackson, Berry	1821	25 c	VA
Jackson, Bomby	1804	25 b	NJ
Jackson, Clement	1811	23	DE
Jackson, Daniel	1818	34 b	DE
Jackson, David	1818	22 b	NY
Jackson, Demcy	1807	21	NC
Jackson, Elisha	1807	31	NC
Jackson, Emanuel	1820	20 b	DE
Jackson, Francis	1819	30 y	DE
Jackson, Gabriel	1811	24 b	DE
Jackson, George	1801	23	CT
Jackson, George	1809	22	MD
Jackson, George	1810	33 b	VA
Jackson, George	1812	25 b	DE
Jackson, George	1823	31	MD
Jackson, Henry	1816	23	NY
Jackson, Isaac	1804	25 b	MD
Jackson, Jacob	1798	19 b	PA

Jackson, Jacob Morton
                    1807 16   PA
Jackson, Jacob Lambert
                    1811 21 b CT

Jackson, James	1804	22 b	DE

bound servant to Mathew Pearce, Phila. merchant.
attachment: 1 May 1810 this day produced proof
of having obtained his freedom

Jackson, James	1809	28	MA
Jackson, James	1811	24	NY
Jackson, James	1814	26 y	VA
Jackson, James	1819	19	ME
Jackson, James	1819	21	PA
Jackson, James	1820	15 y	PA
Jackson, James	1820	16 y	PA
Jackson, James	1823	22 y	PA
Jackson, John	1801	21	RI
Jackson, John	1806	21 b	NY
Jackson, John	1807	37 b	MA
Jackson, John	1807	21 b	PA
Jackson, John	1807	35 b	NJ
Jackson, John	1808	0	MA
Jackson, John	1809	29 b	CT
Jackson, John	1809	0	MA
Jackson, John	1809	23	PA
Jackson, John	1811	20 c	MD
Jackson, John	1812	18	MD
Jackson, John	1819	31 b	NY
Jackson, John	1821	23	MA
Jackson, John	1821	26	NY
Jackson, John	1822	27 s	MD
Jackson, Joseph	1804	19 b	MD
Jackson, Joseph	1811	00	MD
Jackson, Joseph	1818	22	PA
Jackson, Joseph	1822	25 y	RI
Jackson, Jr., Jacob	1814	22 b	NY
Jackson, Moses	1810	24 b	VA
Jackson, Moses	1811	19 b	MD
Jackson, Obadiah	1821	21 y	NY
Jackson, Peter	1803	30 b	St Croix
Jackson, Peter	1823	21 y	DE
Jackson, Philip	1822	30 b	MD
Jackson, Richard	1798	25	MA
Jackson, Robert	1811	22	MA
Jackson, Robert	1812	00	
Jackson, Samuel	1804	20 b	MA
Jackson, Samuel	1804	23 b	DE
Jackson, Samuel	1807	25 b	MD
Jackson, Samuel	1810	29 b	VA
Jackson, Shadrick	1810	19 b	MD
Jackson, Thomas	1808	27	NY
Jackson, Thomas	1810	23 y	NJ
Jackson, Thomas	1811	37	RI
Jackson, Thomas	1811	29 b	NY
Jackson, Thomas	1815	28 b	MA

Jackson, Thomas	1823	21 s	NY
Jackson, Thomas	1823	22 y	MD
Jackson, William	1804	28 b	NY
Jackson, William	1804	21 b	NY
Jackson, William	1804	22 b	NY
Jackson, William	1807	22 b	NY
Jackson, William	1809	23	PA
Jackson, William	1809	23	DE
Jackson, William	1811	25 b	MD
Jackson, William	1815	24 y	MD
Jackson, William	1816	21 b	NY
Jackson, William	1819	23 y	MD
Jackson, William	1823	30	MA
Jackson, Wm.	1809	23 m	MA
Jackson, Wm.	1818	26	PA

born Elfriths Alley No. 27 between Arch & Race

Jackston, Arthor	1809	25	NJ
Jacobs, Henry	1822	29 s	DE
Jacobs, James	1823	23	MD
Jacobs, Jesse	1823	26 b	PA
Jacobs, Richard	1805	22	NC
Jacobs, Richard	1805	22	NC
Jacobs, Rus	1815	28 b	CT
Jacobson, Matthias	1795	0	
Jafharson, Thomas	1808	24	PA
James, Aaron	1798	25 b	RI
James, Aron	1797	0	RI
James, Ferman	1821	25 m	NJ
James, Isaac	1815	19	RI
James, John	1809	26 y	LA
James, John	1814	0	
James, John	1816	24	NY
James, John	1820	21 b	PA
James, John	1822	36	PA
James, Thomas C.	1806	17	NJ
James, Thomas Johnson			
	1817	16 b	PA
James, William	1810	21 y	NY
James, William	1811	22 y	NY
James, William	1815	0	
James, William	1822	24	NY
Jameson, John	1812	26	MD
Jameson, Matthew	1807	25	PA
Jameson, Stephen	1804	21	PA
Jameson, Thomas	1796	0	VA
Jameson, William	1809	22	NJ
Jamison, Alexander	1823	18	PA
Janeau, Armon	1815	17	PA
Jansen, Boote	1806	20	PA
Janson, Peter	1809	29	PA

January, David	1806	39	DE
January, William	1819	21	PA
Jarman, John	1810	38	NJ
Jarman, Samuel E.	1823	20	PA
Jarvis, John	1815	19 b	NY
Jarvis, William	1817	22	MD
Jasper, Benjamin	1810	37 b	MD
Jasson, Francous	1807	22	MS
Javet, George	1805	22	PA
Jaxon, James	1815	19 b	NY
Jefferis, James	1823	18	DE
Jefferis, Joseph	1809	21	PA
Jefferis, Samuel	1821	23	DE
Jefferis, William	1818	23	DE
Jeffers, Isaac	1804	25 b	MD
Jefferson, Richard	1805	24	SC
Jefferson, Richard	1805	24	SC
Jeffery, John	1820	16 b	PA
Jeffery, Samuel	1818	20	DE
Jefferys, Jacob	1805	25	PA
Jeffrey, John	1823	21	NY
Jeffries, Robert	1816	26	VA
Jeffris, Taylor	1810	25	DE
Jematrice, John	1809	27 b	SC
Jenings, Horatio	1807	24	MD
Jenkens, Philip	1798	21 b	PA
Jenkins, Charles	1815	20	MA
Jenkins, Frederick	1816	36	PA
Jenkins, Homer	1810	17 b	NJ
Jenkins, Jacob	1809	27 b	PA
Jenkins, James	1798	44 b	PA
Jenkins, James	1813	22	PA
Jenkins, Peter	1811	26	PA
Jenkins, Peter	1812	00	
Jenkins, Peter	1815	0	
Jenkins, Philip	1806	27 b	PA
Jenkins, Philip	1806	0	
Jenkins, William	1801	22	PA
Jenks, John	1817	18	MA
Jennings, Alpha	1811	21	CT
Jerkins, Thomas	1798	19	VA
Jernegan, Benjamin	1823	33	NC
Jerrell, William D.	1816	18	PA
Jerrit, Abraham	1822	32 y	MA
Jess, Jacob	1814	21	NJ
Jesson, William	1815	22	RI
Jester, James	1823	20	DE
Jewell, James B.	1822	19	PA
Jewell, Wilson	1821	21	PA
Jinkens, Thomas	1810	30	PA
Joachim, Antoine	1806	24	LA
Joachim, Antonio	1808	21	MS

Joachim, Joseph	1809	34	LA
Jobson, James	1819	15	PA
John, Dr., Martin	1803	22	DE
Johns, Thomas	1811	22	PA
Johnsen, Henry	1805	23	MD
Johnsen, Samuel	1809	20	NJ
Johnson, Andrew	1803	34	PA
Johnson, Andrew	1805	34	SC
Johnson, Andrew	1810	21	ME
Johnson, Andrew	1818	23	MA

Johnson, Benjamin 1797 0 NJ
apprenticed to John Holland, Greenwich Twp.,
Cumberland County, cooper

Johnson, Benjamin	1809	14	PA
Johnson, Bernard	1809	32	PA
Johnson, Caleb	1817	31	DE
Johnson, Charles	1805	23	PA
Johnson, Charles	1818	25	NJ
Johnson, Charles	1821	19 b	PA
Johnson, Charles	1822	23 b	NY
Johnson, Cyrus	1812	30 b	VA
Johnson, David	1805	20	NJ
Johnson, Edward	1804	0	
Johnson, Edward	1810	0	
Johnson, Edward	1812	22 b	MD
Johnson, Edward	1812	55	none given
Johnson, Edward	1816	26 b	NY
Johnson, Elias	1821	28	none given
Johnson, Frederick	1804	19	PA
Johnson, Frederick	1804	26 b	NY
Johnson, Frederick	1813	33	none given
Johnson, George	1796	37	
Johnson, Gershom	1807	20	NY
Johnson, Henry	1810	21	PA
Johnson, Henry	1812	24 b	DE
Johnson, Henry	1812	16 b	MA
Johnson, Isaac	1809	23 b	MD
Johnson, Isaac	1812	19	NJ
Johnson, Isaac	1823	35 b	MD
Johnson, Jacob	1817	25	MA
Johnson, James	1801	43	PA
Johnson, James	1801	24	PA
Johnson, James	1804	30 c	MA
Johnson, James	1805	46	MD
Johnson, James	1805	0	PA
Johnson, James	1809	23	NJ
Johnson, James	1810	23	NJ
Johnson, James	1810	21	MD
Johnson, James	1811	18	MA
Johnson, James	1812	26 b	NJ

Johnson, James	1813	14	PA
Johnson, James	1814	0	
Johnson, James	1815	23 m	VA
Johnson, James T.	1815	25	PA
Johnson, James	1816	19	PA
Johnson, James	1820	21	PA
Johnson, James	1821	24	ME
Johnson, James	1823	23	DE
Johnson, Jesse	1809	20	PA
Johnson, Jesse	1815	39	PA
Johnson, Joel	1823	30	VT
Johnson, John	1800	32 b	DE
Johnson, John	1800	19	PA
Johnson, John	1801	28 m	DE
Johnson, John	1801	33 b	DE
Johnson, John	1801	19	PA
Johnson, John	1804	23	PA
Johnson, John	1804	18	DE
Johnson, John	1806	30 b	SC
Johnson, John	1806	25 b	DE
Johnson, John	1807	20	NJ
Johnson, John	1807	21	PA
Johnson, John	1807	17	PA
Johnson, John	1807	31	PA
Johnson, John	1809	16 m	DE
Johnson, John	1809	41 b	MD
Johnson, John	1809	38	LA
Johnson, John	1810	13	PA
Johnson, John	1810	16	DE
Johnson, John	1812	21	PA
Johnson, John	1815	28	MD
Johnson, John	1815	16	PA
Johnson, John	1816	22	PA
Johnson, John	1820	40	none given
Johnson, John	1821	36	PA
Johnson, John	1821	25	DE
Johnson, Joseph	1805	23	CT
Johnson, Joseph	1805	24	NJ
Johnson, Joseph	1807		
Johnson, Joseph	1810	0	
Johnson, Joseph	1816	25 b	PA
Johnson, Lewis	1810	19 b	PA
Johnson, Lewis	1812	00	
Johnson, Nels	1805	29	NY
Johnson, Nels	1810	34	Sweden
Johnson, Nicholas	1801	25	PA
Johnson, Nicholas	1809	32	none given
Johnson, Peter	0000	24 b	NY
Johnson, Peter	0000	24	NY
Johnson, Peter	1804	28 m	NY
Johnson, Peter	1804	29	PA
Johnson, Peter	1808	24	PA
Johnson, Peter	1809	22 b	DE
Johnson, Peter	1809	33	NY
Johnson, Peter	1809	28 b	NY
Johnson, Peter	1812	28	MA
Johnson, Peter	1815	27	MA
Johnson, Peter	1815	31	MA
Johnson, Peter	1815	23	NJ
Johnson, Peter	1816	27	PA
Johnson, Peter	1816	39 b	DE
Johnson, Peter	1820	21	NJ
Johnson, Randle	1813	22	PA
Johnson, Rice	1810	23	CT
Johnson, Richard	1822	24 b	MD
Johnson, Robert	1811	24	PA
Johnson, Robert	1812	38 b	VA
Johnson, Robert	1815	31	VA
Johnson, Royal Jasper	1811	24	MA
Johnson, Samuel	1809	0	
Johnson, Samuel	1813	27 c	MD
Johnson, Samuel	1815	37 b	DE
Johnson, Samuel	1819	19	NY
Johnson, Samuel	1822	30 b	NY
Johnson, Samuel A.	1823	31	MA
Johnson, Simon	1812	32	none given
Johnson, Smith	1811	22 b	MD
Johnson, Stephen	1807	17 b	MD
Johnson, Stephen	1821	22 b	DE
Johnson, Thomas	1804	27	NY
Johnson, Thomas	1810	17	PA
Johnson, Thomas	1810	18	CT
Johnson, Thomas	1818	30	NY
Johnson, Thomas	1818	40	MD
Johnson, Thomas W.	1819	23	DE
Johnson, Tully	1806	25	PA
Johnson, Wiliam	1810	0	
Johnson, William	1803	38	PA
Johnson, William	1804	23	NY
Johnson, William	1805	21 b	SC
Johnson, William	1805	20	PA
Johnson, William	1806	22	PA
Johnson, William	1806	0	NY
Johnson, William	1807	18	NY
Johnson, William	1809	0	
Johnson, William	1809	23	PA
Johnson, William	1809	23	NY
Johnson, William	1810	23	VA
Johnson, William	1810	31	LA
Johnson, William	1810	23 b	DE
Johnson, William	1814	0	
Johnson, William	1815	18 y	CT
Johnson, William	1815	0	
Johnson, William	1817	0	

Name	Year	Age	State
Johnson, William	1817	00	xx
Johnson, William	1817	23	MA
Johnson, William	1817	20	CT
Johnson, William	1822	22 b	ME
Johnson, Zenos	1815	33	NJ
Johnsten, Robert	1809	25	PA
Johnston, Andrew	1810	23	NJ
Johnston, Charles	1798	20	PA
Johnston, Charles	1818	18	MA
Johnston, Daniel D.	1818	39 b	VA
Johnston, David	1806	39	NY
Johnston, David	1821	49 b	VA
Johnston, Ezekiel	1804	25	NJ

Johnston, Francis 1815 27 b Africa
free black man who came to America 14 years
ago from Africa

Name	Year	Age	State
Johnston, Fredrick	1805	23 b	NY
Johnston, James C.	1806	11	PA
Johnston, James	1810	27 b	LA
Johnston, James	1811	24 b	MD
Johnston, John	1804	30	PA
Johnston, John Peter	1804	25	PA
Johnston, John	1805	20	NJ
Johnston, John	1807	23 y	PA
Johnston, John	1809	22	NY
Johnston, John	1810	28 b	NY
Johnston, John	1815	22 y	NY
Johnston, John	1815	29 y	SC
Johnston, John	1815	18	NY
Johnston, John	1815	22 b	DE
Johnston, John	1817	14	MA
Johnston, John	1817	27	DE
Johnston, John	1817	43 b	LA
Johnston, John	1819	19	PA
Johnston, John	1822	25 y	NY
Johnston, Michael	1801	21	MA
Johnston, Michael	1804	25	MA
Johnston, Michael	1805	15 m	NJ
Johnston, Michael	1811	25	MA
Johnston, Perry	1806	22 b	MD
Johnston, Peter	1806	25	PA
Johnston, Plumm	1813	23	PA
Johnston, Reuben	1798	28 m	NJ
Johnston, Robert	1810	24	PA
Johnston, Tobias	1811	23 m	PA
Johnston, Tobias	1811	27 y	PA
Johnston, William	1798	26	RI
Johnston, William	1804	21 b	NY
Johnston, William	1805	33 m	VA
Johnston, William	1805	0	

Name	Year	Age	State
Johnston, William	1810	22	MA
Johnston, William	1810	28 b	NY
Johnston, William	1813	16	PA
Johnston, William	1819	23	MD
Johnston, William	1821	28 y	MA
Johnston, William	1821	39 y	PA
Jones, Allen	1818	20	PA
Jones, Andrew	1821	28	PA
Jones, Benjamin Sixley			
	1815	21	PA
Jones, Charles	1811	18	NJ
Jones, Charles	1812	00	
Jones, Charles	1812	32 y	DE
Jones, Charles	1812	00	
Jones, Charles	1812	00	
Jones, Charles	1812	22 b	DE
Jones, Charles	1813	0	
Jones, Charles	1813	0	
Jones, Daniel	1807	22 m	DE
Jones, David	1808	21	VA
Jones, David	1812	23	none given
Jones, David	1813	20	DE
Jones, Ebenezer	1813	21	NY
Jones, Edward	1801	20	SC
Jones, Edward	1822	18	PA
Jones, Elias	1809	15	DE
Jones, Elias	1812	00	DE
Jones, Elijah	1811	20	NJ
Jones, Evans	1809	32 b	VA
Jones, Ezra	1822	32	PA
Jones, Gilbert	1809	16	NJ
Jones, Harbert	1798	32	PA
Jones, Heeler	1810	19 b	MD
Jones, Henry	1815	24	NY
Jones, Henry	1818	24 y	MD
Jones, Henry	1822	19 b	PA
Jones, Humphrey	1804	20	PA
Jones, Isaac	1807	34 b	PA
Jones, Isaac	1809	0 b	PA
Jones, Isaac	1823	19 y	MD
Jones, Israel	1816	21 y	MD
Jones, Jacob	1823	19	DE
Jones, James	1801	21	PA
Jones, James	1801	21	PA
Jones, James	1803	27	PA
Jones, James	1806	38 m	PA
Jones, James	1810	33	PA
Jones, James	1811	00	
Jones, James	1811	23	VA
Jones, James	1811	24	MD
Jones, James	1812	00	
Jones, James	1820	50 b	NY

Name	Year	Age		State
Jones, James	1820	27		PA
Jones, Jasper W.	1821	25		NY
Jones, Jeremiah	1815	15	m	DE
Jones, Jeremiah	1823	21	b	PA
Jones, Joel Dean	1823	15		PA
Jones, John	1798	16		PA
Jones, John	1801	23		PA
Jones, John	1804	28		DE
Jones, John	1804	26		PA
Jones, John	1805	47	b	SC
Jones, John G.	1806	42		CT
Jones, John G.	1806	0		
Jones, John C.	1807	27		PA
Jones, John	1807	23		NY
Jones, John	1808	25		NY
Jones, John	1809	21		MD
Jones, John	1809	22		SC
Jones, John	1810	28	b	VA
Jones, John	1810	0		VA
Jones, John	1810	31	b	PA
Jones, John	1811	38		DE
Jones, John	1812	23	y	MD
Jones, John	1817	22		MA
Jones, John	1819	19	b	PA
Jones, John	1821	50	b	CT
Jones, Joseph	1804	21		PA
Jones, Joseph	1804	23	b	VA
Jones, Joseph	1805	20		NJ
Jones, Joseph	1806	23		PA
Jones, Joseph	1808	23		NJ
Jones, Joseph	1810	26	b	DE
Jones, Joseph	1811	28		PA
Jones, Lewis	1823	34		none given
Jones, Major	1807	27	b	MD
Jones, Major	1821	25		VA
Jones, Matthew	1806	30		MA
Jones, Michael	1811	37		LA
Jones, Nathan H.	1803	31		CT
Jones, Nathan	1818	25	y	SC
Jones, Nathaniel	1807	32	b	SC
Jones, Nathaniel	1812	00		
Jones, Owen Win	1809	0		
Jones, Owin Win	1808	23		MA
Jones, Paul	1809	27	b	SC
Jones, Peter	1815	26		NY
Jones, Peter	1815	34	b	MA
Jones, Peter	1816	27	b	NY
Jones, Richard	1803	25	b	MA
Jones, Richard	1811	24	b	DE
Jones, Richard	1813	25		MD
Jones, Richard	1818	55		MA
Jones, Richard	1822	21		PA
Jones, Robert	1807	16		LA
Jones, Robert	1810	15		PA
Jones, Robert F.	1812	26		NJ
Jones, Robert	1813	0		
Jones, Robert	1813	0		
Jones, Robert	1819	20		MA
Jones, Rowland	1811	46		MA
Jones, Samuel	1803	33	b	PA
Jones, Samuel	1804	22		NJ
Jones, Samuel	1805	0		
Jones, Samuel	1805	19		MD
Jones, Samuel	1810	35		NJ
Jones, Samuel	1811	26	b	DE
Jones, Samuel	1811	00		
Jones, Samuel S.	1814	18		PA
Jones, Samuel	1817	40	b	NY
Jones, Simon	1804	40	b	MD
Jones, Simon	1806	0		
Jones, Solomon	1810	39	y	PA
Jones, Thomas	1801	22		MD
Jones, Thomas Miller	1801	25		NC
Jones, Thomas	1805	26		MS
Jones, Thomas	1806	0		
Jones, Thomas	1806	0		
Jones, Thomas	1806	32		NJ
Jones, Thomas	1807	26		MA
Jones, Thomas	1807	22		PA
Jones, Thomas	1807	29		PA
Jones, Thomas	1809	18		MD
Jones, Thomas	1809	35	b	PA
Jones, Thomas	1810	17		PA
Jones, Thomas	1811	00		
Jones, Thomas	1811	00		
Jones, Thomas	1815	22	y	MD
Jones, Thomas	1823	32	s	MA
Jones, Uriah	1807	18		PA
Jones, William	1799	23		PA
Jones, William	1801	45		PA
Jones, William	1807	20		PA
Jones, William	1809	19		PA
Jones, William	1809	21		DE
Jones, William	1809	35		NY
Jones, William Nelson	1810	29	b	MD
Jones, William	1811	31		MD
Jones, William	1812	23		PA
Jones, William	1815	19		MA
Jones, William	1819	21		NJ
Jones, William	1820	17		PA
Jones, William	1820	40	b	NJ
Jones, William	1821	16		PA
Joneson, James	1816	0		XX
Jonston, Abraham	1804	19	b	MD

Jonston, John	1807	34		PA	Kaiser, Jacob	1804	16	PA
Jontz, John	1816	26		PA	Kane, Daniel	1820	25	PA
Jordan, Alexander	1805	24		PA	Kane, John	1815	23	NY
Jordan, Alexander	1806	25		PA	Kane, Mathias	1814	27	PA
Jordan, Naler	1804	28		MA	Kanel, John	1823	34	SC
Jordan, Robert	1803	22		PA	Kankey, Stephen H.	1805	30	MD
Jordan, Samuel	1813	16		PA	Karns, Jesse	1813	22	PA
Jordan, Samuel F.	1821	18		MA	Kartsher, John C.	1821	20	PA
Jordan, Thomas	1807	30	b	VA	Kates, Samuel	1810	21	PA
Jordan, Thomas	1819	22		MA	Kates, Samuel	1810	0	
Jordan, William	1812	21		NY	Katts, Michael	1811	20	PA
Jordon, William	1810	21	m	VA	Katz, John	1804	13	PA
Jori, John	1807	23		MS	Kavanagh, John M.	1816	19	PA
Joseph, Andreas	1805	25		MS	Kay, Alexander	1821	15	PA
Joseph, Anthony	1807	26		LA	Kay, Charles	1807	16	NJ
Joseph, Anthony	1807	22		MS	Kay, Charles	1816	25	NJ
Joseph, Antonio	1806	18		LA	Kean, Henry	1805	19	PA
Joseph, Edmond H.	1821	22	b	PA	Kean, Roger	1807	19	PA
Joseph, Eli	1809	39		LA	Kearney, James	1800	35	PA
Joseph, Francis	1809	30		LA	Kearny, Christopher	1806	21	PA
Joseph, John	1808	46		MS	Kearwin, John	1804	20	VA
Joseph, John	1810	33	b	LA	Keates, Charles	1821	21	NY
Joseph, John	1810	26		MA	Keath, James	1823	16	PA
Joseph, John	1815	25		VA	Keaton, Michael	1799	30	
Joseph, John	1818	27		MD	Keech, Robert W.	1813	24	NY
Joseph, John	1822	21		NC	Keef, Andrew	1805	22	NJ
Joseph, Manuel	1816	28	s	NY	Keef, Ephraim	1811	22	ME
Josey, Anthony	1807	24		LA	Keehmle, Leonard, Jr.	1811	14	PA
Joshua, John	1806	22	b	NC	Keel, John Randel Pitt	1807	22	VA
Joslin, Isaac	1798	16		RI	Keeling, Henry	1817	30	VA
Joue, Thomas	1806	30		NY	Keemer, David	1819	23	PA
Jourdan, Aaron	1817	25	b	VA	Keemer, Thomas	1818	30	PA
Jowsey, John	1820	25		PA	Keemle, Isaac	1810	16	PA
Joy, Bennett	1811	18		MD	Keemle, Isaac A.	1819	25	PA
Joze, Francis	1811	18		LA	Keen, Daniel	1810	24	PA
Judy, Joseph	1811	19		PA	Keen, Elisha	1806	21	PA
Jummers, John	1804	18		NJ	Keen, John B.	1811	18	PA
Jungerick, John, Jr.	1811	23		NY	Keen, Joseph S.	1809	20	PA
Junkins, Richworth	1815	20		MA	Keen, Joseph Jr.	1815	21	PA
Jurden, Wiliam	1807	23		NY	Keen, Laurence	1803	19	PA
Jurdon, David	1809	30	y	MD	Keenan, John	1810	34	PA
Jurkins, Henry	1805	22		PA	Keenan, Thomas	1809	28	CT
Justice, Charles	1804	18	b	DE	Keenen, Thomas	1812	00	
Justice, Charles	1810	0			Keeter, Isaac	1810	22	VA
Justice, John	1811	25		PA	Kehrum, John	1810	21	PA
Justice, John	1811	23		NJ	Kehrum, John	1814	0	
Justice, Joseph	1809	25		PA	Kehrum, Thomas	1819	27	PA
Justice, Samuel	1807	16		NJ	Keith, John	1815	24	PA
Kaern, John	1798	40		PA	Keith, Neal	1810	24	SC
Kahmar, Rheinard	1809	0			Keller, George	1814	18	PA
Kahmen, Rhunard	1807	18		PA	Keller, Jacob	1815	16	PA
Kain, Daniel	1812	19		PA	Kelley, James	1801	30	PA

Kelley, James	1803	20		DE	Ker, James	1815	16	PA
Kelley, Robert	1823	24	y	PA	Ker, Nelson	1822	27 b	VA
Kellogg, Stephen	1804	18		DE	Ker, Nelson	1822	27 b	VA
Kellum, Liba	1807	25		NJ	Kerby, Thomas	1822	28	NY
Kelly, Henry	1807	18		PA	Kerlin, John Savage	1805	20	PA
Kelly, Henry	1809	0		PA	Kerns, William	1815	17	PA
Kelly, Henry	1811	18 y		PA	Kerr, John	1812	45	Ireland
Kelly, Henry	1812	00			Kerr, Peter	1801	19	PA
Kelly, John	1805	32		NJ	Kerr, William	1796	0	No.Br.
Kelly, John	1810	23 b		MD	Kewell, William	1809	22	NY
Kelly, John, Jr.	1811	15		PA	Key, John	1811	34	NJ
Kelly, John	1817	16		MD	Key, William	1807	14	PA
Kelly, Joseph	1801	29 m		VA	Keys, Alexander	1796	19	Ireland
Kelly, William Douglass					Keys, Elijah	1804	21	DE
	1820	21		NJ	Keys, William	1811	24	MA
Kelsay, Robert	1796	24		NJ	Keyser, Daniel	1809	37	PA
Kelsay, Robert	1798	0		NJ	Keyser, Daniel	1809	0	
Kelsey, Peter	1809	21 y		PA	Keyser, John	1806	24	PA
Kelson, Francis B.	1822	16		MD	Keyser, John	1810	0	
Kelton, Robert	1810	17 b		PA	Keyser, Nathan L.	1815	20	PA
Kely, James	1811	22		MA	Kibby, John	1815	35	VA
Kemble, George, Jr.	1809	16		PA	Kid, James P.	1819	16	PA
Kemble, Joseph	1810	14		PA	Kidd, Thomas	1815	22	MD
Kemble, Samuel	1822	16		PA	Kidman, John	1809	21	PA
Kempenfell, William	1808	38 m		MA	Kiel, Jacob	1805	23	PA
Kenard, Menan	1809	20		NJ	Kilbey, Peter Thomas	1804	16	PA
Kendal, John	1810	23		MA	Kilborn, Enos	1804	19	MA
Kendrick, John	1815	20		PA	Kilburn, Thomas	1809	28	MA
Kennar, James	1815	28		NJ	Kile, George	1809	18	PA
Kennard, Francis A.	1817	19		DE	Kilhower, Marlin	1815	22	PA
Kennard, Richard Tilghman					Kilhower, Martin	1818	26	PA
	1811	19		DE	Killingsworth, John	1810	15	DE
Kennard, Richard T.	1812	00			Killo, Dennis	1807	18	DE
Kenneday, Edward	1805	19		PA	Killroy, Henry	1809	24	NY
Kennedy, Alexander L.	1818	13		PA	Killy, Shoubel	1798	30	MA
Kennedy, Alexander	1822	20		PA	Kimberly, Charles	1823	16	CT
Kennedy, Andrew	1801	32		SC	Kimm, Richard	1798	20	PA
Kennedy, Charles	1822	14		PA	Kimsey, William	1813	22	NJ
Kennedy, David	1810	14 b		MD	Kin, John	1811	25	NY
Kennedy, James	1817	24		MD	Kin, Joseph	1815	21 b	SC
Kennedy, James	1821	27		PA	Kinder, John	1817	26	NY
Kennedy, William	1807	22		MD	Kindig, George	1817	18	PA
Kennedy, William	1815	15		PA	King, Charles	1821	15	MD
Kenny, Daniel	1812	23		CT	King, Daniel,Jr	1805	28	NJ
Kenny, Georege	1815	29		PA	King, Edmund	1823	33	NY
Kenny, James	1804	20		PA	King, George	1807	21	PA
Kenny, James	1804	20		PA	King, Henry	1809	19	DE
Kenny, John	1798	26		Gr.Br.	King, Henry	1810	20 b	MD
Kent, Joseph	1810	25		PA	King, Henry	1811	00	DE
Kent, Josiah	1804	20		RI	King, Israel	1809	18	NJ
Kepplee, John H.	1819	20		PA	King, James	1797	30	NY
Ker, Jack	1810	25 y		VA	King, James	1823	28	NY

King, Job	1815	23	NJ		Knap, Joseph	1809	19	PA
King, John	1806	21		none given	Knap, Samuel	1805	18	MD
King, John	1807	21	VA		Knapp, James	1821	36	CT
King, John	1807				Knapp, Ruben	1796	0	CT
King, John W.	1815	21	PA		Knapp, Samuel	1812	24	MD
King, Joseph	1803	21	NY		Kneass, Fullerton Tully	1822	18	PA
King, Joseph	1809	0			Kneath, David	1807		
King, Joseph	1815	18 b	PA		Knight, David	1818	18	MA
King, Joseph	1816	22	GA		Knight, George	1796	0		Ireland
King, Lawrence	1817	20 y	NJ		Knight, Isaac C.	1823	19	PA
King, Malen	1815	00			Knight, Joel	1815	25	MA
King, Malin	1809	21	NJ		Knight, John	1815	22	RI
King, Mifflin	1812	21 b	PA		Knight, Samuel	1815	24	MA
King, Peter	1804	21 b	DE		Knight, Thomas	1818	47	MA
King, Richard	1822	20	MD		Knight, William	1812	16	MA
King, Samuel	1807	22	PA		Knight, William	1815	21	NJ
King, Thomas	1805	26	VA		Knop, Henry	1815	22 b	MD
King, Thomas	1806	25	PA		Knowland, Andrew	1818	44	MA
King, William	1810	29	NJ		Knowles, John	1805	21 b	PA
King, William	1815	12	PA		Knowles, John	1810	21	PA
King, William	1818	18	PA		Knowles, Norton	1807	19	PA
King, William	1818	39	PA		Knowles, Thomas	1804	19	PA
King, Wm.	1814	26	PA		Knowles, William	1801	17	PA
Kingston, William	1810	27	NY		Knowlton, David	1818	34	MA
Kinmy, Stephen	1798	28	NJ		Knox, Caeser	1798	23 b	NY
Kinnard, William	1807	30	MD		Knox, Charles Lynd	1810	18	PA
Kinndar, Joshua	1812	22 b	DE		Knox, James	1823	20	CT
Kinnison, James	1822	19	ME		Knox, Nehemiah	1811	27	DE
Kinny, Bartlet	1809	37 m	VA		Knox, Nehemiah	1823	41	DE
Kinsey, James	1809	23 m	MD		Knox, Robert	1804	19	NY
Kinsey, Thomas	1804	21	NJ		Knox, Robert	1809	0	
Kinsinger, John	1798	25	PA		Knox, Thomas Jr.	1815	35	MA
Kinsley, Richard	1801	34	MA		Kochenspenger, Martin, III			
Kinsman, John	1798	21	RI			1817	15	PA
Kintzing, Harbeson	1818	23	PA					
Kiran, Michael	1801	21	DE		Koff, Isaac	1810	22 y	NY
Kirby, Benjamin	1810	21	PA		a free Indian; skin color given as yellow			
Kirby, Jonathan	1809	15	NJ					
Kirk, Andrew	1809	26	PA		Koffskey, John P.	1820	26	SC
Kirk, Henry	1798	16	NY		Kollack, Lewis	1818		
Kirk, Henry	1819	35	MA		Kollock, Lewis	1815	33 b	DE
Kirk, Joseph L.	1815	16	PA		Koockogey, Thomas	1821	24	PA
Kirkham, Samuel	1815	28	CT		Koockogie, Thomas	1814	17	PA
Kirkoff, Christian	1820	24	NJ		Kopp, John	1798	30	PA
Kite, James A.	1818	29	NC		Korkoff, Christian	1815	19	NJ
Kits, John	1803	24	PA		Kracht, Martin	1809	25	PA
Kitts, Joseph	1812	25	PA		Kubey, Epraim	1806	26	PA
Klein, Abraham	1811	23	NY		Kugler, Benjamin	1817	28	PA
Kleyn, Frederick	1807	32	NY		Kugler, John	1804	25	PA
Kline, Jacob	1811	22	PA		Kugler, John	1807		
Kloss, Peter	1814	20	PA		Kuhn, Ceaser	1811	00	
Klotz, John	1822	21	PA		Kuhn, Ceaser	1811	17 b	MA

Kuhn, Lewis	1810	17	PA
Kuhn, Michael	1812	22	PA
Kuhn, William	1798	24	PA
Kuhn, William	1815	14	PA
Kuhn, William	1818	17	PA
Kurtz, Daniel L.	1811	21	PA
Kurtz, Henry	1819	17	PA
La Fitte, John	1809	25	LA
Lacave, Alfred P.	1822	14	MA
Lace, William W.	1806	16	PA
Lachlen, William	1804	23	NY
Lacombe, John Baptiste			
	1816	17	PA
Lacombe, Peter	1807	36	LA
Lafetra, Daniel A.	1810	29	NJ
Lafong, John	1822	41	NC
Lagreeze, John	1811	21 y	PA
Laidley, James Jr.	1815	18	none given
Lainhoff, Godfrey	1818	21	PA
Lair, Philip	1810	20	MA
Lake, Benjamin	1815	33	RI
Lake, James	1803	23	MD
Lake, John	1811	43	MA
Lake, Thomas	1805	28	PA
Lake, William,Jr	1805	21	PA
Lakes, James	1805	16	PA
Lam, George	1807	26	PA
Lamb, Caleb	1804	28	MD
Lamb, Peter	1808	28	NY
Lamb, William	1807	25	PA
Lambe, Robert	1806	22	MD
Lamberg, Charles	1811	21	PA
Lambert, James	1804	18	VA
Lambert, James	1805	0	
Lambert, John	1814	22	MD
Lambert, Lewis	1805	34 b	PA
Lambert, Richard	1796	0	Gr.Br.
Lambert, Thomas	1812	19	MA
Lamoth, Jacob	1817	56 b	DE
Lampheer, James	1810	19	SC
Lampheer, James	1812	00	
Lampley, Richard	1811	29	DE
Lampley, Richard	1812	00	
Lamplugh, Jacob	1823	27	PA
Lamply, John	1804	18	PA
Lampshear, Nathan	1817	17	RI
Lamuth, Jacob	1809	40 b	DE
Lanbert, Joseph	1817	31	LA
Lance, John Philip	1805	20	PA
Landenburg, Samuel	1816	24	PA
Landers, Samuel	1822	19	DE
Lane, John	1801	21	NY

Lane, John	1804	26	MA
Lane, John	1811	00	
Lane, John	1815	22	MA
Lane, Joseph	1818	25	MA
Lane, Samuel	1815	17	NJ
Lane, Samuel	1819	21	NH
Lane, Thomas	1812	22	NC
Lane, William	1809	22	PA
Lane, William	1811	39	NJ
Lang, Benjamin	1815	22 m	PA
Lang, Charles	1804	34	DE
Lang, James K.	1818	26	NH
Lang, Samuel	1811	14	PA
Lang, William	1817	23 b	PA
Langdon, Benjamin	1820	28	NY
Lange, Frederick	1803	23	PA
Langley, Davis	1806	22	NJ
Langley, Nehemiah	1809	28	NJ
Langley, Samuel	1816	18	PA
Langwill, Robert	1820	19	MD
Lanine, John	1815	23	NY
Lank, David	1799	22	DE
Lanning, Samuel	1815	15	NJ
Lansdey, James	1810	16	NY
Lapond, Charles	1809	15	LA
Larbonet, John	1803	38	PA
Lardner, James L.	1820	17	PA
Larmeth, Jacob	1812	00	
Larmouth, Jacob	1815	00	
LaRoche, Peter	1817	17	CT
Larrabe, Abraham	1818	28	MA
Latcham, John	1811	27	DE
Lathberry, Samuel	1804	26	NJ
Latimer, George	1801	23	MD
Latimer, George	1803	32	VA
Latimer, George	1804	0	
Latimer, George	1805	0	
Latimer, James	1810	30	MD
Latimer, James Bond	1820	16	PA
Latimer, John	1815	19	PA
Latimer, Robert	1817	23	PA
Latour, Amede	1811	13	VA
Lattimore, Robert	1818		
Lauck, Benjamin	1817	25	PA
Lauder, Charles	1812	18	PA
Lauder, Matthew	1807		
Laudon, Friedrick	1806	21	PA
Lauer, Philip	1809	22	PA
Laughead, Robert	1811	00	
Laughlin, Richard E.	1818	15	VA
Laurent, Peter Augustin			
	1811	31	none given

81

Lavalets, Lewis	1822	22 y	NY
Lavell, Joseph	1804	16	PA
Lavina, John	1817	18 b	PA
Lavit, John	1820	22	ME
Law, Alexander	1814	33	
Law, Samuel, Jr.	1823	23	PA
Lawder, Mathew	1805	23 b	MD
Lawes, William	1811	22 m	VA
Lawler, Edward	1815	15	PA
Lawler, Mathew, Jr.	1811	17	PA
Lawler, William F.	1811	15	PA
Lawless, James	1804	28	PA
Lawrence, Antonio	1810	25 b	MS
Lawrence, Daniel	1811	22	NJ
Lawrence, George	1821	29 y	NY
Lawrence, Jabish	1805	31	CT
Lawrence, John	1804	15	NJ
Lawrence, John	1809	19	NJ
Lawrence, John	1809	19	NJ
Lawrence, John	1815	37 m	LA
Lawrence, John H.	1822	33	NJ
Lawrence, Jonathan	1803	22	NJ
Lawrence, Joseph	1811	22	LA
Lawrence, Joseph F.	1822	16	PA
Lawrence, Josiah	1820	26	PA
Lawrence, Nicholas	1806	23	PA
Lawrence, Nicholas	1806	0	
Laws, Caleb	1810	25 b	DE
Laws, James	1804	19 y	DE
Laws, James	1807	22 c	DE
Laws, James	1811	19	MD
Laws, James	1811	19	MD
Laws, James	1812	00	
Laws, Peter	1818	24 b	DE
Laws, Stringer	1809	23	DE
Laws, William	1811	26	DE

Lawson, James   1815 45   Norway
born Fredericks Hall, Norway. Landed NY 1775;
married in Albany, NY; has 3 children; wife deceased.
Served 2 years on U.S. frigate *Constellation*.

Lawson, John Peter	1811	13	PA
Lawson, John Peter	1812	00	
Lawson, Mathew	1815	32	none given
Lawson, Peter	1804	38	NJ
Lawson, Peter	1808	0	
Lawson, Peter	1809	0	
Lay, Peter	1821	23 y	PA
Layland, James	1810	17	PA
Layland, James	1815	22	MA
Layton, Charles	1804	27	DE

Layton, Charles	1807	30	DE
Layton, Edward	1809	28	DE
Layton, Edward	1810	0	
Layton, William	1821	21 b	DE
Lazarus, John	1817	49	none given
Le Coney, James	1809	21	NJ
Lea, James	1821	20	NJ
Lea, Jesse	1811	00	
Lea, John	1805	22	PA
Leach, Charles	1823	32	MA
Leach, George	1814	19	NY
Leach, John	1809	25	NH
Leach, William	1823	26	CT
Leach, Wittshere	1817	30 y	NJ
Leadler, Thomas	1805	25	PA
Leahy, John	1811	23	PA
Leak, Robert	1815	20	England
Leamer, Anthony, Jr.	1818	16	PA
Leaming, James	1810	21	NJ
Leaming, Persons	1811	21	NJ
Leamy, Simon	1811	19	MD
Lean, William	1806	23	MD
Lear, Timothy	1809	25 b	NY
Lears, Jonathan	1815	16	MA
Leary, Berrey	1812	24 m	DE
Leathen, Thomas	1813	22	PA
Leatherbarrow, Paul	1806	30	NY
Leaver, Francis	1797	0	MD
Leaverton, James	1809	21	MD
Lebertine, Andrew	1801	38	NY
Lebeter, George	1803	13	MA
Lebrang, Solomon	1810	20 m	MD
Lebrang, Solomon	1814	20 y	MD
Lechler, Anthony	1807	21	PA
Lechler, George Ernst	1805	23	PA
Leconey, James	1815	00	
Leconey, James	1817	00	NJ
Lecount, Jesse	1821	16 y	DE
Lecount, Jesse	1822	17 y	DE
Lecount, Sevin	1821	25	VA
Leddy, John	1815	24	NY
Ledent, Lambert	1815	15	PA
Ledent, William	1818	16	PA
Lederstrom, Jonas	1807	28	
Ledru, Joseph	1803	21	PA
Leduc, Cadet	1810	22	MS
Ledyard, John Washington			
	1810	21	CT
Lee, Abel	1812	28	NJ
Lee, Charles	1815	23	NY
Lee, David	1815	22	NJ
Lee, Edward	1803	28	PA

Name	Year	Age		State
Lee, George	1810	27		VA
Lee, Henry W.	1811	15		PA
Lee, Jacob	1805	37	b	DE
Lee, Jacob	1810	0		
Lee, James	1823	22		NJ
Lee, Jesse	1809	22	m	MD
Lee, John	1801	30		PA
Lee, John	1804	31	m	PA
Lee, John	1806	0	b	
Lee, John	1807	22	y	VA
Lee, John	1808	0		
Lee, John	1808	21		NC
Lee, John W.	1813	18		VA
Lee, John	1818	22		MA
Lee, John	1822	35		none given
Lee, Joseph	1801	22		PA
Lee, Joseph	1814	18		PA
Lee, Joseph OSullivan	1820	19		NY
Lee, Joshua Clark	1804	23		MD
Lee, Lawrence	1806	22	b	VA
Lee, Richard	1804	23	b	MD
Lee, Richard	1804	23	b	MD
Lee, Robert	1799	28	b	DE
Lee, Roger	1811	20	b	MD
Lee, Samuel Browbn	1818	28		PA
Lee, Thomas	1815	15	m	NJ
Lee, William	1809	18		SC
Lee, Yarmouth	1822	44	y	DE
Leedom, James	1809	24		MA
Leeds, William	1815	26		CT
Leeman, John	1812	23		VA
Lees, John	0000	23		PA
Lees, John	0000	23		PA
Lees, Samuel D.	1819	21		PA
Lees, Thomas J	1811	18		NJ
Leets, Thomas	1815	23		NJ
Lefevre, John	1807	22		NY
LeGeyt, Phillip	1808	23		LA
Legg, Joseph	1818	20		MD
Legrove, Philip	1810	28		MA
Lehman, Nathan	1810	24	b	NJ
Lei, Charles	1817	25		NY
Leich, Andrew	1823	42		MA
Leich, James	1823	17		PA
Leighton, Daniel	1819	24		MA
Leighton, Nathaniel	1818	21		MA
Leiper, William	1822	14		PA
Leland, John	1813	22		NY
Lelar, Henry, Jr.	1823	17		PA
Lemaitre, Louis Henry	1815	25		LA
LeMare, Joseph	1816	36		LA
Lemeke, Friedrick	1806	29		PA
Lemmon, Francis	1809	24		PA
Lemmon, Francis	1811	00		
Lemons, Francis	1816	34		none given
LeMottais, Philip	1798	22		MA
Lemunyon, David	1804	33		NJ
Lemunyon, Stephen	1804	23		NJ
Lenard, John	1817	21		PA
Lenderman, John	1810	18		MD
Lennard, John	1806	22		PA
Lenoff, John	1809	25		PA
Lentz, Henry, Jr.	1821	21		PA
Leonard, James	1805	24		NJ
Leonard, James	1809	18		PA
Leonard, James	1815	00		
Leonard, John	1811	00		
Leonard, John	1815	18		NJ
Leonard, Robert	1813	28		NY
Leownsbury, John	1815	17		PA
Lepini, Benjamin	1800	20		PA
Leppey, Henry	1803	35		PA
Lercy, Morris	1797	27		
Lericke, Lewis Victror	1816	28		XX
LeSage, John	1823	32		LA
Lescaille, Frederick	1817	21		LA
Leshe, Zachariah	1804	25		PA
Lesher, George	1819	21		PA
Lesher, Henry	1810	19		PA
Leson, J. Christn	1821	32	y	PA
Lester, Robert	1805	24		PA
Leston, John	1801	20	b	VA
Lestrade, Joseph	1813	23		VA
Letts, William	1809	36		PA
Leveck, Peter	1805	44	y	PA
Levering, William, Jr.	1812	20		PA
Levery, John	1809	30		MA
Levery, John	1810	0		
Levis, Jesse	1806	23	b	VA
Levis, Samuel P.	1804	19		PA
Levy, Abraham	1821	29	y	PA
Levy, Jonas P.	1823	16		PA
Levy, William	1820	31		MD
Lewis, Adam	1807	22		NY
Lewis, Adam	1810	0		
Lewis, Benjamin	1797	0		Gr.Br.
Lewis, Benjamin	1804	28	b	DE
Lewis, Benjamin	1805	0	b	
Lewis, Benjamin	1816	50	b	NY
Lewis, Charles	1817	21	y	MD
Lewis, Cornillius	1803	22		MD
Lewis, David	1819	23	b	MD
Lewis, Henry	1800	23		PA
Lewis, Henry	1810	23	b	DE

Name	Year	Age		State
Lewis, Henry	1810	0		DE
Lewis, James	1806	39	b	DE
Lewis, James	1807		b	
Lewis, James	1811	25	b	PA
Lewis, James F.	1822	17	l	MA
native American				
Lewis, John	1805	23		NY
Lewis, John	1806	25	b	NJ
Lewis, John	1807	17	y	MS
Lewis, John	1809	21		MA
Lewis, John	1809	24	b	DE
Lewis, John	1809	27	y	MD
Lewis, John	1810	21		PA
Lewis, John	1810	16		MA
Lewis, John	1810	24		LA
Lewis, John	1810	17		MD
Lewis, John	1811	29	m	LA
Lewis, John	1811	22	y	MA
Lewis, John	1814	21		PA
Lewis, John	1815	17		PA
Lewis, John	1815	30	b	LA
Lewis, John	1815	18	y	PA
Lewis, John	1815	00		
Lewis, John	1815	00		
Lewis, John	1815	25	s	DE
Lewis, John	1820	16	b	PA
Lewis, John	1822	30		PA
Lewis, Joseph	1812	21		NJ
Lewis, Joseph	1813	22		NJ
Lewis, Joseph	1814	30	b	LA
Lewis, Joseph	1815	26		MA
Lewis, Michael	1812	45		PA
Lewis, Michael	1816	50		PA
Lewis, Peter	1806	24	b	MD
Lewis, Peter	1807	20	y	MD
Lewis, Peter	1807	22	b	DE
Lewis, Peter	1809	18		RI
Lewis, Peter	1810	29	b	PA
Lewis, Peter	1815	28	b	MA
Lewis, Peter	1823	24	b	DE
Lewis, Richard	1805	37	y	MD
Lewis, Richard	1805	37	y	MD
Lewis, Robert	1810	18		MA
Lewis, Robert	1820	16	y	PA
Lewis, Samuel	1820	21		PA
Lewis, Samuel	1821	30		NH
Lewis, Samuel	1823	37	s	NJ
Lewis, Stephen	1798	23		DE
Lewis, Thomas	1805	22		MA
Lewis, Wharton	1809	18		PA
Lewis, William	1805	18		PA
Lewis, William	1809	22		MA
Lewis, William L.	1810	28		VA
Lewis, William G.	1823	16		PA
Lewis, Zalmon	1823	34	y	CT
Lewistown, Lewis	1812	11	b	DE
Lework, Charles Fredrick				
	1804	0		
Lexcey, Joseph	1809	0		
Lexley, Joseph	1807	28	b	NJ
Ley, Daniel, Jr.	1818	21		PA
Ley, John	1811	17		PA
Liautier, Joseph Stewart				
	1805	18		PA
Libby, John	1818	27		MA
Libby, Joseph	1821	24		ME
Light, John	1807	33		NH
Likens, Parker	1809	23		PA
Lilly, Simeon	1811	17		MA
Liming, John	1796	0		NJ
Liming, William	1814	19		PA
Linbar, John	1810	25		PA
Linch, George	1810	32		DE
Lincoln, Abel	1803	29		MA
Lincoln, Benjamin	1806	29		MA
Lincoln, Charles	1816	29		MA
Lincoln, Charles	1817			
Lincoln, Freeman	1816	30		RI
Lincoln, Jonathan Jr.	1819	30		MA
Lincoln, Marshall	1803	16		MA
Lincoln, Moses	1815	22		PA
Lincoln, Samuel C.	1820	16		MA
Lincoln, William	1815	24		MA
Lindbom, Andrew Peter				
	1810	30		PA
Lindsay, David	1801	28		PA
Lindsay, Hugh A.	1821	16		PA
Lindsay, James	1809	17		PA
Lindsay, John	1811	23		NY
Lindsay, Robert	1801	30		PA
Lindsey, James	1805	23		DE
Lindsey, John	1809	28	b	NY
Lindsey, John	1811	00		
Lindsey, William	1806	0		
Lindsey, William	1806	17		PA
Lindsey, William	1809	28		SC
Lindsey, William	1812	00		
Lindstrom, Benjamin	1809	28		NY
Linen, William	1808	0		
Liney, Thomas	1801	18		NY
Linin, William	1805	28		Pa
Linn, Robert	1809	21		PA

Linn, William	1809	0	
Linnen, William	1809	0	PA
Linston, Peter	1806	29	DE
Linthicum, Thomas	1810	22	NJ
Linton, Joseph	1804	26	PA
Lippey, Henry	1807		
Lippincott, Benjamin	1811	22	NJ
Lippincott, Collins P. P.			
	1809	23	NJ
Lippincott, William	1809	21	NJ
Lipringer, John	1811	21	NJ
Lipscomb, Ambrose	1807	29	PA
Lipscomb, Major	1815	30	VA
Lisha, Stephen	1822	25 y	RI
Lisk, Aaron	1807	29 b	MD
Lisle, Charles Palmer	1805	15	Tortola
Lisle, Thomas	1823	30	PA
List, James	1804	12 b	DE
List, Moses	1804	22 b	MD
List, Moses	1815	27	CT
Lister, Conrad	1810	25	PA
Lister, James	1808	31	
Liston, David	1809	18 b	DE
Liston, David	1810	0	
Liston, David	1810	18 b	MD
Liston, Jeremiah	1821	28 b	DE
Liston, John	1815	24 b	DE
Liston, Perry	1799	33 b	DE
Liston, Perry	1810	40 b	DE
Lithgow, John	1818	28	NY
Litlar, Richard	1815	26	MA
Littin, Joseph S.	1804	25	none given
Little, Archibald	1805	28	DE
Little, Archibald	1818	45	Ireland
Little, Daniel	1820	22	ME
Little, Edward	1820	24	NY
Little, Samuel	1823	17	NY
Little, Thomas	1814	11	PA
Little, William	1818	20	CT
Littlefield, John	1815	30	MA
Littlefield, Samuel	1823	25	ME
Lively, James	1823	24 y	NY
Livesley, Thomas	1815	37	CT
Livingston, James	1797	22	RI
Livingston, John	1804	27	MA
Lloyd, John	1806	38	NJ
Lloyd, John	1810	0	
Lloyd, John	1810	0	
Lloyd, Peter	1809	25 b	SC
Lloyd, Robert Burton	1805	25	NJ
Lloyd, Robert	1810	25	PA
Lock, Charles	1811	33	GA

Lock, John	1806	17	NJ
Lock, John	1807		
Lock, Nathaniel	1815	24	MD
Lock, William	1809	22	CT
Locke, William	1819	23	MA
Lockman, Abraham	1810	30	NY
Lockwood, Charles	1810	17	NY
Lockwood, Jacob	1823	25	CT
Lockwood, Oliver, Jr.	1823	16	PA
Lodewijk, Johan	1807	19	PA
Lodine, John	1804	36 b	DE
Lodine, Joshua	1805	20 b	DE
Lodor, Benjamin	1811	16	PA
Loffly, Levi	1820	19 b	NJ
Lofield, John	1815	19	NJ
Lofish, Thomas	1811	33	LA
Logal, Francis William	1815	31	MD
Logan, Samuel	1817	21	MD
Logue, Richard	1796	24	CT
Lohra, Lindia	1820	25 y	PA
Lolly, John	1809	16 b	DE
Lombard, Daniel	1818	23	NY
Lombard, Levi W.	1804	29	MA
Lomis, Jonathan	1809	19	NJ
Lonard, John	1809	15	VA
London, James Washington			
	1812	22 b	PA
London, James	1815	00	
London, Joseph	1810	23 b	VA
London, Robert	1812	13 b	NY
Loney, William	1806	26	PA
Long, Constant	1817	21	NJ
Long, David	1819	24	NJ
Long, James	1810	14	PA
Long, Jesse	1807	24	MA
Long, John G.	1811	22	PA
Long, Lewis	1812	40 b	MD
Long, Nathan	1819	22	NJ
Long, Robert	1809	29	none given
Long, Samuel	1816	39 b	PA
Long, Samuel	1821	20	PA
Long, William	1807	21	MD
Long, William	1810	21	NJ
Longcope, James Elliott			
	1811	12	PA
Longcope, James E.	1813	0	
Longcope, Thomas M.	1822	22	PA
Longcope, William	1822	17	PA
Longe, John	1810	21	NJ
Longfellow, Amos	1812	22	MD
Longshore, George	1811	12	PA
Longshore, Thomas	1809	15	PA

Lonnon, Barnabee	1812	18 b	MA
Loper, John Eldrige	1818	22	MA
Loper, Lyons	1815	47	NY
Loper, Zacheus	1809	21	NJ
Lopez, Antonio	1809	25	LA
Lopez, Joseph	1807	32	
Lord, Benjamin	1810	43	MA
Lord, John	1820	18	ME
Lorentsen, Peter	1801	22	PA
Lorentzen, Peter	1804	0	PA
Lorentzen, Peter	1804	26	PA
Lorentzen, Peter	1807		
Lorentzen, Peter	1808	0	PA

Loring, Elpalet 1799 34 MA
lived in New Kent County, VA, since before
Independence

Loriol, John B.	1801	47	
Lort, Charles	1812	25	DE
Loscombe, John	1798	21	VA
Lossius, Nicholas	1810	19	PA
Louderback, John	1809	21	NJ
Loughead, Robert	1809	24	NJ
Loughead, Robert L.	1821	16	none given
Loughead, Thomas	1797	26	PA
Loughead, Thomas	1805	0	
Loughery, Alfred	1809	27	none given
Louis, John	1810	30	LA
Louman, Francis	1815	22	none given
Love, Archibald	1817	23	NH
Love, Daniel	1804	26	MA
Love, George	1810	18	PA
Love, George	1815	23	RI

Love, George 1817 00
cast away in Brig *Isabella* from Philadelphia
to Kingston, Jamaica

Love, Henry	1812	18 y	MA
Love, Isaac Bathurst	1818	51 y	VA
Love, Peter	1811	47	LA
Love, Peter	1811	47	LA
Love, Robert	1805	17	NY
Lovel, Thomas	1798	24	VA
Loveland, Daniel	1815	28	CT
Loveless, William	1796	0	NY
Lovell, Benjamin	1807	16	MA
Lovell, William	1817	36	PA
Lovell, William	1819	45	MD
Lovering, Charles F.	1816	19	VA

Lovet, James	1803	20	MA
Low, Elisha	1819	19	NH
Low, Jacob	1807	49	MA
Low, John	1798	27	CT
Low, John Christian	1806	28	PA
Low, John Brown	1816	38	VA
Low, Joseph	1808	29	PA
Low, Joseph	1809	0	PA
Low, Joseph	1815	29 y	NY
Low, Michael	1811	22	NJ
Low, Thomas	1807	23	PA
Lowden, Samuel	1809	21	NJ
Lowder, John	1810	20	PA
Lowder, Moses	1809	18	PA
Lowdine, Benjamin	1820	19 y	DE
Lowdon, Joseph	1816	20 c	PA
Lowe, Richard	1818	23	MA
Lowe, Samuel	1805	16	PA
Lowe, Thomas H.	1815	21	PA
Lownsbury, Carpenter	1812	44	NJ
Lowry, Andrew	1805	22	PA
Lowry, James	1820	27 y	PA
Lowry, Robert	1804	19	PA
Loxley, Charles T.	1818	13	PA
Loxley, John	1817	14	PA
Loyd, Nathaniel	1819	36 b	PA
Lozout, Jean Edouard	1804	36	none given
Luberg, John Christian	1811	26	DE
Lubke, John	1798	35	PA
Lucas, Daniel	1811	24 b	PA
Lucas, Francis	1809	30	LA
Lucas, James	1807	31	VA
Lucas, James	1808	24	NH
Lucas, James	1809	0	VA
Lucas, John	1811	13 m	PA
Lucas, Robert	1807	17	Pa
Luce, Jonathan	1807	34	MA
Ludham, James	1810	25	
Ludington, William	1811	28	
Ludington, William	1810	27	MD
Ludlam, Cornelius	1799	19	NJ
Ludlam, Daniel	1815	28	NJ
Ludlam, Norton	1810	22	NJ
Ludley, Aron	1798	24 b	NJ
Ludlo, Adam	1815	45 b	NJ
Ludlum, Adam	1798	0 b	NJ
Lue, Mon	1808	20 b	MD
Lufberry, Samuel	1806	23	PA
Luff, Anthony	1823	22 b	DE
Lugg, Thomas	1798	23 b	MA
Lukes, Henry	1810	15	PA
Lum, Joseph	1810	26	CT

Lumber, James	1823	23	VA
Lumber, William	1823	29	VA
Lumberd, Thomas	1823	26	VA
Lummis, Jacob F.	1822	22	NJ
Lundbeck, Jacob	1805	19	NJ
Lunnar, Francis	1815	25 y	PA
Luno, Francis	1807	15	LA
Lunt, Abel	1818	19	MA
Lupton, John, Jr.	1811	21	NY
Lusk, Francis	1809	18	PA
Lusk, Francis	1811	00	
Lusk, John	1805	42	
Lyle, Abraham Jones	1812	21	PA
Lyle, Benjamin	1818	21	PA
Lyle, Charles	1804	22	PA
Lyle, Charles	1804	22	PA
Lyle, Walter	1820	20	PA
Lyman, Jacob	1807	29	NC
Lyman, Jacob	1811	00	
Lyman, James Wilkinson			
	1816	19	MA
Lynam, George	1797	24	NJ
Lynch, Edward	1812	30	SC
Lynch, Elias	1806	21 b	MD
Lynch, James	1818	32	MD
Lynch, John	1810	28	MD
Lynch, John	1811	00	
Lynch, Joseph S.	1798	0	
Lynch, Michael	1808	17	VA
Lynch, William	1817	17	SC
Lynn, William	1821	28	PA
Lyons, Henry	1811	17	NJ
Lyons, Jacob	1822	32	PA
Lyons, John	1805	27	SC
Lyons, Mathew	1815	17	none given
Lyons, Moses	1818	14	PA
Lyons, Samuel	1815	19	MD
Lyons, Solomon	1811	16	PA
Lyons, Solomon J. J.	1811	16	PA
Lysaght, Isaac	1798	19	NY
M'Dowell, Nathaniel	1816	16	PA
MacAbee, John	1809	22	MD
Macahan, John	1809	20	PA
MaCalahn, John	1810	0	
Macaland, James	1809	0	
Maccue, James	1818	15	PA
Mace, Francis	1803	22	DE
Mace, Henry	1818	17	MA
Mace, Joseph N.	1810	19	MD
Macintosh, Alexander	1798	18	NY
Mackaby, John	1817	30	MD
MacKay, George	1796	22	NY

Mackenzie, Charles	1805	35	NY	
Mackey, Alexander	1804	36	VA	
Mackey, Charles	1816	27	MA	
Mackey, Daniel	1807	15	DE	
Mackey, Robert	1811	20	PA	
Mackey, William	1801	16	PA	
Mackey, William	1805	0	PA	
Mackie, Robert	1811	00		
Mackie, William	1821	15	PA	
Macky, Robert	1807	21	MD	
Macomber, James	1821	18	ME	
Macomber, Robert	1817	23	MA	
Macoy, William	1805	25	NY	
Macpherson, Joseph Stout				
	1806	18	PA	
Macpherson, Joseph S.	1806	18	PA	
Macpherson, Joseph S.	1807			
MacPherson, William	1819	37	MA	
Macy, Henry	1810	19	MA	
Madden, David	1804	23 b	MD	
Maddis, John	1811	00		

SPC lost when Brig *Eliza* captured by the British. Plundered of wearing apparel and papers. Alias: Anthony Medicine

Maddison, Thomas	1818	42	MD	
Maddock, Charles	1805	20	PA	
Maddock, Charles	1811	00		
Maddock, Thomas	1805	22	PA	
Madrin, James	1819	19	NC	
Maffet, David R.	1816	18	PA	
Maffet, John	1805	17	PA	
Maffet, John	1805	19	PA	
Maffet, John	1809	25 b	DE	
Maffet, John	1811	00		
Maffet, John	1818	32		
Maffet, Richard	1799	21 b	DE	
Maffett, John	1806	0		
Magathenes, Jose Homem de				
	1811	26	LA	
Magee, Bernard	1810	21	PA	
Magee, Charles	1815	33		none given
Magee, Hugh	1801	22	PA	
Magee, John	1809	20	DE	
Magill, John	1804	22	MD	
Maginnes, Daniel	1810	31		
Magraw, Samuel	1815	17	NJ	
Maguire, John	1820	32		Ireland
Maguire, Thomas	1809	21	PA	
Mahon, William	1805	23	MA	
Mahoney, James	1792	0		

Mahy, William	1804	49	NY		Mansfield, Joseph	1816	23	MA
Main, Charles	1803	26	PA		Mansfield, Zenas	1811	17	MA
Main, William	1806	21	PA		Manship, Joseph	1804	16	MD
Main, William	1808	0	PA		Mansise, Cornelius	1806	33	MA
Mairwine, Samuel	1806	26	PA		Manson, James	1809	28	PA
Major, Abraham Jones	1819	18	PA		Manson, Jeremiah	1808	22	PA
Major, Francis	1809	18	NJ		Mansure, John	1807	28	
Major, Francis	1810	0			Manuel, George	1800	26 b	RI
Majos, Antoney	1807	22 m			Many, Peter	1811	27	NY
Makins, James N.	1809	21	PA		Maples, John	1805	22 b	NJ
Malcolm, James	1801	20	PA		Maran, William	1813	24 y	MD
Malcom, Neill G.	1805	20	PA		Marble, Enos	1819	21	MA
Male, Jean	1807	36	LA		March, John	1811	19	MD
Mallet, James	1810	13	NJ		Marchand, Lewis	1811	22 y	PA
Mallet, John Lewis	1806	24	PA		Marel, James	1809	17	PA
Mallon, John	1805	30	SC		Mareren, Joseph	1817	36	LA
Maloney, John	1804	20	PA		Marie, Joseph	1807	28	MS
Maloney, John	1811	27	none given	Mariner, Andrew	1796	0		France
Maloney, John	1815	00			Mariner, Henry	1822	20	PA
Maloney, Joseph	1820	24 c	PA		Mariner, James	1815	19 y	PA
Malony, John	1822	25 b	DE		Mariner, Joshua	1815	42	NY
Maloy, Philip	1805	23	PA		Mark, Joseph	1806	23 b	VA
Maloy, Philip	1805	23	PA		Markoe, Francis	1815	14		none given
Maloy, Philip	1807				Marks, Daniel	1809	26	PA
Maloy, Philip	1807	23	PA		Marks, James	1802	0		Denmark
Malry, John	1816	21 s	VA		Marks, James	1804	30		Denmark
Man, Benjamin	1798	25 m	NY		Marks, James	1822	19	PA
Manchester, John	1820	37	RI		Marks, John	1815	24	LA
Mander, Arthur	1807	37	NY		Marks, Samuel	1820	30 b	PA
Manderfield, Charles	1816	25	PA		Marky, Thomas	1810	22	NJ
Manderfield, George	1810	29	PA		Marlet, Joseph	1822	44	NY
Manfield, Stephen	1810	23 m	NJ		Marley, William	1803	23 m	PA
Manlove, Alexander	1806	20	DE		Marll, Charles	1801	28	PA
Manlove, Alexander	1807	21	DE		Marlue, John	1803	24	NJ
Manlove, David	1801	21	DE		Marotty, John Battis	1809	0 b	
Manlove, David	1804	24	DE		Marquis, Simon	1798	31	
Manlove, David	1808	0			Marr, Edward	1823	22	MA
Manlove, Matthew	1815	21	DE		Marriner, Fenwick	1813	45	DE
Manluff, George	1815	23 b	PA		Marriner, Fenwick	1819	16	PA
Mann, Charles	1807	34	MA		Marriner, George K.	1814	20	DE
Mann, Charles	1810	38			Marrs, Thomas	1815	29	MA
Mann, Charles	1816	25	VA		Marsh, Goldsborough	1822	21 b	DE
Mann, Joseph	1812	24 b	DE		Marsh, John Nubley	1809	17	PA
Mannery, John	1809	16	NJ		Marsh, John	1811	19	PA
Mannery, Richard	1821	28	NJ		Marsh, Marcus	1798	33	NJ
Manney, Enoch	1821	58	NJ		Marsh, Marcus	1798	33 b	NJ
Manning, James	1814	21	NH		Marsh, Ottis	1818	21 s	MA
Manning, John	1815	26	CT		Marsh, Stephen	1803	42	MA
Manning, Thomas	1804	16	NH		Marsh, William	1804	18 m	NJ
Manning, Thomas	1815	16	PA		Marshal, Henry	1803	25	PA
Manning, William	1822	18	PA		Marshal, James	1799	0	PA
Mansfield, John	1801	18	PA		Marshall, Alexander	1813	23	PA

Marshall, Henry	1822	22	DE
Marshall, James	1804	19	DE
Marshall, James	1804	15	PA
Marshall, James	1804	0	
Marshall, James	1822	27	PA
Marshall, John	1803	24 b	VA
Marshall, John	1818	16	MA
Marshall, John	1819	26	PA
Marshall, Lenox	1810	22	MD
Marshall, Levi	1809	18	PA
Marshall, Thomas	1804	21	DE
Marshall, Thomas	1806	0	
Marshall, William	1821	24	NJ
Martain, Robert	1815	16	PA
Marten, Cornelis Sirinas			
	1815	28	LA
Marten, John	1815	25 b	PA
Martien, John	1805	0	
Martien, John M.	1809	0	
Martien, John M.	1811	00	
Martien, Joseph Lisle	1812	20	PA
Martin, Abraham	1810	17	PA
Martin, Anotole	1818	25	PA
Martin, Anthony	1812	21	PA
Martin, Charles	1809	14	PA
Martin, Drummond	1805	25	LA
Martin, Edward	1805	25 b	NY
Martin, Francis	1812	26	PA
Martin, George	1806	19	PA
Martin, George	1810	22	PA
Martin, George	1815	00	
Martin, George	1817	31	PA
Martin, Henry	1801	26	PA
Martin, Jacob Lewis	1811	14	PA
Martin, James	1796	0	PA
Martin, James	1803	19	MA
Martin, Jebo	1810	25	LA
Martin, Joel	1809	23	VA
Martin, John M.	1804	14	PA
Martin, John	1807	24	MS
Martin, John M.	1807		
Martin, John	1807	23	MD
Martin, John	1809	24 y	LA
Martin, John	1809	25	DE
Martin, John	1810	35	LA
Martin, John	1810	24 y	LA
Martin, John	1811	24	DE
Martin, John	1811	16	VA
Martin, John Baptiste Eugene			
	1812	21	none given
Martin, John	1815	26	MA
Martin, John Woodside	1815	14	PA

Martin, John	1816	20	NY
Martin, John Batice	1816	24	LA
Martin, John	1816	24	PA
Martin, John	1820	27	NY
Martin, Joseph	1807	17	DE
Martin, Joseph	1807	19	PA
Martin, Joseph Turner	1809	17	PA
Martin, Joseph	1818	22 b	PA
Martin, Joseph	1819	17	DE
Martin, Major	1804	23	MA
Martin, Mathew	1801	26	
Martin, Michael	1801	16	MA
Martin, Peter	1810	24	LA
Martin, Peter	1815	34	LA
Martin, Philip	1798	23	MD
Martin, Reinhart	1809	22	PA
Martin, Robert	1798	48 b	PA
Martin, Robert	1807	15	MD
Martin, Robert	1811	34	MD
Martin, Robert	1817	19	PA
Martin, Samuel	1801	19	PA
Martin, Thomas	1807	21	PA
Martin, Thomas Gull	1810	21	PA
Martin, Thomas	1815	25	PA
Martin, William	1815	50	PA
Martin, William	1815	19	MA
Martin, William	1816	23 s	NY
Martin, William	1819	21	NJ
Martin, William	1820	22	NJ
Martin, William	1821	23	NJ
Martin, William	1822	21 b	PA
Martin, William	1823	24	PA
Martindale, Charles N.	1820	22	MD
Martinez, Ferdinand	1807	20	LA
Martinis, Manoah	1809	29	LA
Martz, John	1810	22	PA
refused duplicate SPC because he is not			
an American citizen			
Marval, Philip Collins	1810	33 c	PA
Marwick, Andrew	1822	31	ME
Masden, Thomas	1819	22	NJ
Masen, Elijah	1817	25 b	DE
Mash, William	1809	0	NJ
Mashman, John	1811	21	NC
Mason, Charles A.	1816	23	RI
Mason, Francis	1810	12	PA
Mason, Francis	1812	00	
Mason, George	1805	23	PA
Mason, James	1821	40 b	MA
Mason, James	1823	21	NY

Name	Year	Age	State
Mason, John	1804	24	PA
Mason, John	1805	25	VA
Mason, John	1809	18	PA
Mason, John Felix	1811	17 b	LA
Mason, John	1813	0 c	
Mason, John	1821	15	PA
Mason, Lewis	1801	19	PA
Mason, Nathaniel	1814	21	NJ
Mason, Robert	1806	26	PA
Mason, Robert	1806	15	NY
Mason, Thomas	1798	18	NY
Mason, Thomas	1805	0	NY
Mason, Thomas	1815	00	
Mason, William	1822	21	ME
Mason, William	1823	23 b	MD
Massey, Joseph	1811	21	MD
Massey, Joseph	1811	00	
Massey, William	1801	23	MD
Massoner, Matthias	1823	38	PA
Masters, Joseph	1804	21	NC
Mastors, William	1803	24	DE
Mather, Henry	1807	20	MD
Mather, John H.	1818	23 y	CT
Mather, Samuel	1810	30	PA
Mathews, Charles	1809	18	NH
Mathews, George	1806	21	PA
Mathews, George	1820	36	DE
Mathews, James	1797	20	NY
Mathews, William	1804	25	NY
Mathews, William	1806	27	PA
Matlack, Benjamin	1801	21	NJ
Matlock, Abraham Karsper			
	1822	17	PA
Matsinger, John	1807	23	PA
Matson, Cutting	1815	29	MA
Mattee, Thomas	1810	20 b	MD
Mattee, Thomas	1815	00	
Matteson, John Christian			
	1807	20	PA
Matthaws, Isreal	1801	23	PA
Matthews, Daniel	1822	27 b	NJ
Matthews, Hugh	1823	31	NY
Matthews, James	1807	27	PA
Matthews, John	1798	25	NY
Matthews, John	1805	25 b	NJ
Matthews, John	1808	19	MA
Matthews, John	1817	27	DE
Matthews, John	1823	31	GA
Matthews, Joseph	1816	21 s	PA
Matthews, Uriah	1817	18	VT
Matthews, William	1811	22 c	NJ
Matthews, William	1812	24	MA
Mattson, Worrell	1809	16	PA
Maul, Alexander	1810	27	NJ
Maull, James	1809	15	PA
Mauran, Ira	1807	21	RI
Mauraw, Jeremi	1807	26	NY
Maxfield, John	1803	34 b	VA
Maxfield, Thomas	1817	26	DE
Maxfield, William Webster			
	1823	25	ME
Maxwell, Daniel Franklin			
	1811	21	NC
Maxwell, David	1818	24	MA
Maxwell, George	1810	32	SC
Maxwell, Henry	1810	24	PA
Maxwell, John	1809	20	PA
Maxwell, John	1823	28	ME
Maxwell, Solomon	1810	15	DE
Maxwell, Solomon	1814	0	
Maxwell, Thomas	1817	23	NY
Maxwell, Trusty	1809	25 b	PA
Maxwell, Trusty	1810	0	
Maxwell, Trusty	1810	0	
Maxwell, Trusty	1814	0	
Maxwell, Trusty	1819	12 b	
May, Georege	1815	18	NJ
May, George	1809	36	NJ
May, James	1815	19	MA
Mayberry, Mathew	1823	7	Ireland
Maycox, James	1822	22 b	PA
Mayers, Henry	1809	28	PA
Mayers, Nicholas	1811	25	PA
Mayfield, George	1811	18	RI
Mayne, John	1815	20	MD
Mayne, Joseph	1810	28	PA
Mayne, Thomas	1797	22	SC
Mayns, Henry	1820		none given
Mayo, Simeon	1803	32	MA
Mayors, John	1801	22	PA
Maysey, John	1804	22	PA
Maysey, John	1809	27	PA
Maze, Benjamin	1816	19	PA
Maze, William	1809	22	PA
Mazley, William	1820	28	VA
Mc Claskey, William	1809	20	PA
McAdams, James	1818	20	PA
McAfferty, William	1811	18	PA
McAnimy, James	1806	24	NJ
McArthur, Alexander	1818	21	PA
McBride, Henry	1806	29	none given
McBride, John	1806	40	none given
McBryan, Charles	1822	16	PA
McCafferty, Hugh	1808	21	PA

Name	Year	Age		Place
McCahen, Samuel Charless	1817	12		PA
McCale, Robert	1822	30	b	DE
McCall, George	1811	13		PA
McCall, William	1821	19		DE
McCalla, John	1810	20		NJ
McCarney, James	1812	26		none given
McCartey, John	1817	00		
McCarthey, John	1803	14		PA
McCarthy, James	1808	21		PA
McCarthy, James	1811	00		
McCarthy, John	1806	18		PA
McCarthy, Raymond	1823	48		ME
McCartney, Thomas	1820	27		MA
McCarty, Alexander	1810	15		PA
McCarty, John	1817	26		NY
McCarty, John	1821	26		MD
McCaskey, John Hamilton	1822	24		PA
McCasland, James	1804	22		PA
McCauley, Charles Stewart	1807	13		PA
McCauley, George	1816	19		PA
McCawley, Cornelius	1805	23		NH
McClain, Daniel	1811	25		VA
McClain, John	1807	22		NY
McClaskey, William	1823	18		PA
McClatchie, Alexander	1810	30		NJ
McClatchie, Alexander	1811	00		
McClay, John	1807	24		DE
McClay, John	1809	26		DE
McCloud, John	1812	31		PA
McCloud, John	1815	00		
McCloud, Oliver	1823	23		ME
McClure, James	1809	24		PA
McClure, Theophelas	1800	14		PA
McClure, Theophilus	1809	23		PA
McCobley, George	1810	14		PA
McColagan, James	1798	29		Ireland
McCollick, Cato Waterford	1815	27	b	NJ
McComb, Thomas	1798	27		Ireland
McConiche, Peter	1818	23		NY
McConnel, John	1817	20		NJ
McConnell, Edward	1809	27		none given
McConnell, John	1806	20		PA
McConnell, Matthew	1809	21		PA
McCord, Robert	1805	22		PA
McCormack, Daniel	1809	18		NJ
McCormick, Isaac	1806	18		PA
McCormick, John	1810	26		PA
McCormick, John	1817	25		PA
McCormick, Martin	1817	25		MA
McCormick, Martin	1821	26		Ireland
McCormick, William	1815	46		PA
McCowen, Francis	1807	28		PA
McCoy, Edward	1823	23	b	NJ
McCoy, James	1809	17		PA
McCoy, James	1809	0		
McCoy, William	1813	20		PA
McCoy, William	1819	22		PA
McCrea, Robert	1810	14		PA
McCrea, Robert	1815	19		PA
McCrea, Robert	1819	24		PA
McCrearey, John	1798	30		Ireland
McCredie, George	1823	19		VA
McCue, Henry	1804	21		PA
McCue, Henry	1804	21		PA
McCullagh, Robert	1810	15		DE
McCullagh, Robert	1811	25		PA
McCullagh, Robert	1812	00		
McCulloh, George B.	1806	15		PA
McCulloh, George Bell	1806	15		PA
McCullough, Joseph	1811	23		PA
McCullough, William	1806	34		PA
McCully, Thomas S.	1822	16		PA
McCurdy, James A.	1806	20		MA
McDaniel, Duncan	1804	21		PA
McDaniel, John	1805	24		PA
McDermond, Andrew	1814	23		PA
McDermont, Michael	1807	28		VA
McDermott, Stephen	1820	16		PA
McDonald, Charles	1821	22		PA
McDonald, Daniel	1804	37		NC
McDonald, Daniel	1809	28		PA
McDonald, Dennis	1798	28		MD
McDonald, Edward	1820	9	y	PA
McDonald, Henry	1810	13		PA
McDonald, Henry	1815	00		
McDonald, James	1815	20		PA
McDonald, James	1821	26		PA
McDonald, Jeremiah	1815	25		NJ
McDonald, John	1810	27		PA
McDonald, John	1810	21		PA
McDonald, John	1816	33		PA
McDonald, John	1823	21		NY
McDonald, Joshua	1818	22		NY
McDonald, William	1819	26		
McDonaled, Charles	1817	32		NY
McDonnald, Henry	1812	00		
McDonnough, George	1815	21		PA
McDougale, John	1815	18		PA
McDovett, James	1817	42		VA
McDowell, James	1805	28		PA

Name	Year	Age	Extra	State
McDowell, James	1810	13		PA
McElivee, Thomas	1810	27		NJ
McElroy, Herbert	1815	16		PA
McElroy, William	1810	20		PA
McElroy, William	1815	00		
McElwain, George	1809	19		PA
McFadon, John, Jr.	1809	19		MD
McFall, John	1801	29		PA
McFarlan, Andrew	1819	13		PA
McFarlan, William, Jr.	1823	14		PA
McFarland, Arthur	1812	21		NJ
McFarland, George	1805	25		MA
McFarland, Samuel	1821	20		MA
McFarland, Walter	1823	15		PA
McFarlane, John	1799	26		PA
McFarlane, John	1815	24		PA
McFarlane, Walter	1806	35		none given
McFarlane, Walter	1807			
McFarlane, Walter	1807			
McFaul, James	1798	20		NY
McFayden, Edward	1803	38		PA
McFox, James	1810	16		PA
McGarvey, John	1806	21		NJ
McGarvey, John	1810	27		NJ
McGaryle, William	1815	24		NY
McGee, John	1822	19		PA
McGee, Robert	1798	19		PA
McGee, Samuel	1803	29		VA
McGee, Thomas	1806	24		PA
McGee, Thomas	1809	24		none given
McGee, William	1810	33		PA
McGill, John	1805	18		MD
McGill, John	1808	13		PA
McGill, John	1815	00		
McGill, Joseph R.	1821	24		NJ
McGill, Mathias	1798	22		NJ
McGill, Matthias	1810	0		
McGinley, Samuel	1812	25		PA
McGinnis, John	1813	16		NY
McGinniss, Barney S.	1815	24		PA
McGlassin, James	1809	23		PA
McGlathery, James, Jr.	0000	0		
McGlathery, James, Jr.	1812	13		PA
McGlathevy, James	1814	0		
McGowan, John Peter	1804	22		NJ
McGowan, John Patrick	1804	22		NJ
McGowan, John	1812	15		PA
McGowan, John	1819	14		PA
McGrath, James	1815	30		NY
McGraw, John	1815	21		VT
McGregor, Archibald	1800	17		PA
McGuffin, Robert	1806	26		PA
McGuffin, Thomas	1811	23		NJ
McGuire, Hugh	1810	0		GA
McGuire, Hugh	1810	17		GA
McGuire, Lewis	1817	25	c	LA
McGuire, William	1805	16		DE
McHall, Levin	1822	22		MD
McHam, Daniel N.	1821	32		DE
McHurd, Charles	1811	26	b	MD
McIlvain, Isaac	1821	19		PA
McIntire, James	1811	21		PA
McIntire, William	1801	33		PA
McIntire, William B.	1821	18		DE
McIntosh, James G.	1801	32		NH
McIntosh, Mountain	1798	30	b	
McIsaac, James	1820	21		NY
McKay, David	1812	22		DE
McKay, George	1801	23		PA
McKay, William	1820	23		NY
McKean, George	1817	25		NY
McKean, Thomas	1820	17		NJ
McKee, John	1815	43		DE
McKee, John	1815	17		PA
McKee, Joshua	1798	20		NY
McKellar, Neill	1804	33		PA
McKenlay, James	1819	21		NY
McKenney, William	1811	23		NJ
McKenzie, Alexander	1799	26		
McKenzie, George	1799	30	b	VA
McKenzie, Kenneth	1819	29		PA
McKenzie, Reuben	1815	25		MA
Mckever, James	1810	30		PA
McKever, James, Jr.	1803	19		MD
McKever, Reese W.	1809	19		PA
McKinnel, James	1810	20		MD
McKinney, Thomas	1806	28		MA
McKinney, William	1816	40	b	MD
McKinnon, Archabald	1807	18		MA
McKinsey, Jacob	1803	49		none given
McKinzie, William	1801	21		PA
McLaughlin, Charles	1811	17	y	PA
McLaughlin, Daniel	1809	30		none given
McLaughlin, George	1805	17		PA
McLaughlin, John	1811	13		PA
McLaughlin, Patrick	1799	20		PA
McLaughlin, Robert	1815	23		PA
McLean, James	1814	22		DE
McLean, Thomas	1805	15		VA
McLearn, William	1823	15		PA
McLeod, John	1809	19		MD
McLeod, John	1821	25		ny
McLeveen, Myles Thornton				
	1819	17		PA

McLoud, Daniel	1798	20	PA	
McLoud, Daniel	1807			
McLoude, Daniel	1811	32	PA	
McLughlin, Edward	1810	32		Ireland
McMahon, Thomas Pinckney				
	1811	18		none given
McMan, William	1807	26	NJ	
McManus, John	1817	24	MA	
McMeaken, William Greves				
	1815	17	NY	
McMichael, William	1823	21	NJ	
McMickel, James	1806	36	PA	
McMollin, John	1818	45		Ireland
McMullan, John	1807	25	PA	
McMullen, John	1803	54		none given
McMullen, Joseph	1821	21	PA	
McMullen, Michael	1799	31		Ireland
McMullin, Alexander	1809	26	PA	
McMullin, Daniel	1808	20	NY	
McMullin, Robert	1819	18	PA	
McMurdy, Benjamin	1809	22	DE	
McMurphy, Thomas	1804	24	DE	
McNally, Robert	1810	30	PA	
McNary, Morris	1822	27	CT	
McNeal, Alexander	1799	21 b	PA	
McNeal, Israel	1812	00		
McNeal, John	1798	22	PA	
McNeal, John	1804	25	PA	
McNeal, John	1811	28	NY	
McNeal, John	1812	00	NY	
McNeiledge, James	1811	21 y	DE	
McNeilledge, Alexander				
	1810	18	NY	
McNeilledge, James	1816	0		
McNeilledge, James	1817	00	DE	
McNelly, Robert	1815	00		
McNelly, Robert	1818	37	PA	
McNiel, Israel	1811	18 b	PA	
McNullidge, James	1812	00		
McNutty, James	1815	26	PA	
McPhail, John	1796	26	PA	
McPhail, John	1798	0	PA	
McPhatridge, Thomas	1804	20	DE	
McPherson, Edward	1819	15	PA	
McPherson, Hugh	1799	0		Sweden
McPherson, Hugh, Jr.	1817	18	PA	
McPherson, John	1804	24 b	PA	
McPherson, John	1815	27	PA	
McPherson, Michael	1817	19	VA	
McPherson, Robert	1810	24	PA	
McPherson, Robert	1812	00		
McPherson, Robert	1820	15	PA	

McPherson, William	1811	17	PA	
McQuaid, John	1816	16	PA	
McQuhae, William	1805	25		Scotland
McQuillen, Hugh	1810	18	PA	
McTaggart, John	1805	22	SC	
McVicar, Nevan	1806	19	VA	
McWilliam, David	1806	26	NJ	
Meade, George	1818	19	PA	
Mean, Henry	1815	20	CT	
Meany, Cornelius	1809	17	PA	
Meany, Cornelius	1815	00		
Meany, Edward	1809	19	NY	
Mearing, Thomas	1805	25	PA	
Mears, John	1805	21 b	MS	
Mears, Shedrick	1811	00		
Meason, Richard	1815	26	RI	
Mecum, Edward	1806	43	NJ	
Meder, Timothy	1820	30	MA	
Medicine, Anthony	1810	36	LA	
See note John Maddis aabove.				
Medicis, Anthonio	1812	00		
Medkiff, Ephraim	1822	20	MD	
Medlyn, James	1807	15	NY	
Meeker, James	1809	26 y	NJ	
Meeker, Wakeman	1806	18	CT	
Meekins, Isaac	1815	28	MD	
Meer, John Jackson	1823	14	PA	
Meers, Shedrack	1806	29 b	VA	
Meganliss, Edward	1809	23	PA	
Megill, John	1811	00		
Meginnes, Stephen	1811	28		none given
Megonigal, John	1810	22	PA	
Meilburne, Thomas	1807	24	NY	
Mein, Charles	1812	00		
Mejeat, Jan	1811	19	LA	
Mellar, William	1798	23	PA	
Mellinby, Henry	1811	22	PA	
Mellon, Peter	1810	33	NJ	
Meloy, Joseph	1798	26	NJ	
Melward, George	1798	19	MA	
Mende, Peter	1803	35	SC	
Mendenhall, Thomas, Jr.				
	1818	25	DE	
Menn, John Henry	1805	19		
Mennen, William	1809	19	NY	
Mentz, Joseph	1809	18	PA	
Meny, Silas	1819	25 b	NJ	
Mequillin, James	1807	14	PA	
Mercier, Charles, Jr.	1823	18	PA	
Meredeth, James	1798	25	MD	

Meredith, David	1804	20 b	DE
indented to Benjamin C. Wilcocks and goes			
to sea with his consent			
Meredith, David	1809	0 b	DE
Meredith, David	1810	0	
Meredith, Hugh	1821	14	PA
Meredith, James	1810	14	PA
Meredith, William	1817	31	RI
Merit, William	1807	24	NY
Merkeel, Abraham	1822	20 y	VA
Merlin, Lewis	1823	21	PA
Merrick, Alexander P.	1812	21	PA
Merrick, Alexander P.	1812	00	
Merrick, Joseph	1820	20	PA
Merrill, Richard	1815	35	CT
Merrit, Charles	1809	20 y	NY
Merritt, Nathaniel	1817	24	MA
Merritt, William	1811	29	PA
Merrow, Zachariah	1804	17	NJ
Merry, James	1815	23	PA
Merryman, John	1816	45	VA
Merryman, Joseph	1819	31	CT
Merryman, Timothy	1811	23	MA
Meryo, Brisstol	1804	22 b	PA
Mesnage, Lewis	1809	31	none given
Mettz, George	1806	21	PA
Metz, John Bern	1811	24	none given
Metzger, Charles D.	1805	17	NJ
Meyer, Thomas	1815	25	PA
Meyerdircks, Henry	1823	18	MA
Meyers, David	1818	19	
Meyers, Frederick	1803	26	PA
Meyers, John J.	1806	29	GA
born Broton Street, Savanna, GA			
Meyers, John	1806	40	PA
Meyers, John	1809	24	NJ
Meyers, John	1810	23	NJ
Meyers, Peter C.	1812	23	PA
Michael, John	1806	40 b	MD
Michael, John	1811	59 b	LA
Michael, Joseph	1817	14	PA
Michaels, John	1807	31	MS
Micken, John	1806	32	LA
Mickerson, Stephen	1803	22	MA
Mickle, John W.	1817	25	NJ
Middleton, Benjamin	1810	36 b	MD
Middleton, James	1805	23	SC
Middleton, James	1810	0	
Middleton, James	1819	16	NY

Middleton, John, Jr.	1807	24	NJ
Middleton, John	1811	18	PA
Middleton, John	1815	00	
Middleton, Levin	1812	23 b	MD
Middleton, Michael	1795	0	MA
Middleton, Samuel	1819	20	PA
Middleton, Thomas	1808	29	PA
Middleton, Thomas	1811	22	PA
Middleton, Thomas	1812	22	DE
Middleton, William	1807	18	PA
Midlen, Walter, Jr.	1815	20	PA
Midlen, William	1808	16	PA
Midlen, William	1811	00	
Miercken, David	1808	0	PA
Miercken, Henry	1821	14	PA
Miercken, John W.	1815	20	PA
Mierckon, David	1804	35	PA
Miers, Thomas	1823	18	NH
Mierse, Christian D.	1801	20	PA
Mies, Abraham	1807	22 b	NY
Mifflin, Edward	1820	14	PA
Mifflin, Henry	1815	14	PA
Milbery, William, Jr.	1811	23	MA
Mildorn, William	1820	24 y	MD
Miles, Benjamin	1805	23	PA
Miles, Benjamin	1805	0	
Miles, Charles	1809	26	PA
Miles, Charles	1810	0	
Miles, James	1822	22	PA
Miles, John	1798	21	DE
Miles, Mitchell	1809	23	MA
Miles, Samuel	1812	19	PA
Miles, Suthey	1796	0	MA
Miles, William	1811	16	PA
Miles, William	1814	21	PA
Millar, Charles	1821	26	PA
Millbourn, William	1804	21 y	MD
Millegan, James	1809	21 b	DE
Millen, David	1809	17	DE
Miller, Andrew	1811	30	MD
Miller, Charles	1804	21 m	DE
Miller, Charles	1810	0	
Miller, Charles	1818	29	PA
Miller, Charles	1819	26	LA
Miller, Curtis	1809	38 b	DE
Miller, Curtis	1810	0	DE
Miller, David	1810	24 b	DE
Miller, David	1811	00	
Miller, Edward	1798	19	RI
Miller, Elias	1809	24	NJ
Miller, Elijah	1804	44	CT
Miller, Elijah	1814	22 b	DE

Miller, Francis	1812	14	PA
Miller, George	1807	24	PA
Miller, Henry	1799	21	PA
Miller, Henry	1805	28	NC
Miller, Henry	1809	26 b	MA
Miller, Henry	1810	0 b	
Miller, Isaac	1817	00	
Miller, Isaac	1817	25 b	PA
Miller, Isaiah	1798	22	DE
Miller, Jabez	1823	25	ME
Miller, Jacob	1806	22	PA
Miller, Jacob	1807	27	PA
Miller, James	1806	19	SC
Miller, James Y.	1807	22	MA
Miller, James	1808	22	PA
Miller, James	1809	27 b	NJ
Miller, James	1810	0	
Miller, James	1810	24	PA
Miller, James	1810	36	DE
Miller, James	1820	33	PA
Miller, Jeremiah	1816	24	NY
Miller, John	1805	21 b	PA
Miller, John	1806	21	PA
Miller, John	1807	22	PA
Miller, John	1807	17 b	DE
Miller, John	1807	15	PA
Miller, John	1808	29	PA
Miller, John	1809	0	VA
Miller, John	1809	22	NY
Miller, John	1809	29	PA
Miller, John	1809	22	PA
Miller, John	1810	27	PA
Miller, John	1810	18	RI
Miller, John Jacob	1811	28	PA
Miller, John	1812	00	
Miller, John	1813	0	
Miller, John	1820	33	NY
Miller, John	1821	20	PA

Miller, Jonathan	1804	13 b	DE

indented as a free black boy to Dorcas Montgomery

Miller, Jonathan	1809	20 b	DE
Miller, Joseph	1809	19	DE
Miller, Joseph	1816	21	PA
Miller, Mark	1812	23 b	DE
Miller/Miles, Curtis	1809	38 b	DE
Miller, Nicholas J.	1798	30	PA
Miller, Peter	1804	21	VA

Miller, Richard Christian

	1804	19	MD

Miller, Robert B.	1817	16	PA
Miller, Robert	1822	28 s	VA
Miller, Thomas	1809	25 b	MD

Miller, Thomas Harrison

	1810	23	none given
Miller, Thomas	1811	23 m	PA
Miller, Thomas	1820	28	PA
Miller, Timonten B.	1818	25 b	MD
Miller, William	1801	21	NC
Miller, William	1804	25	NY
Miller, William	1804	25	NY
Miller, William	1812	25	PA
Miller, William	1812	26	none given
Miller, William F.	1818	21	DE
Miller, William B.	1818	15	DE
Miller, William E.	1820	21	PA
Miller, William	1823	22	NJ
Milligan, John	1798	25	PA
Milliken, Alexander Jr.	1817	18	MA

Milliken, Charles Austin

	1817	9	MA
Milliner, James	1822	23	VA
Millington, David	1800	20	SC
Millner, William	1805	22	NY
Mills, Alexander	1807	39	PA
Mills, Elijah	1815	28 b	MA
Mills, George	1810	17	NY
Mills, Henry	1805	28	PA
Mills, Henry	1807	31	PA
Mills, James	1821	22 y	NY
Mills, John	1809	31	PA
Mills, John	1810	15	NC
Mills, John	1819	21	NY
Mills, Joseph	1807	24	DE
Mills, Joseph	1822	28	NH
Mills, Matthew	1821	26	NY
Mills, Peter	1799	0	PA
Mills, Robert	1819	23	MA
Mills, Samuel	1805	20	NY
Mills, Thomas	1807	21	VA
Mills, Thomas	1812	11 m	PA
Mills, Thomas	1814	23	PA
Mills, William	1822	19	NJ
Millward, John	1817	28	PA
Milner, Robert	1799	18	
Milner, William B.	1823	21	PA
Milward, George	1805	26	MA

Milward, Richard Buckler

	1809	19	NY
Mines, Christopher	1817	21	MD
Mingle, William	1807	14	PA
Mingle, William	1812	00	

Mink, Reinhard	1803	36	PA
Minos, William	1809	27 b	DE
Mint, Rose	1817	21	SC
Minto, John	1810	24	MA
Miskell, Martin	1811	24	MA
Mitchel, Charles	1807	30	NJ
Mitchel, Daniel Baker	1815	28	VA
Mitchel, Henry	1823	20	NY
Mitchel, Joseph	1803	23	NY
Mitchel, Walter	1803	27	NY
Mitchell, Abraham	1821	20	ME
Mitchell, Adam	1805	18 c	MD
Mitchell, Adam	1806	24 b	NY
Mitchell, Alexander	1815	22	NY
Mitchell, Anthony	1804	23	MD
Mitchell, Anthony	1809	0	
Mitchell, Charles	1810	32 b	MA
Mitchell, Charles	1819	38	MA
Mitchell, David	1807	24	MA
Mitchell, Ezekiel	1811	22	MA
Mitchell, George	1817	22	PA
Mitchell, James	1810	18	RI
Mitchell, James, Jr.	1815	25	VA
Mitchell, James	1817	32	PA
Mitchell, John	1796	0	VA
Mitchell, John	1799	21	PA
Mitchell, John	1804	26	MA
Mitchell, John	1807	22 b	DE
Mitchell, John	1808	56 b	LA
Mitchell, John	1810	21	NH
Mitchell, John	1812	19	LA
Mitchell, John	1817	26	SC
Mitchell, John	1817	24 b	NJ
Mitchell, John	1822	25 b	DE
Mitchell, Jonathan	1806	56 b	PA
Mitchell, Joseph	1810	21 c	LA
Mitchell, Joseph	1812	00 b	LA
Mitchell, Paschall	1811	21	PA
Mitchell, Thomas	1810	30	MA
Mitchell, Thomas	1816	20	PA
Mitchell, William	1805	13	PA
Mitchell, William	1806	0	
Mitchell, William	1806	33	NY
Mitchell, William	1806	34	MA
Mitchell, Young	1817	30	NY
Mix, Charles Ash	1815	15	PA
Mix, Charles Ashe	1817	17	PA
Mixo, Juan	1807	25	MS
Mode, John	1810	20 y	DE
Moderwell, James	1815	18	PA
Moffet, Gerard	1818	18	PA
Moffett, Thomas Jr.	1815	26	NJ

Mohere, Richard	1817	00		
Moist, Henry	1823	44	PA	
Molbon, John	1811	26 y	VA	
Molde, John	1806	17	NY	
Moleneux, William	1809	19	PA	
Moler, Fortune	1809	19 c	PA	
Moles, Cage	1804	21	VA	
Moles, Cage	1804	21	VA	
Moliere, Richard	1815	15	PA	
Moliere, Richard	1818			
Moliere, Thomas	1815	16	PA	
Molineax, Benjamin E.	1807	17	PA	
Molle, Christian	1815	36		Prussia
Molledore, John	1809	21	PA	
Molliston, Solomon	1812	20 b	DE	
Molliston, Stephen	1812	00		
Molliston, Stephen	1812	22 b	DE	
Molloy, Arthur	1816	20	VA	
Molloy, Joseph C.	1823	20	NY	
Molony, Berry	1823	27 s	PA	
Molony, Daniel	1820	21	PA	
Mondoza, Charles	1820	25 y	NJ	
Monfort, Francis	1809	25	LA	
Monfree, James F.	1814	23	SC	
Monham, William	1818	23	PA	
Monk, Joseph	1811	15	PA	
Monroe, Henry	1805	21	PA	
Montgomery, Charles	1806	28	MA	
Montgomery, Ephram	1809	21 b	NJ	
Montgomery, Francis	1804	25	MA	
Montgomery, Jacob	1811	25	DE	
Montgomery, John	1807	40	NJ	
Montgomery, John	1810	0		
Montgomery, John	1811	00		
Montgomery, John	1811	22 m	NY	
Montgomery, Samuel Powell				
	1807	17	PA	
Montgomery, William G.				
	1809	22	PA	
Montgomery, William	1817	19	PA	
Montieth, Edward R.	1815	12	PA	
Montinjelot, Francisco	1808	35	LA	
Montville, Peter	1816	0		
Moody, George M.	1811	17	PA	
Moody, James	1801	23	DE	
Moody, Joshua	1806	35	MA	
Moody, Joshua	1809	0	MA	
Moody, Samuel	1809	21	DE	
Moody, Samuel	1815	00		
Moody, William	1810	23	DE	
Moon, George	1820	23 b	NJ	
Moor, James	1798	25	NH	

Name	Year	Age		State
Moor, James	1801	15		PA
Moor, Justus	1804	21		CT
Moor, Thomas	1805	39		NY
Moore, Alexander	1810	17		DE
Moore, Andrew	1804	26	b	NC
Moore, Andrew	1810	33		MD
Moore, Andrew	1811	00		
Moore, Benjamin	1822	18		ME
Moore, Charles	1810	31	b	PA
Moore, Daniel	1806	19		PA
Moore, Daniel, Jr.	1811	23		PA
Moore, Edward	1810	20	c	NY
Moore, Edward	1811	00		
Moore, George	1820	23	b	NJ
Moore, Henry	1811	19	b	MD
Moore, Isaac	1806	24		PA
Moore, James	1807	25		PA
Moore, James	1814	26		NJ
Moore, John	1796	25	c	
Moore, John	1798	20		DE
Moore, John	1804	28	b	MA
Moore, John	1806	0		DE
Moore, John	1806	26		SC
Moore, John	1806	26		SC
Moore, John	1807	25	b	MD
Moore, John	1809	15		NY
Moore, John	1809	23		RI
Moore, John	1810	37	b	NY
Moore, John	1810	0		
Moore, John P.	1810	15		PA
Moore, John	1811	27	b	MD
Moore, John	1814	29		PA
Moore, John	1823	26		PA
Moore, Jonathan	1804	16		PA
Moore, Joseph	1817	20		PA
Moore, Mathias	1820	50	b	MD
Moore, Richard	1810	30	b	PA
Moore, Richard	1812	30	m	NJ
Moore, Robert	1805	23		PA
Moore, Samuel	1817	27		PA
Moore, Samuel	1818	22		NH
Moore, Shandy	1810	16	b	NY
Moore, Shandy	1811	00		
Moore, Thomas	1799	25		DE
Moore, Thomas	1804	38		NY
Moore, Thomas	1805	0		NY
Moore, Thomas	1806	0		
Moore, Thomas	1807			
Moore, Thomas E.	1817	21		NJ
Moore, Thomas	1821	14		PA
Moore, William	1804	25		MA
Moore, William	1807		b	DE
Moore, William	1810	19		NY
Moore, William	1812	00		
Moore, William	1812	34		NY
Moore, William	1817	29		NY
Moore, William	1819	23	b	PA
Moore, Zalmon	1807	37		NY
Moose, John	1815	16		PA
Moose, John	1817	19		PA
Moran, James	1820	18		NY
Moran, John	1818	23		NY
Moran, William	1804	22		MD
Moran, William	1809	20		DE
Morang, Samuel	1815	21		MD
Mordant, John	1815	28		LA
More, David	1809	19		NJ
More, John Homer	1811	19		MA
More, Moses M.	1821	17	b	PA
Morel, Peter	1818	20		PA
Morgan, Francis	0000	0		PA
Morgan, Francis	1804	28		PA
Morgan, Geroge Washington	1819	16		PA
Morgan, Henry	1809	43		NY
Morgan, James	1815	30	b	MD
Morgan, John	1805	20		NJ
Morgan, John	1806	21		NJ
Morgan, Jonathan	1798	21		MD
Morgan, Joseph C.	1809	25		PA
Morgan, Platt	1809	21	m	NY
Morgan, Reuben O.	1819	24		DE
Morgan, Thomas	1805	33		PA
Morgan, Thomas	1808	29		VA
Morgan, Thomas	1809	20		PA
Morgan, Ward	1805	18		NJ
Morgan, Ward	1805	17		NJ
Morgan, Ward	1809	0		
Morgan, Ward	1818	28		NJ
Morgan, William	1807	13		PA
Morgan, Wm.	1812	34		MD
Morin, Raphael	1806	18		LA
Morison, Condy	1804	21		DE
Morison, Condy	1807			DE
Mority, John Battis	1809	20	b	DE
Morlen, John	1818	25		NY
Morney, Robert	1798	26		VA
Morose, Dominica	1804	32		none given
Morrell, Abraham	1810	19		PA
Morrell, Jacob	1816	27	y	SC
Morrell, Johnson	1798	25		NJ
Morrell, Richard	1804	21		PA
Morret, John	1809	27		LA
Morrill, Charles M.	1820	20		MA

Morris, Abraham	1810	0	
Morris, Abraham	1810	21 b	MD
Morris, Abraham	1821	14	ME
Morris, Barnabas	1816	31	MA
Morris, Benjamin	1810	30 b	NJ
Morris, Benjamin	1815	25	MA
Morris, Benjamin	1815	00	
Morris, Caesar Augustus			
	1798	23 m	NY
Morris, Charles	1810	25 b	LA
Morris, Charles	1823	18 b	PA
Morris, Cyrus	1809	25 b	DE
Morris, Ebenezer	1803	27	NY
Morris, Edmond	1805	24 b	DE
Morris, Elisha	1810	24	DE
Morris, George	1806	17	NY
Morris, George	1807	19	PA
Morris, George	1809	0	
Morris, George Farquhar			
	1810	20	PA
Morris, George	1811	00	
Morris, George	1815	40 b	PA
Morris, Isaac	1804	25 b	PA
Morris, Isaac	1809	21 m	NY
Morris, Isaac	1810	19 b	MD
Morris, Isaac	1811	00	
Morris, Isaac	1816	0	
Morris, Isaac	1817	20 b	PA
Morris, Isaac	1818	39 b	DE
Morris, Jacob	1799	39 b	MD
Morris, Jacob	1815	39 y	DE
Morris, James	1805	21 b	GA
Morris, James	1811	15 b	PA
Morris, James	1821	25 b	DE
Morris, Jesse	1797	21	PA
Morris, John	1796	0	NH
Morris, John	1805	24	PA
Morris, John	1811	20	NC
Morris, John	1812	24	DE
Morris, John	1812	26	NY
Morris, John	1815	15	PA
Morris, Joseph	1809	21	DE
Morris, Mitchell	1818	27 b	LA
Morris, Richard	1821	55 b	PA
Morris, Robert	1815	26 b	MA
Morris, Samuel	1798	20	MA
Morris, Samuel	1808	20 b	NY
Morris, Samuel	1809	21 b	NY
Morris, Samuel	1811	19	MA
Morris, Stephen	1805	28 b	MD
Morris, Thomas	1812	20	MD
Morris, William	1806	23	MA
Morris, William	1807	23	MD
Morris, William	1811	25	NY
Morris, Zebulan	1809	22 b	NY
Morrison, Andrew	1809	17	PA
Morrison, Candy	1808	0	
Morrison, Dependence	1815	00	
Morrison, Dependence	1815	24	VA
Morrison, Jacob	1815	27	NY
Morrison, James	1803	26	PA
Morrison, James	1804	0	
Morrison, James	1804	0	
Morrison, James	1805	26	LA
Morrison, John	1798	19	PA
Morrison, John	1801	24	MA
Morrison, John	1807	16	PA
Morrison, John	1822	19 b	PA
Morrison, Robert	1815	21	NY
Morrison, William	1809	18	PA
Morrisson, Charles	1815	24	PA
Morrow, Matthew	1804	25	NJ
Morse, Daniel	1796	36	MA
Morse, John	1817	17	MA
Morse, Levi	1818	21	MA
Morss, Isaac	1809	32	MD
Morss, Robert	1805	28	NJ
Mortimer, Francis Joseph			
	1815	24	LA
son of Peter Jerome Mortimer, merchant			
of New Orleans			
Mortimer, John	1822	39	VA
Mortimor, Lester	1807	20 b	CT
Morton, George	1801	24	VA
Morton, John	1798	25	PA
Morton, John	1815	17	NJ
Morton, Samuel	1821	24	DE
Moses, Ezekiel	1811	21 b	VA
Moses, Ezekiel	1816	22 b	VA
Moses, Isaac	1818	31 b	VA
Moses, Israel	1823	23 b	VA
Mosher, James	1803	18	MD
Mosher, John	1804	22	PA
Moslander, John	1821	23	NJ
Moss, Aza	1823	21	NC
Moss, Banjamin	1809	21	DE
Moss, James	1811	17	NY
Moss, John	1798	17	PA
Moss, Robert	1804	22	VA
Moss, Theo F.	0000	18	
Moss, Theo. F.	????	18	
Moss, William	1807	24	VA

Mosson, John Hill	1823	35	SC
Mott, Gessham	1806	22	DE
Mott, John	1798	27	DE
Mould, James	1805	25	MA
Mould, William	1815	33	MA
Moulder, Joseph	1815	22	PA
Mount, Edwards	1804	22	NJ
Mount, Forman M.	1813	20	NJ
Mount, Josiah	1820	18 c	PA
Mount, Thomas	1820	19 y	PA
Mountain, James M.	1807	16	DE
Movran, Richard	1806	28	MD
Mowberry, William	1821	22	DC
Mowbray, John	1801	22	PA
Mower, George	1817	33	NJ
Mowlan, William	1809	16	DE
Mowlan, William	1811	19	DE
Mowlan, William	1815	00	

Mowlar, William 1814 0
SPC lost 25 Oct. 1812 aboard U.S. Frigate
Unitod States

Much, Adam	1809	21	PA
Much, Jeremiah, Jr.	1807	25	PA

Muckleroy, Samuel 1813 40 PA
held prisoner on board his B. M. prison ship
Massau lying at Chatham, England

Muhlenberg, Peter, Jr.	1806	19	PA
Muir, Thomas	1801	22	CT
Mulford, Thomas	1801	18	NJ
Mull, Jacob	1823	19	VA
Mullen, John	1800	22	PA
Muller, Friedrick C.	1807	23	PA
Muller, Hinrick	1804	23	PA
Muller, Peter	1813	23	PA
Mulligan, Michael	1809	22	MD
Mulligan, Michael	1810	0	MD
Mullikin, William	1810	21	MD
Mulloy, James	1810	23	MA
Mumford, Richard	1821	18	NY
Munay, Jacob	1803	25	PA
Muncy, Daniel	1809	21	NJ
Mundeville, Peter	1810	40 b	LA
Mundorus, William	1812	00	
Munger, Peter	1811	19	NY
Munger, William	1815	18	NY
Munrow, Job	1807	20	NJ
Munsell, John	1807	27	LA
Murat, John	1813	18	NJ

Murdock, John	1798	0		Scotland
Murduck, John,Jr.	1805	20	PA	
Murduck, Jonathan	1811	29	PA	
Murmer, Frederick	1815	21 c	PA	
Murmery, Benjamin	1822	22	PA	
Murphey, John	1815	16	PA	
Murphy, David	1806	23	NJ	
Murphy, David	1809	26	NJ	
Murphy, Enos	1820	16	PA	
Murphy, Francis	1807	24	NJ	
Murphy, George	1817	15	CT	
Murphy, Isaac	1811	26 y	DE	
Murphy, James	1810	25	DE	
Murphy, James	1817	26	PA	
Murphy, John	1805	24	NJ	
Murphy, Joseph	1807	25	PA	
Murphy, Joseph	1807	24 b	VA	
Murphy, Joseph	1807			
Murphy, Michael	1807	21	PA	
Murphy, Peter	1806	20	PA	
Murphy, Philip	1804	14	MD	
Murphy, Thomas	1805	25	DE	
Murphy, Thomas	1807	20	NJ	
Murphy, William	1810	28 b	MD	
Murray, Abendigo	1815	23 b	PA	
Murray, Abraham Bennett				
	1821	18 y	PA	
Murray, Abraham	1823	25 b	PA	
Murray, Andrew Tod	1809	32	NH	
Murray, Cotton	1811	21	MA	
Murray, George	1807	16	MD	
Murray, Isaac	1806	28 m	DE	
Murray, James	1804	20	DE	
Murray, James	1806	22	PA	
Murray, James	1812	00		
Murray, James	1812	27	NY	
Murray, James	1815	33	MA	
Murray, John	1797	0	MD	
Murray, John	1804	17	NY	
Murray, John	1811	16 m	PA	
Murray, John	1820	22		none given
Murray, Joseph	1811	26	MA	
Murray, Manwall	1809	37 b	MD	
Murray, Nathan	1809	32 b	PA	
Murray, Nathan	1815	00		
Murray, Stephen	1803	22 y	MD	
Murrey, Hambelton	1815	27 b	MD	
Murrey, Isaac	1807	29 b	PA	
Murrey, James	1804	28 m	VA	
Murrey, Samuel, Jr.	1812	22 c	MD	
Murry, Isaac	1809	32 y	VA	
Murry, Jacob	1809	0		

Murry, James	1814	0	
Murry, James	1815	00	
Murry, Nicholas	1809	22	PA
Murry, William	1815	25	PA
Murtetus, Samuel	1815	26	PA
Murtetus, Samuel	1818		
Murttus, Samuel	1812	22	PA
Muschert, George	1804	21	VA
Musquett, Thomas	1806	23	PA
Musquett, Thomas	1809	0	
Myer, John, Jr.	1803	19	PA
Myer, John	1810	21	PA
Myer, John	1811	00	
Myer, William	1809	14	PA
Myer, William	1810	0	
Myerle, Benjamin	1819	22	PA
Myerle, Frederick	1822	24	PA
Myers, Charles H.	1822	22	NY
Myers, Daniel	1815	24	NJ
Myers, David	1821	38	NY
Myers, Edward	1815	23	MD
Myers, Frederick	1798	30	PA
Myers, Frederick SPC stolen in Russia	1804	0	PA
Myers, George	1807	18	NJ
Myers, George	1809	22	PA
Myers, George	1814	0	
Myers, George	1815	00	
Myers, Henry	1809	29	PA
Myers, James	1804	19 b	PA
Myers, James	1818	29 b	NY
Myers, John	1806	0	
Myers, John	1810	27	LA
Myers, John P.	1815	22	PA
Myers, John	1821	16	PA
Myers, John	1822	13	PA
Myers, Joseph	1809	24 b	MD
Myers, Joseph	1811	21	PA
Myers, Samuel Davis	1810	17	PA
Myers, Samuel	1815	17	PA
Myers, Thomas	1801	18 y	NY
Myers, Thomas	1805	21	PA
Myers, Thomas	1814	22	NJ
Myers, William	1806	20	MD
Myers, William	1815	20	PA
Myrick, Jethro	1804	23	MA
Myrick, John	1804	33	RI
Myrick, John	1807	44	NY
Myrick, Samuel	1815	23	MA
Nace, Joseph	1817	19	PA

Nailer, David	1805	27 b	PA	
Namette, Eli A.	1807			
Nante, Daniel	1809	20	LA	
Napier, James	1806	25	MA	
Napier, James	1815	14	PA	
Nargney, James	1809	24		none given
Nartigue, John Edward	1815	19	PA	
Nary, Michael	1816	28	MD	
Nash, James	1806	40 b	NY	
Nash, William	1818	23 b	DE	
Nassan, Michael	1814	28	PA	
Nat, John	1807	22	PA	
Nat, John	1812	00		
Nathans, David	1811	18	PA	
Navaria, Joseph	1819	20	NY	
Nave, Benjamin	1801	17	NJ	
Nayle, Michael	1811	17	PA	
Naylon, Thomas	1796	21	PA	
Naylor, William	1806	22	NJ	
Nead, Guy	1809	23 b	PA	
Neadus, Richard	1817	22 b	PA	
Neafus, Mahlon T.	1810	26	NJ	
Neal, Anderson	1822	23 b	NC	
Neal, Benjamin T.	1819	23	NH	
Neal, David	1804	21	PA	
Neal, David	1805	23	PA	
Neal, Jacob	1817	21 b	NJ	
Neal, John	1815	22	MA	
Neal, John	1822	21	PA	
Neal, Parmenio	1808	22	MA	
Neal, William	1821	22	PA	
Neath, George	1823	24	PA	
Nedley, James	1805	21	PA	
Needham, James	1807	23 y	DE	
Needs, Richard	1817	00		
Neen, William	1808	19	SC	
Negles, Henry	1805	15	MA	
Negles, Michael	1816	23	MA	
Negley, William	1822	48	PA	
Negus, Stephen W.	1811	19	PA	
Neill, John	1804	26	PA	
Neill, William C.	1809	19	MD	
Neilledge, Alexander M.	1818			
Neilson, Noble, Jr. C.	1822	21	PA	
Neilson, Stephen	1798	32	MD	
Nelson, Andrew	1807	25	NJ	
Nelson, Andrew	1810	0		
Nelson, Andrew	1817	00		
Nelson, Davis	1807	2	NJ	
Nelson, Fredrick	1817	34	PA	
Nelson, Henry	1815	21	NY	
Nelson, Isaac	1804	22	NJ	

Nelson, James	1821	15	PA
Nelson, Jocob	1807	20	PA
Nelson, Joshua	1806	28	NY
Nelson, Nicolas	1807	23	NJ
Nelson, Oliver	1821	36	MA
Nelson, Robert H.	1804	27	
Nelson, Thomas	1809	14	DE
Nelson, William R.	1805	25	SC
Nepean, Evan	1817	35	Africa
Nesbit, George	1799	27	PA
Nesbit, Richard	1813	0	
Nesbitt, George	1805	0	
Nesbitt, Thomas	1804	28	PA
Nestell, William	1816	18	NY
Nevin, John	1807	26	MA
Nevin, Thomas	1817	18	
Nevin, William	1798	22	MA
New, John	1804	22	PA
Newark, Jesse	1810	18	NJ
Newark, William	1809	35	NJ
Newberry, Daniel	1805	23	CT
Newburey, Daniel	1810	32	CT
Newby, Richard	1796	0	VA
Newcomb, Ephriam	1807	26	NJ
Newcomb, John	1805	19	NJ
Newell, James	1815	18	PA
Newell, John	1809	20	PA
Newell, John	1819	26	MA
Newell, Samuel	1807	18	NJ
Newgent, Levi	1810	17	MD
Newhouse, John	1816	26	DE
Newman, Charles	1804	18 b	DE
Newman, Daniel	1815	40	PA
Newman, George	1823	22	CT
Newman, Henry	1815	25	NY
Newman, John	1805	14	CT
Newman, John	1806	0	
Newman, John	1806	22	DE
Newman, John	1823	15	PA
Newman, Peter	1808	19	PA
Newman, Thos. H.	1817	16	PA
Newport, Ceasar	1805	26 b	PA
Newport, George	1809	24 b	PA
Newson, Bricon	1809	43	VA
Newton, Isaac	1814	23	
Newton, James	1810	18	NJ
Newton, John	1812	20	PA
Newton, Nathan	1809	21	NJ
Newton, William	1804	39 b	SC
Nice, Anthony	1804	24	NJ
Nice, Anthony	1804	24	NJ
Nice, Anthony	1805	25	NJ

Nice, George	1815	19		PA
Nicholas, Adam	1804	22 y		PA
Nicholas, Felix	1817	24		
Nicholas, John	1809	21 b		PA
Nicholas, John	1809	26 y		PA
Nicholas, John	1810	24 b		NY
Nicholas, Noar	1815	25 b		CT
Nicholas, Samuel	1803	23		PA
Nicholes, John	1821	30 b		LA
Nicholls, James	1809	23		DE
Nicholls, Parker	1809	18		DE
Nichols, Arthur St. Clair				
	1805	18		PA
Nichols, Dennis	1798	53		NC
Nichols, Edward	1805	22 b		RI
Nichols, Francis	1798	30		RI
Nichols, John	1809	20 m		DE
Nichols, John	1823	38 b		NJ
Nichols, Samuel	1816	22		CT
Nichols, William Francis				
	1810	27		PA
Nichols, William	1812	52		none given
Nicholson, Chalres	1804	15		VA
Nicholson, Charles	1805	16		VA
Nicholson, Isaac	1806	25 y		PA
Nicholson, James	1809	26 y		NJ
Nicholson, Jesse	1817	36		PA
Nicholson, Mathew	1805	26		NY
Nicholson, Samuel	1823	33 b		MD
Nicholson, Thomas	1799	20		PA
Nicholson, William	1806	27		PA
Nicholson, William	1823	22 b		NJ
Nick, John	1803	21		PA
Nickel, Edward	1805	18		VA
Nickel, Edward	1809	0		VA
Nickel, Edward	1811	00		VA
Nickels, John	1810	0		NY
Nickels, John	1816	24		PA
Nickerson, John	1811	20		NJ
Nickerson, Samuel	1801	18		DE
Nickerson, Shubal	1823	17		MA
Nickols, James	1811	22		NJ
Nickolson, John	1813	24		VA
Nickolson, Joseph	1823	26 s		MD
Nickson, Thomas	1823	17 b		DE
Nicols, James	1807	19		NY
Nicolson, William	1810	24		VA
Niel, Josiah	1815	27		VA
Nightingale, Joseph	1821	24 y		RI
Niles, George	1807	26 b		NY
Niles, Robert	1815	27		RI
Niles, William	1822	15		MA

Nimrod, Joseph	1820	49 b	VA
Nisbet, Richard	1810	26		Island of Nevi
Nisbett, William	1809	28	MA
Nivin, John M.	1823	21	DE
Nixon, Hannibal	1807		
Nixon, Hannibal	1807	20 c	NJ
Nixon, Primes	1805	25 m	PA
Nixon, Primes	1806	0	
Nixon, Robert, Jr.	1803	25	NJ
Nixon, Robert	1821	34	PA
Nixon, Silas	1798	16 m	PA
Nixon, Silas	1817	38 y	PA
Nixon, William	1801	23	DE
Nixon, William	1804	20	NY
Nixon, William	1809	25 b	VA
Noar, Mark	1803	24 b	NJ
Noble, Anthony	1810	17 b	MD
Noble, Anthony	1811	00	
Noble, Ormond, Jr.	1817	18	VT
Nocho, Samuel	1813	32 m	MD
Nocti, John B.	1809	21	LA
Noe, Elias	1796	0	NJ
Noe, Elias	1798	24	NJ
Nones, Emanuel	1807	16	LA
Nones, Henry B.	1817	13	PA
Noonan, John	1823	25	ME
Nooney, William	1812	23	DE
Norbury, Joseph	1813	23	PA
Nordike, Benoin de	1818	22	NJ
Nordike, John	1817	26	NJ
Nordstrom, Peter	1810	39		Sweden
Nordyke, Thomas	1811	21	NY
Norgrave, Jeremiah	1805	23	PA
Norman, John	1806	26	DE
Norqua, William	1796	23	PA
Norqua, William	1796	0	PA
Norris, George	1798	21	PA
Norris, Isaac	1823	16	PA
Norris, Jervis	1815	26		none given
Norris, John	1795	0	VA
Norris, John	1798	26	MA
Norris, John	1804	30	NY
Norris, John	1806	0	NY
Norris, Joseph	1809	21	PA
Norris, Joseph	1810	28	LA
Norris, Richard	1809	24	NJ
Norris, Robert	1806	24	MD
Norris, Samuel	1822	35	MA

owner and master of oyster boats sailing from
Philadelphia

Norris, Thomas	1796	20	NJ

Norris, Thomas	1805	45	MA
Norris, Thomas	1809	49	MA
Norris, Thomas Lloyd	1819	16	PA
Norris, William	1796	0	PA
Norris, William	1806	25	MD
Norrisk, John	1816	21	VA
North, George	1808	26	MD
North, Josiah	1807	20	NJ
North, Thomas	1805	30	MD
North, William	1823	16	PA
Northam, Joseph, Jr.	1811	45 c	GA
Northrop, Enoch,Jr.	1805	21	PA
Northrop, Jeremiah	1807	17	PA
Norton, Andrew	1822	28 s	VA
Norton, David	1818	22	RI
Norton, George	1811	25	PA
Norton, John	1795	0	PA
Norton, John	1795	22	PA
Norton, John P.	1804	21	MA
Norton, Joseph W.	1820	20	DE
Norton, Nathan	1803	35	MA
Norton, Richard	1811	26	MA
Norton, Thomas	1811	26	PA
Norwood, Benjamin	1805	33	NY
Norwood, Benjamin	1805	33	NY
Norwood, Joseph	1818	37	DE
Nosgraze, Jeremiah	1812	00	
Notsan, John	1813	36		none given
Nottingham, George	1821	25 b		WestIndies
Nourse, Richard	1810	40 n	PA
Novrin, Stephen	1823	19	NY
Nowlan, Daniel	1817	17	PA
Nowlan, John	1807	18	PA
Nowlan, Miles	1815	21	NH
Nowland, Edward Ford	1819	22	NJ
Nowland, Henry	1805	22	DE
Nuby, Francis	1812	32 b	SC
Nugen, Felix	1806	17	PA
Nugent, Richard	1799	26	NJ
Nutt, William	1811	21	NJ
Nutter, Henry	1812	24	NH
Nye, Robert	1823	33	PA
Nyman, John	1823	38		Denmark
O'Brien, George A.	1819	17	
O'Connor, John	1811	14	PA
O'Connor, Scipo	1805	0	

cast away from ship *Wilmington* off coast of
Holland

O'Dunavan, Michael	1800	30	PA
O'Neil, John	1816	23		none given

Oakeley, Robert S.or L.	1812	17	PA
Oakey, Edward	1817	23 b	VA
Oakey, Robert	1821	19	DE
Oakley, John	1813	37	NY
Obear, Zebulon	1806	44	MA
OBrien, Gabriel A.	1823	20	Algiers
OConnor, Nicholas	1807	24	Ireland
OConway, James Mathias			
	1810	19	LA
Odenheimer, William Henry			
	1800	14	PA
Odenheimer, William Henry			
	1806	14	PA
Odenheimer, William Henry			
	1809	18	PA

Odlin, Elisha	1815	30	

wrecked 29 Sept 1812 in ship *Pres. Dadma,*
Capt. John Adamson, on coast of China

Odlin, Peter G.	1807	19	RI
ODonnell, Dennis	1807	35	
Ofton, John	1811	00	
Ogden, James	1803	23 y	NY
Ogden, Jeremiah	1806	21	NJ
Ogden, Michael	1816	42	NY
Ogden, Michael	1820	47	NY
Ogden, Thomas	1803	25 b	NJ
Ogden, Thomas	1805	0	
Ogden, William	1805	33	PA
Ogden, William	1805	0	
Ogg, Samuel	1804	25 b	DE
Ogle, Francis J.	1809	15	DE
Ogle, Howard	1809	19	DE
OHara, Charles	1820	16	PA
Ohardy, Charles	1798	18	NJ
Okey, Joseph	1817	31 b	PA
Okie, Robert	1818	26 y	PA
Oldden, Thomas H.	1806	19	PA
Olden, John	1800	22	DE
Olden, John	1804	26	PA
Olden, Seth	1815	20 b	PA
Olden, Seth	1816	21 s	PA
Oldenburg, Jacob	1804	23	PA
Oldenheimer, W. H.	1815	00	
Olding, James	1809	23	SC
Oldmixon, Edward	1822	26	PA
Oliphant, Benjamin	1823	14	PA
Oliphant, Uzziel	1813	38	NJ
Oliver, Andrew C.	1820	20 b	PA
Oliver, Isaac	1810	20 b	NJ
Oliver, James	1810	13	PA

Oliver, James	1814	16	PA
Oliver, James G.	1821	24	PA
Oliver, James	1823	22 b	PA
Oliver, John Lynch	1797	29	Africa
Oliver, John	1809	24	LA
Oliver, John	1810	13	PA
Oliver, John	1815	17	PA
Oliver, John	1818	49 b	MS
Oliver, Lawrence	1807	32	
Oliver, Nathaniel	1807	32	PA
Oliver, Nicholas	1807	20	PA
Oliver, Paul Ambrose	1809	13	PA
Oliver, Robert	1819	24 y	MD
Oliver, Samuel	1807	36	PA
Oliver, Thomas	1810	27	MA

Oliver, Thomas	1812	00	

SPC lost when taken prisoner aboard the *James*
of New River, NC, by New Providence privateer

Oliver, William	1807	29	MA
Olives, John	1810	23	LA
Ollaway, James	1806	38	MA
Olliver, Joseph	1807	22	DE
Olmstead, Ezekiel	1810	27	MA
Olmsted, Moss	1803	24	CT
Olmsted, Oliver	1808	21	CT
Olney, Banjamin B.	1813	38	RI
Olsen, Michael	1801	46	PA
Olsen, Michael	1803	0	Denmark
Olsen, Michael	1804	48	none given
Olsen, Nicholas	1809	25	PA
Olson, William	1811	32	Denmark
Oman, Richard	1818	30	CT
Omensetter, Peter	1798	17	PA
Omer, Aaron	1818	20	PA
ONeale, John	1810	25	
ONeale, John	1810	25	
ONeill, Edward	1810	28	PA
Onen, John	1808	21	PA
Onetto, Joseph	1823	27	PA
Onion, Thomas	1818	32	MD
Ooms, Simon	1805	33	NY
Oram, John	1817	22	NJ
Orchardson, Thomas	1804	22	MD
Orgen, James	1815	23	RI
Orosmane, John Frederick			
	1811	25 y	MA
Orr, Robert	1804	35	MA
Orum, Aaron	1809	21	NJ
Orvis, Abraham	1811	26	VT
Osbon, John	1806	29	CT

Osborn, James	1815	28	VA
Osborn, William	1811	21	PA
Osborne, Jacob	1820	17 y	MD
Osborne, John	1815	27	PA
Osbourn, Douglass	1823	16	PA
Osbourn, John	1809	24 b	MA
Osgood, Robert	1807	41	MA
Osgood, Samuel W.	1811	28	MA
Ostran, John	1810	21	NY
Oswold, Henry	1816	31 y	PA
Ott, Christian	1807	27	NY
Ott, Christian	1807		
Otterbridge, David	1811	00	
Ottinger, Douglass	1823	19	PA
Ottinger, Isaiah	1804	23	PA
Ottinger, William	1810	21	PA
Otto, John A.	1811	25	PA
Otway, Nicholas	1807	22	MD
Outterside, William	1812	25	MA
Outterside, William	1817	31	MA
Ovington, Lemuel	1817	30 b	NC
Owen, John	1823	33	MA
Owen, William	1806	19	NC
Owen, William	1823	22	ME
Owens, Enoch D.	1815	20	NY
Owens, Evan	1810	25	DE
Owens, Henry	1809	20	PA
Owens, James	1816	19	DE
Owens, John	1810	28 b	MD
Owens, Michael	1821	33	NY
Owens, Robert	1805	21	PA
Owens, Thomas	1822	25	NJ
Owens, William	1809	26	MA
Owings, John	1800	20	MD
Owner, William	1809	16	PA
Oxford, Charles	1806	26	SC
Ozeas, John	1809	17	PA
Paaten, William	1815	21 c	MA
Paca, Isaac	1810	26 b	MD
Packer, Mason R.	1817	17	CT
Paddack, George	1810	18	MA
Paddon, Ebenezer	1818	24	VA
Page, Ely	1807	20	MA
Page, Ely	1807		
Page, Isaac	1801	21	CT
Page, Joseph	1823	29 b	MD
Page, Robert N.	1804	25	VA
Page, William	1809	19	NH
Pain, Mark	1811	14 y	PA
Pain, Mark	1812	00	NJ
Paine, Ephraim	1807	25	SC
Painter, Jacob	1820	25	PA
Painter, Samuel	1812	25 b	NJ
Pairpoint, William Scady			
	1807	21	NJ
Paleske, Lewis	1815	20	PA
Palmer, David	1809	28	NH
Palmer, George Fox	1803	21	NJ
Palmer, James	1804	20	PA
Palmer, James Engle	1823	16	PA
Palmer, John	1809	21	PA
Palmer, John	1810	0	
Palmer, Philip	1815	21	NJ
Palmer, Richard, Jr.	1818	16	PA
Palmer, Robert	1812	20	NJ
Palmer, Robert	1813	21	NJ
Palmer, Robert	1817	21 m	LA
Palmer, Thomas	1804	27	NC
Palmer, William	1811	19	NH
Palmer, William F.	1815	17	PA
Palmer, William	1815	23	NY
Pancoast, Joseph	1811	17 c	PA
Pantostier, Antonio	1806	23	LA
Parc, Samuel	1821	22	NJ
Parcells, Christopher	1822	21	PA
Parcells, Jacob	1818	39	NY
Pardell, Paris	1819	21 y	PA
Pardy, Thomas	1817	25	PA
Parent, John	1811	21	NJ
Parish, Peter	1817	29	
Park, John	1820	28	PA
Park, William	1806	24	VA
Park, William	1807		
Park, William	1810	24 b	NJ
Parke, Thomas	1813	21	NJ
Parker, Aaron	1818	22 m	DE
Parker, Alexander	1812	21	PA
Parker, Avery F.	1815	19	MA
Parker, Charles	1818	18	MA
Parker, David	1796	0	
Parker, Dominick	1812	33 b	MA
Parker, Edward	1818	19 y	PA
Parker, Elisha	1810	24	PA
Parker, George	1804	22 m	NY
Parker, George	1822	34	NY
Parker, Gilbert	1807	30	NY
Parker, Isaac	1818	21	NJ
Parker, Jacob	1820	20 b	PA
Parker, James	1815	21	PA
Parker, John	1801	24	MD
Parker, John	1811	18	VA
Parker, John	1811	18	RI
Parker, John	1812	00	
Parker, John	1820	23	MA

Parker, John, Jr.	1820	14	PA
Parker, Sacker	1804	33	VA
Parker, Samuel	1810	28 b	LA
Parker, Samuel	1812	00	
Parker, Samuel	1812	00	
Parker, Selby	1806	23	VA
Parker, Thomas	1804	15	PA
Parker, Thomas	1804	15	PA
Parker, Thomas	1804	15	PA
Parker, Thomas	1807	25 y	NY
Parker, Thomas	1816	34 m	NY
Parker, William	1806	20	PA
Parker, William	1809	20	DE
Parker, William	1810	0	
Parker, William	1811	23	DE
Parker, William	1816	25	MA
Parker, William	1818	22	MA
Parkhill, James	1811	32	PA
Parkhurst, George	1822	20	NY
Parkin, Joseph	1805	19	PA
Parkin, Joseph	1808	21	PA
Parkin, William	1806	17	PA
Parks, James	1806	20	PA
Parks, John	1805	20	MA
Parks, John	1810	24	MD
Parks, John	1818	25	MD
Parks, Robert	1810	24	MA
Parks, Vincent	1811	23	DE
Parmor, Gideon	1807	25	NJ

Parncuth, Neptune Charles
1809 16
born at sea near America.

Parncuth, Neptune Charles
1809 0

Parr, James	1805	19	PA
Parr, James	1808	22	PA
Parris, John	1815	28 b	NJ
Parry, John	1810	23	NJ
Parsons, Charles	1809	21 b	PA
Parsons, Isaac	1805	21	DE
Parsons, John	1805	22	DE
Parsons, John	1822	19 b	DE
Parsons, Joseph	1811	20	DE
Parsons, Samuel	1822	42	NJ
Parsons, William	1801	24	NJ
Parsons, William	1801	23	
Parsons, William	1804	0	
Parsons, William	1806	0	
Parsons, William	1806	0	
Parsons, William	1811	00	

Parvin, Beniah	1812	23	NJ
Parvin, Silas	1806	28	NJ
Parvis, James	1795	0	NY
Paschal, John	1815	00 b	
Pasfield, George	1812	22	PA
Paskill, John	1809	21 b	DE
Pasko, John	1813	19	VA
Pastorius, John	1815	38	PA
Pastorius, Samuel	1815	28	PA
Pate, Matthias	1806	21	PA
Paterson, William	1821	34 b	MA
Patorson, John	1798	23	MA
Patrick, Owen	1810	19	NJ
Pattan, Richard	1807		
Pattan, William	1816	0	
Patten, William	1809	24	MD
Patterson, Cornelius	1798	36	PA
Patterson, David	1810	23	CT
Patterson, David	1823	35	ME
Patterson, Edward	1809	28	DE
Patterson, Eyre	1811	19	PA
Patterson, Jacob	1812	23 b	PA
Patterson, James	1798	32	MD
Patterson, James	1819	18	PA
Patterson, John	1801	26 b	DE
Patterson, John	1804	30 b	DE
Patterson, John	1809	22	NY
Patterson, John	1817	33 y	LA
Patterson, John	1822	14	PA
Patterson, Joseph	1822	17	PA
Patterson, Robert	1812	20	PA
Patterson, Robert	1813	23	NJ
Patterson, Samuel	1811	19	NJ
Patterson, William	1806	21	PA
Patterson, William	1809	24	PA
Patterson, William	1822	23 m	ME
Patton, James	1810	18	PA
Patton, James	1812	00	
Patton, John	1804	23	DE
Patton, Joseph	1810	19	PA
Patton, Joseph	1817	27	PA
Patton, Richard	1804	17	DE
Patton, Samuel	1817	21	PA
Patton, William	1812	00	
Paul, Abraham	1809	26	NJ
Paul, Alexander	1806	23	MA
Paul, Daniel	1823	18	PA
Paul, Daniel	1823	18	PA
Paul, Gabriel P.	1809	29	LA
Paul, John	1815	33 y	LA
Paul, Jonathan	1812	32	PA
Paul, Jonathan	1813	0	

Paul, Nathan, Jr.	1807	12	NJ		Pedley, Richard	1823	37	VA
Paul, Philip	1797	0		Prussia	Pedrick, Henry	1821	23	NJ
Paul, Richard	1804	23	NY		Pedrick, Silas	1815	20	NJ
Paul, William	1798	24	PA		Pedrick, Young	1822	16	NJ
Paul, William W.	1812	00			Pee, Abraham	1807	26 b	PA
Paul, William B.	1822	21	PA		Peek, Thomas	1804	0	
Paull, Micah	1810	28	MA		Peel, James	1807	23	PA
Paxine, Benedict	1809	25	LA		Peeper, Andreco	1798	19	NJ
Paxson, James	1822	33	MA		Peeterson, Lorens	1800	25	PA
Payerne, John	1815	16	PA		Peirce, Ephraim	1823	20 b	DE
Payne, Barnard Jr.	1815	14	PA		Peirce, John	1807	20	PA
Payne, Barnard	1815	14	PA		Peirce, John P.	1820	20	PA
Payne, Henry	1817	17	PA		Peirce, Joseph	1816	23	GA
Payne, James	1822	16	PA		Peirce, Samuel	1816	45	NH
Payne, William	1798	27	NY		Peischel, Philip	1805	24	PA
Payne, William	1814	15	NC		Peker, George	1815	25 b	MD
Payne, William	1817	13	PA		Peker, William	1815	26 b	MD
Paynter, Richard	1815	20	DE		Pelesson, Francis	1809	18	LA
Peace, Whitell	1807				Penderbury, William	1803	29	PA
Peach, Ebenezer	1822	18	MA		Pendergrass, William	1813	22 c	NC
Peach, Francis	1809	20 b	DE		Pendleton, Charles L.	1822	20	RI
Peale, Linnaeus	1810	16	PA		Pening, Mars	1807	25	MA
Pearce, Daniel	1805	21	NJ		Penington, Fredus	1815	21	DE
Pearce, Ephraim	1805	20 b	MD		Penlow, James	182	16	PA
Pearce, John	1813	25	NY		Penlow, James	182	16	PA
Pearce, Mathew C.	1822	17	PA		Penn, James	1815	26	RI
Pearce, Robert	1810	21		England	Pennant, John	1819	16	NY
Pearce, Thomas	1805	33	NY		Pennell, Joseph	1815	33	PA
Pearce, William	1821	19	VA		Penner, John	1811	18	DE
Pearse, Thomas	1801	18	MD		Pennewell, Thomas	1807	38	DE
Pearson, Alexander	1816	20	PA		Pennington, George	1807	16	NJ
Pearson, George	1804	30	NY		Pennington, John	1821	42	DE
Pearson, John	1820	19	PA		Pennock, Charles Edward			
Pearson, Jonas	1809	28	PA			1821	16	PA
Pearson, Samuel S.	1822	23	PA		Pentland, Andrew	1810	23	PA
Pearson, Thomas	1807	21	DE		Penuel, Littleton	1815	21	MD
Pearson, Valentine	1806	23	PA		Penuel, Lyttleton	1815	00	xx
Pearson, William	1809	17	NJ		Perce, Abraham	1805	25	NJ
Pease, James	1797	26	MA		Perce, Daniel	1810	26	NJ
Pease, Levi	1823	30	NY		Percy, William	1810	21	NY
Pease, Levi	1823	29	NY		Peres, Peter	1807	18	PA
Peck, David	1809	17	NJ		Perez, Francis	1806	30	LA
Peck, David	1818				Perit, John Webster	1807	26	CT
Peck, Thomas	1813	16	NJ		Perit, Petaiah	1805	20	CT
Peck, William B.	1801	24	MA		Perkin, John	1804	29	MA
Peck, William	1815	14	PA		Perkins, David	1796	17	PA
Peckman, John	1806	29	NY		Perkins, David	1798	19	PA
Peckstein, John Christian					Perkins, Francis	1805	39	PA
	1807	28	MS		Perkins, James	1806	24	MD
Peckworth, Thomas P.	1809	26	MD		Perkins, James T.	1809	21	DE
Peddle, Henry	1823	20	PA		Perkins, James	1810	0	MD
Peddle, Joseph	1817	23	PA		Perkins, James	1812	00	

Perkins, Jeremiah	1805	15	NJ
Perkins, John	1798	23	CT
Perkins, Joseph	1796	0	PA
Perkins, Nathan	1811	21	MA
Perkins, Philip	1823	19 y	PA
Perkins, Samuel	1798	23	PA
Perkins, William	1811	00	
Perkins, William	1813	21	PA
Perot, Henry	1814	22	SC
Perot, Joshua	1814	20	SC
Perrin, William	1815	25	NY
Perrot, John	1817	33	MD
Perry, Adam	1800	29	PA
Perry, Charles	1805	21	VA
Perry, Charles	1809	25	VA
Perry, Darius	1805	30	RI
Perry, Elias B.	1804	20	NJ
Perry, Elias B.	1806	0	
Perry, John	1813	22	PA
Perry, Matthew	1807	36	PA
Perry, Matthew	1808	0	
Perry, Matthew	1816	46	
Perry, Nicholas	1819	24 b	VA
Perry, Owen	1798	24	PA
Perry, Thomas	1809	22	NY
Pesoa, Abraham P.	1814	15	PA
Petaluga, John	1810	26	LA
Petarloga, John	1812	00	
Petelow, Micajah	1823	22 b	MD
Peter, Charles	1815	35 b	LA
Peter, George	1808	22	RI
Peter, John	1809	21	LA
Peter, John	1810	15 b	MD
Peter, John	1810	35 b	
Peter, John	1810	24 b	LA
Peter, John	1810	24 m	LA
Peter, John	1810	30 b	MS
Peter, John	1811	29 b	LA
Peter, Manuel	1808	24	
Peter, William	1809	25 m	MD
Peters, Albert	1812	18 b	DE
Peters, Anthony	1810	28	LA
Peters, Caleb	1821	15 b	DE
Peters, Charles H.	1820	19 y	DE
Peters, Elias	1804	39 b	DE
Peters, George	1804	34	PA
Peters, George	1815	18 b	MA
Peters, Henry	1823	31	PA
Peters, James	1810	24 b	DE
Peters, John	1805	27	NJ
Peters, John	1806	19	PA
Peters, John	1806	18 m	PA

Peters, John, Jr.	1806	21	PA
Peters, John	1807	21	MS
Peters, John	1807	19	LA
Peters, John William	1807	34	NY
Peters, John	1809	25	LA
Peters, John	1810	23	LA
Peters, John	1810	16	LA
Peters, John	1813	36	
Peters, John	1815	29	MD
Peters, John	1815	35	PA
Peters, John	1816	42 b	LA
Peters, John	1816	31	PA
Peters, John	1818	35 b	LA
Peters, John	1822	22 y	LA
Peters, Lamuel	1811	18 y	LA
Peters, Lewis	1805	26 b	PA
Peters, Lewis	1806	25 b	MD
Peters, Peter B.	1818	21	PA
Peters, Robert C.	1811	24	CT
Peters, Rowland	1795	18	NJ
Peters, Samuel	1811	21 b	CT
Peters, Samuel	1819	33 b	CT
Peters, Scipio	1809	36 b	PA
Peters, William	1804	19 b	DE
Peters, William	1807	18 b	MS

Petersen, Teye F.	1818		none given

in 1807 commanded *Three Sisters* owned by
Stephen Kingston, merchant of Philadelphia

Peterson, Abraham	1817	23 b	DE
Peterson, Charles	1806	28 b	MA
Peterson, Charles	1809	30	NY
Peterson, Christian	1815	24	PA
Peterson, Daniel	1810	26 b	PA
Peterson, Enoch	1814	0	
Peterson, Erick	1811	19	NJ
Peterson, George	1797	25	PA
Peterson, Gustaf	1810	28	NY
Peterson, Henry	1809	22	NJ
Peterson, Henry	1821	27	PA
Peterson, Jacob	1807	21	NJ
Peterson, Jacob, Jr.	1809	14	PA
Peterson, Jacob	1809	0	NJ
Peterson, Jacob	1823	24	NY
Peterson, James	1812	23	NJ
Peterson, John	1803	26	PA
Peterson, John	1806	27	LA
Peterson, John	1807		
Peterson, John	1807		PA
Peterson, John	1809	26	NY
Peterson, John	1810	22	LA

Peterson, John	1810	0	PA		Philips, Peter	1807		
Peterson, John	1815	17	PA		Philips, Richard	1821	23	VA
Peterson, Jonas	1810	27	SC		Philler, Andrew, Jr.	1801	20	PA
Peterson, Laurence	1807	35			Phillipes, John	1815	22 s	LA
Peterson, Laurence	1813	0			Phillips, Anthony	1820	25 y	NY
Peterson, Lawrence	1816	23	SC		Phillips, Banjamin	1823	28	PA
Peterson, Matthew B.	1817	27	NY		Phillips, David	1805	19	MA
Peterson, Peter	1811	29	VA		Phillips, Garret	1823	37	NJ
Peterson, Richard	1811	23	MA		Phillips, George	1814	20 b	MD
Peterson, Samuel	1817	29 b	NJ		Phillips, George	1817	15	NJ
Peterson, Thomas	1821	41 y	MD		Phillips, George	1820	33	RI
Peterson, William	1804	22 b	NY		Phillips, Isaac	1817	25 c	MD
Peterson, William	1808	12	PA		Phillips, Jacob	1822	23	NJ
Peterson, William	1811	27 b	MD		Phillips, John	1804	21 b	SC
Peterson, William	1816	18	PA		Phillips, John	1805	20 b	PA
Peterson, William	1821	39 b	DE		Phillips, John	1806	23 b	NJ
Petters, Nels	1810	28	MD		Phillips, John	1806	18	NJ
Petterson, John	1813	17	SC		Phillips, John	1812	21	PA
Petterson, John	1821	41	MA		Phillips, John	1813	24	PA
Pettingale, John	1815	31	MA		Phillips, Joseph	1807	25 y	DE
Pettingell, George D.	1796	22	RI		Phillips, Joshua	1798	25	DE
Pettit, George	1810	30	NJ		Phillips, Peter	1804	26		none given
Pettit, Simeon	1806	25	NJ		Phillips, Peter	1804	0		France
Pettit, Thomas C.	1815	24	NJ		Phillips, Peter	1811	23	NJ
Pettit, Waters	1805	36	NY		Phillips, Robert P.	1819	18	PA
Pettry, Jose	1808	23	LA		Phillips, Stotely	1818	23	RI
Phares, William T.	1823	23	NJ		Phillips, Thomas	1815	17	PA
Phenix, John	1809	20 b	PA		Phillips, William	1808	26	NY
Pheonix, John	1812	00			Phillips, William	1818	35	MD
Pheonix, John, Jr.	1812	18	MA		Phinney, Alvian	1810	32	MA
Pherson, Hugh	1809	19	MA		Phinney, John	1809	38 b	DE
Phetty, John	1809	21	MA		Phinney, Samuel	1810	34	MA
Phifer, Edward	1816	22	PA		Phyney, William	1815	28		Ireland
					Picard, Peter M., Jr.	1809	14	PA
Phifer, John	1819	27	PA		Pickard, Samuel	1806	23 b	NJ

has several deep wounds made by musket
balls in last war

					Picken, John	1806	19	PA
					Pickering, William	1804	28	VA
					Pickering, William	1812	00	
Philip, John	1809	24 b	LA		Pickering, William	1814	27	MA
Philip, John	1810	18 b	LA		Pickering, William	1815	00	
Philipe, John	1815	27	LA		Pidgeon, Robert	1823	26	PA
Philips, Daniel	1810	21 y	MD		Pierce, Aaron	1818	26	MA
Philips, George R.	1809	23 b	PA		Pierce, Abraham,Jr.	1819	22	DE
Philips, James	1797	27 m	VA		Pierce, Samuel	1818	29	MA
Philips, John	1796	0		England	Pierce, Whitehill	1804	23	NJ
Philips, John	1807	27 y	PA		Pierce, William	1821	23	SC
Philips, John	1807				Piersival, George	1806	23	PA
Philips, John	1810	37 b	RI		Pierson, Hans	1796	0	PA
Philips, John	1810	22	LA		Pierson, Hans	1796	38	PA
Philips, John	1810	30 y	LA		Pifer, George	1801	18	PA
Philips, John	1811	00			Pike, Benjamin	1809	20	DE
Philips, Peter	1804	22 b	DE		Pike, Soloman	1801	25	ME

Name	Year	Age		Place	Name	Year	Age		Place
Pile, Joseph M.	1815	20		PA	Pope, John	1816	42		MD
Pile, Joseph M.	1819	24		PA	Poppal, George, Jr.	1821	14		PA
Pillet, Lewis	1807	19		St. Domingo	Popple, Henry	1806	27		KY
Pinder, David	1806	18		MA	Port, Joseph	1807	23		NY
Pinder, William	1815	36		GA	Porter, Charles	1815	21	m	PA
Pine, Clayton	1816	18		NJ	Porter, Charles	1822	31		MA
Pinkham, Peter	1798	32		MA	Porter, David	1805	0		
Pinkham, Thomas	1818	24		ME	Porter, Ezra	1815	23		MA
Pinkus, Aaron	1811	16		PA	Porter, James	1806	32		NY
Pinto, Manuel Vas	1807	28		LA	Porter, James	1810	36	b	NJ
Pinyard, Matthias	1810	24		PA	Porter, John	1806	23	c	SC
Piper, William G.	1820	15		PA	Porter, Robert	1804	22		NJ
Pister, John	1817	21		PA	Porter, Robert	1805	23	b	NJ
Pitman, John	1810	26		MA	Porter, Robert	1806	24	b	NJ
Pittyman, Moses	1815	27	b	DE	Porter, Robert	1807	24	b	NJ
Placy, Lewis	1813	17		PA	Porter, Robert	1821	20		ME
Planter, Abraham	1821	20	b	MD	Porter, Samuel	1801	16		PA
Platt, George	1804	14		PA	Porter, Samuel	1815	21	y	PA
Platt, George	1810	0			Porter, Solomon	1801	19		MA
Plott, Peter	1815	37		NY	Porter, Thomas	1810	21		NY
Plumly, Amos	1798	25		PA	Porter, William	1815	17		MD
Plumly, Amos	1805	0			Porter, William	1816	27		MA
Plummer, George	1815	29		MD	Porter, William G.	1819	19		PA
Plummer, Moses	1820	21		ME	Pose, Hanson	1810	30	m	DC
Plummer, William	1822	34		VA	Possapase, Joseph B.	1814	24	b	MD
Plyer, Ezekiel	1810	17		NY	Post, Levi	1809	20		MD
Piyfalr, William	1815	24		NJ	Pote, Jeremiah	1818	23		MA
Poalk, George Litz	1815	17		PA	Potter, Charles	1811	22		DE
Poalk, Samuel	1812	21		DE	Potter, Edmund	1820	17		DE
Poe, James Jr.	1815	26		PA	Potter, Jacob	1805	21	b	NY
Poggy, Anthony	1807	29		Europe	Potter, Jacob	1805	21	y	NY
Poinset, Solomon	1822	33		NJ	Potter, John	1807	24		VA
Polin, Peter	1804	22		PA	Potter, John	1810	25		CT
Polland, Edward	1805	36	b	MD	Potter, Joseph	1809	26		NY
Pollard, John	1807	12			Potter, Joseph	1813	0		
Pollard, John	1809	15		PA	Potter, Peter	1807	22	y	NY
Pollard, Robert	1798	0		PA	Potter, Peter	1809	0		NY
Pollock, John	1815	35		none given	Potter, Peter	1819	36	y	PA
Polston, Perrey	1807	21	m	DE	Potter, Richard	1800	20		PA
Pomeroy, Peter	1807	27		MS	Potts, Benjamin	1810	22		NJ
Pomroy, William	1813	23		MA	Potts, Marshal	1820	20	m	PA
Pond, Abel	1817	20		NJ	Potts, Thomas	1815	22		NJ
Pool, Garret	1798	29		VA	Poulson, John	1815	42		GA
Pool, George	1807	19		MA	Poulston, Joseph	1803	21	y	DE
Pool, James	1810	23	b	VA	Powell, George	1810	39		NY
Pool, John	1806	22	b	MD	Powell, John	1810	19	b	DE
Pool, Matthew	1804	34		MA	Powell, John	1816	19		SC
Pool, William	1815	21		MA	Powell, John	1823	23		NY
Poole, Edward	1809	26		DE	Powell, Joseph	1815	35	b	PA
Poole, John	1810	43		NJ	Powell, Richard	1807	31		NY
Poole, John	1818	33	b	NY	Powell, Thomas	1809	21		MD
Pope, Dennis	1811	25	c	DE	Powell, William	1798	21		MA

Powell, William	1807	36	LA
Powell, William	1808	24	SC
Powell, William	1809	0	
Powell, William	1813	24	NJ
Powell, William	1819	19	MA
Power, Martin	1822	27	none given
Powers, Edward, Jr.	1807	29	MA
Powers, James	1808	24	PA
Powers, James	1809	22	PA
Powers, James	1815	28	PA
Powers, John	1808	21	MA

Powers, John 1817 29 s NJ
served his time with Judge Griffith of Burlington

Powers, John	1817	28	PA
Powers, Michael	1811	21	MA
Powers, Norris Stanley	1815	21	PA
Powers, Philip Francis	1818	25	PA
Powers, Thomas M.	1810	21	DE
Powrs, John	1815	27	NJ
Pratt, Charles M.	1817	17	PA
Pratt, Emanuel	1813	23 m	DE
Pratt, George	1820	29	MD
Pratt, Isaac	1823	15	PA
Pratt, James D.	1805	16	PA
Pratt, Thomas	1809	30	NY
Pratt, Thomas	1815	00	
Premir, Jacob	1804	21	PA
Presbury, William	1822	20	MD
Prescott, John	1812	35	MA
Pressey, Thomas J.	1819	23	MA
Preston, Ebenezer, Jr.	1809	21	NJ
Preston, Jonas	1811	18	DE
Preston, Thomas Paul	1820	38	PA
Prettiman, Eli	1805	23 b	DE
Prevost, Henry Mallet	1800	18	
Price, Alfred Cox	1822	17	MD
Price, Daniel	1804	16	PA
Price, Daniel	1822	18	PA
Price, Frederick Wm.	1818	38	SC
Price, George	1811	16	PA
Price, Henry	1811	29	MD
Price, Henry	1821	49 y	NY
Price, Isaac	1823	17	PA
Price, Jacob	1800	31	PA
Price, James	1801	33	PA
Price, John	1810	26	NY
Price, John	1813	22	DE
Price, John	1818	21	NJ
Price, John	1822	21	NY
Price, Joseph W.	1814	15	MD

Price, Peter	1809	0	
Price, Peter	1809	22 y	PA
Price, Solomon	1815	24 c	NJ
Price, Telafaro	1798	0	DE
Price, Thomas	1811	20	MA
Price, Walter Lane	1793	0	VA
Price, Walter L.	1800	33	
Price, William	1798	24	PA
Price, William	1805	28	GA
Price, William	1811	22	PA
Price, William	1811	20 y	PA
Price, William	1815	33 m	PA
Price, William	1822	20	PA
Prichard, William	1808	29	PA
Prichet, Jethro	1796	24	MA
Pridaux, James	1804	17	MD
Pride, Thomas	1805	18	DE
Prince, Granvill	1798	25	MA
Prince, Peter	1819	24 b	NJ
Prindle, Robert	1821	17	CT
Prindle, Samuel	1809	25	NY
Pringle, John	1798	24	NY
Prise, James	1809	0	
Pritchard, Gustavus	1822	30	MD
Pritchard, James	1823	23	NY
Pritchart, John	1805	45	MD
Pritchett, Jeremiah	1810	19	VA
Proctor, Henry	1806	23	MA
Proctor, James	1822	28 y	PA
Proctor, Thomas	1815	22 c	MD
Prond, Thomas	1804	24	PA
Prophet, Moses the	1820	59 b	VA
Prout, Charles	1806	24 b	MD
Prout, Charles	1811	00	
Prout, William Richard	0000	35 b	MD
Pruit, Frederic	1814	22	PA
Pruit, William	1819	21	PA
Pryor, Ezekiel	1811	00	
Pugh, Evert	1811	13	NC
Pule, Charles	1804	25 b	VA
Pullinger, Collin	1821	45	none given
Pullman, Solomon	1804	22 m	DE
Puntine, Henry	1815	18	NY
Purchase, James	1810	33	MD
Purdon, John	1804	0	
Purdon, John	1804	14	PA
Purfil, John	1806	21	PA
Purfil, John, Sr.	1806	27	PA
Purfil, John,Jr.	1810	27	PA
Purfil, Joseph, Jr.	1810	21	PA
Purington, Amos	1806	26	MA
Purkin, Nicholas	1809	19	MD

Purnell, Benjamin	1810	23 y	DE		
Purnell, Jacob	1809	30 b	MD		
Purnell, John	1815	24	MD		
Purnell, Stephen	1823	22 b	MD		
Purnell, William	1819	15 s	VA		
Purnell, William	1820	16 b	MD		
Purse, Samuel	1821	21	MA		
Purvis, Jacob	1806	23 y	DE		
Purvis, Robert	1805	26	SC		
Purvis, Robert	1807		SC		
Pusey, James	1809	28 b	PA		
Putnam, Levi	1815	37	MA		
Puttyman, Cato	1811	14 b	DE		
Pyles, James	1822	20	NJ		
Pyross, Abraham	1820	50 b	MD		
Quain, William L.	1809	20	DE		
Quain, William S.	1815	00			
Quam, George	1811	25 b	NJ		
Quans, James	1820	23 b	NJ		
Quart, George	1805	18	PA		
Queckeo, Francis	1807	26			
Queckeo, Francis	1813	0			
Queen, Ralph	1818	27 c	MD		
Queheille, Peter M.	1809	23		none given	
Quess, Henry	1804	22	PA		
Quick, Peter	1810	19	NY		
Quick, William	1815	26	NY		
Quigley, Augustine	1823	16	PA		
Quin, John	1810	23	LA		
Quincy, William A.	1805	38	MA		
Quindlen, Mark	1806	17	NJ		
Quindlen, Mark	1812	00			
Quindlen, Mark	1813	0	NJ		
Quirk, John	1813	19	SC		
Quonn, Limeon	1810	33 B	NJ		
Quonn, Simeon	1812	00			
Rabe, George	1803	28	NJ		
Rabey, John	1815	29	NJ		
Rackets, Samuel	1818	26 b	NY		
Rackleff, Samuel	1815	28	MA		
Rackliff, Chandler	1810	19	MA		
Radney, Casar	1809	23 b	DE		
Radney, Cesar	1809	28 b	PA		
Rae, Robert	1816	27	NY		
Raff, William	1807	35 b	NY		
Rafine, Lot	1804	27 b	NJ		
Rafine, Lot	1815	36 b	NJ		
Ragan, John	1798	0		Ireland	
Rain, William	1809	0			
Raine, William	1805	22	PA		
Rainer, Joseph	1805	26	NJ		
Rainey, John	1805	29	MD		
Rainey, John	1806	23 b	NY		
Rainey, William	1805	26	PA		
Rainey, William	1806	0			
Ralph, Francis	1815	00			
Ralston, John	1821	35 b	DE		
Ralstons, Levan	1810	30 b	DE		
Ramage, James	1808	23			
Ramage, John	1797	0			Gr.Br.
Ramage, William T.	1817	22	NY		
Rambless, Charles	1806	0			
Rambo, Joseph	1811	33	PA		
Rambo, Thomas	1809	24	NJ		
Ramlesss, Charles	1806	24 b	DE		
Ramsdell, Reuben	1823	30	MA		
Ramsdell, William, Jr.	1809	33	MA		
Ramsey, John	1809	19	MD		
Ramsey, Samuel	1796	28	DE		
Ranbaldo, Giaeorno	1807	31	LA		
Randall, Christopher	1804	28	PA		
Randall, Frederick	1812	30	MD		
Randle, John	1811	26 b	MA		
Randolph, Edward	1809	24	NJ		
Ranke, Fredrick Gottlieb					
	1819	37	PA		
Rankin, Alexander	1820	21	PA		
Rankin, George	1813	22	MD		
Rankin, John	1796	22	PA		
Rankin, Robert	1803	31 b	NY		
Rankin, Thomas	1804	25	PA		
Rankins, Titus	1810	26	NJ		
Ransford, Henry	1820	22	PA		
Ransley, James	1818	36		none given	
Ranton, Nathaniel	1811	21	PA		
Raoul, Peter	1807	24	LA		
Rape, Ephraim	1800	22	NJ		
Rape, Nickolas	1805	28	PA		
Rapp, John	1807	27	PA		
Rappsin, Richard	1820	11 y	PA		
Rapuozo, Manuel	1808	35	MS		
Rasper, John	1823	26	PA		
Ratcheller, Francis	1822	21	PA		
Rathbun, Richard	1821	18	NY		
Ratien, Thomas	1820	28	MD		
Rattie, Augustis	1819	26	PA		
Rawlins, Nathan	1798	22 y	MD		
Rawson, George	1813	30	PA		
Ray, Joseph	1823	23	NY		
Ray, William	1806	29	PA		
Ray, William	1810	16	MD		
Ray, William	1810	0			
Raybold, James W.	1821	17	PA		
Raynes, Edward	1815	28	MA		

Raynolds, Charles	1803	22 m	VA
Read, Charles	1809	25	MD
Read, Gabriel	1799	23	NY
Read, George	1810	0	
Read, James	1818	40	VA
Read, John	1807	18	DE
Read, John	1810	23	MA
Read, John	1810	19	VA
Read, John	1815	00	
Read, John	1822	47 b	MA
Read, Jonas	1799	0	
Read, Joseph	1805	30 b	NJ
Read, Robert	1804	16 b	MD
Read, Robert	1815	00	
Read, Vinsent	1818	27	NY
Read, William Morris	1815	18 y	PA
Read, William Francis	1817	16	PA
Read, William	1823	23	NJ
Reading, Augustus	1805	34	NY
Reading, Jesse	1821	21 b	DE
Reading, John, Jr.	1805	28	NJ
Reardon, Patrick	1815	00	
Reardon, Patrick	1815	21	MD
Reasons, William	1810	10 b	PA
Reckhow, Daniel	1821	24	PA
Reddick, Thomas	1818	16	PA
Redgrave, John	1804	22	MD
Redick, David	1807	18	PA
Reding, Daniel	1813	23	MA
Reding, John	1811	20	DE
Redman, Alexander	1805	17 b	SC
Redman, John	1809	52	PA
Redman, Joseph	1807	19	PA
Redman, Joseph	1807	19	PA
Redman, Robert	1810	42	NJ
Redmond, William	1817	20	NC
Redner, William	1811	11 m	MA
Reed, Alexander	1811	22	NY
Reed, Arthur	1821	28	PA
Reed, Charles	1811	21	PA
Reed, Daniel James	1800	25	PA
Reed, David	1822	26 b	NY
Reed, George	1795	0	
Reed, George	1808	21	VA
Reed, George	1820	23	ME
Reed, George	1821	16	PA
Reed, Henry	1820	21 y	PA
Reed, James	1803	24	MA
Reed, James	1804	25	NJ
Reed, James	1816	18	DE
Reed, John	1806	23	DE
Reed, John	1814	17	NY

Reed, John Jr.	1815	21	PA
Reed, John	1815	26	MA
Reed, Jonathan	1811	24	NJ
Reed, Joseph	1804	0	
Reed, Joseph	1804	17 b	DE
Reed, Joseph	1807	34	SC
Reed, Joseph	1808	0	
Reed, Jotham	1823	24	MA
Reed, Magor	1807	23 b	PA
Reed, Philip	1798	26	NJ
Reed, Robert	1804	21 b	PA
Reed, Robert	1806	0	
Reed, Robert	1810	0	PA
Reed, William	1811	24	CT
Reeds, John	1807	17	VA
Reef, Ephraim	1811	22	MA
Rees, Henry T.	1823	24	PA
Rees, James	1801	10	NY
Rees, John T	1823	22	PA
Rees, Joshua	1815	20 y	PA
Reese, Benjamin	1820	27	MD
Reese, Chandler P.	1822	16	MS
Reese, Palm	1810	25 b	DE
Reese, Palm	1810	25 b	DE
Reese, Perry	1801	21 b	PA
Reeve, Robert H.	1811	77	NY
Reeves, Stephen	1818	21	NJ
Reford, George	1796	31	MD
Regden, William	1820	20	PA
Regins, James	1820	21	NJ
Rego, John	1796	37	
Rehn, William	1823	22	PA
Reid, Abraham	1813	19	NY
Reid, George	1818	38	GA
Reid, John	0000	33	NH
Reid, William	1821	15	PA
Reigart, Thomas Edwards			
	1805	16	PA
Reiley, John	1822	17	PA
Reilly, Edward	1806	21	MD
Reily, Edward	1801	28	PA
Reily, John,JR	1819	12	PA
Reinhart, Michael	1809	32	PA
Rejins, Jonathan R.	1809	27	NJ
Remick, Thomas S.	1806	26	MA
Remick, William	1821	19	MA
Remington, John S.	1814	14	PA
Remington, William	1821	14	MA
Renaldo, John W.	1812	23	NH
Renfraw, James	1815	19	PA
Reno, Micheal	1807	20	NY
Renolds, Benjamin	1803	45	DE

Renshaw, Samuel	1804	21		PA	Rice, William	1816	0	
Repsher, Daniel	1819	15		PA	Rich, Frederick	1812	23	PA
Resley, Edward	1815	00			Rich, John	1809	29	MD
Ressner, Samuel	1809	17	y	NJ	Rich, John	1810	0	
Rex, William	1803	27		PA	Rich, Matthias	1811	21	MA
Reymers, Henry	1805	36		NY	Richard, John	1800	32	Ireland
Reynegom, William H. V.					Richardes, Samuel, Jr.	1804	22	PA
	1820	19		NY	Richardet, Samuel, Jr.	1806	0	
Reynegon, Francis W. V.					Richards, Azell	1801	29	PA
	1818	14		NY	Richards, Casper H.	1816	15	PA
Reynegon, William Francis N.					Richards, Charles	1823	19	PA
	1818	16		NY	Richards, David	1807	28 b	PA
Reynolds, Amasa	1806	24		CT	Richards, David	1810	31 b	DE
Reynolds, Benjamin	1810	23		MD	Richards, George	1811	22	PA
Reynolds, Benjamin	1811	00			Richards, Henry	1818	39	MA
Reynolds, David	1822	15		ME	Richards, Jacob	1814	18	PA
Reynolds, Francis, Jr	1810	16		MD	Richards, Jacob	1823	16	PA
Reynolds, James	1823	32		RI	Richards, James	1815	36	PA
Reynolds, John	1806	22		PA	Richards, Job	1804	27	DE
Reynolds, John	1806	29		VA	Richards, John	1803	19 m	PA
Reynolds, John	1811	25	y	MD	Richards, John	1806	22	MA
Reynolds, John	1815	21		NY	Richards, John	1809	26	MD
Reynolds, John	1815	24		DE	Richards, Joseph	1804	0	
Reynolds, Joseph	1801	34		CT	Richards, Joseph	1804	0	England
Reynolds, William	1805	24		MA	Richards, Kendal	1804	28	DE
Reynolds, William	1810	18		NY	Richards, Lewis	1817	23	VA
Rhoads, Robert	1810	0 b		DE	Richards, Richard	1803	28 b	MA
Rhoden, Thomas	1804	20 b		NJ	Richards, Richard	1810	28	PA
Rhodes, Amos	1811	22		MA	Richards, Sothea	1805	18	DE
Rhodes, Robert	1810	23 b		DE	Richardson, Campbell	1819	27	NJ
Rial, John	1818	27	y	NJ	Richardson, Edward	1823	22	NJ
Ribble, George	1805	23		PA	Richardson, Elijah	1821	18	VA
Ribble, George	1806	0			Richardson, George	1811	23	PA
Ribble, Peter	1798	15		PA	Richardson, James	1810	22	VA
Ribble, Peter	1799	16		PA	Richardson, James	1811	00	
Ribble, Peter	1808	0			Richardson, John	1804	21 m	MD
Ricard, John	1821	22		PA	Richardson, John	1804	24	NJ
Rice, Calvin	1807	36		MA	Richardson, John	1805	29	PA
Rice, George	1804	32		DE	Richardson, John	1812	25	DE
Rice, James	1815	24		NY	Richardson, John	1817	39 b	PA
Rice, James	1816	31		MD	Richardson, Joshua	1821	28	NJ
Rice, James	1818	28		MA	Richardson, Peter	1804	21 y	PA
Rice, John	1803	22		PA	Richardson, Robert	1809	17	PA
Rice, John	1804	26		DE	Richardson, Robert	1818	48 c	MD
Rice, John	1823	23		none given	Richardson, Robert	1823	30	NC
Rice, Robert	1810	22		PA	Richardson, Samuel	1804	25 b	DE
Rice, Samuel	1809	28		NH	Richardson, Samuel	1810	21	PA
Rice, Samuel	1815	22		CT	Richardson, Samuel	1811	45 b	MA
Rice, Thomas	1808	20		PA	Richardson, Samuel	1812	00	
Rice, William	1807	20 b		MD	Richardson, Sharon	1815	23	MA
Rice, William	1810	19		MA	Richardson, Thomas	1798	23	none given
Rice, William	1810	0			Richardson, Thomas	1817	30 b	NY

Richardson, William	1804	26	VA
Riche, John	1806	23 b	NY
Richemond, Robert	1810	18	PA
Richerdson, John	1819	28	NJ
Richey, Samuel	1811	17 b	NY
Richey, Thomas	1798	23	PA
Richmond, Charles	1809	25 b	MA
Richmond, Peter	1798	28	PA
Richmond, William	1809	27	PA
Richsteen, John Christian			
	1806	36	NY
Richter, John	1817	34	NY
Rickards, Kendal	1804	28	DE
Rickards, Kendal	1804	0	
Ricker, Nathaniel	1815	29	MA
Rickie, William	1808	28	
Ricraft, William	1807	25	GA
Riddle, Thomas	1810	15	PA
Riddle, Thomas	1823	28	PA
Riden, Jeramiah	1811	26	PA
Rideout, Jacob	1810	38	MA
Ridgeley, Richard	1805	33 y	MD
Ridgway, Charles	1809	40 b	PA
Ridley, John	1810	24	MA
Ridley, Pompey	1804	20 m	NY
Ridley, Samuel	1807	22 b	NY
Ridot, Richard	1807	28 b	MD
Riebsam, John	1798	22	PA
Riel, George	1815	19 y	NJ
Rifferd, John	1810	22	PA
Rifford, Joseph	1819	26	PA
Rifford, Mather	1804	20	PA
Rifford, Matthias	1811	24	PA
Rigbie, William	1809	25 b	MD
Rigden, Thomas	1815	13	PA
Rigg, Jonathan	1810	41	MA
Riggan, Noah	1805	24	MD
Riggins, John	1811	15	NJ
Righley, Charles	1798	20	PA
Right, William	1815	21 b	PA
Rihl, George	1798	21	PA
Rihl, Richard	1810	23	PA
Riley, George	1807	22 b	PA
Riley, George	1821	22	NY
discharged from U. S. Navy			
Riley, Jacob	1816	31 b	NY
Riley, John	1822	22 y	CT
Riley, Richard	1804	26	NJ
Riley, William	1813	26 b	CT
Riley, William	1815	28 c	CT

Rimer, John	1807	25	PA
Rinedolle, Henry	1814	0	
Rinedoller, Henry	1810	16	PA
Rinedoller, Samuel	1818	18	PA
Rines, Thomas	1821	21	ME
Ringell, Joseph	1823	26 y	MD
Ringold, Henry	1809	38 b	DE
Ringsberry, John	1809	22	PA
Rink, John	1813	16	PA
Rink, John	1822	24	PA
Riordan, John	1810	20	MD
Riordan, John	1813	23	MD
Risbrough, John	1810	31	NH
Risdell, Alexander	1813	0	
Risley, George M.	1823	21	NJ
Ritchie, Bowman	1823	17	PA
Ritchie, Robert	1821	24	PA
Ritchie, Thomas	1810	22	LA
Rittenger, William	1810	25	PA
Rittenhouse, John B.	1798	17	PA
River, Morris	1823	21	NJ
Rixon, Lewis	1817	23 b	DE
Roach, Ira	1805	17	PA
Roach, James	1805	26 b	MD
Roach, Nicholas	1798	0	Ireland
Roake, Morgan	1810	37	NY
Roan, John	1801	20	PA
Roan, William	1805	22 y	NJ
Robason, William C.	1798	34	ME
Robb, William	1815	13	NJ
Robbarts, John	1804	27	none given
Robbins, James	1806	14	PA
Robbins, John	1796	0	VA
Robbins, Jonathan	1801	28	CT
Robbins, Joseph	1810	25	PA
Robbins, Samuel	1819	15	MA
Robbins, Thomas	1811	24	NY
Robbins, Thomas	1813	25	NY
Robbinson, John	1811	25	RI
Robenson, James	1815	25 y	MD
Roberson, John	1796	24 b	MD
Robert, John	1815	27 m	VA
Robert, Rufus	1805	0 b	
Roberts, Asahel	1813	21	NY
Roberts, Benjamin	1805	20	PA
Roberts, Benjamin	1815	24	MD
Roberts, Caleb	1804	22 b	DE
Roberts, Daniel	1801	27	NJ
Roberts, David	1822	38 c	NY
Roberts, Edward	1807	25	PA
Roberts, Edward	1811	21 b	MD
Roberts, Edward	1812	00	

Name	Year	Age		State
Roberts, Ellis	1823	16		PA
Roberts, Frederick	1820	21		PA
Roberts, George	1804	38	b	VA
Roberts, George	1818	36		MD
Roberts, Jacob	1801	23		MD
Roberts, James	1798	20		MD
Roberts, James	1820	29		MA
Roberts, Jesse W.	1812	25		PA
Roberts, Joel	1816	29		CT
Roberts, John	1803	27		PA
Roberts, John	1805	24		NY
Roberts, John	1806	25		MD
Roberts, John	1811	25		PA
Roberts, John	1811	23	b	MD
Roberts, John	1811	23		PA
Roberts, John	1811	25		PA
Roberts, John	1816	36		PA
Roberts, John	1821	31	c	PA
Roberts, John	1823	38	b	NY
Roberts, Joseph	1807	20	b	NY
Roberts, Joseph	1808	0		
Roberts, Joseph	1821	26		PA
Roberts, Lewis	1808	25		Portugal
Roberts, Nevelle	1809	31	y	MD
Roberts, Nicholas	1809	22		PA
Roberts, Owen John	1820	27		none given
Roberts, Richard	1807	18		NH
Roberts, Samuel	1809	22		PA
Roberts, Samuel	1810	20	y	DE
Roberts, Samuel	1812	00		
Roberts, Samuel	1812	00		
Roberts, Seth	1810	23		PA
Roberts, Thomas	1809	25		PA
Roberts, Thomas	1811	18		DE
Roberts, Thomas R.	1815	00		
Roberts, William	1815	20		MD
Roberts, William	1821	41		MD
Robertson, Andrew	1799	26		SC
Robertson, David	1804	22		DE
Robertson, James	1806	29		
Robertson, James	1810	17		NY
Robertson, John	1807	20		VA
Robertson, John	1809	19		MD
Robertson, John	1811	24		MD
Robertson, John	1811	21		PA
Robertson, John	1815	17		PA
Robertson, Peter	1798	32		PA
Robertson, Robert	1810	29	b	VA
Robertson, Thomas	1809	22		PA
Robertson, Thomas	1812	00		
Robertson, William	1815	24	b	DE
Robertson, William	1820	23		MA
Robeson, Charles	1810	32	b	LA
Robeson, Christian	1808	34		
Robeson, Daniel	1809	25	y	MD
Robeson, George	1821	41		Germany
Robeson, Thomas Greenwich				
	1805	26		PA
Robin, Peter	1804	23		GA
Robinette, Richard Jr.	1815	19		PA
Robins, Henry Edward	1822	18		PA
Robins, William B.	1818	15		MD
Robins, William	1818	28		MA
Robinson, Ambrose	1807	18	y	MD
Robinson, Anthony	1811	18		PA
Robinson, Charles	1806	21		DE
Robinson, Charles H.	1823	29		MA
Robinson, Daniel	1805	24	b	VA
Robinson, Daniel	1811	00		
Robinson, David	1811	25		MA
Robinson, David R.	1822	29		NJ
Robinson, Edwin	1818	18		RI
Robinson, George	1798	15		PA
Robinson, George	1804	25		MD
Robinson, George	1807	14		PA
Robinson, George W.	1810	17		PA
Robinson, Hale	1818	26	b	PA
Robinson, Henry	1807	26	b	DE
Robinson, Henry H.G.	1810	17		DE
Robinson, Henry G.	1812	18		DE
Robinson, Jacob	1817	27		MD
Robinson, James	1801	22		CT
Robinson, James	1804	28	c	PA
Robinson, James	1804	28	b	PA
Robinson, James	1809	25		PA
Robinson, James	1820	28		MA
Robinson, John	1800	25	b	MD
Robinson, John	1802	0		
Robinson, John	1805	19		PA
Robinson, John	1809	21		NJ
Robinson, John	1809	27		PA
Robinson, John	1809	22		NJ
Robinson, John	1810	0		
Robinson, John	1810	22	c	VA
Robinson, John	1811	15	b	NJ
Robinson, John	1812	19	m	DE
Robinson, John	1814	24		MD
Robinson, John	1815	24		MA
Robinson, John	1815	17		MA
Robinson, John	1815	19		VA
Robinson, John	1816	31		PA
Robinson, John	1817	32		NY
Robinson, John	1818	33	c	MD
Robinson, John	1823	13		PA

Robinson, Joshua	1820	30 c	MD
Robinson, Matthew	1811	19	RI
Robinson, Michael	1813	19	MA
Robinson, Michael	1819	25	MA
Robinson, Noah	1819	24	MD
Robinson, Peter	1817	19 b	DE
Robinson, Philip	1817	20 b	DE
Robinson, Stephen	1822	33	MD
Robinson, Thomas	1804	32	PA
Robinson, Thomas	1805	24	PA
Robinson, Thomas	1807	26	NJ
Robinson, Thomas	1811	27	PA
Robinson, Thomas	1818	29	MD
Robinson, William	1804	32 b	VA
Robinson, William	1806	35	PA
Robinson, William	1810	33	DE
Robinson, William	1817	32 y	SC
Robinson, William	1818	23 y	DE
Robinson, William T.	1822	18	PA
Robinson, William	1823	37 b	VA
Robison, Daniel	1823	22 b	NJ
Robson, John	1804	20	NY
Robson, John	1804	20	NY
Robson, Martin	1819	24	VA
Robson, Ralph	1804	20	VA
Robson, Ralph	1809	0	
Robson, William	1810	22	PA
Rocch, Andrew	1813	22	LA
Roche, David	1807	21	MA
Roche, Laurence	1808	24	
Roche, Lawrence	1806	23	PA
Roche, Ruben	1807	23 b	DE
Rockwood, Luther P.	1815	35	NH
Roco, Anthony	1798	29	
Roddick, James	1811	23	MD
Roden, Thomas	1812	00	
Roderiguez, Antonio	1806	38	LA
Roderiguez, Jacinto	1805	37 y	LA
Rodes, Charles	1810	17	PA
Rodes, Charles	1810	17	PA
Rodgers, Edward	1809	22	NY
Rodgers, Henry	1815	29	NJ
Rodgers, James D.	1807	21	NY
Rodgers, James	1807	20	PA
Rodgers, James	1812	00	PA
Rodgers, James	1816	0	
Rodgers, John	1807	21	MD
Rodgers, Joseph	1821	16 y	PA
Rodgers, Leaban	1815	30	VA
Rodgers, Patrick	1817	50	MA
Rodgers, Robert	1820	17	PA
Rodman, Robert R.	1809	21	PA

Rodman, Robert R.	1812	00	
Rodney, John	1815	34	LA
Rodney, Richard	1800	24 b	MA
Rodney, Richard	1806	0 b	
Rodolph, Joseph	1804	50	PA
Rodriguez, Constantino	1807	19	MS
Roe, Luke	1803	25	VA
Roelf, Francis	1810	25	MA
Roger, Ralph Hazard	1801	23	NY
Rogers, America	1809	20	DE
Rogers, Clement S.	1811	16	DE
Rogers, Daniel N.	1818	29	DE
Rogers, Enoch	1805	35	DE
Rogers, George	1798	0	PA
Rogers, George	1798	20 b	PA
Rogers, Henry	1817	00	
Rogers, James	1806	17	PA
Rogers, James	1811	00	
Rogers, James	1817	30	PA
Rogers, James	1818		
Rogers, John	1803	39	NY
Rogers, John	1805	18	PA
Rogers, John	1806	18	PA
Rogers, John	1809	18	MA
Rogers, John	1813	25	PA
Rogers, John	1817	21	ME
Rogers, Joseph	1809	24	LA
Rogers, Laban Thatcher			
	1823	17	MA
Rogers, Levi	1810	20	MA
Rogers, Michael	1798	28	PA
Rogers, Samuel	1822	26 b	CT
Rogers, Timothy, Jr.	1823	23	MA
Rogers, William	1809	16	MA
Rogers, William	1815	28	NY
Rogman, Peter	1806	0	
Rogman, Peter	1809	0	
Rogmon, Peter	1808	0	
Roiz, Emanuel	1815	26	LA
Rojmans, Peter	1798	25	PA
Rolafs, Gorge	1798	24	PA
Roland, Peter	1809	26	LA
Roland, William	1823	46 y	MD
Rolason, Hugh	1798	24	MD
Roleson, Hugh	1798	0	
Roll, Andrew	1803	20	NY
Roll, Andrew	1806	0	
Romeio, Charles	1809	38 m	NJ
Roney, Benjamin	1809	32 y	PA
Roney, William	1807	26	PA
Ronnels, Abram	1807	41 c	NY
Ronnels, Solomon	1821	27 b	NY

Name	Year	Age	State	Notes
Roosevelt, John Schuyler	1806	23	NJ	
Rorback, George H.	1818	19	MD	
Roscoe, James	1804	28	SC	
Roscoe, James	1804	0		
Rose, Alexander	1797	0		Gr.Br.
Rose, Calvin	1810	24	VT	
Rose, Calvin	1810	0		
Rose, Charles	1815	22	MA	
Rose, James	1809	15	NY	
Rose, John B.	1815	25	MD	
Rose, Robert	1819	16	PA	
Rose, Samuel	1820	30	PA	
Rose, Stacy	1809	17	NJ	
Rose, Stacy	1812	00	PA	
Rose, Stephen	1806	25	MD	
Rose, Thomas	1805	27	NJ	
Rose, William	1806	21	MD	
Rose, William	1815	21	PA	
Rose, William	1817	20 y	MA	
Rose, William	1818	28	NJ	
Rosein, William	1805	29	LA	
Rosengranee, Phillip	1809	0	NY	
Roseycrance, Philip	1809	27 b	NY	
Ross, Barney	1817	23	ME	
Ross, Charles	1804	31	PA	
Ross, Daniel	1804	16	PA	
Ross, David	1822	26		none given
Ross, Fredrick	1801	19	PA	
Ross, George	1819	27	NY	
Ross, James	1807	23 b	NY	
Ross, James	1807			
Ross, John	1798	21	VA	
Ross, John	1800	27	PA	
Ross, John	1805	17	PA	
Ross, John	1811	13	PA	
Ross, Richard	1809	21	NJ	
Ross, Richard	1810	0	NJ	
Ross, Robert	1798	23	PA	
Ross, Thomas	1809	23	NJ	
Ross, Thomas	1813	22	PA	
Ross, William	1818	53 y	VA	
Rosseter, Wm. L.	1809	26	CT	
Rossetter, William	1800	24	PA	
Rosycrance, Philip	1807	26 b	NY	
Rouls, David	1811	28 c	MD	
Round, John M.	1815	00		
Roundy, Benjamin	1809	27	MA	
Rourke, Morgan	1810	0		
Rourke, Thomas	1810	23	PA	
Rouvert, Edmund,Jr	1819	19	PA	
Rovet, John	1811	25	LA	

Name	Year	Age	State	Notes
Rovoudt, Andrew	1816	16	PA	
Row, Henry	1795	22		

apprenticed to Capt. John Thomson, Phila.
mariner, for 3 years

Name	Year	Age	State	Notes
Row, John	1820	22 y	NY	
Row, Thomas	1809	41 b	NY	
Row, William	1813	21		
Row, William	1815	29 b	MA	
Row, William	1820	15 b	PA	
Rowan, Charles	1822	35 b	NJ	
Rowan, James	1807	17	DE	
Rowan, Thomas C.	1823	24		none given
Rowe, Charles	1809	26	MA	
Rowe, Cornelius	1813	24	PA	
Rowe, John	1809	30	MA	
Rowe, John	1810	0		
Rowell, James	1815	24	MA	
Rowen, Charles	1816	25 m	NJ	
Rowland, David	1823	18	DE	
Rowland, William	1816	22	PA	
Rowland, William	1818			
Rownd, Henry Justus	1805	13	DE	
Rownd, John M.	1804	18	MD	
Rownd, John Morris	1807	18	MD	
Roxborough, David	1806	27 m	PA	
Roxbury, John	1809	22 m	NJ	
Roy, Edward	1821	26		none given
Roy, William	1817	25 b	PA	
Rozar, Peter	1815	20	LA	
Rozencrantz, John	1800	16	NY	
Rozencrantz, John	1800	0		
Ruand, Alexis	1818	11	PA	
Ruand, Lewis	1821	16	PA	
Ruben, Sylvander	1815	17 m	NY	
Rubey, Joseph	1804	32 b	MA	
Ruby, John	1798	0	MD	
Ruddach, John	1815	21	PA	
Rudduck, William	1805	18	PA	
Rudkin, William	1810	20	VA	
Ruff, John Henry	1796	17	MD	
Rufus, Robert	1803	22 b	NY	
Rufus, Robert	1805	0		
Rugan, Charles	1807	16	PA	
Rugan, William	1815	17	PA	
Rugans, Lawrence	1803	27	PA	
Rugless, Joseph	1823	27	CT	
Rummall, John	1815	22 y	PA	
Runabout, Barney	1804	23	MD	
Runchey, John	1807	17		
Runchez, John	1812	00		

Runchy, John	1811	00	

SPC issued 1807 taken by a captain in Liverpool
and torn up

Rupel, William	1798	20	VA
Rush, Benjiman	1818	18	PA
Rush, James	1815	25	NY
Rush, John	1807	28	MS
Rush, John	1808	34	PA
Rush, John	1812	00	
Rush, Levi	1823	31 b	MD
Rush, Thomas W.	1820	20	PA
Rusk, Samuel	1812	26	MD
Russel, Henry	1805	17	PA
Russel, Patten	1818	24	MA
Russel, Robert	1817	21	VA
Russel, William	1801	23	
Russel, William	1820	21	NY
Russell, Charles	1823	26	MA
Russell, Edward	1810	21	PA
Russell, James	1810	32	NY
Russell, James	1811	00	
Russell, John	1804	25	NJ
Russell, John	1810	21	NJ
Russell, John	1811	00	
Russell, Joseph	1807	19	LA
Russell, Robert	1818		
Russell, Robert	1819	45	
Russell, Stephen L.	1822	16	PA
Russell, Thomas	1809	26	
Ruston, Thomas	1804	18	PA
Ruston, Thomas	1805	0	
Ruth, William	1807	20 b	NY
Rutherford, Samuel	1823	22	NJ
Rutkins, William	1810	21	NY
Rutter, Edward	1822	21	MD
Rutter, Thomas	1810	22	MD
Ryan, Charles	1816	32	MA
Ryan, David	1807		
Ryan, Henry	1805	21	PA
Ryan, Jacob	1805	35 b	SC
Ryan, James	0000	27	
Ryan, James	0000	27	
Ryan, James P.	1812	22	DE
Ryan, John	1822	18	PA
Ryan, Jonathan	1819	12	PA
Ryan, William	1807	14	PA
Ryan, William	1815	00	
Ryan, William	1817	00	PA
Ryans, David	1807	47 y	DE
Ryans, Luke	1807	26 b	DE
Ryder, John	1810	22	MA

Ryer, James	1810	21 b	DE
Ryerson, Thomas Jr.	1815	17	PA
Sabastin, Nathaniel	1804	32	SC
Saddison, William G.	1822	25 y	NY
Sadler, George	1809	18	PA
Sadler, James	1804	27 b	MD
Sadler, James	1805	28 b	MD
Sadler, William	1810	26	MD
Safford, Abraham N.	1818	15	MA
Said, Moses	1805	23 b	PA
Sailsbury, Charles H.	1820	16	MD
Saint, Anthony	1810	23	LA
Saley, John	1811	29	LA
Saliesbery, Samuel	1809	18	PA
Salkeile, Job	1810	22	PA
Salkeld, Jacob	1822	17	PA
Salkeld, William	1823	29	NJ
Sally, Peter	1806	32	LA
Sally, Peter	1808	0	
Sally, Peter	1810	0	
Salmon, Daniel	1810	20	PA
Salmons, William	1809	19 y	DE
Salonius, Gustaf Rainholdt			
	1813	38	none given
Salsbury, Kendall	1822	21	ME
Salter, Orrey	1809	30 b	NJ
Salters, Orris	1810	0	
Saltez, Joseph	1807	25	MS
Sambelson, Edward	1812	00	PA
Sambow, Isaac	1817	25	RI
Sammon, Lewis	1811	28	PA
Sammons, Uriah	1807	21 y	NC
Sammons, William	1806	32 m	DE
Sampson, Alexander	1798	19 y	VA
Sampson, Daniel	1808	50 b	NY
Sampson, John	1807	34	NY
Sampson, Richard	1803	23	VA
Sampson, William	1822	18	PA
Samson, William	1798	34 y	SC
Samuel, Peter	1811	28 b	GA
Sanborn, Josiah	1809	27	MA
Sander, James	1804	15	NY
Sander, William	1805	24	MD
Sanderlin, Thomas	1806	21	NJ
Sanders, Charles	1815	22	MA
Sanders, Ephraim	1815	35 y	NJ
Sanders, James	1809	15 b	PA
Sanders, John	1807	23	DE
Sanders, John	1811	00	
Sanders, John	1818	20	PA
Sanders, John	1822	50 m	VA
Sanders, John	1823	14 b	PA

Sanders, Joseph	1807	24	DE
Sanders, Mark	1799	28	NJ
Sanderson, William	1819	29	MD
Sandford, Hezekiah	1815	24	MA
Sandford, Peregrin	1807	20	NJ
Sandown, Andrew	1817	29	MD
Sands, Lewis	1822	21 b	NY
Sands, Thomas	1811	19	NJ
Sandy, William P.	1801	17	NC
Sanford, Enoch	1803	20	NJ
Sanford, John C.	1820	19	MA

Sangrine, Oliver 1811 00
SPC given to Consul at Lisbon to procure his
liberation

Sanmantin, Joseph	1807	24	MS
Saracin, John	1818	36	SC
Sarazin, Guillaume	1808	0	
Sargeant, Phineas	1811	24	MA
Sargent, Winthrop	1820	22	ME
Sarmento, James Craig	1804	19	PA
Sarmiento, James Craig	1806	21	PA
Sass, John Peter	1807	19	PA
Sattan, John, Jr.	1804	21	PA
Saunders, Isaac	1810	21	NJ
Saunders, Jabez	1820	49	DE
Saunders, Jobus	1804	30	DE
Saunders, John	1801	28	MA
Saunders, John	1805	28	NJ
Saunders, John	1811	19 b	NY
Saunders, John	1815	34	MA
Saunders, John	1816	17	MD
Saunders, John	1821	23 y	MD
Saunders, Joseph	1810	24 y	NJ
Saunders, Joseph	1810	0	
Saunders, Joseph	1815	24	MA
Saunders, Prince	1803	29 m	NJ
Saunders, Samuel	1813	43	NH
Saunders, William	1818	37	RI
Savage, Absolam	1821	21 b	MA
Savage, Jacob	1809	27	PA
Savage, John	1814	16	PA
Savage, John	1814	0	
Savage, Peter	1809	22 b	PA
Savage, Peter	1810	0	PA
Savage, Thomas	1817	32	VA
Savage, Zadoc	1823	21	NJ
Savolane, Thomas	1811	18	PA
Savoy, Nathaniel	1817	23	MA
Sawer, Thomas	1818	26	PA
Sawers, Samuel	1804	17	PA

Sawny, Silvester	1803	22 m	PA	
Sawyer, Charles	1821	19	ME	
Sawyer, Ebenezer	1811	27	MA	
Sawyer, Elisha	1821	37	ME	
Sawyer, John	1815	38 b	NC	
Sawyer, Jonathan	1817	21	NY	
Sawyer, Jonathan	1818	00	NY	
Say, Isaac	1815	21	NJ	
Scantling, Luke	1796	24	PA	
Scarum, James	1805	25	PA	
Scattergood, Thomas	1823	16	NJ	
Schanck, Benjamin	1805	34	NJ	
Schargell, William	1812	24	PA	
Scheiner, Henry	1812	21	PA	
Schellenger, William	1814	25	PA	
Schellinger, John	1810	20	NJ	
Schemlar, Henry	1798	21	NY	
Schenck, Henry F.	1820	24	NY	
Schenck, John	1815	19	NY	
Schiebur, Nicholas	1810	28	PA	
Schisler, Lawrence	1807	40	PA	
Schmidt, Christiann	1821	24		none given
Schmidt, Jacob Willgaard				
	1820	36		Germany
Schoales, James	1798	36	PA	
Schooles, James	1806	0		
Schoolfield, Thomas P.	1822	30	MD	
Schools, James	1814	22	NY	
Schreiner, Jacob S.	1812	15	PA	
Schreiner, William H.	1822	17	PA	
Schriver, Jacob	1820	41	PA	
Schultz, Frederick	1806	33		none given
Schultz, Jacob	1807			
Schutz, Henry	1798	22	DE	
Schuyler, Charles	1820	31 c	NJ	
Schwartz, John	1813	22	PA	
Scofield, Thomas	1815	21	PA	
Scoin, Henry	1810	0		
Scon, Henry	1801	21	PA	
Scon, Henry	1801	21	PA	
Scores, John Homan	1806	32	MA	
Scot, Robert Jr.	1815	22	PA	
Scott, Alexander	1818	27 b	DE	
Scott, Benjamin	1805	20	PA	
Scott, Edward	1804	29	GA	
Scott, George	1806	23	MD	
Scott, George	1807		MD	
Scott, Hamilton James	1817	23	PA	
Scott, Henry	1805	25	PA	
Scott, Hugh	1803	25	PA	
Scott, James	1805	31	MA	
Scott, James	1806	25	PA	

Scott, James	1811	23 b	NJ		Sebastian, Charles	1823	23 y	PA	
Scott, James	1822	20	PA		Sebastian, Henry	1817	22 y	PA	
Scott, Joel	1810	40	PA		Sebrook, William	1811	20 b	NY	
Scott, John	1799	25	NJ		Seckels, William	1809	23	NJ	
Scott, John	1801	19	CT		Seddenger, Thomas	1806	16	PA	
Scott, John	1805	52 y	PA		Sederstrom, Jonas	1810	0		
Scott, John	1807	27 b	PA		Sedley, William	1809	19	NJ	
Scott, John	1809	15	PA		Seeboth, William	1810	0		
Scott, John	1810	25 c	TN		Seeley, Eden Mersellus				
Scott, John	1815	28 y	PA			1815	27	NJ	
Scott, John	1818	37	NY		Seely, John	1804	30	VA	
Scott, Nicholas	1807	32	MS		Sefry, Peter	1806	0		
Scott, Peter	1807	24 b	NJ		Segiune, Francis	1811	20	NJ	
Scott, Solomon	1817	25 b	DE		Seguine, Francis	1811	20	NJ	
Scott, Thomas K. L.	1804	24	SC		Seidler, Gottfried	1806	33	NY	
Scott, William	1803	26	PA		Selby, Charles	1815			none given
Scott, William	1807	21	PA		Selby, Francis	1810	22 y	SC	
Scott, William	1807	21	PA		Selby, Francis	1811	00		
Scott, William	1809	26 b	VA		Selby, James	1815	40 b	MD	
Scott, William	1810	0			Selby, James	1817	12	PA	
Scott, William	1810	28	MD		Selby, Miles	1815	17		none given
Scott, William	1811	00			Selby, Thomas	1798	35	MD	
Scott, William	1812	00			Selby, Thomas T.	1821	19	PA	
Scott, William Alexander					Selby, William	1797	16	MD	
	1815	23	MD		Selick, John, Jr.	1804	17	PA	
Scott, William	1817	27 y	PA		Selick, John	1816	28		
Scott, William	1819	18 b	PA		Sell, Amos	1804	22	NY	
Scottron, Samuel	1818	21 y	PA		Sellick, John	1810	0		
Scribner, William	1803	30	CT		Semans, David	1809	25	DE	
Scriven, Peter M.	1806	30		none given	Sendal, Philip	1810	25	MA	
Scull, Ebenezer T.	1817	21	NJ		Sephay, Peter	1804	0		
Scull, Hewes	1806	16	PA		Sephay, Peter	1804	27 m	NY	
Scull, Richard	1810	15	NJ		Sequine, Francis	1811	20	NJ	
Scully, Timothy	1804	33	MD		Seras, Francis	1811	30 b	PA	
Scully, Timothy	1806	0			Serine, Joseph	1809	37		Venia
Seaberry, John	1823	23 y	NY		Serres, Thomas	1804	19	PA	
Seabrant, John	1803	33	NY		Serriles, John S.	1822	24	PA	
Seagrin, Peter	1806	22	GA		Service, Abraham	1798	39	NH	
Seam, Jacob	1806	10	PA		Servoss, Charles	1807	16	PA	
Seaman, George	1823			none given	Servoss, Jacob	1807	13	PA	
Seaman, John	1819	24	PA		Servoss, Jacob	1815	20	PA	
Seamans, Samuel Young					Sessions, Robert	1811	34 b	RI	
	1811	18	RI		Setchell, Samuel A.	1816	29	MA	
Seamore, John	1804	26	PA		Sevel, Nathan	1819	20	NJ	
Seamore, John	1805	0			Sevier, William Richard	1811	17	TN	
Searl, Robert	1805	22	PA		Sewell, John	1807	19	MD	
Sears, Green	1809	28	MA		Sewins, Thomas	1816	26 b	MD	
Sears, John	1818	22	MD		Sexton, Banjamin	1815	17	PA	
Sears, Uriah	1809	18	MA		Sexton, James	1807	25	PA	
Sears, William	1809	26	NJ		Seymore, Cato	1816	20 b	DE	
Seaton, Alexander Murry					Seymour, Joseph	1806	14	MA	
	1811	24	CT		Seymour, Joseph	1810	0		

Seymour, Joseph	1810	0	
Seymour, Peter	1823	22 b	DE
Shackenberg, Michael	1806	19	SC
Shaddock, Charles	1814	18	DE
Shade, John	1815	16	PA
Shadrick, John	1813	28	PA
Shallcross, Isaac	1805	29	DE
Shallcross, Morris C.	1807	16	DE
Shallus, George P.	1820	14	PA
Shallus, William Augustus			
	1807	16	PA
Shane, George Lewis	1809	25	PA
Shane, John	1815	00	
Shankland, Benjamin	1823	17	PA
Shankland, Charles	1811	16	PA
Shankland, William	1807	14	PA
Shanklin, Joseph Jr.	1815	15	PA
Shannon, Henry	1817	23	NJ
Shannon, James C.	1806	18	PA
Shannon, John	1804	33	PA
Sharp, Cladius	1808	19	PA
Sharp, Cladius	1808	0	
Sharp, Claudius	1806	16	PA
Sharp, Claudius B.	1810	21	PA
Sharp, John	1806	17 m	RI
Sharp, John	1823	25	NJ
Sharp, Joseph	1821	24	ME
Sharp, Peter	1810	17	NJ
Sharp, Peter	1815	00	
Sharp, Samuel	1806	31	PA
Sharp, Thomas	1804	36	DE
Sharp, William D.	1811	21	PA
Sharp, William D.	1812	00	PA
Sharpe, Charles	1815	17	PA
Sharpe, John	1798	23	England
Sharpe, William	1804	36	MD
Sharphead, David	1798	20	DE
Sharpless, Archibald	1822	26 b	PA
Sharpley, Adam	1805	26	DE
Shaw, Alex	1809	30	PA
Shaw, Ephraim	1805	22	NJ
Shaw, Henry	1805	21	NJ
Shaw, Hiram	1820	16	MA
Shaw, Isaiah	1804	21	NJ
Shaw, James	1807	24	NJ
Shaw, James	1811	25	MD
Shaw, Joseph	1804	16	PA
Shaw, Joshua	1811	35	NJ
Shaw, Leonard	1822	30	NJ
Shaw, Leonard	1822	31	MD
Shaw, Leonard	1822	31	MD
Shaw, M.D., James	1804	23	PA

Shaw, Nathan	1796	17	
Shaw, Robert	1813	23	VA
Shaw, Thomas	1813	23	PA
Shaw, Thompson D.	1820	19	PA
Shaw, William	1809	18	VA
Shaw, William	1809	27	NY
Shaw, William	1815	20	RI
Shawman, John	1811	19	SC
Shay, Harvey	1821	16 b	VA
Shay, Isaac	1814	25	NJ
Shay, John	1809	28	PA
Shay, John W.	1810	0	
Shay, John W.	1810	29	PA
Shay, John W.	1810	0	
Shay, John W.	1812	00	
Shea, John	1823	20	MA
Shea, William	1823	16	ME
Sheaff, Henry S.	1809	21	PA
super cargo of ship *Susquehanna* bound			
for China with Capt. Benner			
Shearman, John	1815	23	NY
Shears, Michael	1806	0	
Shears, Michael	1806	0	
Shearwood, James	1809	21	PA
Shearwood, William	1817	26	PA
Shedaker, William	1803	24	PA
Sheed, Richard	1809	25 b	SC
Sheed, Richard	1812	00	
Sheed, Richard	1812	00	
Sheen, John	1814	17	MD
Sheers, Michael	1805	30	MD
Sheers, Michael	1807		
Sheets, Jacob	1816	24	NJ
Shefer, Adam	1815	21	PA
Sheffel, C. Frederick	1798	30	none given
Shefield, Joseph	1818	43	RI
Shehan, Daniel	1822	25	MA
Shelcutt, Daniel	1819	37	CT
Sheldon, Jesse	1814	20	NJ
Shelly, Samuel	1815	65	not given
Shelter, William	1812	17 b	MD
Shelton, Thomas	1821	20	SC
Shepaherd, Thomas	1809	20	PA
Shepard, James	1815	25	NH
Shepard, Jonathan	1809	23	MA
Shepard, Randal	1798	24 b	VA
Shephard, Alexander	1822	21	PA
Shephard, Henry	1810	32	SC
Shephard, Henry	1822	34	MD
Shephard, Joseph	1817	27	NY

Shephard, Thomas	1801	30 b	NC		Shivily, John	1819	21		NJ
Shephard, Thomas	1817	46	DE		Shnyder, Jacob Knop	1812	00		
Shepherd, Emlay	1804	23 b	PA		Shockley, Samuel	1798	19		MA
Shepherd, Emory	1805	0			Shoemaker, Charles F.	1819	16		PA
Shepherd, Ezekiel	1811	22 b	MD		Shoemaker, David	1805	22		PA
Shepherd, Francis	1804	21	VA		Shoemaker, George	1823	14		PA
Shepherd, Mark	1801	31	MA		Short, John	1806	28		PA
Sheppard, Abraham	1821	26	NJ		Shorter, James	1817	40 b		MD
Sheppard, Emery	1804	23 b	PA		Shorter, Jared	1804	26 b		MD
Sheppard, John	1812	22 y	VA		Shorts, Robert	1812	25		DE
Sheppard, Stephen	1803	23	NJ		Shots, Martin	1805	16		NY
Sheppard, Stephen	1811	21	VA		Shourds, Joseph	1807	25		NJ
Shepperd, Richard	1807	21	PA		Shourds, Joseph	1809	0		
Sherer, John	1801	35	NJ		Shower, William	1815	24		PA
Sherer, Michael	1811	00			Shubert, Cato	1807	32 b		PA
Shering, William	1807				Shubert, George	1810	19		PA
Sherington, Wm.	1814	0			Shull, Jacob	1810	20		NJ
Sherman, Isaac	1822	24 b	RI		Shultz, Charles	1803	26		PA
Sherman, Thomas	1820	20	MA		Shultz, Frederick	1810	21		
Shermer, Christian	1815	22	PA		Shultz, Jacob	1804	37		VA
Sherrington, William	1805	27	MA		Shultz, Jacob	1805	0		
Sherrington, William	1814	0			Shultz, Jacob	1807			
Sherwood, Henry	1810	22	NY		Shultz, John Henry	1806	22		PA
Shesler, Nicholas	1804	22		none given	Shuman, John	1819	22		PA
Shettslive, Michael	1810	21	PA		Shumane, George	1806	19		PA
Shewbert, Cato	1806	32 b	PA		Shurtleff, John	1811	19		PA
Shibe, William	1817	23	PA		Shurtleff, John	1811	00		
Shidel, William	1804	34	MD		Shute, Charles	1818	50		VA
Shields, Charles	1810	0			Shute, George	1806	45		MA
Shields, Charles	1810	18	NJ		Sickels, George Washington				
Shields, Charles	1811	00				1810	22		NY
Shields, James	1801	23	PA		Siddons, Benjamin	1815	16		PA
Shields, Robert	1803	31	PA		Siddons, Jesse	1815	18		PA
Shillingford, Thomas	1821	13	PA		Siddons, John	1805	31		PA
Shillings, William	1815	21	MD		Sides, Cato	1799	24		PA
Shillingsforth, Joseph	1813	20	PA		Sidlinger, Samuel	1809	20		Me
Shin, John	1809	20	NJ		Siepplin, Stephen	1815	27 b		DE
Shinckle, John Hide	1810	20	PA		Siggers, John	1819	22		NY
Shinkle, John	1810	0			Sigorre, Joseph	1811	32		LA
Shipley, Daniel	1809	29	VA		Sikes, Charles	1810	16 y		PA
Shipley, Daniel	1813	0			Silay, William	1800	16		PA
Shipley, John	1812	20	NY		Sill, Richard	1815	22		NY
Shipley, John	1815	0			Silliman, Joseph A.	1823	22		PA
Shipley, Thomas	1823	17	DE		Silva, Francisco	1813	33		none given
Shippen, Richard	1811	16	PA		Silve, John	1806	32		MA
Shipply, John	1807	24	NC		Silvester, Henry	1798	23		NY
Shippy, Charles	1805	27 b	DE		Simes, George Washington				
Shirkey, William J.	1822	15	PA			1816	31 b		MD
Shirley, Charles Redman					Simes, Robert	1798	20		PA
	1823	15	PA		Simkins, John	1818	23		NJ
Shirley, Thomas	1819	28 y	VA		Simkins, Joseph	1818	21		NJ
Shivers, Josiah	1800	32	NJ		Simkins, Thomas	1817	34		MD

Name	Year	Age	State	Note
Simkins, William	182	20	NJ	
Simkins, William	182	20	NJ	
Simler, George	1809	23	PA	
Simmons, Benjamin	1816	31 s	NY	
Simmons, Charles	1803	26 b	MA	
Simmons, Edward,Jr	1811	23	PA	
Simmons, Francis Brown				
	1806	12 b	PA	
	1812	18 b	PA	
Simmons, George	1816	27	MA	
Simmons, George	1817	25	SC	
Simmons, John	1794	33	MA	
Simmons, John	1810	25	NJ	
Simmons, John	1817	28 b	MA	
Simmons, Joseph Jr.	1815	17	PA	
Simmons, Morris	1820	54		none given
Simmons, Nicholas	1811	23	NY	
Simmons, Richard	1801	22 b	DE	
Simmons, Sampson	1801	26 b	MD	
Simmons, Thomas	1819	49 b	MA	
Simmons, Thomas F.	1823	21	NJ	
Simmons, Titus	1807	35 b	MA	
Simmons, Titus	1822	47 b	MA	
Simmons, Titus	1822	47 b	MA	
Simmons, William	1806	22	RI	
Simmons, William	1807	18	CT	
Simmons, William	1808	0		
Simmons, William	1819	19 b	PA	
Simmons, William	1823	16	PA	
Simms, Thomas	1810	32	MD	
Simon, Lewis	1817	16	PA	
Simon, Thomas	1810	54 b	Ny	
Simons, Henry	1812	24 m	DE	
Simons, John	1807	29	VA	
Simons, John	1817	21 b	PA	
Simons, Samuel	1806	23 b	PA	
Simonson, Stephen	1820	23	NY	
Simoson, John	1807	25	NY	
Simpler, John	1821	21	DE	
Simpson, Alexander	1810	23	RI	
Simpson, David	1809	22	PA	
Simpson, Edward	1810	20	MA	
Simpson, George	1805	38	PA	
Simpson, George, Jr.	1806	19	PA	
Simpson, George	1823	14	PA	
Simpson, John	1814	19	PA	
Simpson, John	1815	19 b	MD	
Simpson, John	1820	44 b	NY	
Simpson, Robert P.	1821	16	PA	
Simpson, Thomas	1806	23	NY	
Simpson, Thomas	1823	39	NY	
Simpson, William	1805	23	DE	
Simpson, William	1812	23	NY	
Simpson, William	1815	26	VA	
Simpson, William	1822	22	PA	
Sims, Isaac	1797	23	PA	
Sims, Jeremiah	1811	27 b	MD	
Sims, Jeremiah	1812	00		
Sims, John	1815	26 b	MA	
Sims, William	1804	28 b	NY	
Simson, Isaac	1820	22 c	MA	
Sinclair, Archibold	1806	34	VA	
Sinclair, Daniel	1812	39	NY	
Sinclair, David	1812	26 b	MD	
Sinclair, James	1810	19	SC	
Sinclair, Robert	1798	24	MA	
Sinclair, Robert	1821	33	MA	
Sinclare, George	1805	23	NY	
Singelton, James	1810	21	PA	
Singer, Cornelius	1807	23 b	MD	
Singer, Cornelius	1814	0		
Singer, John	1805	22 b	MD	
Singer, John	1806	22 b	MD	
Singer, Thomas	1809	16	NJ	
Singer, Thomas	1810	27 b	MD	
Singer, Thomas	1810	0		
Singer, Thomas	1814	0		
Singer, Thomas	1816	28 b	MD	
Singers, Wm.	1823	32	NY	
Singleton, James	1811	00		
Singleton, James	1813	25 b	DE	
Singleton, James	1815	00		
Singleton, Joshua	1806	19 y	NJ	
Singleton, Robert	1809	28 b	DE	
Sinista, Lewis	1812	50	LA	
Sinister, Francis	1805	29	MD	
Sinnett, John	1815	30		none given
Sinnison, James	1822	41 b	PA	
Sins, Solomon	1822	38	NH	
Siple, Benjamin	1805	22 b	DE	
Sippel, London	1813	28 b	DE	
Sippet, Charles	1807	21	MD	
Sippett, Charles	1810	0		
SPC lost in wreck of ship *Apollo*				
Sipple, James	1823	23 b	DE	
Sipple, Moses	1809	22 b	DE	
Sipple, Moses	1815	00		
Sipple, William	1823	16 y	DE	
Sisinger, John	1804	22	PA	
Sisinger, John	1809	0		PA	
Sissing, William	1821	22 y	MD	
Sitlar, Richard	1815	26	MA	

Sizer, John	1811	31		LA
Skaats, Rinier	1823	27		NY
Skees, John L.	1807	17		PA
Skellenger, Jerimiah	1819	28		PA
Skelton, Robert	1801	22		PA
Skerrett, George	1810	18		LA
Skewne, Henry	1815	35		PA
Skidmore, Joseph	1812	29		NY
Skiff, Stephen	1817	30		MA
Skiff, Stephen	1821	33		MA
Skimer, Johnston	1809	24		
Skinner, Abraham	1808	23		MA
Skinner, Alexander	1805	27		PA
Skinner, Charles William				
	1805	16		MA
Skinner, Francis John	1808	20		MA
Skinner, Henry	1804	47		MA
Skinner, Henry	1808	24		MA
Skinner, James	1800	16		CT
Skinner, John	1801	19		NY
Skinner, Robert	1810	24		PA
Skinner, Thomas N.	1819	18		NJ
Sknyder, Jacob Knop	1810	17		PA
Skolfrield, John	1821	40		ME
Slacum, Manuel	1809	27	b	DE
Slade, Edmund	1819	17		NC
Slade, George	1816	25		NY
Slade, Uriah	1806	29		NC
Slahter, Joseph	1818	36		PA
Slater, Anthony	1813	20		PA
Slater, John	1803	26		DE
Slater, John	1809	27		NY
Slater, William	1798	25		NY
Slaymaker, Samuel C.	1811	17		PA
Sleed, George	1809	27		PA
Slip, James	1807	21		NY
Sloan, James J.	1819	16		MD
Sloan, John	1805	27		PA
Slocum, Solomon	1816	42	y	MA
Sloemn, David	1798	25		RI
Smack, Powell	1814	21		MD
Small, Jesse	1803	22		DE
Small, John	1805	23		PA
Small, Joshua	1803	0		

Small, Peter	1819	25	c	NY

scar from musket ball while on board American
scooner *Allegater* during late war

Small, Thomas	1820	32		MD
Smart, Charles	1794	27		Gr.Br.
Smiley, John	1797	24		MD

Smith, Abel	1809	19		NY
Smith, Abraham	1809	19	b	NY
Smith, Abraham	1811	51		PA
Smith, Abraham	1813	21	b	MD
Smith, Abraham	1822	23	y	PA
Smith, Abram	1807	22	b	NY
Smith, Alexander	1808	16		NY
Smith, Amos	1821	20		ME
Smith, Andrew C.	1805	22		PA
Smith, Andrew	1810	20		MD
Smith, Anthony	1808	17	b	PA
Smith, Anthony	1810	35	b	NY
Smith, Anthony	1813	0		
Smith, Archibald	1810	25		NH
Smith, Bartholomeu	1814	19		MD
Smith, Benjamin	1818	24		DE
Smith, Benjamin G.	1821	29		MA
Smith, Burnham	1822	23		ME
Smith, Caleb	1810	17		MD
Smith, Caleb	1821	22		MA
Smith, Charles W.	1804	15		PA
Smith, Charles	1807	21	y	DE
Smith, Charles	1810	21		DE
Smith, Charles,Jr.	1810	19		PA
Smith, Charles	1815	25		MD
Smith, Charles	1816	28	b	NY
Smith, Charles	1817	18	y	PA
Smith, Chester	1810	22		NJ
Smith, Christiam	1800	28		PA
Smith, Christian	1815	28		none given
Smith, Daniel	1811	30		NH
Smith, Daniel	1813	25		NY
Smith, David	1816	16	b	DE
Smith, David	1817	30	b	NY
Smith, Ebenezer	1823	19		DE
Smith, Edward	1807	23		PA
Smith, Edward	1809	19		PA
Smith, Edward	1811	21		PA
Smith, Edward R.	1817	16		PA
Smith, Edward	1818	19		NY
Smith, Edward S.	1823	26		NY
Smith, Francis	1806	34	b	VA
Smith, Frederick M.	1816	15		PA
Smith, George	1807	21	b	MA
Smith, George	1807	20		PA
Smith, George	1809	21		NJ
Smith, George	1809	26		PA
Smith, George	1809	17		NY
Smith, George	1815	25		MA
Smith, George F.	1815	22		PA
Smith, George	1819	19		PA
Smith, George W.	1821	17		PA

Name	Year	Age		State
Smith, Gilbert	1799	16		PA
Smith, Gilbert H.	1803	18		MD
Smith, Gilman	1804	16		NH
Smith, Greenbury	1817	00		
Smith, Henry	1809	26	y	NY
Smith, Henry	1823	23	y	PA
Smith, Hugh	1819	30		PA
Smith, Isaac	1798	0		PA
Smith, Isaac	1812	24	b	PA
Smith, Jack	1807	23	b	MD
Smith, Jack	1809	0		MD
Smith, Jacob	1804	30		MD
Smith, Jacob	1806	38		NJ
Smith, Jacob	1806	20		PA
Smith, Jacob	1807	25		PA
Smith, Jacob	1807	21		PA
Smith, Jacob	1810	27		PA
Smith, Jacob	1810	32	y	NY
Smith, Jacob	1811	24		NJ
Smith, Jacob W.	1818	33		DE
Smith, Jacob G.	1823	15		PA
Smith, James	1796	20		PA
Smith, James	1801	22	m	MD
Smith, James	1803	23	m	VA
Smith, James	1804	40		VA
Smith, James	1804	28		NJ
Smith, James	1804	28		PA
Smith, James	1807	19		NY
Smith, James	1807	29	b	NY
Smith, James	1807	22		MA
Smith, James	1807	17		DE
Smith, James	1809	22	b	MD
Smith, James	1810	0	n	
Smith, James	1810	17		MA
Smith, James	1810	27		NY
Smith, James	1810	34		PA
Smith, James	1811	00		
Smith, James	1811	14		MA
Smith, James	1811	22	b	DE
Smith, James P.	1814	19		NY
Smith, James	1815	24	b	LA
Smith, James	1815	25		NY
Smith, James	1817	28	b	DE
Smith, James M.	1823	21	b	NY
Smith, John	1796	0		PA
Smith, John	1796	0		VA
Smith, John	1797	0		none given
Smith, John	1798	19		PA
Smith, John	1800	21		PA
Smith, John	1801	29		PA
Smith, John	1803	28		PA
Smith, John	1804	16		PA
Smith, John	1804	18		PA
Smith, John C.	1804	19		PA
Smith, John	1804	21		NJ
Smith, John	1804	24		PA
Smith, John	1805	24		VA
Smith, John	1805	24		NY
Smith, John	1805	26		PA
Smith, John	1805	25		PA
Smith, John	1805	37		PA
Smith, John G.	1806	19		PA
Smith, John E.	1807	40		LA
Smith, John	1807	20		NC
Smith, John	1808	0		
Smith, John	1808	20		PA
Smith, John W.	1809	22		RI
Smith, John	1809	20		NY
Smith, John	1809	0		NY
Smith, John	1809	20		NJ
Smith, John	1809	29		PA
Smith, John	1809	22		LA
Smith, John	1809	23		NJ
Smith, John	1809	24		NY
Smith, John	1809	22		MD
Smith, John A.	1810	0		
Smith, John A.	1810	27		VA
Smith, John	1810	24		MD
Smith, John	1810	12	b	DE
Smith, John	1810	21		NY
Smith, John	1810	19		PA
Smith, John	1810	25		MD
Smith, John	1810	20		NY
Smith, John	1810	32		LA
Smith, John	1810	25	b	NJ
Smith, John	1810	25		NY
Smith, John	1810	18		NY
Smith, John	1811	20		NY
Smith, John	1811	25		MA
Smith, John	1811	16		NY
Smith, John	1811	22		MD
Smith, John	1811	26		NJ
Smith, John	1812	00		
Smith, John	1812	00		
Smith, John	1812	00		
Smith, John	1812	00		
Smith, John	1812	22	c	MD
Smith, John H.	1813	15		PA
Smith, John	1813	34		MA
Smith, John	1813	35		NY
Smith, John	1815	0		
Smith, John	1815	25		NJ
Smith, John	1815	22		NJ
Smith, John	1815	23		MA

Name	Year	Age		State
Smith, John	1815	37	y	RI
Smith, John	1815	16		PA
Smith, John	1815	37		none given
Smith, John	1815	27	b	MD
Smith, John	1815	24		MD
Smith, John	1815	25	b	NJ
Smith, John	1815	27		NY
Smith, John	1816	0		
Smith, John A.	1817	17		PA
Smith, John	1817	42		NJ
Smith, John	1817	18		PA
Smith, John	1818	30	b	NY
Smith, John	1818	19		PA
Smith, John	1819	19	b	MD
Smith, John	1821	17		PA
Smith, John	1821	22	b	VA
Smith, John	1821	26	b	PA
Smith, John	1821	22		NJ
Smith, John	1821	28		PA
Smith, John	1822	27		ME
Smith, John	1823	25		NC
Smith, John	1823	23	b	PA
Smith, John E.	1823	22		NY
Smith, Jonathan	1805	22	b	DE
Smith, Jonathan F.	1806	23		NJ
Smith, Jonathan F.	1812	00		
Smith, Joseph	1797	38		NJ
Smith, Joseph	1805	24		NJ
Smith, Joseph	1809	26		NJ
Smith, Joseph	1809	0		NJ
Smith, Joseph	1810	21	b	MD
Smith, Joseph	1811	15		NY
Smith, Joseph	1816	20		LA
Smith, Joseph	1818	25		NH
Smith, Joseph	1819	25		MD
Smith, Joseph	1820	26		MD
Smith, Lewis	1820	22	y	PA
Smith, Lewis	1822	27	y	MA
Smith, Marcus D.	1820	16		PA
Smith, Michael	1815	23		PA
Smith, Minor	1807	27		NY
Smith, Nathaniel	1810	32	c	VA
Smith, Nicholas	1809	19		PA
Smith, Peter	1823	25	b	PA
Smith, Philip	1818	18		PA
Smith, Rial	1811	27		MA
Smith, Richard	1807	20		NJ
Smith, Richard	1809	42		NJ
Smith, Richard	1809	18		NY
Smith, Richard	1811	27	y	MD
Smith, Richard	1815	00		
Smith, Richard	1816	35		MD
Smith, Robert	1801	20		DE
Smith, Robert	1803	23		NY
Smith, Robert	1804	19		PA
Smith, Robert	1805	22	b	DE
Smith, Robert	1807	22		MD
Smith, Robert	1810	22		DE
Smith, Samuel	1803	33		MA
Smith, Samuel	1804	0		
Smith, Samuel B.	1805	20		VA
Smith, Samuel	1807	25	b	DE
Smith, Samuel	1810	28	b	MD
Smith, Samuel	1810	21		PA
Smith, Samuel	1811	23		MA
Smith, Samuel	1812	00		
Smith, Samuel	1813	18		NJ
Smith, Samuel	1814	0		
Smith, Samuel	1815	25	m	DE
Smith, Samuel	1820	15		PA
Smith, Samuel C.	1820	22	y	PA
Smith, Samuel	1823	49		MA
Smith, Samuel F.	1823	19		DE
Smith, Solomon	1809	29		NJ
Smith, Solomon	1812	00		
Smith, Thomas	1798	25		DE
Smith, Thomas	1801	22	b	MD
Smith, Thomas	1801	23		MA
Smith, Thomas	1805	32		NY
Smith, Thomas	1805	25	b	NY
Smith, Thomas	1806	0		
Smith, Thomas	1806	28		NC
Smith, Thomas	1807	21		PA
Smith, Thomas	1807	16		MA
Smith, Thomas	1809	24		MA
Smith, Thomas	1809	23		PA
Smith, Thomas	1809	0		
Smith, Thomas	1810	29		MA
Smith, Thomas	1810	22		PA
Smith, Thomas	1810	32		MD
Smith, Thomas	1815	00		
Smith, Thomas	1815	22		MD
Smith, Thomas	1818			
Smith, Thomas	1821	36	m	MD
Smith, Thomas	1821	22		MA
Smith, Thomas	1822	23	b	MD
Smith, Thomas	1822	28	y	VA
Smith, Thomas, Jr.	1823	23		PA
Smith, Thomas	1823	18		NY
Smith, Uriah	1814	21		NJ
Smith, Wallin	1819	26	b	MA
Smith, William	1796	22		CT
Smith, William	1797	0		MD
Smith, William	1798	20		PA

Smith, William	1803	28	PA
Smith, William	1804	24	PA
Smith, William	1804	19	PA
Smith, William	1804	18	NJ
Smith, William	1804	20	PA
Smith, William	1804	20	PA
Smith, William	1804	20	PA
Smith, William	1806	37	MA
Smith, William	1806	20	PA
Smith, William P.	1806	22	PA
Smith, William	1807	26	PA
Smith, William	1808	20	CT
Smith, William	1809	29	PA
Smith, William	1809	33	GA
Smith, William	1809	22	VA
Smith, William	1809	25	MA
Smith, William	1810	0	
Smith, William	1811	29	MA
Smith, William	1811	20	NY
Smith, William	1811	00	
Smith, William	1811	26 b	NJ
Smith, William	1811	28	RI
Smith, William	1813	0	
Smith, William	1814	22	VA
Smith, William	1815	00	
Smith, William	1815	37	RI
Smith, William	1815	28	MD
Smith, William	1815	19	LA
Smith, William	1816	23	DE
Smith, William	1816	22	NY
Smith, William	1817	24	NY
Smith, William	1817	29	NJ
Smith, William	1817	21	PA
Smith, William	1818	18	NC
Smith, William	1819	25	NJ
Smith, William	1820	47	MA
Smith, William	1821	18	PA
Smith, William Sidney	1822	18	PA
Smith, William	1822	15	PA
Smith, Willm.	1798	0	
Smith, Winthrop	1818	22	CT
Smith, Zekiel	1817	19	NJ
Smock, James	1815	18	NJ
Smother, Moses	1818	17 m	NJ
Smothers, Henry	1818	33 y	MD
Smull, William	1805	37	MD
Smullutt, Thomas	1807	21	NY
Smyth, Clarkson Z.	1815	20	PA
Smyth, Richard	1804	31	NY
Snack, Jacob	1804	0	PA
Snack, Jacob	1804	23	PA
Snaders, Eli	1811	17	MD

Snell, Charles	1810	19	PA
Snell, James	1812	55	Gr.Br.
Snell, Matthias M.	1805	45	
Snelling, John	1807	23	PA
Snelling, John	1815	28	PA
Snook, Joseph	1805	28	NY
Snow, Abial	1823	26	ME
Snow, Emery	1815	15	MA
Snow, Emery	1821	21	ME
Snow, Henry	1803	22	MA
Snow, James	1811	25	MA
Snow, John M.	1821	17	MA
Snow, Stephen	1803	23	MA
Snowden, Charles	1811	16	PA
Snowden, Charles	1814	20	PA
Snowden, John	1805	21	MA
Snowton, John	1805	29 b	PA
Snyder, Charles	1815	23	MD
Snyder, George K.	1815	23	PA
Snyder, George Frederick			
	1815	15	PA
Snyder, Henry	1823	25	PA
Snyder, Jacob	1798	25	PA
Snyder, Jacob	1819	29	PA
Snyder, John	1804	22	PA
Snyder, John	1804	22	PA
Snyder, John A.	1810	15	PA
Snyder, John	1813	13	PA
Snyder, John	1815	00	
Snyder, John	1815	20	PA
Snyder, Lewis	1803	18	MD
Snyder, Peter	1807	25	PA
Snyder, Thomas	1815	22	NJ
Snyder, William	1813	23	PA
Snyder, William	1818	19	PA
Snyder, William G.	1821	15	PA
Socket, Joseph	1815	25	NY
Soloman, David	1807	24 m	NJ
Solomon, Steven V.	1815	18	MD
Somberson, Edward	1810	21 c	PA
Somberson, Thomas	1810	24 b	NJ
Somers, Constant	1810	16	NJ
Somers, Cyrus	1822	30 b	DE
Somers, John	1807	17	NJ
Somers, John, Jr.	1807	15	NJ
Somers, Joseph	1810	21	NJ
Somers, Richard	1798	19	NJ
Somers, William	1809	16	NJ
Somes, Henry	1806	28	MA
Sommerlot, William	1810	23	PA
Sommers, Francis	1811	43	MD
Sommers, John	1821	24	PA

Sonder, Peter	1815	00		
Songrain, Oliver	1805	32		
Sonntag, William Lewis, Jr.				
	1810	22		PA
Soper, John	1817	23		NY
Souder, Daniel	1807	32		PA
Souder, Peter	1810	26		NJ
Souders, Peter	1809	18		NJ
Souders, Webster	1809	22		NJ
Soupp, Antony	1823	33	y	NJ
South, Richard	1809	24		NJ
Sowerby, Robert	1807	14		PA
Spalding, William M.	1803	36		MA
Spangler, James	1813	19		NJ
Spanison, John	1815	32	b	SC
Sparkes, William	1822	27	b	MD
Sparks, Bowman H.	1822	24		NJ
Sparks, Henry Darroch	1808	15		PA
Sparks, Henry	1811	13		PA
Sparks, Henry	1811	00		
Sparks, Henry D.	1812	00		
Sparks, Henry	1813	15		PA
Sparks, Isaac W.	1819	23		PA
Sparks, James	1809	28	b	MD
Sparks, John	1806	64		NY
Sparks, Mathew	1823	17		MD
Sparks, Randall	1821	14		NJ
Sparrow, Stephen	1815	22		MA
Spears, John P.	1804	23		RI
Spears, Joseph	1804	22		NJ
Specht, John	1809	24		PA
Specht, John	1810	0		
Speed, George	1804	22		PA
Speel, Henry	1821	19		PA
Speer, John	1809	17		PA

Spees, William Renynold

1795 18

indentured to Mathias Pinyard, Philadelphia
cooper for 2 years, 7 months, 6 days.

Spence, S. James	1807			
Spence, Thomas	1811	24	b	PA
Spencer, Archbold	1810	31	b	DE
Spencer, Edward	1805	22	b	PA
Spencer, George	1817	23	b	DE
Spencer, Henry	1818	28	b	NY
Spencer, Jacob	1811	16		PA
Spencer, Jessee	1807	18		DE
Spencer, S. James	1805	32		
Spicer, Walter	1813	24		PA
Spiegelberg, John	1809	22		PA

Spier, Abraham	1806	0	b	DE	
Spiers, Abraham	1803	28	b	DE	
Spillwerth, John	1807	27		PA	
Spinel, Charles	1807	28		LA	
Spinney, Josephus M.	1821	17		ME	
Spinney, Nathaniel	1820	24		NH	
Spires, Abraham	1809	41	b	DE	
Spires, Abraham	1809	42	b	DE	
Spires, John	1807	24		PA	
Spofford, Jacob	1804	28		MA	
Spofford, Jacob A.	1820	18		PA	
Spofford, Willien	1820	14		PA	
Spooner, William	1823	34		KY	
Spotswood, James C.	1820	20		MA	
Spraggs, Joseph	1814	27		DE	
Sprague, Richard	1811	49		RI	
Spratt, Sampson	1800	24		MA	
Spratt, Sampson	1804	0			
Spratt, Sampson	1807				
Springer, Charles	1817	23		PA	
Springer, Hudson	1810	20		NJ	
Springer, John	1811	21		NJ	
Springer, John M.	1822	18		PA	
Springer, Levy	1798	26		MD	
Springer, Peter	1811	16		DE	
Springer, Samuel R.	1810	21		NJ	
Springer, Thomas H.	1821	19		DE	
Springsteen, Garret	1804	20		NY	
Sprogell, Thomas Y.	1810	39		PA	
Sprong, Garrett	1818	29		NJ	
Spruce, William	1809	19	y	LA	
Spry, Ebenezar	1803	36	m	MD	
Spyers, Joseph	1807	26		MD	
Spywood, Ezekiel	1807	16	y	RI	
Squerl, Luke	1815	32	y	NJ	
Squire, Philip	1805	0			
Squire, T.C. Charles	1805	36		NY	
Squires, Charles	1809	0			
Squires, John	1817	22	y	MA	
Squires, Philip	1804	27		SC	
Squires, T.C. Charles	1808	0		NY	
Squires, Thomas C.Charles	1807				
Squirrel, Amariah	1817	21		NJ	
St.Clair, James	1799	35		PA	
St.John, John	1804	0			Ireland
St.John, John	1804	32			none given
Stacey, Samuel	1815	28		LA	
Stackly, John Galt	1820	22		PA	
Stafford, David	1818	19		PA	
Stafford, Israel	1807	19		NJ	
Stafford, James	1804	18		MD	
Stafford, James	1811	26		PA	

Stafford, John	1805	17	PA
Staley, George	1806	17 m	PA
Stalker, David	1803	24	SC
Stanbrough, Josiah	1811	32	NJ
Stancliff, William	1810	10	NJ
Standford, James	1805	29	MA
Standley, Joshua	1822	24	ME
Standley, Richard	1809	22	DE
Stanes, Robert	1816	36	MD
Stanfield, Robert	1804	20	PA
Stanfield, Robert	1807	23	PA
Stanford, Alexander	1804	26	DE
Stanford, Thomas	1810	21	DE
Stanford, Thomas	1816	32	PA
Stange, Frederick	1820	51	XX
Stanley, Thomas	1796	24	PA
Stansbury, Dixon	1820	30	MD
Stanton, Jonathan	1805	24	PA
Stanwood, Peleg	1819	26	MA
Stanwood, William	1819	40	MA
Stanze, John Christian	1809	25	PA
Stapalton, Thomas	1808	38	PA
Staples, John	1804	28	NY
Starboard, William G.	1810	20	MA
Starkey, John	1804	39	DE
Starkey, John	1804	39	DE
Starkey, John	1805	41	DE
Starkey, Thomas	1809	25	NJ
Starks, William	1818	29 b	NY
Starling, Adam	1805	23	NY
Starnes, Eben	1822	19	ME
Starr, John	1815	18	DE
Starr, Noah	1805	19	CT
Starr, Samuel F.	1801	0	
Starr, Samuel F.	1801	26	DE
Starr, Samuel F.	1809	0	
Starrett, James	1810	23 c	PA
Staven, Frederic	1816	26	LA
Stawell, George	1821	36	VA
Staylor, John	1810	22	PA
Stedman, Joseph C.	1809	14	PA
Stedwell, Richard	1817	47 b	PA
Steel, James	1815	34	NY
Steel, John	1808	20	NJ
Steel, Meritt	1803	25 b	DE
Steel, Peter	1809	22 b	PA
Steel, Peter	1812	00	
Steel, Peter	1813	0	
Steel, Peter	1814	0	
Steel, Peter	1823	23	DE
Steel, Robert	1798	20	PA
Steel, Thomas S.	1823	17	DE

Steele, Robert L.	1811	14	NY	
Steele, Robert L.	1813	0		
Steele, Samuel R.	1820	26	VT	
Steell, Henry N.	1820	18	NJ	
Steelman, John	1811	19	NJ	
Steelman, John	1812	00		
Steelman, Samuel	1810	22	NJ	
Steer, John	1807	24	MS	
Steer, John	1808	0	LA	
Steinbaugh, Nicholas	1805	24	PA	
Steinbaugh, Rudolph	1805	27	PA	
Steinhauer, Joseph	1813	20	PA	
Steinmetz, Andrew	1806	36	PA	
Steinmetz, Andrew	1817	00		
Steinmetz, John	1804	22	PA	
Stell, Henry S.	1816	23		none given
Stellwagen, Daniel	1799	24	PA	
Stensee, Thomas	1800	21 m	NJ	
Stephens, Abel	1822	25 b	VA	
Stephens, Henry	1810	37 b	PA	
Stephens, Henry	1811	23	MA	
Stephens, Jack	1813	21 b	VA	
Stephens, John	1803	29	PA	
Stephens, John	1810	32 y	LA	
Stephens, John	1811	21	NJ	
Stephens, Joseph	1805	23 b	VA	
Stephens, Littleton	1806	22 b	VA	
Stephens, Littleton	1809	0	VA	
Stephens, Loyd	1820	39 b	MD	
Stephens, Perry	1815	24 b	MD	
Stephens, Robert	1806	32	NJ	
Stephens, Samuel	1819	28	MA	
Stephenson, Abraham	1804	18 b	MD	
Stephenson, Alexander	1805	25	PA	
Stephenson, Christopher				
	1816	45	MA	
Stephenson, James	1808	27	PA	
Stephenson, John	1804	22	NJ	
Stephenson, John	1812	24	DE	
Stephenson, Paul	1817	19	MA	
Stephenson, Peter	1810	38 y	MD	
Stephenson, William	1815	18	PA	
Stephenson, Zekariah	1818	41 b	MD	
Stetar, William	1810	28	PA	
Stetson, William	1820	20	ME	
Stevens, Amos	1805	24	NY	
Stevens, Charles F.	1796	0	NH	
Stevens, Daniel M.	1818	18	NJ	
Stevens, Daniel	1819	15	MA	
Stevens, George	1810	25 b	MD	
Stevens, Hardy	1809	33	NC	
Stevens, Henry	1810	0		

Name	Year	Age		Place
Stevens, Henry	1811	00		
Stevens, Henry	1821	19		NJ
Stevens, Jacob	1815	23	b	MD
Stevens, Jacob	1818	29	y	NY
Stevens, John	1804	22		NY
Stevens, John	1805	19		NJ
Stevens, John	1807	49	b	PA
Stevens, John	1810	22	b	MA
Stevens, John	1810	25		MA
Stevens, John	1816	23		MA
Stevens, John	1820	35		NY
Stevens, John	1822	34	y	VA
Stevens, Joseph	1803	26		DE
Stevens, Loyd	1818	28		NJ
Stevens, Obadiah	1811	25		PA
Stevens, Samuel	1815	26	b	MD
Stevens, Samuel	1821	18		MD
Stevens, Stanton Jr.	1819	13		CT
Stevens, Thomas	1815	24		MA
Stevens, William	1810	16		MA
Stevens, William	1811	22	b	MD
Stevens, William	1811	29		CT
Stevenson, Abraham	1804	0		
Stevenson, Henry	1809	21	b	NJ
Stevenson, Hugh	1805	15		PA
Stevenson, Hugh	1806	0		
Stevenson, Hugh	1807			
Stevenson, James	1819	23	y	MD
Stevenson, John Lea	1806	22		PA
Stevenson, John	1807	21	b	MD
Stevenson, John	1807	13		PA
Stevenson, John	1809	29		NJ
Stevenson, John	1811	22	b	NY
Stevenson, John	1817	30	b	MD
Stevenson, Joseph	1811	23	b	MD
Stevenson, Levi	1809	18	b	MD
Stevenson, Levi	1810	0		
Stevenson, Lloyd	1803	18		MD
Stevenson, Peter	1819	20		PA
Stevenson, Ralph	1799	18		PA
Stevenson, Robert	1804	23		MD
Stevenson, Robert	1804	23		MD
Stevenson, Samuel H.	1807	28		NJ
Stevenson, William	1798	10		PA
Stevenson, William	1807	21		PA
Stevenson, William B.	1818	16		PA
Steward, Charles	1806	23	b	NJ
Steward, Eben	1823	20		PA
Steward, Eli	1803	19		NJ
Steward, Eli	1805	20		NJ
Steward, Eli	1815	00		NJ
Steward, Henry	1815	22	y	MD
Steward, James	1820	18		PA
Steward, John	1807	27	b	MD
Steward, William	1811	23		MA
Stewart, Alexander	1797	0		Ireland
Stewart, Alexander	1809	27		
Stewart, Charles	1816	23		PA
Stewart, Charles	1821	18		DE
Stewart, Edward B.	1821	22		MD
Stewart, James	1796	25		CT
Stewart, James	1804	29		MA
Stewart, James	1807	24		PA
Stewart, James	1810	21		DE
Stewart, James	1812	22		NJ
Stewart, John	1801	24		NY
Stewart, John	1809	17		PA
Stewart, John	1810	35		PA
Stewart, John	1811	00		
Stewart, John	1811	18		NY
Stewart, John	1811	29		none given
Stewart, John	1811	29		none given
Stewart, John	1815	00		
Stewart, John	1816	24		PA
Stewart, Joseph	1821	20		MD
Stewart, Matthias	1810	16		PA
Stewart, MD, Josiah	1812	21		PA
Stewart, Newport	1818	37		MA
Stewart, Peter	1823	31	y	MD
Stewart, Richard	1821	28		NJ
Stewart, Robert	1803	25		PA
Stewart, Samuel	1803	23	b	DE
Stewart, Scipio	1820	31	b	LA
Stewart, Stephen	1805	0		
Stewart, Stephen	1807	34	m	NJ
Stewart, Thomas	1804	26		NJ
Stewart, Thomas	1814	0		
Stewart, William	1805	23		PA
Stewart, William	1811	22	m	VA
Stewart, William	1816	27	b	NC
Stewart, William.Jr.	1809	14		NJ
Stewart, Wm	1820	25	b	MA
Stewer, Daniel, Jr.	1806	20		PA
Steynmetz, John	1807	22		NY
Stibbins, Stephen	1813	28		NJ
Stickling, Charles	1815	18		PA
Stickney, Albert A.	1810	26		MA
Stidham, David	1821	29		CT
Stile, Mark	1804	33	b	NJ
Stile, Thomas	1804	22		DE
Stiles, Joseph	1818	16		PA
Stiles, Joshua	1798	24		NJ
Stiles, Josiah	1798	27		NJ
Stiles, Levi	1809	28		NJ

Name	Year	Age	State
Stiles, Page	1814	23	NJ
Stiles, Richard, Jr.	1813	0	
Still, Charles	1807	28 b	NJ
Still, Mark	1806	39 b	NJ
Stillwell, John	1804	19	PA
Stillwell, Savage	1809	33	NJ
Stilwell, Jonathen	1797	0	PA
Stimble, Daniel Lyng	1810	18	PA
Stimel, Albert	1813	22	PA
Stine, Samuel	1813	23	PA
Stine, Samuel	1815	00	
Stinemets, Andrew	1817	00	
Stinemetz, Andrew	1809	0	PA
Stinemetz, Andrew	1810	0	
Stinemetz, Andrew	1810	0	
Stinson, John	1813	26	MD
Stirling, Francis	1819	37	NC
Stirling, James	1806	28	PA
Stirling, James	1807		
Stites, Francis W.	1815	20	PA
Stites, Humphrey Shaw			
	1815	25	NJ
Stites, John	1815	19	PA
Stites, Joseph	1809	14	NJ
Stites, Joseph	1811	00	
Stites, Richard, Jr.	1810	19	PA
Stites, Samuel	1815	15	PA
Stites, Samuel	1817	17	
Stites, Townsend	1809	24	NJ
Stoakes, William	1807	25	PA
Stockley, Frederick	1815	17	PA
Stockley, George	1809	23 b	VA
Stockley, Siras	1811	21 b	NY
Stockton, Douglass	1805	21	NJ
Stockton, John, Jr.	1809	21	DE
Stoddard, Bruce	1803	22	MA
Stoddard, Luther	1818	18	MA
Stodhart, Thomas	1801	23	RI
Stokely, Fera Scarborough			
	1806	25	DE
Stokely, Job	1805	28	DE
Stokely, John	1810	21 b	VA
Stokely, Martin	1820	22 b	VA
Stokely, William	1810	27	DE
Stokes, Alexander	1821	17	PA
Stokes, James	1809	21	PA
Stokes, James	1810	0	
Stokes, Jeremiah	1823	15	PA
Stokley, Cyrus	1815	00	
Stokley, James	1810	23 b	DE
Stoms, Jacob	1804	21	NJ
Stone, Benjamin	1806	22	NJ
Stone, Henry	1812	18	PA
Stone, John	1808	23	CT
Stone, John	1812	00	
Stone, Joseph	1814	19	MA
Stone, Robert	1798	23	NJ
Stone, Samuel	1813	22	PA
Stone, William	1812	19	NJ
Stoops, John	1822	30	DE
Stoots, George	1798	19	PA
Stophel, Anthony	1810	19	PA
Storm, John	1810	25	none given
Story, Henry	1821	14	PA
Story, John	1801	15	MD
Story, John	1819	19	PA
Story, Patrick	1820	13	PA
Story, William	1815	42	England
Stotz, Jacob	1814	23	PA
Stout, James	1813	23	NJ
Stout, Jeremiah	1809	18 b	DE
Stout, John	1816	17	PA
Stout, Leager	1815	28	NJ
Stout, Peter	1809	23 b	DE
Stout, Peter	1811	22 b	DE
Stout, Richard	1807	23	NY
Stout, Scudden	1811	21	NJ
Stout, Seymour, Jr.	1812	22	NY
Stowe, Jeremiah	1798	24	PA
Stowe, Jeromyah	1815	00	
Stran, James	1807	26	VA
Stran, James	1822	36	PA
Stran, William	1798	35	VA
Strane, James	1823	24	SC
Strang, Daniel	1823	19	NY
Strang, William	1805	20	NJ
Strange, Thomas	1805	22 b	SC
Strange, William	1809	23	NJ
Strattan, Isaac	1815	26 b	NJ
Stratton, Daniel	1804	24	MA
Stratton, Gilbert	1806	17	CT
Stratton, Jonathan	1818	14	PA
Stratton, Samuel	1819	27	NJ
Strawbridge, James	1809	22	PA
Strawbridge, Thomas	1805	21	NY
Streder, Charles	1808	24	VA
Street, Asa	1810	23 y	DE
Street, William	1815	21	MD
Street, William	1822	17	PA
Stricklen, John	1804	39	NY
Strong, Charles	1809	30	NJ
Strong, Peter G.	1813	13	PA
Stroud, John	1822	32	PA
Strouse, Martin	1813	22	PA

131

Stuart, Andrew	1807	19	MD
Stuart, Charles	1803	23	NY
Stuart, Charles	1806	0	
Stuart, Henry	1807	27	NY
Stuart, James	1804	21 b	MD
Stuart, James, Jr.	1823	15	PA
Stuart, John	1814	24	PA
Stuart, Robert	1796	0	
Stuart, Robert	1804	39 b	NY
Stuart, William	1803	24	PA
Stuart, William	1810	38	VA
Stuart, William	1810	34	PA
Stuart, William	1811	00	
Sturdingbaugh, Benjamin			
	1814	20	PA
Sturges, John	1811	19	VA
Sturges, John	1811	22	PA
Sturges, Joseph	1807	26	CT
Sturges, William	1798	0	
Sturges, William	1801	22	MD
Sturgis, George	1823	18	PA
Sturgis, Nathaniel	1805	16	MD
Sturing, John	1805	22	NY
Subers, James	1817	23	PA
Suez, Francis Emanuel			
	1810	28	LA
Sulevan, John	1808	25	
Sullenden, John	1814	0	
Sullender, Charles	1809	23	PA
Sullender, John	1809	21	PA
Sullender, Thomas	1804	24	PA
Sullivan, Daniel	1811	26	PA
Sullivan, John	1819	27	MA
Sullivan, Murthy	1817	33	NY
Sullivan, Nehemiah	1821	47	DE
Sullivan, William	1798	24	NY
Summer, William	1814	0	
Summerfield, Cornelius	1821	26	PA
Summerl, William	1809	16	DE
Summers, Andrew	1815	17	PA
Summers, Francis	1804	20	NY
Summers, George	1804	14 b	DE
Summers, George	1814	18	PA
Summers, George Washington			
	1815	15	PA
Summers, Hugh	1804	23	NY
Summers, James	1807	23	PA
Summers, James	1810	22	NY
Summers, James W.	1820	15	PA
Summers, James Wickham			
	1821	16	PA
Summers, John	1804	18	NJ
Summers, John	1816	25	NY
Summers, Joseph Higby			
	1815	14	PA
Summers, Samuel Myers			
	1809	20	PA
Summers, William	1815	21 b	VA
Sunnoks, John	1804	22	PA
Surgent, Henry	1804	23	PA
Sutherland, John	1813	27	NJ
Sutter, Peter	1809	31	PA
Sutter, Peter	1814	0	
Sutter, Peter	1815	00	
Sutton, George Harvey	1809	22	NY
Sutton, John	1809	27 b	MD
Sutton, Jonathan	1817	22	NJ
Sutton, Thomas	1801	24	DE
Sutton, Thomas	1806	26	NY
Sutton, William	1810	20	NJ
Swaih, Michael	1805	21	PA
Swain, Benjamin	1808	18	PA
Swain, Benjamin	1812	20	PA
Swain, Henry	1810	22	MA
Swain, Henry	1815	21	NY
Swain, James	1818	24	MD
Swain, Jonathan W.	1822	16	PA
Swain, Joshua, Jr.	1823	19	NJ
Swain, Michael	1819	32	PA
Swain, Samuel	1815	30 b	PA
Swain, Thomas C.	1815	17	PA
Swain, William B.	1816	21	NJ
Swain, William	1821	19	NJ
Swaine, Michael	1813	0	
Swan, John	1800	19	NY
Swan, John	1822	22 b	NY
Swan, Robert	1808	24 b	MA
Swan, Samuel	1809	0	
Swan, William	1804	0 b	
Swan, William	1816	28 s	PA
Swan, William	1816	22 b	PA
Swann, Samuel	1808	24 y	PA
Swanton, John	1810	22	PA
Swanton, John	1811	00	
Swasey, Seth	1809	26	MA
Sweeny, Doyle E.	1815	23	PA
Sweeny, William	1804	21	MD
Sweetland, Nathaniel	1799	21	PA
Sweetser, John	1821	22	ME
Swenson, John	1810	32	MA
Swift, Benjamin	1815	16	MA
Swift, Francis	1823	24	PA
Swift, Jarvis	1820	33	MA
Swift, Silas	1815	19	MA

Name	Year	Age	Place
Swift, Thomas	1806	21	NJ
Swift, William	1815	31	NJ
Swiney, Michael	1810	21	PA
Swinfin, Tyler	1810	21	PA
Sword, William	1798	34	SC
Sybert, William	1811	21	PA
Sykes, John	1811	24	NY
Sykes, Solomon	1801	19	VA
Sykes, Thomas	1816	0	
Sykes, Thomas	1816	23 y	PA
Sylvaine, Daniel	1798	26	PA
Sylvester, John, Jr.	1821	22	MA
Symonds, Jonathan	1810	21	MA
Syng, John	1813	20	NJ
Syrus, Peter	1811	24 b	NJ
Tabaux, Haven	1817	23	MD
Taber, Daniel	1818	34	MA
Taff, Anthony	1815	27	SC
Taff, Henry	1809	22	PA
Tage, Benjamin	1815	18	PA
Tage, Benjamin	1816	0	
Taggart, Francis	1812	16	PA
Taggart, James	1805	14	PA
Taggart, Robert L.	1815	00	
Taggart, Robert L.	1815	14	MD
Taggart, Robert L.	1817	00	
Tague, John Burveal	1815	17	DE
Taigers, Anthony	1813	21	LA
Tallentine, John	1796	0	
Talley, Cyrus	1805	24	DE
Tallman, Francis	1805	24	MA
Tallman, James	1822	21	NJ
Tallman, John D.	1822	16	PA
Tally, George	1806	27 b	MD
Talman, James M.	1800	24	NJ
Talman, James M.	1806	30	NJ
Tammen, John	1818	22 b	NY
Tamplen, John	1807	16	NY
Tange, Francis	1810	24	none given
Tanner, Jacob	1805	30	NJ
Tantum, Newbury	1804	23	NJ
Tarris, Emanuel J.	1817	15	PA
Tate, William	1809	25 b	MD
Tatem, George P.	1811	26	NJ
Tatem, Jackson	1821	19	PA
Tatem, John	1817	21	NJ
Tatem, Robert S.	1811	19	PA
Tatham, Benjamin	1798	38	England
Tauffe, James	1815	23	NY
taylor, William	1801	22	NJ
Taylor, Adam	1807	22	MA
Taylor, Alexander	1812	47	PA
Taylor, Alexander	1817	41	Scotland
Taylor, Benjamin	1801	16	DE
Taylor, Charles	1815	18	PA
Taylor, Daniel	1815	19	MA
Taylor, Edward	1809	39	MA
Taylor, Elias	1815	18	NJ
Taylor, Elias	1818	25	NJ
Taylor, Elisha	1805	27	NJ
Taylor, Ezra R.	1806	18	PA
Taylor, Gardiner R.	1820	21	PA
Taylor, George	1810	21	NY
Taylor, George	1811	26	DE
Taylor, George	1816	24 b	MD
Taylor, George	1817	25	NY
Taylor, George	1820	17	PA
Taylor, George	1823	24	PA
Taylor, Gideon	1823	24	NJ
Taylor, Henry	1800	17	VA
Taylor, Henry	1807	23	CT
Taylor, Henry	1810	29	MD
Taylor, Isaac	1815	26	PA
Taylor, Israel	1818	23	NY
Taylor, Jacob	1807	26 b	MD
Taylor, Jacob R.	1810	17	PA
Taylor, Jacob	1814	22	
Taylor, James	1809	28	NY
Taylor, James	1809	21 b	PA
Taylor, James	1811	20	DE
Taylor, James	1816	23 b	PA
Taylor, James	1822	17	PA
Taylor, John	1798	31	MD
Taylor, John	1799	31	PA
Taylor, John	1805	21	PA
Taylor, John	1805	22	PA
Taylor, John	1806	25 l	NJ
Taylor, John	1810	19	NC
Taylor, John	1810	19	NJ
Taylor, John	1813	0	
Taylor, John	1815	14	NJ
Taylor, Joseph R.	1804	17	PA
Taylor, Joseph	1814	23	NJ
Taylor, Joseph	1818	21	DE
Taylor, Joseph	1822	27	PA
Taylor, Peter	1798	30	Guinea
Taylor, Peter	1805	26	PA
Taylor, Peter	1817	19	PA
Taylor, Philip	1815	22	NY
Taylor, Richard	1822	28	PA
Taylor, Robert	1814	17	MD
Taylor, Robert R.	1819	17	PA
Taylor, Sampson	1818	19 b	PA
Taylor, Selbay	1804	22	MD

Taylor, Shadrack	1807	24		VA	Thomas, Aaron	1809	25 b		MA
Taylor, Thomas	1801	21		DE	Thomas, Adam	1818	35 b		NY
Taylor, Thomas	1808	22		PA	Thomas, Andrew	1810	20 b		DE
Taylor, Thomas	1809	19		PA	Thomas, Benjamin, Jr.	1811	21		PA
Taylor, Thomas	1809	21		DE	Thomas, Caleb Davis	1807			
Taylor, Thomas	1810	24		NY	Thomas, Caleb Davis	1807	29		MA
Taylor, Thomas	1812	45		none given	Thomas, Charles	1810	25		LA
Taylor, William	1798	32		PA	Thomas, Charles	1811	30 b		LA
Taylor, William	1798	32		PA	Thomas, Charles	1815	18		PA
Taylor, William	1815	20		PA	Thomas, Colbert	1815	18 b		MD
Taylor, William	1817	23		PA	Thomas, David Bevan	1806	19		DE
Taylor, William	1820	14		PA	Thomas, David Bevan	1807			
Taylor, William	1821	23		MD	Thomas, David	1810	19		PA
Taylor, William	1822	23		NJ	Thomas, Edmund	1815	17		MD
Taylor, Zadock	1807	40		MD	Thomas, Edward	1810	27		So.Wales
Taylor, Zadock	1809	0			Thomas, George	1807	17 y		PA
Teal, Harvey	1809	22		NJ	Thomas, George	1809	20 y		PA
Teammer, Andrew	1817	25		NY	Thomas, George	1809	26 b		MD
Tear, John	1798	13		PA	Thomas, George	1816	29 b		MD
Tear, John	1810	25		PA	Thomas, George	1823	21 b		PA
Tear, William	1805	15		PA	Thomas, Gidyen	1805	30 b		MD
Teel, David	1803	25		NJ	Thomas, Hartshorn R.	1817	25		NJ
Teel, David	1804	26		NJ	Thomas, Henry	1812	35 n		MD
Teel, Jesse	1810	37		NJ	Thomas, Henry	1816	0		
Teel, John	1818	15		DE	Thomas, Henry	1816	27 b		MD
Teer, William D.	1821	18		NY	Thomas, Horace	1811	22 y		MD
Teese, Frederick	1807	19		PA	Thomas, Isaac	1804	25		PA
Teide, John	1803	29		NY	Thomas, Isaac	1805	28 b		PA
Tell, John Thornthwaite	1804	0		NY	Thomas, James	1801	23		NY
Temple, Clement	1809	17		PA	Thomas, James	1805	46		PA
Temple, Clement	1810	0			Thomas, James	1816	28		VA
Temple, Clement	1810	0			Thomas, James	1816	36		PA
Temple, Clement	1811	00			Thomas, James Sherson				
Tenbrink, John	1818	14		PA		1817	14		NJ
Tenbrink, John	1823	18		PA	Thomas, James	1822	22 y		NY
Tenike, James	1810	26		NY	Thomas, John	1803	23		PA
Tenike, James	1815	33		NY	Thomas, John	1804	25 b		MD
Tennant, Christopher	1809	20		PA	Thomas, John	1805	25 b		PA
Tennant, Samuel	1809	24 m		PA	Thomas, John	1805	21		PA
Tennery, John M.	1798	28		NJ	Thomas, John	1807	21 b		NY
Tennery, John B.	1819	21		DE	Thomas, John	1807	22		CT
Terason, Stephen	1804	26		none given	Thomas, John	1807	29 b		PA
Terhoeven, John	1807	26		PA	Thomas, John	1808	20		DE
Terpine, Thomas	1815	21		NJ	Thomas, John	1809	22 b		LA
Terry, David	1823	33		NJ	Thomas, John	1809	0		
Tesshey, John	1809	33		MD	Thomas, John	1810	28 y		MD
Thayer, Barzilla	1805	21		MA	Thomas, John	1810	20 b		NY
Thayer, Laban	1810	27		MA	Thomas, John	1810	0		
Theadore, Peter	1807	22 y		DE	Thomas, John	1810	23 b		MA
Theodore, Lewis	1820	22		TN	Thomas, John	1813	20		PA
Thiell, Henry,Jr.	1822	12		PA	Thomas, John	1815	16		PA
Thom, George	1803	27		RI	Thomas, John	1815	16		RI

Thomas, John	1815	00	
Thomas, John	1815	25	PA
Thomas, John	1815	28	VA
Thomas, John	1815	27	NH
Thomas, John	1817	23 b	DE
Thomas, John	1818	18 b	MD
Thomas, John	1820	21 b	PA
Thomas, John	1820	17	PA
Thomas, John	1823	17	PA
Thomas, Jonas	1812	22	NJ
Thomas, Joseph	1807	21	MS
Thomas, Joseph	1816	32	PA
Thomas, Joseph S.	1822	13	PA
Thomas, Joshua	1815	18	PA
Thomas, Louis	1798	18	NC
Thomas, Philip	1811	36	MS
Thomas, Richard	1822	18	PA
Thomas, Samuel	1815	27 m	GA
Thomas, Spencer	1811	26 n	MD
Thomas, Stephen	1821	35	DE
Thomas, Stephen	1822	23 b	MA
Thomas, Thomas Whittemore			
	1798	23	MA
Thomas, Thomas	1812	33 b	NY
Thomas, Timothy	1812	19	NJ
Thomas, Timothy	1813	0	
Thomas, Timothy	1814	0	
Thomas, Timothy	1817		
Thomas, William	1804	35	PA
Thomas, William	1805	20	SC
Thomas, William	1808	23	DE
Thomas, William	1809	28 y	LA
Thomas, William	1810	27	NY
Thomas, William	1811	23 b	DE
Thomas, William	1811	23	NY
Thomas, William	1811	30 b	at sea

a free Negro, born at sea "within the U. S."

Thomas, William	1812	14	PA
Thomas, William	1816	19	NC
Thompkins, Benedick	1815	13 b	PA
Thompson, Alexander	1813	22 b	MD
Thompson, Andrew	1822	28	RI
Thompson, Barnet	1815	25	NJ
Thompson, Benjamin	1822	30	NY
Thompson, Charles	1806	29	PA
Thompson, Charles	1806	21 b	MD
Thompson, Charles	1818	36 y	VA
Thompson, Christopher	1805	24	PA
Thompson, Christopher	1807	23 b	MD

Thompson, Daniel	1815	19 b	NY	
Thompson, David	1804	25	NY	
Thompson, David	1809	24	PA	
Thompson, David	1818	22 b	NY	
Thompson, Francis	1819	18	PA	
Thompson, George	1807	25	VA	
Thompson, George	1818	17	PA	
Thompson, George Harison				
	1821	16	PA	
Thompson, Henry Levingston				
	1804	18	PA	
Thompson, Henry	1817	21	VA	
Thompson, Henry	182	20	NY	
Thompson, Henry	182	20	NY	
Thompson, James	1798	22	CT	
Thompson, James	1804	21	DE	
Thompson, James	1807	19	NJ	
Thompson, James	1810	23	PA	
Thompson, James	1810	17	PA	
Thompson, James	1815	22	NY	
Thompson, James	1818	25	NJ	
Thompson, John	1799	12	DE	
Thompson, John	1803	19	NY	
Thompson, John	1805	28	PA	
Thompson, John	1805	21	NJ	
Thompson, John	1807	20	MA	
Thompson, John	1807	19	PA	
Thompson, John	1807	24	MA	
Thompson, John	1807			
Thompson, John	1807	26	PA	
Thompson, John	1809	21 b	DE	
Thompson, John	1809	31	PA	
Thompson, John	1810	24 b		Africa
Thompson, John	1811	26	MD	
Thompson, John	1811	35	DE	
Thompson, John	1811	00		
Thompson, John	1811	21	RI	
Thompson, John Lockton				
	1811	14	DE	
Thompson, John	1811	21	PA	
Thompson, John	1814	0 b		
Thompson, John Lockton				
	1815	18	DE	
Thompson, John	1815	00	NJ	
Thompson, John	1815	21	MA	
Thompson, John	1817	19	PA	
Thompson, John	1817	23	NY	
Thompson, John	1817	25	SC	
Thompson, John	1817	20	SC	
Thompson, John	1819	18	PA	
Thompson, John	1819	23 b	MD	
Thompson, John	1820	36	DE	

Thompson, John	1821	25		NY
Thompson, John	1823	22		PA
Thompson, John	1823	33		RI
Thompson, Joseph	1821	30	y	PA
Thompson, Lewis	1805	23	b	PA
Thompson, Matthew	1812	20	b	NJ
Thompson, Nathan	1805	24		NJ
Thompson, Nathan	1807			
Thompson, Nelson	1811	25	b	PA
Thompson, Nicholas	1803	23		PA
Thompson, Peter	1808	22		PA
Thompson, Peter	1809	28		GA
Thompson, Preston	1821	23		MA
Thompson, Robert	1803	25		MD
Thompson, Robert	1809	21		MS
Thompson, Samuel	1805	20		NY
Thompson, Samuel	1807	24	b	NY
Thompson, Samuel	1809	0		NY
Thompson, Thomas	1804	20		PA
Thompson, Thomas	1807	18		NJ
Thompson, Thomas	1807	26		NC
Thompson, Thomas	1811	00		
Thompson, Thomas	1821	22		ME
Thompson, Walton	1808	30		MD
Thompson, William	1798	25		DE
Thompson, William	1807	21		MD
Thompson, William	1809	23	b	NY
Thompson, William	1809	47		NJ
Thompson, William	1810	22		NJ
Thompson, William	1810	23		NC
Thompson, William	1810	22		PA
Thompson, William	1811	00		
Thompson, William	1815	19		none given
Thompson, William	1816	24		
Thompson, William	1818	29		none given
Thompson, William	1819	26	b	CT
Thompson, William	1821	21		MD
Thomson, Alexander	1796	0		MA
Thomson, Benjamin	1798	0		
Thomson, Edmund R.	1815	20		PA
Thomson, Edward	1809	19	b	MD
Thomson, Enoch	1804	36		PA
Thomson, George	1817	25	b	MA
Thomson, George, Jr.	1821	15		PA
Thomson, Isaac	1806	23		PA
Thomson, Jesse	1807	37	b	NJ
Thomson, John	1803	28		NY
Thomson, John	1809	18		NY
Thomson, John	1809	29	b	MA
Thomson, John	1809	18		NY
Thomson, John	1810	21		NJ
Thomson, Joseph	1798	13		DE

Thomson, Lyde	1801	32		PA	
Thomson, Nathan	1805	17		NJ	
Thomson, Richmond	1805	27	b	MD	
Thomson, Thomas	1801	23	y	SC	
Thomson, Thomas	1806	25	b	NY	
Thomson, William	1801	25		CT	
Thomson, William	1810	18		SC	
Thomson, Wm.	1803	19	m	RI	
Thones, Simon	1808	31			
Thorn, John	1817	30		NJ	
Thorn, Joseph	1807	11		PA	
Thorne, Richard Jr.	1815	16		PA	
Thorne, Wm.	1804	24		NY	
Thornton, Edward	1817	23		MD	
Thornton, Henry	1809	24		DE	
Thornton, John	1800	27		PA	
Thornton, John	1807	21		VA	
Thornton, Robert	1817	36	b	NY	
Thornton, Thomas	1805	19	b	NY	
Thornton, Thomas	1817	26		DC	
Thornton, William	1819	25		VA	
Thorp, Walter, Jr.	1806	18		CT	
Thorp, William	1820	32		NY	
Thrasher, Josiah	1810	42		MA	
Threlfall, Robert	1823	29		MD	
Thrift, Jesse	1819	25		MA	
Thrift, Stephen	1815	16		VA	
Thum, Charles Donaldson					
	1823	15		PA	
Thum, Jacob	1806	30		PA	
Thurston, John	1823	24		NY	
Thurston, Samuel F.	1809	22		RI	
Thusten, Daniel	1818	21		MA	
Tice, James H.	1822	26		PA	
Tice, John	1810	37		NY	
Tichenor, Richard	1811	22		NJ	
Tiebout, William	1816	44		LA	
Tiedman, Nicholas	1818	34			none given
Tiel, Johan	1807	16		PA	
Tiffin, Robert	1805	12		NY	
Tiffin, Robert	1809	16			
Tilden, John B.	1821	23		MD	
Tildon, William	1815	21		MD	
Tilghman, Henry	1822	20	b	DE	
Tilghman, Jacob	1805	21	b	DE	
Tilghman, Jacob	1819	23	b	DE	
Tilghman, Thomas	1821	46	y	MD	
Tilghman, William	1810	15		PA	
Till, Andrew, Jr.	1821	21	s	DE	
Till, John	1815	22		PA	
Till, Samuel	1805	23	b	DE	
Till, Samuel	1809	0		DE	

Till, Samuel	1815	26 s	DE
Till, William	1809	30	PA
Tillman, Thomas	1816	32 b	NJ
Tillon, Peter	1809	14	MS
Tilly, George	1816	23	NY
Tilly, Richard	1809	23	PA
Tilly, Richard	1810	0	

SPC taken by Capt. Rob. Barry, British frigate *Pomone* in Straits of Gibralter

Tilly, Richard	1811	0	
Tilman, John	1812	26 b	DE

served his time with Robert Hamilton, Esq. of Wilmington, DE, and is a free black man

Tilson, John	1806	18	PA
Tilton, Edward Gibson	1821	16	DE
Tilton, Nehemiah	1809	16	DE
Timbrell, William	1805	21	MA
Timmons, Annanias	1801	22	MD
Tindall, Francis	1810	22	MD
Tindoll, Francis S.	1815	00	
Tine, John	1817	14	PA
Tine, Joseph	1810	36	PA
Tingle, John	1810	22	MD
Tipney, Thomas	1810	23	PA
Tisdale, Edward D.	1815	26	MA
Tittermary, David	1815	17	PA
Tittermary, John R.	1804	24	PA
Tittermary, William W.	1819	22	PA
Titus, Peter	1804	27 b	NY
Titus, Robert	1815	23	NJ
Toalson, Jerry	1821	39 s	VA
Tobias, John	1822	27 y	CT
Todd, Charles	1804	23 b	PA

African descent; goes to sea with consent of his master Francis Ingraham

Todd, David W.	1818	19	NY
Todd, William Patterson			
	1807	26 m	MA
Toel, Joseph	1809	21	PA
Toland, Henry Ward	1809	18	
Tolman, John	1809	20	NY
Tomat, Peter	1816	23	LA
Tombs, David	1805	22	PA
Tomkins, Jesse	1818	29 b	NJ
Tomkins, Joseph	1821	39	NC
Tomkinson, George	1815	38	RI

Tomlin, Hudson	1807	20	NJ
Tomlin, Issac	1822	24	NJ
Tomlin, Stokes	1809	21	NJ
Tomlin, William	1809	21	NJ
Tomlinson, Elijah	1805	22	PA
Tomlinson, John Jr.	1815	18	PA
Tomlinson, John	1818	21	PA
Tomlinson, Joseph	1807	20	PA
Tomlinson, Joseph	1811	28	NJ
Tompkins, Stockton	1815	32 b	NJ
Tomsen, Henri	1804	19	DE
Tonken, Robert	1804	0	
Tonken, Robert	1804	42	MA
Tonnell, Isaac	1815	20 b	DE
Toothaker, John	1811	22	MA
Torbert, John, Jr.	1823	15	DE
Torrance, John	1819	31	MD
Torton, Benj.	1821	24	PA
Tory, Maximo	1818	21	PA
Totten, Mark	1822	39	NY
Town, John	1821	21	PA
Town, Joseph	1811	22	PA
Town, Nicholas	1811	21	NJ
Townsen, Thomas	1821	25 c	NY
Townsend, Ebzey	1811	24 b	DE
Townsend, Edward	1807	18 b	PA
Townsend, Job	1815	24	NJ
Townsend, John	1823	20	MD
Townsend, William B.	1804	22	MD
Townsend, William, Jr.	1806	21	DE
Townsend, William	1807	18	PA
Townsend, William	1810	23	PA
Toy, Andrew	1809	39	PA
Toy, John	1805	22	PA
Toy, John	1809	23	PA
Toy, Thomas	1820	18	PA
Toy, William	1799	21	NJ
Tozer, Samuel	1805	23	MA
Trafton, Stephen	1820	18	ME
Train, Jacob	1807	24	DE
Traner, Samuel	1822	22	PA
Trask, John	1812	41	MA
Travaso, Antone	1808	24	MS
Travers, Frederick	1814	50	MD
Travers, Henry	1817	22	DE
Travers, Jeremiah	1810	32	MD
Travers, Matthew	1810	20	MD
Travis, George	1810	20	MD
Travis, John J.	1809	22	PA
Travis, William	1807	26	MD
Treadaway, Henry	1815	23	NJ
Treat, Richard H.	1815	21	NJ

Tree, John Evans	1820	19	PA
Tree, Samuel Williamson			
	1823	21	PA
Tremans, Ashbel	1815	19	NY
Tremble, Matthew	1804	16	MA
Tremells, James McCarty			
	1820	16	PA
Tremells, John, Jr.	1810	18	PA
Tremells, Robert	1803	16	PA
Trenchard, Thomas	1820	23	NJ
Trevett, Benjamin	1810	21	MA
Tribbles, George	1814	22	CT
Tribe, Jesse	1806	20	NY
Trigge, John	1816	21	LA
Trimble, Job	1820	28	MD
Trimble, Matthew	1805	0	
Tripanny, Francis	1814	24	MD
Tripe, Seth Martin	1817	19	NH
Tripp, Adam	1813	16	PA
Tripp, Godfreay	1807	40	MA
Trippe, Adam, Jr.	1810	14	PA
Troll, John	1815	23	PA
Trott, Frederick W.	1813	24	PA
Trott, Lemuel	1820	25	MA
Trotter, Charles	1805	21	PA
Trotter, Richard	1807	26	VT
Trout, James	1817	20	NJ
Trout, John T.	1816	21	PA
Trout, John S.	1823	21	NJ
Trout, Nathaniel	1815	54	MA
Trout, Samuel B.	1817	20	NJ
Trout, William	1810	22	MA
Trow, John	1812	44	MA
Troy, Charles	1804	47	PA
True, Joseph	1823	29	ME
Trufry, Joel	1815	24	MA
Truit, Miers Fisher	1803	14	DE
Truit, Richard	1806	25 b	DE
Truitt, Elijah	1815	20	DE
Trusty, Jacob	1809	19 b	PA
Trusty, James	1809	29 b	MD
Trusty, John	1816	21 m	PA
Trusty, Joseph	1815	28 c	DE
Trusty, Perry	1809	23 b	PA
Truxton, John	1823	19	DE
Tucker, George C.	1821	28	MA
Tucker, Henry	1798	30	NY
Tucker, James	1807	34	NJ
Tucker, James	1811	00	
Tucker, John	1801	23	NY
Tucker, John	1811	28 y	VA
Tucker, John	1820	42 b	VA
Tucker, Reuben	1807	28 y	VA
Tucker, William	1806	22	MA
Tucker, William	1810	0	
Tuder, John Jr.	1806	22	PA
Tudis, Francis	1798	30	NJ
Tufts, Amos	1815	22	MA
Tulane, Lewis Stephen	1815	20	NJ
Tuley, Thomas	1807	21	VA
Tull, John	1817	45	PA
Tull, Joshu	1819	35	MD
Tull, Richard	1804	23	PA
Tull, Samuel	1809	15	PA
Tullock, Robert	1804	23	NY
Tullock, Robert	1810	0	
Tully, George Rees	1812	14	PA
Tully, John	1815	14	PA
Tumbline, Thomas	1813	0 b	
Tumbling, Thomas	1812	17 b	DE
Tune, John	1801	18	PA
Tunis, Banjamin H.	1813	19	PA
Tunis, William	1804	21	PA
Tunis, William	1804	21	PA
Tunison, Matthias Ten Eyck			
	1815	22	NJ
Tunnell, Henry	1810	35	VA
Turk, John	1805	26	MD
Turley, Enoch	1823	14	PA
Turlington, William	1820	21	VA
Turnbull, Charles Nesbet			
	1819	15	PA
Turner, Arch.	1821	27	SC
Turner, Daniel	1798	26	NJ
Turner, David	1823	27	MA
Turner, Edmund	1809	21	VA
Turner, George	1816	19	PA
Turner, Henry	1803	32	PA
Turner, Hugh	1812	21	NJ
Turner, Job	1821	26 b	NJ
Turner, John	1805	22	DE
Turner, John	1806	22	DE
Turner, John	1811	25 b	VA
Turner, John	1811	28 c	NY
Turner, John	1811	00 c	
Turner, John	1817	19	PA
Turner, Joseph	1804	25 m	MD
Turner, Joseph Mason	1806	20	PA
Turner, Joseph, Jr.	1817	11	PA
Turner, Joseph, Jr.	1823	20	PA
Turner, Levi	1815	23 b	DE
Turner, Levi	1823	22 b	DE
Turner, Levi	1823	23 b	DE
Turner, Mirazah	1801	25	MD

Turner, Philip	1804	22	GA
Turner, Prince	1818	21 b	NY
Turner, Robert	1798	22	PA
Turner, Robert	1811	26	PA
Turner, Robert	1814	23 y	NJ
Turner, Samuel	1811	16	NJ
Turner, Samuel	1817	28 b	DE
Turner, Shirley C.	1823	17	VA
Turner, Stephen	1810	17	MA
Turner, Thomas	1818	36	NH
Turner, Valentine	1823	19	VA
Turner, William	1815	21	NY
Turner, William	1817	24	VA
Turney, Daniel	1815	31	PA
Turney, George	1819	36	PA
Turve, John C.	1819	21	NY
Tusler, William	1805	31	PA
Tusleson, Nilsen	1809	25	PA
Tuston, Thomas	1817	18	NJ
Tutton, Jenkins P.	1810	25	PA
Tutton, John W.	1809	38 b	NJ
Tweed, Caldwell	1811	21	PA
Twiford, William Augustus D.S.S.			
	1822	20	VA
Twines, Isaac	1805	18	NJ
Tyler, William	1809	21	MD
Tyler, William	1810	18	NJ
Uhler, George	1804	18	PA
Ulary, Edward	1823	16	PA
Ulary, William Hudson	1820	17	PA
Ulick, Henry	1811	41	NY
Ulings, Nathniel	1813	34	NJ
Ulmer, William	1819	31	not given
Ulrich, Caspar	1812	00	
Ulrich, Casper	1810	17	PA
Underwood, Benjamin	1811	22	PA
Underwood, John	1815	00	
Urlich, Peter	1805	15	PA
Ustick, Daniel Gano	1814	18	PA
Utley, Elisha	1798	23	PA
Vackaler, Fredrick	1809	23	
Vahette, E.A. F.	1808	0	
Vale, William	1800	18	PA
Valentine, James	1796	52 b	VA
Valentine, Simon	1809	26 b	MA
Vallance, William	1805	37	PA
Valleau, William F.	1810	33	NY
Vallette, Eli A. F.	1807	00	
Vallette, Eli Aug. F.	1811	00	
Vallette, Elie Augustus Frederick			
	1805	15	VA
Vallette,William Russell	1813	23	VA

Vallette, William Russell	1814	0	
Van Dusen, Matthew	1815	27	PA
Van, Isaiah	1807	17 m	DE
Van, Isaiah	1810	19 b	DE
Van Ness, Isaac	1812	23 y	NY
Van Padden, John	1812	26	MA
Van Pelt, Peter	1804	27	NY
Van Syckle, Ralph	1815	23	NJ
VanAllen, John I.	1798	20	NY
Vanaro, John Frederick	1804	27	MA
Vance, Arthur	1820	21	PA
Vance, Bartholomew	1817	22	PA
Vance, David	1805	21	PA
Vance, William	1810	19	NC
VanCleve, George W.	1822	28	PA
Vandegrift, Abraham	1800	0	PA
Vanderbelt, Cornelius	1815	18	PA
Vanderbelt, Cornelius	1817		PA
This is not THE Cornelius Vanderbilt.			
Vanderhachin, Francis	1817	24	MD
Vanderslice, Andrew	1807	24	PA
Vanderslice, Charles	1815	14	PA
Vanderslice, Henry	1796	0	PA
Vanderslice, Thomas W.			
	1817	15	PA
Vandersloot, Charles Augustus			
	1823	14	PA
Vandine, George	1821	35	PA
Vandine, Peter	1821	20 y	NJ
Vandiver, Matthew	1810	16	DE
Vandrell, Isaac	1804	28 b	PA
Vaness, Isaac	1812	00	PA
Vanhorn, David	1811	19	PA
Vanhorn, John	1810	16	DE
VanMetere, Israel	1822	37 y	NJ
Vannatta, John D.	1811	28	NY
Vanneman, John, Jr.	1811	17	PA
VanPelt, Alexander	1815	18	NJ
Vansant, Isaac	1809	19	DE
Vanscivor, Imlay	1807	21	NJ
Vanstollen, Christian	1810	21	NY
Vantine, Allen	1819	19	NJ
Vanuxem, Lewis C.	1810	21	PA
Vanvicle, Marc	1820	26 y	NJ
Vanvoorhis, Robert	1804	0	
Vanwinkle, Presley A.	1805	24	DE
Vanwyck, Thomas	1809	32	NY
Vanzandt, Garrett H.	1822	22	PA
Varick, James	1823	20	NY
Varnar, John	1815	30	PA

Varney, John	1822	21	PA
Varnum, George	1804	18	NY
Vask, Felix	1806	29	LA
Vasse, Charles	1821	27	PA
Vauguelin, Francis	1798	24	France
Veacock, James	1818	14	PA
Vearney, Joseph	1806	22	LA
Vedt, Thomas	1806	22	PA
Veitch, George	1810	38	MA
Venables, Jacob	1823	44 m	PA
Venice, Joseph	1815	28	NY
Venson, James	1796	35	MD
Verger, Peter	1804	0	France
Veron, Lewis	1812	19	MA
Verwer, John	1809	26	PA
Vessels, Sylvester	1809	23	NJ
Vice, David	1809	20	PA
Vickery, Edward	1810	46	NJ
Vickray, John	1804	37	GA
Victor, John	1815	18 b	PA
Victor, William	1807	26	MS
Villar, Lewis	1823	14	PA
Vincent, John	1815	31	PA
Vincent, John	1821	29	MA
Vincent, Joseph	1808	44	MS
Vincent, William	1806	19	NY
Vincent, William	1806	0	
Vincent, William	1809	0	
Vinsent, William	1820	41 b	VA
Vinson, James	1811	48	VA
Vinyard, James	1809	21	PA
Vinyard, William	1798	29	PA
Vitry, Benj. A.	1821	20 y	PA
Viwson, Abraham	1800	21 m	MD
Vizey, John	1811	22	MD
Voigt, Henrich	1806	24	PA
Voorees, Perry	1812	22 b	MD
Voorhees, Julius	1805	22	NY
Voris, Philip	1812	22	NY
Vorkees, William	1822	22 y	PA
Vorse, David	1820	21	NY
Voshall, Daniel	1813	26	MD
Voss, Matthias	1818	38	PA
Vurley, James	1822	29	MA
Wacker, Fredrick	1823	23	PA
Wade, George	1806	25	MA
Wade, Jacob Brush	1821	21	NJ
Wade, John	1804	23	PA
Wade, John L.	1805	26	MA
Wadsworth, James	1799	22	CT
Waggoner, John	1812	37	PA
Wagner, Jacob	1818	16	PA

Wagner, John	1811	16	Pa
Wagner, Peter Jr.	1815	30	PA
Wagner, Samuel	1810	21 c	PA
Wagner, Samuel	1815	23	PA
Wagner, William	1816	21	PA
Wahab, John	1811	12	PA
Waheven, John	1809	25	DE
Waihsmuth, John	1808	23	PA
Wake, Leroy	1817	24	VA
Waldington, James	1804	21	PA
Wale, Joseph	1806	30	SC
Wales, Edmond	1819	14	PA
Walker, Aaron	1809	17	PA
Walker, Aaron	1813	0	
Walker, Benjamin	1821	32 y	MD
Walker, George	1804	26	PA

Walker, James   1804   27 b   VA
born on Rappehannock River, VA. Bound to
Samuel Duffield, Phila. and served until 21 years
old in 1798. Now free.

Walker, James	1805	19	PA
Walker, James	1806	21	MD
Walker, James	1807		
Walker, James	1809	0	
Walker, James	1810	0	
Walker, John	1800	18	PA
Walker, John	1801	20	PA
Walker, John	1804	19	PA
Walker, John	1805	21	PA
Walker, John	1815	32	none given
Walker, John	1817	17	PA
Walker, Joseph P.	1815	21	PA
Walker, Joseph	1820	27	NH
Walker, Nathaniel	1809	37	MA
Walker, Richard	1812	52	DE
Walker, Richard	1815	41 b	PA
Walker, Richard	1823	23 b	MD
Walker, Robert	1822	46	PA
Walker, Thomas	1801	21	DE
Walker, Thomas	1809	19	MA
Walker, Thomas	1810	32	ME
Walker, Thomas	1811	00	
Walker, William	1800	26	PA
Walker, William	1803	41	VA
Walker, William	1806	21	PA
Walker, William	1812	22	NH
Wall, Daniel	1804	45	CT
Wallace, Alexander	1815	13	PA
Wallace, Benjamin	1806	26	PA
Wallace, Isaac	1810	19	MD

Wallace, Issac	1822	22 y	DE
Wallace, James	1807	28	NY
Wallace, James	1811	29	MD
Wallace, John	1804	51	VA
Wallace, John	1806	22	DE
Wallace, Lewis	1823	30 b	NC
Wallace, Thomas	1807	19	PA
Wallace, Thomas	1810	0	
Wallace, Thomas	1812	35 m	VA
Wallace, William	1804	31	NJ
Wallace, William	1821	20	MD

grape shot wound received aboard ship
early in late war with Great Britain

Wallen, Aaron	1798	24	NJ
Waller, William	1799	22	DE
Walless, Isaac	1810	24	NJ
Walley, Francis	1810	21	PA
Wallin, Emanuel	1815	24	LA
Walling, James	1815	34	NJ
Wallington, Edward	1798	22	DE
Wallington, Samuel E.	1821	18	PA
Wallop, David	1817	18	VA
Wallop, Levi	1821	43 b	VA
Wally, Daniel	1810	17 b	DE
Waln, Jacob S. , Jr.	1806	22	PA
Walsh, John	1809	25	
Walsh, Keyran, Jr	1805	23	NH
Walter, John	1809	24 b	LA
Walter, John	1817	28	NJ
Walter, Peter	1804	16	PA
Walter, Peter P.	1809	30	PA
Walter, William	1809	19	VA
Walters, Major	1818	25 b	NY
Walters, Nicholas	1806	26	PA
Walters, Nicholas	1809	0	
Walters, Peter	1806	21	PA
Walters, Richard	1821	31 y	MD
Walters, Thomas	1799	26	SC
Walters, William	1806	29	MD
Walters, William	1809	23	PA
Waltman, Samuel V.	1817	17	PA
Walton, Charles	1815	31 m	MA
Walton, Isaac	1806	21	PA
Walton, William	1818		
Walton, Wm.	1818	31	PA
Wansie, Elijah	1799	27 b	DE
Wansley, Elijah	1821	44 m	DE
Wansor, Henry	1811	25	NY
Wanwood, Wally	1817	20 b	RI
Ward, David	1810	25	CT

Ward, Ebenezar B.	1810	17	MA	
Ward, Enoch	1805	21	NC	
Ward, Ichabod	1810	21	CT	
Ward, James	1809	44	NJ	
Ward, James H.	1819	42	NY	
Ward, John	1810	17	NY	
Ward, John	1811	00		
Ward, Joseph	1810	21 b	NY	
Ward, Joseph	1810	25	MD	
Ward, Joseph	1811	00		
Ward, Joseph	1821	26	RI	
Ward, Mason	1812	23	NJ	
Ward, Mexico	1805	22 b	NJ	
Ward, Peter	1806	18	MA	
Ward, Robert	1809	19	NJ	
Ward, Robert	1811	00		
Ward, Robert	1815	00		
Ward, Samuel	1798	0	NJ	
Ward, Samuel	1815	22	NJ	
Ward, Samuel	1815	39	NJ	
Ward, Solomon	1804	19	PA	
Ward, Thomas	1811	40 y	NJ	
Ward, William	1805	18	NY	
Ward, William S.	1812	35 b	NY	
Warden, Appleton	1804	30	CT	
Warden, John	1811	19	PA	
Wards, Joseph	1807	20 b	MS	
Wardwell, Moses H.	1815	16	NH	
Ware, Charles	1815	26	MD	
Ware, George	1806	18	NJ	
Ware, Thomas	1819	29	NJ	
Ware, William	1804	28	PA	
Ware, William	1804	28	PA	
Ware, William	1805	29	PA	
Ware, William	1805	29	PA	
Ware, William	1809	33	PA	
Ware, William	1809	34	PA	
Wark, Francis	1813	42		Flanders
Warner, Adam	1820	20	PA	
Warner, Edward	1807	29 b	MD	
Warner, Edward	1809	0	MD	
Warner, George	1815	21	PA	
Warner, James	1804	22	DE	
Warner, James	1805	0		
Warner, James C.	1809	23	PA	
Warner, James	1810	0		
Warner, James	1812	00		
Warner, Jas C.	1815	00		
Warner, Joseph Moore	1807	13	PA	
	1812	00		
Warner, Joseph	1807	23 b	DE	
Warner, Joseph	1811	28 b	DE	

Warner, Mark	1804	16		PA
Warner, Samuel	1801	20		PA
Warner, Stephen	1813	21		DE
Warner, Thomas B.	1822	28		NY
Warner, William	1807	20	b	DE
Warner, William	1809	28		LA
Warner, William	1809	21		PA
Warnick, Daniel	1823	21		PA
Warran, Clark	1808	18		MD
Warrance, John	1812	19		PA
Warrant, Emory	1821	29	b	MD
Warren, Asa	1823	23	b	DE
Warren, George	1821	25		MD
Warren, John	1798	26		MD
Warren, John	1816	46	y	MD
Warren, Thomas C.	1821	19		PA
Warren, Thomas	1823	22		NJ
Warren, William	1821	22		ME
Warterford, Israel	1810	21	c	NJ
Warwick, Darius	1810	22		NJ
Warwick, John	1815	24		NJ
Warwick, John	1819	20		NJ
Warwick, Richard	1817	20	m	PA
Wasgatt, William	1810	23		MA
Washington, George	1807	39	b	PA
Washington, George	1810	54		PA
Washington, James	1805	0		
Washington, James	1805	22		PA
Washington, James	1805	22		PA
Washington, Samuel Richard				
	1804	35	b	VA
Washington, William	1811	21	y	SC
Wastmay, John	1791	0		
Wat, Lesley	1809	19		PA
Waterford, Essex	1816	50		PA
Waterford, Israel	1809	23	b	NJ
Waterman, William	1811	21		PA
Waterman, William	1815	24		PA
Waterman, William	1817	25		
Waters, Daniel	1800	26		VA
Waters, George	1815	21		PA
Waters, George	1822	27	b	PA
Waters, Isreal	1807	31	b	MD
Waters, John S.	1809	25		SC
Waters, Major	1815	21	b	MD
Waters, Robert	1810	25		MA
Waters, Robert	1811	20		MA
Waters, Robert	1812	30	b	MD
Waters, William	1798	29	m	NY
Waters, William	1809	28	b	NJ
Watkins, Banjamin	1810	0		
Watkins, Benjamin	1807	21		NJ

Watkins, Benjamin	1809	0		
Watkins, Benjamin	1810	0		NJ
Watkins, Daniel	1815	24		NJ
Watkins, Peter	1809	18		NJ
Watkins, Richard	1819	22		PA
Watkins, Thomas	1809	20		NY
Watkins, Thomas	1817	29	b	NY
Watkins, Thomas	1819	34	b	PA
Watkins, William	1809	13		VA
Watkins, William	1810	27	b	MA
Watkins, William	1819	40		MD
Watkins, William	1820	20		PA
Watkinson, Thomas W.				
	1819	17		PA
Watson, Alexander	1815	28		CT
Watson, Andrew	1819	39		MD
Watson, David	1807	36		MD
Watson, David	1815	0		
Watson, Exum	1812	24	M	NC
Watson, Feilder	1807	25	b	PA
Watson, George	1817	25		NY
Watson, Jacob	1809	0		DE
Watson, Jacob	1814	0		
Watson, Jacob	1816	35	y	DE
Watson, James	1795	28		MD
Watson, James	1810	23		NY
Watson, John	1806	18		PA
Watson, John	1807	19		NY
Watson, John	1808	19		PA
Watson, John	1811	21		DE
Watson, John	1815	00		
Watson, Joseph	1809	23		DE
Watson, Richard	1809	19		NJ
Watson, Richard	1821	20		PA
Watson, Thomas Jos.	1817	17		PA
Watson, Thomas	1818	32	b	VA
Watson, Thomas	1819	29	n	VA
Watson, William Henry	1803	21		PA
Watson, William Henry	1807			
Watson, William	1809	28		
Watson, William	1812	22		SC
Watt, George	1806	17		PA
Watt, James	1798	33		PA
Watt, John Joseph	1815	30		LA
Watt, John	1819	25		MD
Watt, Lesley	1809	0		
Watt, William	1807	17		PA
Watterson, Thomas	1801	44		PA
Watts, Stephen	1807	18		MS
Watts, William	1805	22		MD
Watts, William	1819	18		PA
Wattson, George	1804	26		MA

142

Wattson, Holbert	1803	23	DE
Wattson, William K.	1815	19	PA
Wattson, William	1819	23	PA
Way, Hiram	1816	17	PA
Way, John W.	1822	17	NJ
Way, Joshua	1798	22	PA
Wayman, Philip	1821	15 b	PA
Wayman, Samuel, Jr.	1818	17	PA
Wayne, James Stokes	1823	18	PA
Wayne, Thomas	1810	14	PA
Weaks, Thomas	1815	0	PA
Weatherby, Joseph, Jr.			
	1811	21	PA
Weatherstine, Joseph	1808	23	PA
Weaver, George	1810	21	NJ
Weaver, George, Jr.	1821	15	PA
Weaver, George	1822	48 y	MA
Weaver, John	1822	29 b	VA
Weaver, Philip	1805	31	PA
Weaver, William	1806	27 b	MD
Weaver, William	1814	10	NJ
Webb, Alexander	1817	25 y	PA
Webb, Ambrose	1822	18	PA
Webb, Charles	1810	23 b	NY
Webb, Frederick	1818	17	MA
Webb, James	1806	29	NY
Webb, James	1809	18	NJ
Webb, John	1806	30	DE
Webb, John, Jr.	1817	15	PA
Webb, Joseph	1811	27	CT
Webb, Joseph	1814	0	
Webb, Kendal	1813	23	MD
Webb, Perry	1815	18	MD
Webb, Thomas, Jr.	1806	17	PA
Webb, Thomas, Jr.	1807		
Webb, Thomas, Jr.	1809	0	PA
Webb, Thomas H., Jr.	1812	00	
Webb, William R.	1804	22	MD
Webb, William	1806	34	MA
Webb, William	1817	37	NY
Webber, John	1811	32	NY
Webber, Moses	1815	14	MA
Webster, Charles	1809	25	PA
Webster, Elijah	1803	24	MD
Webster, Henry	1811	25	PA
Webster, John	1803	32	MA
Webster, John Lee	1817	22 b	PA
Webster, Thomas	1818	24 c	NH
Webster, William	1815	32	NY
Weddle, James	1808	24	MA
Wedmore, Nathaniel	1815	21	CT
Weed, William B.	1821	21	PA

Weekes, Thomas	1812	35 y	PA
Weeks, Charles	1821	17	NY
Weeks, Ezekiel	1813	21	NJ
Weeks, George	1810	25 b	MD
Weeks, James	1806	22	NJ
Weeks, James	1810	0	
Weeks, Jeremiah	1813	23	NJ
Weeks, Joel	1819	24	NJ
Weeks, Thomas	1813	32	NH
Weeks, William	1803	24	MA
Weeks, William	1804	32	MS
Weir, David	1801	41	PA
Weise, Philip	1810	23	PA
Welch, John	1820	37	MD
Welch, Thomas	1809	37	PA
Welcome, William	1806	36 b	MD
Welcome, William	1809	37 b	MD
Welcome, William	1815	00	
SPC lost in New Castle after voyage to Russia			
Weld, John	1797	40	MA
Welden, Alexander	1799	21	NJ
Weldon, David	1805	19	NJ
Weldon, Thomas	1810	20	DE
Wellbur, Daniel	1815	27 b	PA
Wellcorn, Joseph	1815	28	PA
Wellford, Thomas	1815	39	none given
Wells, Daniel	1807	21	NJ
Wells, Edward	1806	30	PA
Wells, George	1807	26	DE
Wells, George	1809	25 m	PA
Wells, John	1816	29	MD
Wells, Rufus	1819	19	MA
Wells, Samuel	1807	40	CT
Wells, Samuel	1815	41	none given
Wells, William	1807	23	NJ
Wells, William	1810	21	CT
Welser, William	1809	17	PA
Welsh, Jacob	1819	33	DE
Welsh, John	1804	28	PA
Welsh, John	1805	22	NY
Welsh, John	1813	23	NY
Welsh, John Hall	1815	14	PA
Welsh, Nicholas	1803	21	PA
Welsh, Philip	1823	22	PA
Welsh, Thomas	1813	21	PA
Welsh, William	1815	21	MD
Wendel, William	1798	24	NY
Wert, Peter	1811	24	PA
Wescoat, Leonard	1823	19	NJ
Wescot, William	1817	16	MA

Wesnaar, John	1809	33	LA
Wessell, Samuel	1809	16	NJ
West, Adam	1818	22 c	VA
West, Anthony	1809	20	NY
West, Anthony	1811	00	
West, Elijah	1814	22	MD
West, James	1815	22 y	PA
West, James	1816	26	NY
West, James	1819	16	PA
West, John	1809	20	NJ
West, John	1809	0	
West, John Wharton	1818	20	PA
West, Peter	1805	39 b	MA
West, Peter	1818	23 y	VA
West, Richard	1813	17	PA
West, Samuel	1823	16	PA
West, Thomas	1815	30 b	MD
West, Washington W.	1817	16	NY
West, William R.	1807	17	NJ
West, William	1809	16	PA
Westcoatt, Henry	1806	0	NJ
Westcott, Henry	1804	15	NJ
Westerber, John	1804	23	NY
Westerhood, Bernard H.			
	1807	20	PA
Westland, Henay	1819	15	PA
Westley, George	1814	23	DE
Weston, George	1796	24	
Westphal, John William			
	1820	18	PA
Westwick, William	1812	29	NJ
Westwood, Thomas	0000	21	PA
Westwood, Thomas	1807		
Wetherby, Calvin	1806	33	MA
Wetherill, Henry E.	1820	23	NY
Wever, Thomas	1812	18	PA
Whaley, Daniel	1807	19	DE
Wharf, John	1807	21	MA
Wharton, Elisha	1810	27	DE
Wharton, John, Jr.	1799	26	PA
Wharton, Joseph B.	1815	15	PA
Wharton, Thomas	1804	26	PA
Wheatly, Edward	1810	22 y	MD
Wheaton, Amos	1809	19	NJ
Wheaton, Enoch	1801	25	NJ
Wheaton, Enoch	1804	27	NJ
Wheaton, Enoch	1804	27	NJ
Wheeler, David	1817	40	NY
Wheeler, J. Jones	1812	00	
Wheeler, James	1801	30	MA
Wheeler, James	1807	25 b	CT
Wheeler, James T.	1822	26	PA

Wheeler, John	1806	23	PA
Wheeler, John	1807	22	VA
Wheeler, John	1807	22 y	MS
Wheeler, Jonathan	1807	15	PA
Wheeler, Samuel, Jr	1805	21	PA
Wheeler, Samuel	1809	20	CT
Wheeler, Thomas	1807	16	MA
Wheeler, Thomas	1815	42	VA
Wheeler, William	0000	0	
Wheeler, William	1804	19	PA
Wheeling, James	1798	26	MD
Whelan, Charles E.	1821	19	PA
Whelan, Matthew	1815	16	PA
Whelen, James	1817	21	NH
Whelldin, Thomas Vaughan			
	1804	22	NJ
Wheobee, Joseph	1798	21	NC
Wherry, John	1812	22	PA
Whetick, Joseph	1807	17	PA
Whipper, Cyrus	1811	36 m	MD
Whipple, John	1796	28	
Whipple, John	1819	25 b	NH
Whipple, Joseph	1811	25	RI
Whipple, Joseph	1811	00	
Whiston, Obadiah	1812	38	MA
Whitaker, James	1812	21	PA
Whitall, Benjamin Gilbert			
	1822	20 b	NJ
Whitall, John Mickle	1816	15	NJ
Whitall, Richard M.	1798	0	NJ
White, Cato	1811	23 b	PA
White, Charles	1812	26	VA
White, David	1801	23	PA
White, Ephraim	1805	41	MA
White, Francis	1798	23	NJ
White, Francis	1804	21 y	PA
White, Francis	1809	25 y	PA
White, Francis	1809	0 m	PA
White, Francis	1815	25 m	PA
White, George	1805	24	PA
White, George	1805	32	PA
White, George Philip	1821	21	DE
White, George	1823	27	MA
White, Geroge	1798	24 m	PA
White, Gorham	1820	18	MA
White, Isaac	1810	22	PA
White, James	1806	25	NH
White, James	1810	28	NJ
White, James	1818	24	VA
White, James	1820	28	MA
White, James	1820	29	DE
White, John	1804	29	NC

White, John	1804	21	MA
White, John	1805	20	SC
White, John	1805	24	NY
White, John	1806	23	MA
White, John	1807	18	PA
White, John	1807	17	PA
White, John	1809	26	DE
White, John	1811	31	PA
White, John	1811	22 m	LA
White, John	1814	0	
White, John	1814	17	PA
White, John	1815	00	
White, John	1815	22	PA
White, John	1818	24	PA

"bearer is an imposter"

White, Joseph	1801	24	PA
White, Joseph	1806	15	PA
White, Joseph	1817	30	NC
White, Joshua	1821	25	DE
White, Lewis	1801	21	PA
White, Lewis	1816	36	MA
White, Mark	1818	18 s	PA
White, Michael	1815	25	MD
White, Michael	1817	00	

SPC and baggage lost at Battle of Bladensburg

White, Nathaniel	1810	29	MD
White, Philip	1812	17	DE
White, Phillip	1815	00	
White, Richard	1823	18	PA
White, Richard	1823	17	PA
White, Robert	1810	29	NJ
White, Samuel	1807	22	PA
White, Samuel	1807		
White, Samuel	1811	20	DE
White, Samuel	1811	00	
White, Samuel	1814	28	NY
White, Samuel	1815	15	PA
White, Samuel	1815	23	DE
White, Samuel	1815	26	NY
White, Solomon	1804	27 y	NY
White, Solomon	1805	0	
White, Stephen	1813	25	NJ
White, Thomas	1806	26 b	PA
White, Thomas	1807		
White, Thomas	1809	15	MD
White, Thomas	1811	24	DE
White, Thomas	1812	19 b	PA
White, Thomas	1814	21	MD

White, Thomas	1815	18	PA
White, Thomas	1818	21	MD
White, William	1808	17	PA
White, William	1809	17	NY
White, William	1815	26 m	DE
White, William	1817	22 m	NY
White, William	1819	30	ME
Whiteburgh, Christian	1807	20	PA
Whiteford, James	1817	23	PA
Whitefore, Robert	1804	36	none given
Whitehead, Benjamin	1798	29	SC
Whitehead, Benjamin	1799	30	PA
Whitehead, Daniel	1815	27	NY
Whitehead, Elias	1813	21	NJ
Whitehead, Whillet	1807	16	NY
Whitehead, William	1796	23	PA

baptised Christ Church and St. Peters, Phila.;
son of Matthew and Elizabeth Whitehead.

Whitell, James W.	1819	19	NJ
Whiteman, John	1811	20	NJ
Whiteman, Michael	1806	22	PA
Whiteman, William	1815	20	PA
Whiteside, Bamber	1799	0	
Whiteside, Bamber	1818	43	PA
Whitesides, Henry	1821	27	PA
Whitesides, John	1819	18	PA
Whitmill, Francis	1809	25	PA
Whitney, Simeon	1807	16	MA
Whittall, Charles West	1822	18	NJ
Whitten, Elisha	1811	29	MA
Whitten, Elisha	1814	0	
Whitten, William	1796	0	Ireland
Whitten, William	1796	32	
Whittin, Elias	1821	24	ME

born in Kennibeck, Readfield County MA, now
"Main"

Whitton, William	1799	32	SC
Whitty, Thomas	1805	18	MA
Wiatt, John	1821	24	VA
Wickes, Benjamin Jr.	1817	35	MD
Wickes, Samuel	1811	15	PA
Wickham, Joseph	1811	33	RI
Widdecomb, William	1821	27	MA
Widdrington, Robert W.	1811	31	NY

"confest to be a liar -- therefore no further
confidence can be places in his oath. SPC cancelled.

Name	Year	Age		State
Widmann, James	1809	44		
Wiegand, John	1815	14		PA
Wiessell, George F.	1823	14		PA
Wiggins, Benjamin P.	1811	21		NJ
Wiggins, Michael	1805	33		MA
Wiggins, Michael	1809	0		MA
Wiggins, William	1809	35	b	MA
Wight, John	1815	26		ME
Wigins, William	1809	0		
Wilbank, Solomon	1815	24	b	DE
Wilbey, Charles	1821	21		PA
Wilbey, John	1816	28		DE
Wilbour, John	1811	16		RI
Wilbour, Reuel	1815	24		MA
Wilcox, Adam	1820	25		RI
Wilcox, James	1810	20		PA
Wilcox, William	1806	33		CT
Wilder, Skinner	1807	26		VA
Wildes, Job	1812	16		NJ
Wildes, Job	1815	20		NJ
Wildes, Thomas	1805	17		NJ
Wildes, William	1813	21		NJ
Wilding, Philip	1815	36		PA
Wiley, Alexander	1812	21		DE
Wiley, George	1810	26		DE
Wiley, James	1806	44		VT
Wiley, John	1805	27		NY
Wiley, Nathaniel	1811	24		MA
Wilkeson, James	1798	22		NY
Wilkie, William	1801	24		NY
Wilkins, Aaron	1811	21		NJ
Wilkins, Charles	1815	22		NJ
Wilkins, George	1811	21		DE
Wilkins, Henry	1822	34		PA
Wilkins, John	1805	30		PA
Wilkins, John	1816	29		MA
Wilkins, Lemuel	1809	24		DE
Wilkins, Lemuel	1812	00		
Wilkins, Thomas, Jr.	1810	15		NJ
Wilkins, William H.	1809	17		NJ
Wilkins, William H.	1812	00		
Wilkinson, George	1820	26		PA
Wilkinson, James	1813	23		MA
Wilkinson, Thomas	1810	20		PA
Wilkison, John	1805	21		PA
Wilkison, John	1810	30	b	RI
Will, Francis	1810	26		LA
Willcox, George	1816	22		NY
Willcox, Parker	1814	26		RI
Wille, Lewis	1815	15		MA
Willeby, Thomas	1816	25	b	MA
Willes, Brookes	1809	21	b	NJ
Willes, John Trey	1813	22		SC
Willet, Brooks	1809	0	b	NJ
Willet, Brooks	1811	00		
Willet, Brooks	1812	00		
Willett, Edward	1817	20	m	NJ
Willett, Edward W.	1823	19		PA
William, John	1798	21		PA
William, John	1801	22	b	MD
William, Samuel	1811	20		LA
Williams, Aaron	1821	44		NY
Williams, Abraham	1816	45	b	PA
Williams, Abram	1810	24	l	MA
Williams, Adin	1818	22	y	PA
Williams, Alexander	1809	24		DE
Williams, Alfred	1804	25		NJ
Williams, Andrew	1805	21		LA
Williams, Andrew	1807	40	b	MD
Williams, Benjamin	1805	23	b	MD
Williams, Benjamin	1807	21		MA
Williams, Benjamin	1811	00		
Williams, Benjamin	1817	00		
Williams, Benjamin	1823	26		PA
Williams, Charles	1812	29	b	MD
Williams, Charles	1816	22	b	xx
Williams, Charles	1818	25		NJ
Williams, Charles	1822	19	b	PA
Williams, Charles	1823	25		VA
Williams, Charles V.	1823	24		PA
Williams, Christopher	1809	22		PA
Williams, Daneil	1800	20	b	MD
Williams, Daniel	1812	21		PA
Williams, David	1805	23		PA
Williams, David	1815	37	c	DE
Williams, Elijah	1798	22		CT
Williams, Elijah	1806	22	b	DE
Williams, Enos	1806	20	b	PA
Williams, Friday	1808	27	y	SC
Williams, George	1805	23	b	SC
Williams, George	1806	22	b	DE
Williams, George	1807	23	b	DE
Williams, George	1807	21		MD
Williams, George	1808	27		PA
Williams, George	1809	21		LA
Williams, George	1810	26	b	VA
Williams, George	1811	23	y	MD
Williams, George	1812	22		MA
Williams, George	1812	23		NY
Williams, George	1820	22	b	MD
Williams, Haton	1815	26	b	NJ
Williams, Henry Gibson	1809	22		DE
Williams, Henry	1813	25		CT

Williams, Henry	1817	26 b	LA
Williams, Henry	1819	22 b	PA
Williams, Henry	1820	24 b	PA
Williams, Henry	1821	27 b	DE
Williams, Isaac	1807	26	NJ
Williams, Isaac	1810	28 b	PA
Williams, Isaac	1811	29	MA
Williams, James	1804	20	NC
Williams, James	1807	21	NY
Williams, James	1808	28	MA
Williams, James	1809	22	SC
Williams, James	1809	22	SC
Williams, James	1809	16	NJ
Williams, James	1811	00	
Williams, James	1816	24 b	NY
Williams, James	1817	24 y	PA
Williams, James	1818	26	MA
Williams, James	1821	29 b	MD
Williams, James	1821	27 b	NY
Williams, James	1821	21 y	PA
Williams, James	1821	30 b	NJ
Williams, James	1822	33	ME
Williams, James	1822	22 b	MA
Williams, Jeremiah	1806	24	DE
Williams, Jesse	1811	00	
Williams, Jesse	1811	35 b	NJ
Williams, John	1798	23	MD
Williams, John	1799	27	PA
Williams, John	1801	22	DE
Williams, John	1801	19	PA
Williams, John	1801	0	
Williams, John	1803	24	CT
Williams, John	1804	35 b	NY
Williams, John	1804	27 m	MA
Williams, John	1804	17 b	PA
Williams, John	1804	28 b	PA
Williams, John	1805	25 b	NY
Williams, John	1805	36 b	MD
Williams, John	1805	59	NJ
Williams, John	1805	17	PA
Williams, John	1805	19	MA
Williams, John	1805	25 b	NY
Williams, John	1806	23 m	PA
Williams, John	1806	39	PA
Williams, John	1806	20 b	NJ
Williams, John	1807	22	NJ
Williams, John	1807	22 y	PA
Williams, John	1807	30	SC
Williams, John	1807	24	MA
Williams, John	1807	27	PA
Williams, John	1807	19 y	NY
Williams, John	1808	19	PA

Williams, John	1809	22	NJ
Williams, John	1809	28	MD
Williams, John	1809	22 b	DE
Williams, John	1809	21	PA
Williams, John	1809	23 b	PA
Williams, John	1810	26	MS
Williams, John	1810	26 y	MD
Williams, John	1810	28	MD
Williams, John	1810	28	LA
Williams, John	1810	28	NY
Williams, John	1811	00	
Williams, John	1811	28 y	NJ
Williams, John	1811	22	VA
Williams, John	1811	31 b	NY
Williams, John	1811	29	DE
Williams, John	1812	00	
Williams, John	1812	29 c	MD
Williams, John	1814	36 b	MT
Williams, John	1815	20	MD
Williams, John	1815	24	NJ
Williams, John	1815	22	MD
Williams, John	1815	32 b	MD
Williams, John	1815	23	MD
Williams, John	1816	48	CT
Williams, John	1816	25 m	NY
Williams, John	1816	17	NJ
Williams, John	1818	21 c	PA
Williams, John	1818		
Williams, John	1818	57 y	PA
Williams, John	1819	22	DE
Williams, John	1819	20 b	NY
Williams, John	1819	23 b	VA
Williams, John	1820	25 b	NJ
Williams, John	1820	28	MA
Williams, John	1820	25	VA
Williams, John	1822	16 b	MA
Williams, John	1823	24	MA
Williams, Joseph	1799	23 b	PA
Williams, Joseph	1801	35	PA
Williams, Joseph	1811	31	VT
Williams, Joseph	1812	22	LA

Williams, Joseph	1815	00	

SPC stolen while a prisoner aboard recaptured prise of privateer of Baltimore; had served aboard ship *Harmons*, Capt. Ansley,bound to Bombay

Williams, Joseph	1823	33 b	MD
Williams, Judiah	1812	19 y	NJ
Williams, Judiah	1818	24	NJ
Williams, Kinsay	1800	30 b	MD
Williams, Leven	1817	25 b	MD

Williams, Levin	1811	35 b	MD		
Williams, Levin	1817	26 y	VA		
Williams, Lewis Henry	1809	10 b	PA		
Williams, Lloyd	1810	20	MA		
Williams, Matheu	1804	22	PA		
Williams, Nathan	1809	18	NJ		
Williams, Peter	1810	20 b	PA		
Williams, Peter	1811	23 b	LA		
Williams, Peter	1815	29 c	VA		
Williams, Richard	1805	25	NJ		
Williams, Robert	1818	26	MD		
Williams, Samuel	1810	26 b	DE		
Williams, Samuel	1814	21	CT		
Williams, Samuel	1815	29 b	NY		
Williams, Samuel	1818	20	NY		
Williams, Samuel	1822	21 y	PA		
Williams, Sanford	1817	23	CT		
Williams, Sanford	1817	23	CT		
Williams, Sanford	1817	23	CT		
Williams, Scipio	1805	35 b	VA		
Williams, Scipio	1807	b			
Williams, Stephen	1809	19 b	PA		
Williams, Stephen	1822	24 b	DE		
Williams, Thomas	1801	27	SC		
Williams, Thomas	1805	21	PA		
Williams, Thomas	1805	40	NY		
Williams, Thomas	1806	24	NC		
Williams, Thomas	1807	20	NY		
Williams, Thomas	1810	30 b	NY		
Williams, Thomas	1810	19	DE		
Williams, Thomas	1812	21	MD		
Williams, Thomas	1815	40	CT		
Williams, Thomas	1815	00			
Williams, Thomas	1815	33 c	NY		
Williams, Thomas	1816	33		Denmark	
Williams, Thomas	1817	28	DE		
Williams, Thomas	1818	16	NJ		
Williams, Thomas	1820	42	MD		
Williams, Thomas	1822	19 b	DE		
Williams, Walter	1806	22	PA		
Williams, William	0000	0	PA		
Williams, William	0000	18	PA		
Williams, William	1797	14	MA		
Williams, William	1803	23	RI		
Williams, William	1806	20 b	NY		
Williams, William	1807	16	DE		
Williams, William	1809	19	PA		
Williams, William	1809	22 m	DE		
Williams, William	1809	25	PA		
Williams, William	1816	17	MD		
Williams, William	1821	18	VA		
Williams, William	1821	26		Gr.Br.	

Williams, William	1822	20	NY		
Williams, William	1823	21	ME		
Williams, Willis	1823	27	VA		
Williams, Wm. E.	1823	20	NY		
Williamson, George	1806	22	PA		
Williamson, George	1808	0			
Williamson, George H.	1815	31	VA		
Williamson, Henry	1808	26	PA		
Williamson, Henry	1809	0			
Williamson, Henry	1809	27	NJ		
Williamson, James C.	1803	27	NJ		
Williamson, James	1809	28	MD		
Williamson, James	1819	24 b	NY		
Williamson, John	1803	18	PA		
Williamson, John	1803	18	PA		
Williamson, John	1804	22	GA		
Williamson, John	1806	28	LA		
Williamson, John	1807	47	NJ		
Williamson, John	1807	38	PA		
Williamson, John	1808	22	LA		
Williamson, John	1809	0	PA		
Williamson, John	1820	32	PA		
Williamson, Joseph	1811	15	PA		
Williamson, Joseph	1811	00			
Williamson, Peter	1805	28	SC		
Williamson, Samuel	1810	17	PA		
Williamson, Thomas	1807	24	MA		
Williamson, Thomas	1822	21 y	MD		
Williamson, William	1816	28	VA		
Williamson, William	1817	21	PA		
Williamson, William R.	1821	21	PA		
Willig, Edward	1811	19		none given	
Willing, Deunard	1807	19 b	MD		
Willing, Richard Peters	1821	14	PA		
Willing, Thomas	1820	17	PA		
Willis, Henry	1821	25 b	MD		
Willis, James	1818	26	NY		
Willis, Thomas	1805	17	PA		
Willis, Thomas	1808	30	NC		
Willis, Thomas	1810	0			
Willis, William	1809	20	PA		
Willits, Isaac	1822	22	NJ		
Willks, William	1815	22	MD		
Willman, James	1800	21	PA		
Wills, Brooks	1810	24 c	NY		
Wills, Hugh	1813	20	PA		
Wills, Samuel	1814	21	NJ		
Wills, Samuel	1821	23	NJ		
Willson, Alexander	1805	24	VA		
Willson, Frederick	1804	26	MD		
Willson, Frederick	1804	0			
Willson, Henry	1810	24	MD		

148

Willson, Henry	1811	22 y	PA
Willson, Henry	1812	00	
Willson, James	1823	21	PA
Willson, John	1805	28	MA
Willson, Joseph	1811	42 b	MD
Willson, Peter	1807	19	MA
Willson, Thomas	1804	26	
Willson, William	1815	22	RI
Willson, William	1823	23	ME
Willyard, William	1809	25 y	MD
Wilman, William Horton	1809	17	PA
Wilmer, Thomas	1821	20	PA
Wilmert, Henry	1801	10	PA
Wilmerton, John	1811	21	NJ
Wilmore, Isaac	1819	0 c	
Wilmore, Joseph	1809	28 b	NY
Wilson, Andrew	1818	32	SC
Wilson, Anthony H.	1821	15	PA
Wilson, Charles	1809	16	CT
Wilson, Charles	1809	28 b	PA
Wilson, Charles	1812	00	
Wilson, Charles	1813	16 m	MD
Wilson, Charles	1817	37 b	MD
Wilson, Charles	1818	20	PA
Wilson, Charles	1819	30	MA
Wilson, Christopher	1811	19	DE
Wilson, Daniel	1807	23 b	NJ
Wilson, David	1804	23 b	MD
Wilson, David	1804	23 b	MD
Wilson, David	1805	27	CT
Wilson, David	1805	26	PA
Wilson, David	1807		
Wilson, Fredrick	1819	19	LA
Wilson, George	1810	30	PA
Wilson, George	1810	23	RI
Wilson, George	1810	23	PA
Wilson, Henry	1801	22	PA
Wilson, Henry Robert	1811	15	
Wilson, Henry	1812	28 b	MD
Wilson, Henry	1822	19	MD
Wilson, Isaac	1811	27 y	NY
Wilson, Isaac	1812	00	
Wilson, Jacob	1815	33 b	DE
Wilson, James	1804	25 b	NY
Wilson, James	1805	37	PA
Wilson, James	1805	26 b	VA
Wilson, James	1811	24	NJ
Wilson, James	1815	19	MA
Wilson, James	1815	27	NY
Wilson, James	1816	28	VA
Wilson, James	1818	18 y	NH
Wilson, James	1823	37	PA

Wilson, Jessee	1821	35 s	MD
Wilson, John	1801	26	NC
Wilson, John Peter	1805	26	NY
Wilson, John	1805	21	MD
Wilson, John	1806	0	MA

SPC taken from him by lieutenant of British sloop
of war *Arab* at Senegal

Wilson, John	1807	27	LA
Wilson, John	1807	29	NC
Wilson, John	1809	31	PA
Wilson, John	1810	27 b	VA
Wilson, John	1815	23	PA
Wilson, John	1815	24	DE
Wilson, John	1816	0	
Wilson, John	1816	31	NY
Wilson, John	1819	28	MD
Wilson, John	1822	23 b	MD
Wilson, Joseph	1810	25	PA
Wilson, Matthew	1801	22	PA
Wilson, Peter	1804	23	DE
Wilson, Peter	1814	0	
Wilson, Richard	1807	24 y	PA
Wilson, Richard	1809	33	NH
Wilson, Richard	1816	22	SC
Wilson, Robert M.	1821	16	PA
Wilson, Samuel	1821	23 s	NY
Wilson, Thomas	1798	0	CT
Wilson, Thomas	1803	22	PA
Wilson, Thomas	1804	25 b	DE
Wilson, Thomas	1804	26	NC
Wilson, Thomas	1805	28	MA
Wilson, Thomas	1807	28 b	MD
Wilson, Thomas	1807	22	PA
Wilson, Thomas	1809	26 m	PA
Wilson, Thomas	1811	20	NJ
Wilson, Thomas	1813	27 y	PA
Wilson, Thomas	1817	37 m	MA
Wilson, Timothy "Tim"	1817	43 y	SC
Wilson, William	1798	16	PA
Wilson, William	1800	21	PA
Wilson, William	1804	23	PA
Wilson, William	1807	47	PA
Wilson, William	1812	28 b	MD
Wilson, William	1814	0	
Wilson, William	1816	27	MA
Wilson, William	1821	22	MA
Wiltberger, Peter, Jr.	1810	18	PA
Wiltberger, Peter, Jr.	1810	18	PA
Wimer, John	1799	26	PA
Winans, William W.	1821	23	NY

Winberg, Jones	1803	0		Sweden	Witmer, Abraham	1816	23	PA
Winch, James	1809	26	DE		Witmer, Henry	1804	24	PA
Winch, James	1813	0			Witmer, Henry	1805	0	
Winchester, Bronson V.	1818	27	NJ		Witmer, Henry	1807		PA
Winder, Samuel	1809	31	MA		Witt, James	1815	36	NY
Windhorft, Herman	1809	20	PA		Wittenter, John	1817	16 b	MD
Window, John	1821	21	NY		Wittenton, John	1803	17 b	PA
Windsor, James	1807	28	NJ		Witter, James	1821	21 b	PA
Windsor, Samuel	1809	31	MA		Witter, Mathew	1815	23	SC
Wine, Andrew	1810	18	MD		Wittick, John	1818	20	PA
Winemore, Jacob	1810	15	PA		Wittry, John	1798	19	PA
Winemore, Jacob	1813	0			Wityck, Joseph	1807		
Winemore, Philip	1798	13	PA		Witz, Philip	1815	27	PA
Winemore, Philip	1807	20	PA		Woelpper, Charles	1823	16	PA
Winemore, Philip	1809	22	PA		Woladr, Martin	1805	34	NC
Winemore, Thomas	1805	14	PA		Wolbert, Charles	1803	19	PA
Winford, Charles	1805	25 m	CT		Wolbert, Fred George, Jr.			
Winford, Charles	1807	25 c	CT			1818	19	PA
Wing, Jacob	1801	20	PA		Wolf, Martin	1804	22	MD
Wing, John	1817	16	MA		Wolfe, David	1811	28	PA
Wing, Joshua	1811	20	MA		Wolland, Martin	1812	00	
Wing, LeRoy Anderson	1823	22	MA		Wollard, John	1815	22	NC
Winkelmann, Laois Frederick					Wolpard, Jacob	1804	40	PA
	1808	18	PA		Wolt, Peter	1813	22	PA
Winkler, Jacob	1805	35	PA		Wonderly, Jacob	1815	21	PA
Winkler, Jacob	1806	38	PA		Wood, Charles	1809	20	PA
Winn, Henry	1809	22 b	MD		Wood, Charles J.	1815	21	PA
Winn, Isaac	1810	56 b	MD		Wood, Edward	1817	28	MA
Winn, Richard	1814	22 b	MD		Wood, Elliott	1807	21	NJ
Winnemare, John	1820	21	PA		Wood, George	1810	24 b	PA
Winnemore, Philip	1807				Wood, Isaiah	1806	27 b	MD
Winser, John	1815	28	NJ		Wood, James	1807	16	PA
Winslow, Charles	1820	30	MA		Wood, James H.	1822	22	MA
Winslow, John	1809	27	MA		Wood, John	1808	30	MS
Winter, Josiah R.	1823	20	PA		Wood, John	1815	34	MA
Winter, Lewis	1796	25	PA		Wood, John	1819	31	NJ
Winter, William	1812	21	NJ		Wood, John	1819	17	
Winter, William	1812	21	NJ		Wood, Joseph	1820	25	MA
Winterfield, Roderick	1804	16	PA		Wood, Loftan Seaton	1815	29 b	VA
Winters, Peter	1809	22 b	DE		Wood, Matthew	1808	23	DE
Winters, Peter	1812	00 b	DE		Wood, Michael	1808	18	NY
Wirden, George	1819	14 b	PA		Wood, Mordecai C.	1812	24	PA
Wire, Peter	1812	22	MA		Wood, Peter	1810	19	PA
Wise, Henry W.	1821	24	VA		Wood, Robert	1799	24	MD
Wise, Southey	1809	21	VA		Wood, Robert	1801	19	PA
Wiseman, Joseph	1815	20	PA		Wood, Thomas	1804	18	PA
Wiser, Martin	1798	19	PA		Wood, Thomas	1806	0	PA
Wisey, Joseph	1801	22	NJ		Wood, Thomas	1810	0	
Wiske, John	1818	30	PA		Wood, Thomas	1810	20	PA
Witcraft, Abner	1815	22	DE		Wood, Thomas	1811	50	DE
Witcraft, William	1815	28	DE		Wood, Thomas	1815	15 m	DE
Witman, Charles	1817	22	PA		Wood, Zachariah	1823	29	NJ

Woodberry, Peter	1811	24	MA
Woodby, John	1804	21 m	PA
Wooden, James	1815	22	DE
Woodert, Peter	1815	23 c	PA
Woodford, Joseph	1809	0	
Woodford, Joseph	1809	23	CT
Wooding, John B.	1823	29	NJ
Woodland, Charles	1822	27 b	MD
Woodnutt, Thomas	1809	27	NJ
Woodruff, Asa	1818	25	NJ
Woodruff, David	1809	23	NJ
Woodruff, David	1816	21	NY
Woodruff, John	1814	19	PA
Woodruff, Samuel	1796	28	NJ
Woodruff, Samuel	1806	0	
Woodruff, Samuel	1815	25	MA
Woodruff, Samuel	1823	19	NJ
Woodruff, William	1807	22	PA
Woodruff, William	1811	14	PA
Woods, John	1804	18	NJ
Woods, John	1813	0	
Woods, Thomas	1819	26 b	MD
Woods, William	1805	21 m	NY
Woods, William	1823	21	NY
Woodsides, James Duthie			
	1797	16	PA
Woodwan, Mathias	1797	23	
Woodward, Anthony	1810	15 b	PA
Woodward, Anthony	1811	00	PA
Woodward, Anthony	1811	22 b	PA
Woodward, Anthony	1814	0 c	
Woodward, Anthony	1817	19 b	PA
Woodward, James	1804	16	SC
Woodward, Peter	1806	21 b	DE
Woodward, William	1823	21	VA
Woolard, Martin	1805	33	NC
Woolf, Jacob	1815	21	PA
Woollcock, Nicholas	1811	30	CT
Woollens, Joseph, Jr.	1810	26	PA
Woolly, John	1809	34	NY
Woolly, John	1809	34	NY
Woolson, Aaron	1823	19	NJ
Woolson, John L.	1823	22	NJ
Wooten, John	1812	21	DE
Worenton, Jacob	1806	18 b	DE
Workman, Samuel	1811	24	PA
Worn, Samuel H.	1805	15	PA
Worrell, Benjamin M.	1810	32	PA
Worrell, James	1811	23	PA
Worrell, Jesse	1813	21	PA
Worrell, Richard	1811	32	PA

Worth, Andrew	1810	29	MA
Worthy, Joseph L.	1804	21	PA
Wouters, Jacob	1817	43	PA
Wraight, Henry	1800	20	NJ
Wran, Charles	1810	33	NY
Wrangham, Bartlett	1807	36	VA
Wren, Frederic	1822	27	PA
Wright, Absalom	1819	22 y	PA
Wright, Alexander	1811	30	NJ
Wright, Amos	1809	26	PA
Wright, Anthony	1817	23	MA
Wright, George L.	1810	0	PA
Wright, George Lancaster			
	1810	22 b	PA
Wright, George	1811	27 b	DE
Wright, George	1823	26 b	MD
Wright, Hector	1810	24 b	PA
Wright, Hector	1812	00	
Wright, Isaac	1814	25	MA
Wright, Jacob	1823	45	MD
Wright, James	1806	21 b	DE
Wright, James	1809	25	PA
Wright, James	1811	24	CT
Wright, James	1816	21	PA
Wright, John	1805	27	PA
Wright, John	1806	24	NJ
Wright, John	1807		
Wright, John	1809	25	PA
Wright, John	1811	20	PA
Wright, John	1811	25	RI
Wright, John	1819	30	NY
Wright, John	1819	32	PA
Wright, John	1822	45	VA
Wright, John	1822	21 b	DE
Wright, Joseph	1806	22	VA
Wright, Joseph	1822	22 y	VA
Wright, Lewis	1810	21	PA
Wright, Lewis	1811	00	
Wright, Noell	1823	24	MD
Wright, Peter F.	1810	26	DE
Wright, Simeon	1810	44	CT
Wright, Thomas	1815	21	NY
Wright, Thomas	1822	14	PA
Wright, William	1798	21	NJ
Wright, William	1808	21 y	PA
Wright, William	1815	24	PA
Wright, William	1815	24	NY
Wright, William	1822	27 b	DE
Wrighter, Dedrick	1815	30	NY
Write, Jonathan	1798	21	PA
Write, Jonathan	1798	20	PA
Wroe, Samuel	1807	23	VA

Wyes, John	1812	19		MA
Wylee, James	1804	42		none given
Wyman, David L.	1818	19		CT
Wymen, John	1805	26		PA
Wynekoop, John W.	1815	20		PA
Wynemore, Philip	1813	0		
Wynemore, Philip	1813	0		
Yagins, Daniel	1798	25		NY
Yard, Archabald William				
	1815	18		PA
Yard, Shandy Ephraim	1812	15	b	PA
Yard, William	1811	25		NJ
Yard, William	1811	27	m	PA
Yarington, Luther	1815	32		PA
Yarnal, Benjamin	1811	16		PA
Yarnall, William,Jr.	1818	28		PA
Yates, Charles	1798	29	y	MD
Yates, John	1811	26		DE
Yates, John	1814	53		KY
Yates, John	1814	0		
Yates, John Henry	1816	30		NY
Yeager, Benjamin	1806	16		PA
Yeager, Michael	1804	25		PA
Yeager, William	1820	16		PA
Yearman, Perry	1817	30	b	DE
Yeates, John	1811	18		DE
Yeoman, John William	1810	30		NY
Yoest, John	1815	24		DE
Yoreous, Andrew	1805	19		PA
York, Isaac	1804	23	m	PA
York, John	1815	16		MA
Yorke, Joseph	1809	23		NY
Yorke, Lewis L.	1820	17		NJ
Yorke, Peter	1804	39		PA
Yorke, Thomas	1810	24		NJ
Yorke, William C.	1822	19		PA
Yorker, David	1818	13	b	PA
Yorker, George	1805	30	b	MD
Youman, James	1804	25		MD
Young, Abiathar	1806	19		RI
Young, Banjamin	1806	24		PA
Young, Benjamin	1809	26		PA
Young, Benjamin	1810	0		
Young, Benjamin	1815	19		PA
Young, Benjamin	1818	23		PA
Young, Charles	1807	27		NY
Young, Charles	1818	17		MA
Young, George	1806	20		NY
Young, George	1820	31		LA
Young, Henry	1815	19		NY
Young, James	1810	34	b	NH
Young, James	1817	18		PA

Young, Jesse	1818	27		NJ
Young, John	1806	27		CT
Young, John	1807	21		PA
Young, John	1807	16		PA
Young, John Jacob	1810	0		
Young, John Jacob	1810	17		PA
Young, John	1810	21		PA
Young, John	1811	30		PA
Young, John	1813	23	y	PA
Young, John	1817	20		MA
Young, John	1818	29		PA
Young, John	1818	18		LA
Young, John	1818	28		MA
Young, Joseph	1822	20		ME
Young, Peter	1798	27		PA
Young, Peter	1816	24		MS
Young, Robert	1815	22		NY
Young, Seth	1807	19		NJ
Young, Stephen	1799	19		NJ
Young, Thomas	1811	32		PA
Young, William	1806	19		PA
Young, William Brothers				
	1811	23		PA
Young, William	1811	21		MD
Young, William B.	1815	28		MA
Young, William	1815	23		PA
Young, William	1815	17		PA
Young, William	1817	26		MD
Younger, William	1815	36		NY
Youngs, Alexander	1809	23		NY
Yowart, William	1797	29		NY
Zane, Nathan Shenton	1815	18		DE
Zane, Nathan Shenton	1818	00		PA
Zane, Timothy Hanson	1815	15		DE
Zane, Wilkins	1806	24		NJ
Zane, William	1801	21		PA
Zane, William	1807	28		PA
Zanes, John	1809	17		NY
Zebley, Samuel	1805	19		PA
Zibley, Samuel	1806	20		PA
Zilli, Antonio	1810	39		LA
Zollinger, Henry	1811	21		PA
Zorns, Philip	1805	28		PA

Introduction to Supplement

Seamen's Protection Certificate Applications
Port of Philadelphia
1796-1861

This supplement adds some 640 names to the two earlier indexes to Seamen's Protection Certificate Applications filed in the Port of Philadelphia. One earlier index covers the years 1796-1823; the other 1824-1861. This supplement spans the entire period of 1796-1861.

After the publication of the earlier indexes, two additional boxes of applications which had been separated from the bulk of these records were located by an archivist. There is no obvious explanation for their having been separated from the main files. They are not all from one area, nor from one era. They are not all young nor old, black or white. They seem typical of the records organized earlier.

These 640 records have now been filed by year and alpha by surname with the those organized earlier.

Data in this index is given in the same order as in earlier indexes: seaman's name, year of application, age at time of application, color, state or country of birth. Please see page 7 for a more detailed explanation.

Acco, Nain	1811	27 b	NJ	
Adams, Joseph	1850	18	CT	
Alden, James C.	1857	19	NY	
Allen, Jervis	1846	0		
Allen, John	1806	38	DE	
Allen, William	1850	49	ME	
Alln, Isaac	1850	25	RI	
Anderson, James	1838	24	NY	
Anderson, Robert	1861	28	PA	
Anderson, William	1850	25	MA	
Andrews, Edward	1857	22	PA	
Arey, William	1857	22	ME	
Argerett, George	1838	25 y	GA	
Ashmead, Thomas E.	1857	17	PA	
Ashton, Henry	1857	20 b	MA	
Atkins, John	1838	21		Ireland
Ayres, Walter B.	1861	26	NJ	
Bacon, William	1850	29 c	DE	
Bailey, Ezra	1850	12	ME	
Baker, Joel A.	1827	19	MA	
Baker, Joseph	1838	25	ME	
Bantorn, Charles	1840	19 s	PA	
Barber, William	1838	24 c	MD	
Barbour, James	1844	26	NJ	
Barge, William	1846	0		
Barret, Matthew B.	1861	22	NY	
Barron, John	1857	25	NY	
Baxter, Abraham	1857	25 b	MA	
Bayard, Stephen Henry	1850	19 m	MD	
Bayne, Peter	1857	50 m	PA	
Bell, Joseph	1797	21	DE	
Berry, Henry W.	1857	17	ME	
Berry, John Henry	1850	25 b	RI	
Bird, Edward	1840	22 b	PA	
Bisco, Allen	1857	31 b	DE	
Bishop, William	1861	22	MD	
Black, Richard H.	1857	18 c	PA	
Bohanan, Joseph	1838	21	ME	
Bolten, John	1838	32	NY	
Borlase, William J.	1850	23	MA	
Botley, James	1857	20 b	MA	
Bowen, Charles B.	1857	32	RI	
Bowen, John	1828	0		
Bowen, Richard S.	1861	23	MA	
Bowen, William	1838	22	PA	
Boyd, James	1861	28	DC	
Bradfield, James	1861	22	MA	
Bradley, Albert C.	1861	22	CT	
Bradley, Hugh	1817	0		
Bradley, John Joseph	1838	21		England
Bradshaw, George	1838	27	VA	
Brice, Henry	1857	26	NC	
Brittan, James H.	1861	20	NY	
Britton, Isaac	1854	20 b	PA	

Brooks, John	1838	23 c	PA	
Brooks, Noah	1861	25 b	MD	
Brooks, William	1838	23 y	DC	
Broom, Thomas	1822	23	PA	
Brown, Charles	1838	28 b	PA	
Brown, James	1857	27	NY	
Brown, John	1857	26 m	NY	
Brown, John	1838	25 b	NJ	
Brown, John	1857	32	NY	
Brown, Stillmon	1838	23	ME	
Brown, Thomas	1838	29 c	DE	
Brown, Thomas	1801	26 b	VA	
Brown, Titus A.	1857	22 m	PA	
Brown, William	1850	39 c	PA	
Browne, James	1803	35		
Brunswick, John C	1838	23 c	DE	
Bryson, Robert	1838	19		England
Buckley, William M.	1850	30	PA	
Buell, Samuel F.	1844	20	VT	
Burchell, John	1861	32	MA	
Burke, William	1825	28	PA	
Burns, James	1850	23	PA	
Burns, William	1850	25	MA	
Burrill, Edward M.	1857	17 m	VA	
Butler, William	1838	46	PA	
Caesar, Glaucestor	1798	0 b		
Callanan, William	1850	29	MA	
Campbell, Daniel	1838	25 c	DE	
Campbell, Joseph J.	1850	22	NJ	
Card, Samuel	1861	22	ME	
Carey, James M.	1838	19	DE	
Carlisle, Joseph	1861	35 s	PA	
Carll, William	1822	25	ME	
Carmichael, Samuel	1804	0		
Carson, Joseph	1839	45	MA	
Cash, Michael	1850	38	ME	
Cassady, Edward J.	1854	25	PA	
Casson, Nathan	1827	24 b	DE	
Cate, Daniel, Jr.	1839	25	ME	
Chace, Cyrus A.	1861	27	NY	
Chalkley, Moses	1838	34 b	DE	
Chambers, Christopher	1833	29 b	PA	
Chambers, David	1857	35 b	DE	
Chandler, Edward T.	1857	26	ME	
Chase, Eldridge	1861	27	MA	
Chew, John	1857	42 c	MD	
Christian, Charles	1857	46		Prussia
Clark, James F.	1861	15	MA	
Clark, Jeremiah	1850	25 c	DE	
Clark, John S.	1844	16	PA	
Clark, John Severing	1838	23	PA	
Clark, Stephen	1857	31 b	MD	
Coffin, Charles	1861	22 I	MA	
Comery, Isaac	1838	18	ME	

Connor, Ebenezer	1850	53	ME
Conway, Daniel	1861	21 b	DE
Conwell, William	1850	15	DE
Conyers, William	1800	21	PA
Cooley, Thomas	1850	36 c	MA
Cooper, Atwill	1838	30 s	DE
Cooper, George H.	1838	12	PA
Cooper, Isaac	1847	18 b	MD
Cooper, John	1850	21	ME
Cooper, William	1857	25 b	NY
Cooper, William	1861	26 b	MD
Copeland, Richard	1840	23 b	PA
Corey, James M.	1838	19	DE
Cornish, William	1850	26	ME
Corson, Amos S.	1838	21	NJ
Craft, Edward	1839	24	PA
Crane, John L.	1861	19	ME
Cresee, Smith	1861	18	NJ
Crocker, Francis W.	1857	48	MA
Crosby, Edward	1838	40	MA
Crowell, Edwin	1861	27	MA
Cummings, James	1828	0	
Cunningham, James	1857	18	PA
Cunningham, James F.	1861	28	NY
Curry, Wesley	1838	23 c	DE
Dalton, Thomas	1857	22 m	CT
Danenhower, Charles	1857	16	PA
Davis, Charles	1857	17	ME
Davis, Henry	1828	0	
Davis, Levin	1822	19 y	VA
Davison, Isaac	1838	31	PA
Dawson, James	1861	29 b	PA
Deamer, James	1822	15	PA
DeGrate, Alfred H.	1857	30 b	MA
Denny, James	1835	26 b	VA
Depass, Henry	1850	38 b	MD
Derby, Josiah G.	1857	37	NY
Derrickson, Jacob	1857	30 b	DE
Devons, Thomas	1857	16	ME
Dexter, Sumner	1838	23	MA
Dickinson, William	1850	45	ME
Dill, Eliza	1857	29 b	PA
Doan, Joseph	1797	20	PA
Donahoe, Matthew	1861	19	DC
Donahue, Patrick	1861	27	NY
Dorman, James	1839	24	ME
Dom, James	1855	24	NH
Dorsey, Benjamin	1838	22 c	MD
Douglass, William	1857	21 m	PA
Drain, Solomon	1861	23 m	DE
Duane, Charles	1850	24	NY
Duffell, Samuel	1861	22	NJ
Duncan, John	1858	31	TN
Dwier, William W. W.	1850	20	PA
Earley, Dennis	1850	22	MD
Eaton, Henry H.	1850	38	ME
Eckard, Henry G.	1857	18	PA
Edwards, Bertine	1850	25	NJ
Elliott, William	1838	21	MD
Ellis, Albert	1861	17	MA
Ellis, Charles E.	1857	28	ME
Ellis, Peter	1857	28 b	MD
Ellis, Spencer P.	1861	23	MA
Ellison, Swan P.	1857	24	NY
Emery, Isaac H.	1861	24	ME
Ennis, Frederick	1850	35 b	MD
Ettridge, Isaac	1850	21	DE
Evans, David	1850	24	ME
Evans, James	1850	29	MD
Evans, Richard	1797	23	PA
Eveington, William	1838	24	NC
Everett, Isaac	1838	25	MA
Fenna, Robert B.	1861	39	NY
Fetherston, Thomas V.	1850	24	ME
Fields, James	1855	21	PA
Fillmore, John	1850	21	ME
Finn, John G.	1857	14	MO
Fitzgerald, Enoch	1850	24	ME
Fitzmaurice, John	1861	18	RI
Fletcher, Stephen	1838	60 b	VA
Flint, Benjamin	1857	20	MA
Ford, James	1861	23	NY
Fowler, James	1857	33	NY
Fowler, Simeon E.	1838	23	ME
Frazer, Caleb	1838	28 y	MD
Frederick, John	1844	33	NY
Freeburger, John Seaborn	1835	17	PA
Freeman, Frederick	1857	21 m	MA
Frost, George W.	1857	19	ME
Fuller, Martin	1850	29	CT
Fullman, William	1844	14 y	PA
Fulton, William J.	1857	19	PA
Gale, Coltson	1838	28	VA
Gardner, Jonathan	1800	23	MA
Gardner, William	1839	22	NY
Garwood, William P.	1838	19	PA
Gehret, Adam	1857	24	PA
George, James T.	1850	19	AL
Gerden, Thomas	1846	0	
Gibbs, Shadrack F.	1861	23	MA
Gibson, Henery	1857	19	MD
Giles, William	1828	0	
Gilliams, John	1861	15	PA
Gilman, John S.	1835	17	NJ
Gitten, Robert	1850	26	NY
Glasgow, John	1838	25 s	NJ
Godfrey, Edward	1838	27	MA
Godfrey, Harrison	1856	15	NJ

Godwin, Samuel M.	1861	21	NC
Golder, Jacob M.	1857	27	NY
Gorham, Stephen	1861	38	MA
Gorman, John B.	1850	23	DC
Gorwaiz, Joseph	1850	19	MA
Gould, Ephraim	1861	29 b	NJ
Graham, Robert	1850	21	PA
Gran, Thomas S.	1857	31	MA
Grant, Joseph	1857	23 b	NY
Green, James	1796	24	MA
Green, John	1828	0	
Griffin, Anthony	1838	19 s	ME
Griffin, William	1797	32	PA
Gumbs, William T.	1857	20 b	NY
Hall, Henry	1838	25	NJ
Hall, James M.	1828	0	
Hall, John	1850	34	MA
Hall, William	1850	25	MD
Hallowell, Christopher	1857	22	PA
Halstead, Leonard	1847	47	NY
Hamilton, Richard	1861	31	CT
Hamilton, Samuel	1861	18	PA
Hand, George	1850	24 b	RI
Hand, Joseph	1847	23	NJ
Harding, William	1838	24 s	DE
Harman, Lemuel	1847	22 c	DE
Harper, George	1850	32 c	DE
Harrington, William L.	1861	22	ME
Harris, George	1857	26 b	DE
Harris, John	1850	23	MD
Harris, Peter	1838	19	PA
Hays, Perry	1838	38 c	DE
Hazard, James O.	1861	20	DE
Hebbern, James Henry	1838	15	DE
Heffeerson, John	1828	0	
Helms, Job	1844	21	PA
Henckley, James S.	1861	18	MA
Henry, Samuel	1857	16	PA
Herbert, William	1838	22	PA
Hern, Ephraim	1857	23 b	VA
Hevelo, George	1857	21 b	DE
Hewitt, James	1838	16	NJ
Hickman, John	1857	18	DE
Hicks, Charles H. W.	1850	20 c	DE
Highat, John	1825	40	PA
Hill, Frederick	1861	27 b	MD
Hill, James	1847	32	NH
Hill, St.Vestin	1838	19 y	DE
Hill, Thomas	1861	26	PA
Hodge, Sidney A.	1861	29	NY
Hoffa, Abraham M.	1838	29	PA
Holden, Henry	1850	27	ME
Holmes, John	1857	36	PA
Hooper, John	1838	35 b	DE

Hopkins, John	1820	23 b		
Housman, John Allen	1838	19	PA	
Howard, John	1857	40	NJ	
Howard, Walter	1861	27	MA	
Hudland, Henry	1859	35 b	MD	
Hughes, Henry	1861	60	NY	
Hughes, Robert	1850	17	ME	
Hughes, Thomas	1857	23 b	PA	
Hull, David	1828	0		
Humphreys, David M.	1861	22	ME	
Humphreys, Frederick Clinton	1838	14	MA	
Hurt, William	1850	28 c	DE	
Ingersoll, Joseph N.	1861	24	NJ	
Jacks, William G.	1857	24 b	NH	
Jackson, George	1861	23 b	NJ	
Jackson, Henry	1835	42 c	NY	
Jackson, John	1857	22 b	MD	
Jacob, Antony Benjamin	1850	23 c	DE	
Jarvis, James	1857	22 b	NY	
Jenkins, Edgar	1861	23	MA	
Jewell, Henry Weber	1847	28		England
Johnson, Charles	1857	22 b	NY	
Johnson, David H.	1861	21	DE	
Johnson, Henry	1838	21 b	MD	
Johnson, John	1833	25 b	PA	
Johnson, John	1828	0		
Johnson, John	1857	20	NY	
Johnson, John A.	1857	22	NY	
Johnson, Lott	1850	25 c	VA	
Johnson, Orrick	1850	25	VA	
Johnson, Robert	1838	26 s	NY	
Johnston, John	1861	18	IL	
Jones, John	1850	23	NY	
Jones, William	1833	24 b	PA	
Jordan, Henry	1800	28 b	NY	
Kassenaus, Cristoffel	1800	24	VA	
Keeler, Daniel	1858	20	MA	
Keen, William	1838	23	NY	
Kehail, Arthur	1861	27	ME	
Kelley, David G.	1839	0		
Kelley, Zeno	1861	25	MA	
Kelly, Edwin	1838	17	PA	
Kempsy, Robert	1850	22	NY	
Keniston, Edward C.	1861	18	ME	
Kennedy, George W.	1861	21	NJ	
Kidd, Robert	1838	20	MD	
Kiff, William Henry	1850	17	ME	
Killoch, William	1857	38	ME	
Kline, George W.	1857	18	PA	
Kyle, John	1861	20	PA	
Lambert, Charles R.	1850	23	PA	
Langham, John, Jr.	1857	16		England
Lawton, Russell James	1850	24	RI	
Lee, Sydney Smith, Jr.	1857	20	DC	

Leighton, Aaron	1861	32	ME
Leighton, George W.	1861	21	ME
Leighton, William	1861	19	PA
Leo, James W.	1861	30	NY
LeRoy, Daniel	1838	28	NY
Lewis, Joseph A.	1857	23 b	ME
Lewis, Raymond	1850	24	CT
Lewis, William	1857	20	DE
Lewis, William	1838	18	ME
Liddle, James W.	1850	21	PA
Linden, William	1850	21	ME
Lindon, James	1797	0	PA
Lines, Thomas	1847	18	NJ
Little, Henry F.	1861	15	PA
Lloyd, William	1847	19	NY
Locke, William	1850	22	MA
Lockhart, Charles	1838	27	W. Indies
Logan, Andrew	1850	23	PA
Lopez, Bartholomew	1808	34	MS Terr.
Lorimer, John	1857	30	Scotland
Lousen, Christopher	1857	24	NY
Lowber, Caleb G.	1856	21 b	DE
Lowrey, William	1804	0	
Lucas, John	1846	0	
Lyons, John	1844	19	MD
Macartney, William	1838	32	PA
MacKeither, Moses	1840	21	SC
Mansfield, Wm.	1828	0	
Manwaring, George A.	1854	25	CT
Marks, John	1857	25	NY
Martin, Elijah A.	1861	21	NJ
Martin, Ephraim	1800	26	MA
Martin, George	1828	0	
Martin, James	1861	23	Ireland
Mason, James	1838	27	DE
Mason, Jonathan	1847	22 b	DE
Mason, Joseph Sharp	1850	15 m	PA
Masterman, Cornelius	1857	21 b	NY
McBratnie, John	1850	23	NY
McBride, John	1846	0	
McCarter, Warren B.	1857	17	PA
McClain, Leander	1850	21	ME
McCormick, Wm.	1850	17	LA
McCosker, James	1850	20	DE
McCullough, Thomas	1857	26	NJ
McCully, John	1838	27	PA
McDonald, Francis	1861	25	ME
McDowell, William	1827	20	PA
McFarland, Alphonso	1850	16	ME
McGlathry, James D.	1844	17	ME
McKenzie, John	1857	29	ME
McLane, James	1838	37 b	NY
McMillen, John	1850	26	ME
McMitchel, James	1828	0	
McNeall, Joseph	1807	22	NC
McNeilly, James	1861	21	DE
Mehlman, Solomon	1838	23	MA
Melville, John	1828	0	
Mendham, Robert	1850	19	PA
Meyers, Jno. H. C.	1850	25	Germany
Middleton, Charles	1840	18	NJ
Miers, Gerard	1838	21	Germany
Miller, Edward	1850	18	ME
Miller, Garnson	1850	37 b	NJ
Miller, George A.	1861	29	ME
Miller, John	1828	0	
Miller, Robert	1835	41 c	NJ
Mills, Frederick	1838	24	NY
Minus, Richard	1857	26 b	DE
Mires, Benjamin	1838	27 s	PA
Moore, Charles W.	1850	22	MA
Moore, Nathaniel	1844	39	PA
Morris, Edward	1838	22	DE
Morris, John	1839	32	DC
Morris, William	1838	22 b	PA
Morse, William	1838	19	MA
Morslander, David Y.	1850	20	NJ
Mosley, Robert	1850	25 m	DE
Mullen, John F.	1857	23	MA
Mullen, Lawrence	1806	0	
Mullin, John	1828	0	
Murphy, John	1861	40	Ireland
Murray, Androw	1838	23	MA
Murray, Isaac	1839	29 c	MD
Murray, John	1850	21	RI
Murray, John	1850	28	NY
Myers, Charles	1850	28 c	MA
Nelson, Andrew	1846	0	
Nelson, William	1838	34	NY
Newcome, Samuel S.	1861	32	MA
Nicholls, John	1850	29	MD
Nickerson, Eleazar	1861	21	MA
Nickerson, Joel S.	1861	16	MA
Norton, Jeremiah B.	1857	27	ME
Null, C. Remington	1857	17	NJ
Nutting, John	1827	22	MA
O'Leary, Henry	1857	37	PA
OConnor, William	1822	42	PA
Oliver, James	1850	23	Corfu
Oney, James	1850	22	CT
Ormson, James	1809	0	
Ormson, James	1808	22	PA
Orr, James	1806	0	
Orskins, William	1861	35	DE
Otis, Lorenzo	1822	30 b	MA
Painter, Samuel	1861	21 b	DE
Palmer, Thomas	1861	24	ME
Parker, Charles	1857	23 c	PA

Name	Year	Age	State	Note
Parker, Charles	1850	21	NY	
Parker, Charles F.	1861	28	MA	
Parker, Miles	1857	21 c	PA	
Parkinson, William L.	1838	23	NJ	
Parsell, Thomas	1797	23	NY	
Pascal, James	1838	23	MD	
Passon, John	1857	25 I		Chili
Patterson, William D.	1838	21	MA	
Payne, John	1838	24	VT	
Peabody, Andrew E.	1850	19	ME	
Penosey, Charles	1838	60	LA	
Peters, George	1803	30	PA	
Peters, Smith	1838	21	MA	
Peterson, John	1857	24 b	NJ	
Pilbrow, James	1850	16	PA	
Pinkham, Handy	1850	21	ME	
Pointer, Nathan	1850	28 b	DE	
Port, Joseph H.	1861	23	MA	
Porter, John	1850	18	ME	
Powers, Henry R.	1861	30	ME	
Pratt, Dennis	1850	22	MA	
Prescott, John	1838	22	NY	
Price, George	1857	37	ME	
Price, George T.	1861	24	DE	
Pride, Selby	1861	26 I	DE	
Priest, George	1853	27	VA	
Pultz, Norman S.	1861	21	NY	
Rankin, John	1796	0		
Ray, Saml. M.	1839	24	MA	
Redman, John E.	1856	21	ME	
Renck, Thomas P.	1857	24	NY	
Richards, Richard	1857	26 b	NY	
Richards, Thomas F.	1838	29	ME	
Ricketts, Samuel D.	1861	20	DE	
Riddle, Richard K.	1838	18	DE	
Riggin, Charles W.	1850	21	DE	
Riley, David	1838	19	MA	
Roberts, Edward	1799	26 y	MD	
Roberts, William	1850	24	ME	
Robertson, George	1850	17	MA	
Robins, John C.	1850	29	VA	
Robinson, Edward	1850	26	NY	
Robinson, John	1857	22	CT	
Robinson, Richard	1857	27	MA .	
Rone, Thomas	1857	28 b	MA	
Rook, James	1857	39 s	MA	
Ross, Charles M.	1838	26	MD	
Ross, George	1857	16	PA	
Rousseau, Louis VanDyke	1861	21	PA	
Rowan, Edward N.	1856	25	PA	
Roy, William	1838	26	NY	
Royal, Jarvis	1844	27	NJ	
Royal, Joseph	1848	22	PA	
Rutenhusen, Charles	1857	30		
Ryan, William	1861	23	PA	
Ryan, William	1850	18	VA	
Sampson, William	1857	28 c	MD	
Samuels, Robert	1857	22 b	NY	
Sanford, John	1839	21	RI	
Scott, John	1850	23	NY	
Scott, William	1856	27 b	PA	
Scull, Elisha	1861	27	NJ	
Searell, Charles T.	1861	21	MA	
Seaton, William	1850	22	MA	
Seewald, Harry	1861	24	OH	
Sessor, Oscar	1861	24 m	NY	
Shankland, Alexander T.	1861	41	PA	
Shankland, Alexander T.	1838	19	PA	
Sharp, George A.	1857	16	PA	
Shippey, Nathaniel	1797	22	RI	
Shirley, William	1850	21	NY	
Shockley, James	1861	36 b	DE	
Shockley, John	1861	30 b	DE	
Sias, Nathaniel C.	1850	17	MA	
Silver, Aaron	1857	45	LA	
Simpson, James	1850	21	ME	
Small, Augustus	1850	27	LA	
Smith, Charles Carroll	1857	18	PA	
Smith, Charles E.	1857	22	CT	
Smith, Edward	1857	34 b	NY	
Smith, George H.	1861	24	RI	
Smith, George W.	1839	23	NJ	
Smith, Henry	1857	29	RI	
Smith, Jacob S.	1861	21	NJ	
Smith, James	1850	29	NY	
Smith, James	1797	32	PA	
Smith, James	1850	50	ME	
Smith, John L.	1850	38	MD	
Smith, Joseph	1838	16	PA	
Smith, Richard L.	1838	19	PA	
Smith, Sidney	1838	20	MA	
Smith, William	1846	0	PA	
Smith, William	1850	39 c	MA	
Spencer, George	1857	21	NJ	
Spencer, Mark A.	1861	23 b	DE	
Sprague, Benjamin	1850	24	ME	
Stafford, Robert	1844	22	PA	
Stanwood, Amasa C.	1850	23	ME	
Staves, William	1850	20	MA	
Steelman, Deristus B.	1861	29	NJ	
Steelman, John B.	1861	28	NJ	
Sterling, John	1850	22	ME	
Stevens, Charles L.	1861	22 m	NJ	
Stevens, Edward J.	1838	18	MD	
Stevens, John	1857	23 b	CT	
Stevens, William	1861	40 m	VA	
Stevenson, Asael	1850	27	DE	
Stevenson, John S.	1857	23 b	MA	

Stewart, William	1861	30 m	DC
Stout, James Wilson	1850	18	PA
Stout, William	1861	53	PA
Stratton, John	1857	35	NJ
Stute/Stule, Jeremiah	1857	18	NJ
Sullivan, James	1838	30	MA
Sullivan, John	1857	21	ME
Summers, Henry	1828	0	
Sutton, Richard	1850	22	ME
Swan, William	1797	26 b	
Sweeten, William Tully	1850	35	NJ
Sylvester, Robert H.	1838	24	MD
Taylor, James	1819	19	NY
Taylor, Joseph	1797	33	DE
Taylor, Thomas W.	1850	23	NJ
Teir, Mark	1838	43	NY
Thiesen, Abraham	1838	15	PA
Thomas, Charles	1850	21 b	NJ
Thomas, Frankling	1838	27 s	MA
Thomas, William	1850	18	NY
Thompson, Edward R.	1850	58	PA
Thompson, Francis	1850	40 b	NY
Thompson, George W.	1828	0	
Thompson, John S.	1861	29	NJ
Thompson, Lewis	1857	21 b	PA
Thompson, Robert	1857	20	PA
Timmins, Francis J.	1850	0	
Todd, Sylvester	1838	23 s	MD
Todovich, Peter	1840	37	Austria
Toler, Sander	1838	19	NC
Town, Daniel	1827	29	MD
Tronbear, Charles	1828	0	
Truitt, Thomas J.	1861	28 b	DE
Turner, James	1850	29	NY
Turner, Joseph	1861	35	RI
Uval, Levin	1838	29 b	MD
Wade, William	1838	21	ME
Walker, John S.	1838	23	NH
Walker, William A.	1857	22	PA
Wallace, John	1839	21	MA
Walsh, William	1850	22	NY
Ward, Charles J.	1857	25	Ireland
Warren, Charles	1857	29 b	NY
Watson, Henry	1847	18	DE
Watson, Isaac	1861	26	DE
Watson, James	1850	14	PA
Watters, Able	1827	24 b	MD
Weaaver, Edward	1811	0	
Webster, John	1850	29	ME
Weessman, Andrew	1850	22	MD
Welsh, Philip	1838	21	PA
West, Robert	1850	24	ME
Wharton, James H.	1861	20	DE
Whattley, William	1857	22 m	MA

Wheaton, Edmund W.	1861	23	NJ
Wheaton, Elijah T.	1838	34	NY
Whidden, Joseph P.	1850	16	ME
Whildin, Zenas S.	1861	32	MA
White, Henry	1850	54 c	PA
White, Lewis	1838	28 c	DE
White, Samuel	1861	59	PA
White, Thomas	1801	21	PA
Widmer, Francis	1822	28	PA
Wilbour, David W.	1844	19	RI
Wild, George	1850	20	MA
Wild, Robert	1846	0	NY
Willett, Edward W.	1846	0	
Willey, James	1850	18	ME
Williams, Bill	1857	22 m	MD
Williams, Charles	1857	36 b	NY
Williams, Francis	1822	17	PA
Williams, Geo. Henry	1857	26 b	NY
Williams, James	1850	32 b	NY
Williams, Jeremiah	1850	22 b	PA
Williams, John	1844	21	PA
Williams, John	1850	21	PA
Williams, John F.	1857	23	CT
Williams, John H. A.	1838	23	England
Williams, William	1850	22	ME
Williamson, Elbridge	1850	23	ME
Williamson, Thomas Dent	1838	12	CT
Wilson, Henry	1850	28	LA
Wilson, Honry	1857	20 b	NY
Wilson, James	1838	24	MA
Wilson, Richard	1850	19	NY
Wilson, Thos	1840	36	
Wilson, William	1838	23	PA
Wilson, William	1844	19 c	PA
Winch, Samuel	1850	40	MA
Winchenpaw, Augustus	1838	21	ME
Winchester, Jacob	1850	37	MD
Wingrove, William	1838	43	NY
Wood, Alfred	1850	43 b	MD
Woodland, Moses	1857	31 b	DE
Woodsum, Oliver	1838	17	NH
Woodward, John	1828	0	
Wright, John	1857	22 c	NY
Yates, Madison	1850	33	ME
Young, Benjamin H.	1827	28	CT
Young, John	1861	31 b	MD
Yule, Robert	1850	25	ME

NOTE

There is a great deal more information on the original applications than is provided in the indexes. You may find:

- city and/or county of birth
- date and court of naturalization
- dates and courts of manumission or freedom
- name of witness
- relationship of witness to seaman
- height, and color of hair and eyes
- signature of seaman, if literate

Often times the notary who executes the application makes interesting observations about the seaman. In the case of an application for a duplicate "protection" the whole story of how the original one was lost may be told. These are particularly interesting in the early years when the British were impressing our seamen. Date and court of naturalization of father is given when son claims citizenship on that basis. Indenture records appear. Fascinating stories are found in these records, adding flesh to the dry bones of family research.

I will provide a photocopy of an original application filed in the Port of Philadelphia, 1796-1861, for $20.00

I will sort the database by state/county/country for $20.00 per hour.

Your request with the name and date of the seaman or other research specifications and your check should be sent to:

Ruth Priest Dixon, CGRS
10450 Lottsford Road, Mitchellville MD 20721
(301) 925-7297 Email RDGENE@AOL.com